POLITICS EAST AND WEST

POLITICS EAST AND WEST

A COMPARISON OF JAPANESE AND BRITISH POLITICAL CULTURE

CURTIS H. MARTIN • BRUCE STRONACH

An East Gate Book

Routledge
Taylor & Francis Group

LONDON AND NEW YORK

An East Gate Book

First published 1992 by M.E. Sharpe

Reissued 2018 by Routledge
2 Park Square, Milton Park, Abingdon, Oxon OX14 4RN
711 Third Avenue, New York, NY 10017, USA

Routledge is an imprint of the Taylor & Francis Group, an informa business

A Library of Congress record exists under LC control number: 92026273

ISBN 13: 978-1-138-89644-4 (hbk)
ISBN 13: 978-1-138-89645-1 (pbk)
ISBN 13: 978-1-315-17915-5 (ebk)

Contents

List of Tables

Introduction

Britain and Japan have both been considered as paradigms—Britain, the success-ful democratic polity; Japan, the successful postindustrial economy. While Brit-ain by many accounts has been suffering long-term economic decline, at least in a comparative sense, Japan has enjoyed and continues to enjoy relatively strong growth and, more recently, an expansion of influence. Yet Britain's management of economic and imperial decline can be viewed as evidence of its political "success," the maintenance, by and large, of a stable and legitimate political order. In contrast, there is much that can be viewed as "unsuccessful" about Japan's apparent inability, amidst prosperity and a remarkable degree of national homogeneity, to forge strong links of legitimacy between national political insti-tutions and the citizenry. The present work is not a study of economic policies or growth, but it is very much concerned with the political dimension of the com-parison. How true is it that the British polity, in which many generations have become habituated to democratic institutions and rules, can count on a greater degree of legitimacy and support than the Japanese, where democracy is such a recent arrival?

Culture is about the transmission of central social values, and it is accordingly a conservative force (Eckstein 1988: 792–93). Values may not always be suc-cessfully transmitted from one generation to the next, and they may undergo alteration as successive generations reinterpret values, but inertia remains a pow-erful force for continuity in the political culture (Girvin 1989: 31; Inglehart 1990: 19). We can read Lafcadio Hearn on Japan or Walter Bagehot on Britain and recognize some contemporary political values, if in different manifestations and proportions than in the last century. In both countries, values and attitudes have changed. Traditional deference has waned, as have the materialist aspira-tions of the prewar generations. In their place, "postmaterialist" values such as environmentalism appear to have sprung forth. For both Britain and Japan, the prewar and war generations have retired from or are approaching retirement from politics. The material and psychological effects of victory or defeat in

World War II are no longer sufficient directly to explain the attitudes of a majority of Britons or Japanese. Because some of the changes that have taken place are recent, scholars hotly debate their magnitude, causes, and permanence. It is simply unclear at this point whether some of the older attitudes are waning for good, or being subjected to "life-cycle" effects. We ought, perhaps, to accept that both effects are likely. We should expect change. Political cultures do change. But, notwithstanding the precipitous erosion of socialist political cultures in Eastern Europe in the late 1980s, or perhaps because of them, we should be suspicious of the appearance of sudden change, or claims of sudden change in longstanding attributes of societies.

Many scholars have written about political culture and they tend to have their own definitions, but we have decided to rely mainly upon the definition given by Verba (1965: 513–17): "The political culture of a society consists of the system of empirical beliefs, expressive symbols, and values which define the situation in which political action takes place ... [it] refers to the system of beliefs about patterns of political interaction and political institutions. It refers not to what is happening in the world of politics, but what people believe about those happenings. And these beliefs can be of several kinds: they can be empirical beliefs about what the actual state of political life is; they can be beliefs as to the goals or values that ought to be pursued in political life; and these beliefs may have an important expressive or emotional dimension. Political culture forms an important link between the events of politics and the behavior of individuals in reaction to those events. ... Political culture regulates who talks to whom and who influences whom. It also regulates what is said in political contacts and the effects of these contacts. It regulates the ways in which formal institutions operate as well." Many others have added their interpretations as well. Rose (1986c: 116–17) writes that "The political culture concerns intangible but important values, beliefs, and emotions that influence support for authority and compliance with its basic political laws"; Marsh (1977: 30) that "The study of political culture is the study of the way social attitudes and values shape mass political behavior"; and Kavanagh (1985a: 46) that it is comprised of "the values, beliefs, and emotions that give meaning to political behavior." We should also be careful not to judge differences in certain components of political culture as "strengths" or "weaknesses," nor should we be too quick to judge any political system a paradigm. As Richardson and Flanagan (1984: 164) note, "different cultures provide different answers that simply represent different mixes of strengths and weaknesses." Almond and Verba's ideal type of the "civic culture" in Britain may have set up unrealistic and inflated expectations for the political system, leading perhaps inevitably to the revisionist view that the system was in a state of collapse because it no longer appeared to meet the standards of the civic culture model.

Our study will be cautious about assuming that political culture causes or regulates behavior, but we tend to accept, with Richardson and Flanagan (1984:

163), that "culture conditions behavior by providing certain resources that may be drawn upon as a new problem emerges and by setting certain limits on what kinds of solutions to the problem will be compatible with social sensibilities and expectations." We agree with Kavanagh (1985a: 46) that political culture creates a "predisposition for people to behave in a particular way which provides justification for behavior. A society's political culture disposes its members to regard certain forms of political behavior and institutions as 'normal' and others as 'abnormal.' " Robert Jervis (1976: 217) has demonstrated the link between elite attitudes and behavior by demonstrating that formative experiences and values are quite influential in shaping perceptions of and responses to later events, and that major decisions reflect these cognitive models. The role of political culture in setting the bounds of behavior assumes special importance in a polity that lacks a written constitution or bill of rights, as in Britain. But it may also be of particular importance in a society such as Japan, where a written constitution exists, but lacks very widespread legitimacy.

A political culture is not uniform. By no means everyone or even a majority share the same values and attitudes. It is rather that a majority draw upon the same range of values and attitudes and beliefs in their political debates. The political culture sets the parameters of the political game. For example, a characteristic of British political culture is not the absence of ideology in political debate, but its limited role. What distinguishes Britain is the distinct moderation of public beliefs, the absence of politically influential extremes of "left" and "right." There is further, no reason why these parameters cannot encompass contradictions and inconsistencies. Political culture is in a very important sense like Greenleaf's concept of a " 'tradition' of political activity," consisting of "a complex amalgam of different forces and opposing choices, and therefore of internal tensions, which is at the same time in a continual state of flux and development but which nevertheless constitutes a recognizable and acknowledged whole" (Greenleaf 1983a: 13). It is important to note that within each individual, as well as between individuals, values and attitudes may vie for dominance, with results that vary according to the situation. People can have mixed feelings, values, and motives. Japan, which follows a philosophical tradition of nondichotomous thought, enjoys something of an advantage over Britain in comprehending and accepting the contradictions of political and other behavior, but the British polity, no less than the Japanese, exhibits these internal tensions that de facto, coexist.

Political culture can be defined as neutral with respect to attachment to the polity, and can therefore include the attitudes of the populace toward political objects, be they positive or negative, supportive or cynical. Or it can be defined more normatively as the attitudinal underpinning of regime legitimacy, therefore including only positive feelings of trust, patriotism, unity, etc. In the second view, a political culture can be weak (unsupportive of the polity) or strong (supportive) in maintaining system stability. Almond and Verba's model of the civic culture is an example of such a normative classification scheme.

A good deal of literature over the past fifteen years has counseled caution in overreliance on political culture. The concept remains a controversial one (see Elkins and Simeon 1979: 127–43; and Hart 1978: 35). It has been variously criticized as too imprecise, as lacking explanatory value, as too narrowly concerned with "national" culture where other system levels may be at work (e.g., class, individual psychology). Concentrating as it does on mass attitudes and values, the concept comes afoul of the objection that in all countries, politics, and even more so, political philosophy are remote, of little salience to the average person. People are unlikely to have given as much thought as political scientists to "trust" or "legitimacy." Many are unlikely to have thought in any depth about why they support the political system. As a result, it may be very difficult in some instances to define very precisely what attitudes and convictions people have or how deeply they hold them. To date, studies of political culture have rarely focused on the problem of intensity. Surveys are indeed "very blunt instruments for investigating complex and often ill-articulated attitudes," and are "a relatively recent tool making historical generalizations difficult" (Hart 1978: 36). We shall attempt to keep these criticisms and refinements in mind, while defending the importance of political culture to the study of comparative politics. Even if political culture is but one variable, an identification of differences and similarities in the political cultures of Japan and Britain will be of value, if only to lead to further questions and research on the causes and implications of those comparisons. It is important to recall that political culture is but a part of a wider national culture that embraces a very large nonpolitical sphere. We accept, with Almond and Verba (1980: 38), that the political and nonpolitical cultures are closely linked. The impact of such factors as weak levels of trust, deference, or efficacy, will vary with the broader cultural context. Political efficacy may be linked to personal efficacy, or patriotism to satisfactory interpersonal relationships. For example, the potential in Japan for relatively low levels of respect for the Diet or high levels of cynicism to undermine system legitimacy may be mitigated by other cultural norms such as a general sense of fatalism about life, and respect for local political structures. A higher value attached to other social institutions may, to a certain degree, compensate for the low ratings given to national institutions.

One of the greatest obstacles to the study of political attitudes is the lack of coherence among political scientists in their use of basic terms. The degree of confusion over use of terms such as efficacy, trust, deference, support, legitimacy, and behavior should strike any student of politics with trepidation. While we make no pretense to rebuild the collapsed tower of Babel, we do attempt here to establish some internal consistency in our use of the terminology of political culture. By applying the same vocabulary of political culture to each country, we hope to reduce the problems posed by the very different analytical categories and constructs often applied to Japan, such as *omote/ura* or *tatemae* and *honne*. This approach cannot help but risk becoming a procrustean bed, and we are aware that concepts important in one culture may lack the same relevance in the other. Again and again, group identities and pressure can be seen to shape expressed Japanese values, attitudes, and behaviors to a degree that would be nearly incomprehensible to most Britons.

We are not unmindful of the growing body of comparative politics literature warning against preoccupation with intranational (sui generis) explanations for political behavior. Much that once might have been seen as distinctively English, for example, is now treated as European, or advanced capitalist. Studies such as Inglehart's and Barnes and Kaase et al.'s seek to find sources of political behavior in the Western democracies in postindustrial phenomena common to them all. We shall try to keep our discussion in this larger context without attempting to formulate a general theory for these wider classifications. We also take note of the very different problem posed by views stressing the uniqueness of cultural assumptions and traditions (Bull 1972; Bozeman 1984). Postmodernists stress the fragmentation intrinsic in the fact that "each society has its own regime of truth, its general politics of truth" (Foucalt 1981, cited in Rengger 1989: 243). From this perspective, Western political values "cannot be meaningful outside the grid which originally gave them meaning" (Rengger 1989: 245). Presumably Japanese and British political cultures would be subject to the same caveat.

Caught between the view that Japan and Britain represent unique and incomparable political cultures, and the view that they are largely variants of a larger postindustrial society, we would have to conclude that certainly cultures retain their distinctiveness, including different research traditions and assumptions. It is equally evident, however, that societies today are subject to many of the same forces. We shall be satisfied if in comparing these two countries we can contribute to the craft of cross-national comparison, and in the process, can enhance the reader's understanding of politics in Britain and Japan.

When we get down to substantive comparisons, it is to be expected that both similarities and differences will be evident. Much has been written about both political cultures that presents them as possessing certain distinctive features. Unlike the Japanese, the British have a highly developed classical liberal, or individualistic, component to their image of society. Notions of individualism, so important in the intellectual history of the West, including Britain, have scant representation in Japanese thought. However, literature on both Japan and Britain over the past two decades has addressed certain concerns in common as well: collectivism, citizen deference and low levels of participation, links between political and social culture, and legitimacy. Collectivism has been an important feature of the political landscape of Britain and Japan, and while each is a distinctive variant, this shared collectivism constitutes an important common ground. Yet while modern British political development has been influenced by a dialectic between the collectivist and individualist images, this is not the case in Japan. There, individualistic and collectivist concepts compete as in Britain, but for most Japanese, most of the time, collectivism overwhelms individualism.

Another important contrast may be made between the "organic" and "nonorganic" origins of democracy in the two countries. British democracy is almost entirely home grown, the product of internal historical and social forces that have played themselves out in centuries of incremental, nonpurposive growth of political institutions and rules. Japanese democracy, by contrast, is only partly home grown. Many of its political institutions have far younger roots in the history and culture (though other components of the polity have very deep roots indeed, as we shall see). The postwar constitution was implanted by the United States, albeit with some attention to the soil conditions of its host. Even the earlier Meiji constitution was imposed quite purposively from above by the new elite of the period.

The older British polity has been subjected to the stresses of economic decline, national separatism, and racial tension. Japan's new polity, which has enjoyed prolonged economic growth and prosperity and the absence of national or racial strife, lacks a deep reservoir of support for the political system. Japan's government, in many studies, is seen as having successfully negotiated its way through the postwar period, while Britain's has been seen by some as a victim of "overload" or a "legitimation crisis." The implication would be that a long democratic tradition is only one factor in political stability. Our study suggests, however, that neither society is in crisis, and that both polities enjoy fairly widespread support, one despite its "decline," the other despite the "alien" character of its constitution and government. Despite evidence of some erosion of support, political legitimacy in Britain still appears strong. And while it is still early to judge the success of the Japanese democratic implant, there is evidence of growing acceptance of democratic values. Though by traditional survey measures, legitimacy appears weakly developed in Japan, so too does the potential for protest and rebellion. From Japanese experience it appears that a long democratic tradition may not be necessary for democracy to function reasonably well—at least in the absence of an economic or social crisis. What may seem surprising is how little evidence there is that the rather different economic circumstances of Japan and Britain over the past two generations have not produced more pronounced differences in political behavior or support.

One characteristic which observers have noted in both Japan and Britain is political deference. Deference, an attitude normally associated with traditional societies, refers to the trusting concession of decision making to elites. Both Japan and Britain have traditional institutions and values that survived into the industrialization period and beyond, and with them, traditional deferential attitudes. In the case of Britain, these traditional deferential attitudes survived in spite of the enormous social clashes associated with industrialization. In the right combination with more modern participant attitudes, deference was considered a major contributor to democratic stability (Almond and Verba 1963: 31–32). Today, most observers agree that deference is no longer a significant aspect of the political culture, though in certain contexts it is still more prevalent than in other European states. In Japan, traditional deference survived the transition from the Tokugawa period to the present by the maintenance of central authority in the emperor (until 1945), and the continued importance of Confucian ethics. Deferential attitudes have been seen, on the one hand, as contributing to the economic success of the society. On the other, and in contrast to Britain, they have been cited for contributing to a "spectator political culture," lacking the necessary citizen commitment to democratic values and participation. In Japan, deference seems more likely to be associated with apathy and distancing from authority, rather than with the trust that is normally a part of deference. Certainly the populations of both countries do tend rather more than in other polities to minimize political action, to let decisions be made elsewhere. It is our contention, however, that while traditional deference may have declined significantly, *acquiescent* attitudes and behavior still comprise an important element of both British and Japanese political culture. Acquiescence in the exercise of political authority, not deference, explains the continuation of passive behaviors long associated with deference.

British democracy may be defined in terms of strong yet limited government. Most citizens still see their principal political role as expressing an electoral preference, and little more, although expressions of populism and protest behavior are on the increase. If there is a prevailing view, it is still that government is for the people, not by the people. The contract that allows Britons to accept this role is the understanding that individual liberties will not be infringed, even as the government takes what most Britons still see as an interventionist approach to social policy.

This is not dissimilar to the prevailing concept of the citizen/government relationship in Japanese politics. The Japanese perceive, to an even greater degree, the relationship between themselves and the government as one of separate spheres and roles wherein the government is responsible to the people through election. In practice, most people are content simply to elect politicians to office and leave them alone to run the government. What is different, however, is the operative concept of liberty. While Britons are willing to accept what, in essence, they would consider bad policy making by the government as long as fundamental liberties are left intact, the Japanese accept bad policy making because they do not believe it is their role to interfere, although neither do they expect any automatic "contract" that guarantees their liberty as a quid pro quo for support.

Another important distinction between Japan and Britain—two cultures characterized by strong collectivist traditions and acquiescent behavior—is the presence of powerful pressures from the group to follow social norms of behavior in Japan, and their much lower visibility in Britain. In Japan, there is a variety of mechanisms of pressure to adopt the correct attitudes and behaviors, as defined by the appropriate group, what we later term the "terror of the social majority."

If one does not conform to group norms (and the group can be as inclusive as all Japanese or as exclusive as the working group), then real punishments such as nonpromotion or social snubbing will be meted out. This kind of pressure also helps to explain why behavior that appears deferent in Japan is not really a product of trust. This is not to say that in Britain no group norm is operative. The impact of group pressures is well documented in the literature of Western social psychology, and its political impact is suggested in the literature on the "neighborhood effect" in British voting behavior. Group pressures for "correct" behavior account to a degree for British political behavior, too, but nowhere near the extent that we find in Japan. A survey of political studies of Britain quickly reveal that group psychology as an explanation for political behavior lacks the salience in Britain that it has in Japan.

Both Japan and Britain are noted for the absence of a strongly polarized electorate. Rustow's (1970) developmental model of democracy would suggest that the absence of polarization today reflects the past resolution in Britain of conflicts over incorporation. All contesting groups found after long and exhausting struggles that they benefited from democratic rules, and hence accepted them as satisfactory, and of instrumental value. The absence of polarization in Britain is therefore seen as a positive factor. Its absence in Japan has been seen in quite a different light, and as a potential source of concern. In Japan, lack of polarization is seen more to reflect the absence of attachment to democratic values. It is seen as the result of a history by which the value of democratic norms and processes was not experienced by contending segments of society, but rather imposed from above. There was no "hot family feud," as Rustow (1970: 355) would put it, over incorporation of new social classes into the polity, nor was either constitutional order achieved as the result of contest and resolution. It is the absence of this "polarized" prologue in Japan that leads analysts like Flanagan to be concerned over the commitment of the Japanese to democracy.

POLITICS EAST AND WEST

Part I

Political Values and Attitudes

Part I is concerned with the political values and attitudes toward political objects that underlie the political culture. Values address those aspects of political relations and processes that citizens consider true, appropriate, and desirable, such as individual liberty, equality, or social harmony. Attitudes address citizens' disposition toward the political self and other actors (national identity, efficacy, and trust), and toward the system (national pride, compliance, participation). Part I will consider all these but attitudes toward participation, which we defer to Part II. Chapter 1 examines values that lie at the core of the British and Japanese political cultures. Chapter 2 defines and compares their respective senses of national identity and pride. Chapter 3 examines the relative prevalence of political efficacy and trust, and Chapter 4 embarks on a consideration of popular support and regime legitimacy. As we set out, we shall define some of the terms around which our discussion will revolve. Efficacy will refer to the self-confident feelings of citizens about their ability to express demands and act in an influential capacity. Trust will refer to the attitudes citizens have about the honesty of politicians, their willingness to listen, and their ability to produce desired outcomes. In other studies, efficacy is sometimes referred to as "internal efficacy," while trust is sometimes referred to as "external efficacy" (Abramson 1983: 134–45; Barnes, Kaase et al. 1979: 573–74). Acquiescence is the willingness of citizens, for a variety of reasons including trust, pragmatism or tradition, to let supervisors and officials make decisions for them. It is this behavior, not necessarily "deference," that remains prevalent in Britain and Japan. Deference has been one of the most vexing terms in the literature on political culture. After more than twenty-five years, the debate over whether or not deference is dead in Britain has yet to be laid completely to rest. Part of the problem lies in establishing motives for the passive political behaviors often associated with deference. In this study, deference will refer to a particular variant of acquiescence, one based on trust and respect. The distinction is important for a discussion of politics in both Britain and Japan, where generally passive attitudes and behaviors are still more prevalent by some measures than in other industrial states. Not all passive behavior is truly deferent, and there is much evidence that deferential attitudes have indeed declined, or have long been weaker than supposed. Support will refer to the willingness of citizens both to comply with authority and to acquiesce in the exercise of the decision-making power, *and* to fulfill their participant roles. It refers to Almond and Verba's "subject" and "citizen" competencies. In our study, we accordingly distinguish between compliant/subject support, in reference to the former, and participant/citizen support, in reference to the latter. In Part I, we will confine our discussion to the more passive compliant/subject support. Support may be offered out of tradition, through pragmatic acceptance, or through strong normative agreement. People may support the political system, without necessarily feeling that it is morally just, fair, ideal, or ideologically "correct." On the other hand, support as we define it may not be coerced. Legitimacy refers to a particular kind of support that *is* normatively based, and accepts that exercise of authority by the government is right and proper. Perhaps the major question addressed in Part I is the degree of popular support and legitimacy enjoyed by the British and Japanese democracies. We find that evidence of widespread full legitimacy of the political order is elusive for both countries, where the incidence of political cynicism is extensive. It is especially lacking in Japan, which, despite a remarkably homogeneous population, lacks a sense of national pride comparable to the British, who are among the most proud. However, when political support is widely defined, there is, by contrast, ample evidence of nonnormative bases of support. While "legitimacy" is often considered essential, the fact is that "support"—as we use the term— may be perfectly adequate for the effective functioning of the regime. Conversely, support is impossible if people believe the government is unjust, unfair, or ideologically blasphemous. What we are saying is that support, to be effective, may be either normative or value neutral. The fact that politics is of relatively little salience across the industrial democracies should alert us to the possibility that for many, political values and attitudes may be rather weakly developed, and that this may account for the apparent absence of strongly affirmative support.

1

Political Values and
the Political Process

An understanding of values is of such importance to political analysis that politics has been defined by some as the process by which values are allocated for a society and its political system (Deutsch 1974: 12). Values define the parameters of what is right and wrong, acceptable and unacceptable, in the practice and outcomes of politics. They may reflect preferences for policy outputs—such as liberty, security, welfare, or harmony—or process—such as participation, compromise, or consensus. Values are the raw material from which are derived other components of the political culture: attitudes and beliefs about politics, and political behavior. They shape perceptions of role and place vis-à-vis the political system. As Ridley (1984: 4) has observed, for example, "While constitutional traditions shape the formal arrangements made for the redress of grievances, it is society's values that will determine how individuals actually set about complaints against authority." Lastly, political values guide society in the creation, maintenance, modification and replacement of political institutions and practices. Values do not operate on attitudes and behavior in any deterministic way. It is no more possible reliably to infer behavior from values than it is to infer values from behavior. At the individual level, values may be in conflict, or poorly defined, or tentatively held, obscuring the link between thought and action. By the same token, people may act in contradiction of one or more of their values for any number of reasons. Still, where values are widely held in a society, they will affect the normally acceptable parameters of politics. They will most certainly affect political speech and debate, if not always action. Given the importance of language in shaping the meaning of events, this is not an inconsiderable effect (Edelman in Pekonen 1989: 133).

The purpose of this chapter is to identify and explain in broad terms some of the underlying values of the political cultures of Britain and Japan. Our purpose is not to identify all the major values of each system, and though there is much to be learned from comparative study of valued policy outcomes, these lie beyond the scope of this work (see Heidenheimer et al. 1990). We have chosen instead to emphasize three *process* value dimensions, which are especially significant for illuminating and comparing the political cultures of Japan and Britain. The first of these is the individualist/collectivist dimension. It is concerned with the relative value or rank which the polity assigns to individual rights vis-à-vis the rights of wider political community. It subsumes a separate but related authoritarian/libertarian dimension that focuses specifically on the authority relations between the individual and collective society, as embodied in the state. The second, conflictual/consensual dimension, concerns the relative expectation and tolerance of conflict in the normal political process. To what degree do the rules of politics incorporate or suppress competition and the clash of interests? The third, universalistic/particularistic dimension, concerns the extent to which either a rigid framework of interdependent values—that is, an ideology—or a flexible framework of loosely connected values, is applied to the definition and resolution of political problems. This dimension consists of several related scales including the ideological/pragmatic, contractual/legal, and absolutist/relativist.

Each of the above three process values has been shaped or sustained by dynamic, historical influences. One of these most suggestive of the contrast between Japan and Britain has been the extent to which the development of the polity was organic or nonorganic, that is, the extent to which the polity evolved in concert with indigenous social and cultural forces, or was imposed under external pressures and constraints. While this particular developmental variable can be related to all three of the above values dimensions, we might be most concerned with its effect on the conflictual/consensual dimension—not with respect to conflict within society, but with respect to potential conflict between society and polity. The British polity, which is organic, has in the past enjoyed a reputation for widespread political consensus. Even in the light of widely observed challenges to consensus, many observers continue to credit the process of constitutional development with providing stability and legitimacy. To what extent does the absence in Japan of an analogous organic relationship between society and polity suggest a more conflicted constitutional reality? In short, how does the organic/nonorganic origin of the two polities affect their legitimacy? We approach such a sweeping historical question humbly and cautiously, recognizing the obstacles to identifying causality. A fortiori, we do not attempt to answer the generic question of whether a native-grown political system enjoys greater legitimacy than one imposed from without. Such an exploration would have to be far more inclusive of different polities than the scope that the present study permits. Nevertheless, it is an important dimension of the Japan-Britain comparison.

Finally, we wish to consider the issue of value change, which potentially cuts across all three of the other values dimensions we have identified. The concept of political culture stresses continuity of values, but it need not exclude the process of change. As Eckstein (1988: 793) points out, while "continuity is . . . an ideal-type expectation . . . akin to that of inertia in the Gallilean conception of motion," it does not rule out "changes of direction or rest, acceleration, and deceleration." There is extensive evidence of change throughout the industrial democracies that needs to be explained. Where these societies are located along the individualist/collectivist, harmony/conflict, and universalistic/particularistic values dimensions can, like political institutions themselves, be expected to change. Many observers during the 1970s became intrigued with the possibility that values change, stimulated by social and economic change, might be leading to less material and less deferential values—that is, in the general paradigm, to a weakening of centralized or corporatist politics in favor of politics that is less hierarchical, more individualistic and participatory, though generally less harmonious. Postmodernists, on the other hand, rejected the concept of linear values change, and focused instead on the possibility that fragmentation, even incoherence of values, was characteristic of contemporary culture.

Individualist/Collectivist

A central normative dimension of politics in Britain and Japan defines the relative worth assigned to the individual and to the group as actors in society. Along the scale from group-oriented to individual-oriented norms, we shall use "collectivism" to indicate the belief in the preeminence of the interests of the group or community over the needs of the individual, and in the leading role of the group in the articulation of interests. In both Britain and Japan group norms are deeply rooted and pervasive in politics, and are readily visible in political organization and process. But both the basic character, and the relative importance of group norms is quite different in the two countries. In Britain, the balance, or tension, between collectivist and individualist strands represents an important dynamic element in the political culture. The individualist strand can be seen in the enduring British preference for personal liberty, expressed in public opinion and action, and in the neoconservative embrace of the philosophical liberalism of the eighteenth and nineteenth centuries. By contrast, ideas of individual worth or rights had limited circulation or appeal in Japan until the twentieth century. Even in post–World War II democratic Japan, they remain less salient to politics than other norms, though there is some evidence that economic development and increased affluence have significantly increased some aspects of individualism in Japan. The sheer mass of the intellectual foundations of both individualism and collectivism in Britain distinguishes it from the Japanese case, where culture has been much more important than intellectual traditions as a vehicle for the transmission of social and political values.

Collectivism as a political concept appears in two related incarnations. The first emphasizes collectivism as a preference for group-centered political activity and articulation. In this view, individual needs are subordinated to or incorporated into those of the group. Individual needs are identified with and met through the satisfaction of group needs. The individual's needs are believed to find their most effective expression through voluntary associational groups, or in the specific socialist variant, through one's natural social class, and demands are organized and expressed primarily through these groups, rather than through the sum of individual pressure. However, the individual's identification with and dependency on the group is normally far less pervasive in Britain than in Japan. There, in sharp contrast, collectivism is more firmly rooted in the social and psychological dependency of the individual on the group, through such social relationships as *amae* (emotional dependency) and *giri* (mutual obligation). Furthermore, Japanese society is far more clearly defined by numerous concentric, socially cohesive groups, than is Britain. The tradition of individualism is too strong in Britain to permit the general acceptance of the idea that the individual personality must be immersed in the group, though the socialist concept of "fellowship" comes close to this position. In any case, collectivism views the group as an appropriate and rational instrument of political organization and action. It is this "group-centered" aspect of collectivism with which we shall primarily be concerned.

In the second incarnation, collectivism is the assertion of the power of the national community, embodied in the interventionist state, over the individual. It is concerned not with the relative value of the individual and the community, but with the degree of state power over the individual. It assigns a special and significant role to government as first among society's various collectivities. The "collectivist" or "welfare state" mobilizes vast resources and powers, presumably to advance the national, collective good. This "welfare state" manifestation of collectivism has preoccupied much of the literature on British politics, reviewed favorably in Beer's *Modern British Politics* (1926), and critically in Greenleaf's *The British Political Tradition* (1983a). While this view of collectivism could also be applied to Japan, the cultural, holistic aspect is far more often stressed (Richardson and Flanagan 1984: 125–31). Concepts of corporatism, however, themselves collectivist in nature, have frequently been applied to the politics of both countries, and there are certainly ways in which the Japanese state is even more interventionist than that of Britain, for example in its role in planning industrial strategy.

Britain

Collectivism in both of the above senses—as group-centered norms and as intervention of state power—has been influential in the evolution of British politics. What Studlar (1976: 107) calls an "appreciation . . for the emotional benefits of collective human endeavor" has been present from medieval Toryism, to Disraelian paternalism and British socialism in the late nineteenth century, to the "collectivist consensus" of the post–World War II generation. A "vigorous group life" has for centuries been a characteristic of British culture (Kavanagh 1985a: 50), and was embodied in the various estates of society. "Trade unions, nonprofit retail cooperatives, and mutual-insurance societies," writes Rose (1964: 32), "provided means ... to make collective provision for individual needs." The "persistent corporatism" of British social attitudes "is predicated on 'a conception of society as consisting primarily not of individuals, but of sub-societies, groups having traditions, occupational and other characteristics in common.' " Accordingly, " 'where corporatistic attitudes persist, governments tend to be regarded not as sovereign in the Austinian sense, but, in the pluralistic sense, as corporations among many other kinds of corporations' "(Eckstein, cited in Vogel 1986: 272). Election boundary commissioners are expected to represent "communities that are integral human entities which have both a history and a very lively sense of corporate feeling" (Rose 1986c: 13). By the nineteenth century, the ancient estates and geographical notions of community had largely given way to modern class and associational collectives, and to this day class remains located at the center of the British political culture and the study of British political science.

Many aspects of the political process in Britain reflect collectivist values. "Group values tend to determine what individuals in office wish to do" (Rose 1986c: 106). Parliamentary rules and norms reinforce group solidarity. It is one of Britain's constitutional conventions that the government speaks, and is responsible, collectively through the cabinet. The bureaucracy, too, is strongly influenced by collectivist values. Whitehall itself has been compared to a "village culture," where group values prevail (Heclo and Wildavsky 1974, cited in Rose 1986c: 106). Government consultation with relevant groups is an "essential part of the policy process" (Kavanagh 1985a: 50), and numerous advisory committees are "a chief channel of collective consultation" (Rose 1964: 44). This collectivist orientation may be further illustrated by the manner in which the courts process appeals of ministerial decisions. Such appeals "are generally promoted by interest organisations rather than individuals and they often refer to collective rather than individual grievances" (Ridley 1984: 10). In the past century, political parties have by and large embodied a different collectivist view of society, especially as long as "party" was closely linked to "class." Bloc voting within the Labour Party Conference is a further example of the collective expression of interests.

In general terms, even within the British collectivist orientation, the individual maintains his or her identity within the collective, yielding only voluntarily to the good of the group. "When priority is given to a group over and above the interests of the individual," observes Wagatsuma (1984: 374), "the individual is seen as 'subdued,' 'oppressed' or 'buried' without autonomy." On a theoretical level, British socialism does hold out as an "ideal" type, a view of the collective, in which "each person's life would be selfless in the sense that his self and the common 'self' of the community would be merged" (Beer 1982: 129). The field of social psychology has given considerable attention to issues of group behavior and conformity as it applies to Western culture (Paicheler 1988; Moscovici 1976; Moscovici and Personnaz 1980; Janis 1983). Western social psychology, however, unlike Japanese, has been as concerned with minority influence on the majority as with the majority influence on the minority. Generally speaking, discussions in the political science literature of British collectivism deal only cursorily with the group dynamics of political collectives, for example, in terms of society's intolerance for "those who might be labeled 'non-conformist' or 'deviant' " (Fogarty 1985: 233–34). Two areas of the discipline which have attempted to grapple with the group dynamics of values formation in Britain are political socialization and voting behavior.

By long usage, collectivism in Britain refers quite specifically to the historical gathering of powers in the hands of the state to advance the collective good of society. During most of the present century, the liberal, individualistic tradition in British political culture was in relative decline while collectivism was in the ascendancy. The postwar consensus was largely collectivist—founded upon social welfare and full employment guaranteed by the state. Beer concludes that collectivism "pervades the political culture of twentieth century Britain" (1982b: 70), and Kavanagh (1985a: 58) states that since 1918 Labour and Conservatives had "accepted, in different degrees, political, social and economic collectivism." In the same vein, Rose (1964: 44) claims that the birth of the Labour Party and the decline of liberalism left only "contrasting conceptions of collectivism." Unaware of how strong a rebound classical liberalism was to make under Mrs. Thatcher, Birch (1980: 13) observed that "The laissez-faire liberalism which Samuel Smiles advocated did not survive beyond the early years of the twentieth century in Britain." Thatcherism seemed to cast these conclusions into doubt. However, the great success of the Thatcher government at staying in power was never unambiguously translated into her stated goal of abolishing socialist—or collectivist—values in Britain (Jowell and Topf 1988: 121; Curtice 1987: 174; Crewe 1989: 241). Even secular phenomena such as the decline of class and party identification, and a corresponding rise in citizen protest and issue-oriented voting did not necessarily imply a decline of collectivism within the culture. Many of the goals and specific programs of the "collectivist" era remain highly popular. Though Britons are quite ambivalent about bearing an increased personal burden for redistributive goals, large majorities believe that it should be government's responsibility "to reduce income differences between rich and poor," and "to provide a decent standard of living for the unemployed" (Curtice 1987: Table 8.3, 185). After seven years of Conservative government, a plurality of Britons (46 percent) thought the government "should increase taxes and spend more on health, education and social benefits" (Jowell et al. 1987: 209). Other evidence of thriving collectivist values could be found in the increased frequency with which the British turned during the 1980s to new organizations, and channeled their grievances through collective organizations (Ridley 1984).

Despite firm support for economic collectivism in Britain, the concept of central planning never took hold. Andrew Shonfield has observed "the extraordinary tenacity of older attitudes towards the role of public power [in Britain]. Anything which smacked of a restless or overenergetic state, with ideas of guiding the nation on the basis of a long view of its collective economic interest, was instinctively the object of suspicion" (cited in Kavanagh 1980: 159). To some extent, this perspective was possible because, unlike the case in, for example, Germany, France, or Japan, the apparatus of the state did not have to be imposed on a society rent by the crises of industrialization or national unification (Ashford 1980: 14–15). In Britain, late industrialization encouraged an alliance between concentrated economic power in the private sector and "an equally powerful public authority" (Heidenheimer et al. 1990: 22). The state did not assume, or have to assume, a developmental role. It is important to note, however, that one of the factors inhibiting the development of a "dirigist state" in Britain, when it could have been imposed after World War II, was not staunch libertarianism, but the collectivist impulse of labor to resist government interference with the rights of unions to engage in private collective bargaining. The tendency has been to see government as a "coequal partner with no special qualification to speak for a higher national interest" (Kavanagh 1980: 159). As a result, the idea of the state as collective was further inhibited.

The collectivist state may find itself responsible for the provision of economic goods, but it should not be forgotten that a much older responsibility of the state is the maintenance of law and order in the community. The relative importance that society places upon "law and order" can be indicated by Britain's place along the libertarian/authoritarian values axis. Collectivism need not imply authoritarian state power, but a considerable degree of state power is not inconsistent with a collectivist political order. This support for the state is also provided, and this is a point of considerable importance, both from Tory traditions of hierarchy and organicism, and from socialist traditions of collective state power. Indeed, both at the level of elite and mass culture, there is ample support in Britain for the concentration and use of state, or collective, power. At the elite level, the doctrine, if not the practice, of parliamentary supremacy directly contradicts concepts of liberty and pluralism, and secrecy tends to protect the government from the individual. There is considerable survey data that suggest strong public support for using the power of the state to enforce the traditional moral order, for example, through stiffer sentences for crimes and through censorship of publications for moral content (Heath and Topf 1987: 63). Britain's high "repression potential," or tolerance for use of state power to maintain law and order, is suggested in several studies (Marsh 1977; Marsh and Kaase 1979b). The European Values System Survey found that 73 percent of Britons believed it would be "good" if among the changes that might take place in the near future would be "greater respect for authority" (Phillips 1985: Table 6.4,162). Thus, the British emerge as more authoritarian than we might expect in a nation that so highly prizes individual rights. These values are an important underpinning for the practice of "strong government" in the tradition of the British political culture, and tend to contradict to some extent findings of low trust in government that we shall examine in Chapter 3. We must add, however, that despite the moral conservatism evident in some surveys, the strong individualist values of the society have led over the past two decades to far more libertarian legislation on pornography, abortion, and homosexuality. Heath and Topf (1987: 64) suggest the possibility, however, that "authoritarian attitudes in the moral or socio-legal sphere are only loosely related to authoritarian attitudes in the political sphere."

If we were to examine British attitudes toward their political leaders for confirmation of authoritarian or libertarian values, we would find very contradictory evidence. On the one hand, both Tory and Whig traditions encouraged a belief in strong and enlightened leadership, though the former believed in a hereditary claim to leadership, and the latter claimed a "nurture not nature" source of leadership ability. Among today's parties, the Conservatives have the more admiring view of the virtues of strong individual leadership by the prime minister. However, the British show a decided ambivalence about strong leaders. As Bagehot (1966: 262) put it, "our freedom is the result of centuries of resistance, more or less legal, more or less audacious, or more or less timid, to the executive government." "Politics," says Dore (1985: 207) "has kept alive our admiration above all for strength in leadership—for bulldogs and iron ladies—while at the same time keeping alive our distrust of all those who exercise authority." The concept of leadership in Britain has become so important "precisely because the impulse to defy has so commonly to be reckoned with" (Dore 1985: 204). It should not be surprising that Mrs. Thatcher aroused both strong admiration and distrust for her leadership, nor that Mr. Major, her successor, should be praised for his collegiality and criticized for his indecision.

In recent decades, a number of observers claim to have observed an erosion of collectivist institutions and traditions. British culture was said to have become more atomistic, more participant, less deferential, less class bound. Class and party dealignment, as well as the fragmentation and weakening of trade unions, were cited as evidence of waning collectivism. These changes should have worked to the advantage of Mrs. Thatcher and her "enterprise culture." As we saw above, however, collectivist values have remained resistant to erosion. While the years of Thatcherism do not appear finally to have vanquished the collectivist spirit of the British, they do remind us that British political culture still has two strings to its bow. It is by no means limited to different versions of collectivism. Individualistic norms and philosophies have played a much greater role in British politics than in Japanese politics, and in fact continue to vie energetically with the collectivist strain.

Individual liberty is a cornerstone of the culture. "The British have traditionally emphasized a negative view toward liberty, one which left the citizen free to do as he wished, unless the activity was formally proscribed" (Kavanagh 1980: 159). Liberty is the absence of government interference rather than the existence of affirmative rights. Dicey (1959: 207–8) defines the right to personal liberty as "a person's right not to be subjected to imprisonment, arrest, or other physical coercion in any manner that does not admit of legal justification." According to Rose (1986c: 128), "avoiding the abuse of power, rather than effectiveness in its use, is the cornerstone of support for government in England." We noted above that in certain respects, the British are supportive of state coercion. But given the British view of liberty, it should be no surprise that while Britons support the force of the state against lawbreakers, they strongly oppose state interference with law-abiding citizens (Social Survey's Ltd., December 10–15, 1987). Their "collectivism" appears to approve the provision of benefits, but not intrusion into private life. Dore stresses individualism and anti-authoritarianism, as expressed in the "heroic defiance of authority" (Dore 1985: 203), of which the 1990 antitax riots were only a recent manifestation. Despite the pervasiveness of the welfare state, Inglehart (1982: 461) notes, even before Conservative reforms had taken hold in the early 1980s, the persistence of "self-reliance" among the British. Surveys usually show a strong British preference for liberty over equality, compared with other nations, and this "overwhelming preference for freedom over equality shows that concern for individual liberty is a core political value among British people.... The importance placed on freedom is widespread," across class, age, and ideological divisions (Phillips 1985: 160).[1] "Both governors and governed expect that everyone, whether or not he or she agrees with the government of the day, will be free to speak his or her mind" (Rose 1986c:138). A large majority of Britons defend the right of both racists and revolutionaries to publish books, though well under a majority would let either teach in the schools (Young 1984: 27). Defense of basic freedoms such as speech and assembly are among the reasons most frequently cited for either protesting or for breaking the law (Heath and Topf 1987: 58; Marsh 1977: 52; Young 1985: 17).

The British protectiveness of individual rights against government may be traced to ancient sources, and "Fear of centralized power and the danger of its growth was one of the major themes of British politics from at least the seventeenth century onward" (Greenleaf 1983b: 265). Intellectual traditions, most notably classical liberalism in the eighteenth and nineteenth centuries, upheld such a norm. Liberalism was defined and given political circulation through the influential writings of the likes of Richard Cobden, Herbert Spencer, and John Stuart Mill, and while their writings are certainly unfamiliar to most Britons today, they are familiar to the elites who in turn often frame the national debate. Burke's libertarianism sought to delineate a minimum sphere to government action, and served to inspire at least one strand of conservative thought, represented by the Conservative Party's statement in 1976 that "We mean to protect the individual from excessive interference by the State or by organisations licensed by the State, to stop the drift of power away from the people and their democratic institutions, and to give them more power as citizens" (Greenleaf 1983b: 345— from Conservative Central Office, *The Right Approach: a Statement of Conservative Aims*. London 1976: 18). Putnam cites evidence of the persistence of libertarian ideals among elites. "From nine-tenths of the British politicians it is impossible to elicit support for restrictions on extreme political activity," while half refer specifically to values of political freedom as defining democracy (Putnam 1973: 208).

When taken together, all these individualist tendencies have helped encourage the development of values of "limited government" that serve to check on tendencies to "strong government" in British political culture.

Japan

One of the most enduring hallmarks of Japanese society is its collectivist, group-oriented nature. It is for Kyogoku (1987: 41), "[t]he first politically relevant code" of behavior. In the Japanese cultural assumption, however, society, from the beginning, is not basically opposed to individuals. Rather, in contrast to the Western view, group and individual are not in opposition to each other; rather the individual realizes his or her full potential as an individual by acting to perfect the role of group member (Wagatsuma 1984: 374; Kyogoku 1987: 42). An individual is, from the beginning, conceived of as a member of the most fundamental group, the family. As he or she grows, the number of group memberships increases, from family to school to university to company. There are many subgroups within each of these primary reference groups. For example, a university student will also be a member of a campus club and a company employee may also be a member of a faction based upon his university. All groups, however, hark back to the family, in that they tend to be hierarchical and demand the submission of the individual to the will of the group.

There are many explanations for the collectivist orientation of the Japanese, but three interrelated factors seem to predominate. The first has to do with the traditional religious and social culture of Japan. Buddhism teaches the spiritual transcendence of the individual. Through meditation, one tries to transcend the real world, which is encumbered with "things" and "self," to a higher, universal, rational plane. Thus, the world is also ordered into ten realms from those living in hell to those who have attained perfect enlightenment (Moore 1967: 37). This process is, almost by definition, antipolitical in that it creates a religious rationale for the negation of the individual. But it does have importance for political behavior when joined with Confucianism, a set of political and social ethics which outline the relationship between the ruled and rulers. Confucianism transfers the concept of selflessness from the ethereal, religious plane to the practical world and supports the stratification of society into castes, each subservient to the caste above. The history of Japan as a Buddhist/Confucian society has created the contemporary tradition of collective hierarchy.

One can also examine the Japanese group ethic through social psychological concepts such as *ie*, *amae* and *on-giri*. Chie Nakane believes that the "firmly rooted, latent group consciousness in Japanese society is expressed in the traditional and ubiquitous concept of *ie*, the household, a concept which penetrates every nook and cranny of Japanese society" (Nakane 1986: 173). The *ie* is the traditional Japanese household, the fundamental group, but with the decline of the traditional Japanese household in postwar Japan, the *ie* has been transferred to "a social group constructed on the basis of an established frame of residence and often of management organization," i.e., the company and company organizations (Nakane 1986: 174). Within Japanese society it is one's frame, *ba*, that is important, rather than one's attributes. Thus, one tends to define oneself by one's group—the company one works for, or the college one attended—rather than by one's individual attributes such as the work one does or one's profession.

Within the group the most important norms of behavior are *amae* and *on-giri*. *Amae* is defined by L. Takeo Doi as "to depend and presume upon another's benevolence" which is socialized into Japanese children through their dependence on their parents, especially their mothers (Doi 1986: 121). *Amae* behavior, however, does not end with childhood and is exhibited through the adult's need to continue to be dependent upon others in the group. It is especially important when a member of the group does something wrong and then presumes upon his or her relationship with the other members of the group for forgiveness. Group members also have mutual obligations to one another expressed as *on-giri* relationships. *On* is the mutual obligation which implies a reciprocity of helping and support between group members. *On* is "held" by both the person doing the favor and the person receiving the favor and ties the two together by psychological bond much greater than just the need for equal repayment. Both giver and receiver are now bound together, and the burden of *on* is expressed as *giri* (Lebra 1976: 91–93). These ties are extremely strong, can last for a lifetime, can be very burdensome, but are the glue which binds together the members of the group.

The greatest sin is to transgress against the group, and the greatest punishment is to be shunned or ostracized from the group. To avoid ridicule and shame, Japanese people will go to extreme lengths to insure that their every decision and action is in line with the group, even if they believe the group wisdom to be wrong (Kyogoku 1987: 44; Richardson and Flanagan 1984: 145, 193). When American authorities want to teach students in driver's education that speeding can have disastrous results, they show graphic films of death and dismemberment that have occurred as a result of speeding. Contrast this, however, with a film shown by the Japanese National Police Agency to people renewing their drivers' licenses. In the film a man with a loving wife and two children speeds down the street in an effort to get to work on time. He hits and kills an elderly man on a bicycle, but not one drop of blood is shown. Instead, there are many scenes of him, his wife, and his family being shunned by their neighbors and co-workers. Message: the penalty for disruptive behavior (speeding) is not death, but social ostracism.

Lastly, there is the enforced group ethic of an authoritarian political system. One of Karel van Wolferen's basic arguments in his controversial work on Japanese people and their political system, *The Enigma of Japanese Power*, is that the communal aspects of Japanese political and social life are "the result of political arrangements consciously inserted into society by a ruling elite over three centuries ago, and the Japanese today are given little or no choice in accepting arrangements that are still essentially political" (1990: 3). He is speaking of the application of Confucianism to the feudal political system of the Tokugawa period (1615–1868), but the authoritative enforcement of collectivism predates the Tokugawa period, as Buddhism and Confucianism were first joined to form the outline of a hierarchical political system when Prince Shotoku created the Seventeen Article Constitution in 604 A.D. (Tsunoda et al. 1958: 37).

The most recent overt enforcement of collectivism came with the creation of the *kokutai*, or national polity as embodied by the Meiji constitution. In that constitution the divine status of the emperor in Shinto tradition was combined with traditional Confucian ruler-subject relationships and Buddhist morality. The result was an authoritarian government in a society that, while having rid itself of the social and economic castes of the Tokugawa period, still maintained a rigidly hierarchical relationship between the political authorities and the people, with the emperor revered as a father figure to his family of Japanese subjects. This melding of Confucian relationships, Buddhist teaching, and Shinto myths into a centralized, hierarchical authoritarian state was a powerful influence in the socialization of the Japanese people into accepting an hierarchically ordered, authoritarian political system.

But the authoritarian nature of Japanese political culture today is no longer imposed by an authoritarian state backed by repressive laws and the secret police. Rather, contemporary authoritarianism in Japan stems from the social group and social relations. We will use a phrase adapted from J. S. Mill who, interestingly enough, took it from DeTocqueville's description of American society— "the tyranny of the social majority." It cannot be described better than did Mill in *On Liberty* when he wrote:

> But reflecting persons perceived that when society is itself the tyrant—society collectively, over the separate individuals who compose it—its means of tyrannizing are not restricted to the acts which it may do by the hands of all its political functionaries. Society can and does execute its own mandates: and if it issues wrong mandates instead of right, or any mandates at all in things in which it ought not to meddle, it practices a social tyranny more formidable than many kinds of political oppression, since, though not usually upheld by such extreme penalties, it leaves fewer means of escape, penetrating much

more deeply into the details of life, and enslaving the soul itself.[2]

The above quote could well be used to describe the power of social norms of behavior as manifested through the group on the individual Japanese person. While Mill expresses the Western conviction that the social majority "enslaves the soul," the average Japanese would be more inclined to think of it as coddling the soul. Subject behavior in Japan tends as much to be subject to the social group as to political and state institutions. The individual is oriented toward the output of the group more than his or her inputs into the group, and, as Mill points out, while the power of the group is immense, the "laws" determining the relationship are obligatory, implicit, and not contractual. Most Japanese people are socialized into behaving according to social and behavioral norms shared by most other members of the nation. Adherence to these norms and the values upon which they are based become ingrained and are indispensable for a normal life in Japan.

Collectivism as manifested in the Japanese group ethic is both hierarchical and egalitarian. The Japanese sometimes seem obsessed with rank, ordering everything from office employees to universities to sumo wrestlers. The vertical nature of the Japanese group and the necessity of understanding the differences between people with the same attributes exists so that one's place in the hierarchy can be realized. To quote Edwin O. Reischauer (1978: 157), "[Japanese] interpersonal relations and the groups into which they divide are usually structured on the assumption that there will be hierarchical differences." Ranking is absolutely necessary because forms of behavior, speech, bowing, and other mannerisms in Japanese society differ according to the situation and relative levels of the individuals interacting. For example, one would use different levels of formality in speech and bow in different ways when speaking to one's professor, one's classmate, or an underclass student.

Rank in the group is determined not only by attribute, but also by role. The group is held together only as long as every member agrees to perform his or her assigned role. Identification with role is so strong that people are often addressed by their roles in life, or in the group, rather than by their names (Lebra 1976: 84). Elderly women are called "grandmother" (*oba-san*), by everyone, office workers call their manager "manager" (*bucho*), a liquor store owner is called "Mr. Liquor Store" (*sakaya-san*), and a senior member of the group is called "senior" (*sempai*). The harmony of the group depends on everyone understanding his or her role and rank in the group, and fulfilling the functions and behaviors appropriate to them.

However, "[T]he Japanese group is usually characterized by a substantial degree of hierarchy but with qualifications and adaptations that appreciably moderate in practice what might otherwise seem to be quite authoritarian procedures" (Ward 1978: 61). One of those adaptations of the Japanese group leads to the emphasis of the group over the individual to stress egalitarianism even within a hierarchical context. The melding of the individual into the group means that all are subservient to the group, and that while their various roles within the group may have different rankings, no one individual is superior to any other individual in the group. This is reinforced by many behavioral patterns in Japan, often expressed by the phrase "the nail that sticks up gets hammered down." Thus, while everyone in an office is extremely sensitive to the slightest nuance of ranking—who went to which university, whose children are going to which kindergarten, who married into what family—the office is open, everyone has the same desk, carpet, and telephone, the office manager is there in the office with everyone else and has a company work-jacket to put on when he goes down to the shop floor. This situation is in sharp contrast to the "single stature harmonization" of the British workplace, symbolized by separate dining facilities for employers and employees (Dore 1985: 198).

The simultaneously hierarchical and egalitarian nature of Japanese groups meet in collective leadership. In Japan, collective decision making replaces individual leadership. This has been true throughout Japanese history, but is especially important in the modern period. Although Japan under the Meiji constitution was dominated by the figure of the emperor, the emperor himself had relatively little power. It was always those around him who made the decisions as a group. This was true even during the war years when Japan was at its most hierarchical period. But it is also true today. Even though the prime minister is both leader of the government party and leader of the government, he has little individual power and can only act through his membership in groups such as the Liberal Democratic Party's Executive Council.

Collectivity as an assertion of the power of the national community is most clearly manifested in Japan through the tradition of group leadership and is a major factor in the political system of Japan. In the case of Britain, the interventionist state is best known for the state collectivization of resources to be applied to the welfare state. While this has also occurred in Japan since the end of the war, albeit not to the extent of Britain, more important is the collectivity of the state through national leadership. This first occurred in modern Japan with the creation of the *kokutai* during the Meiji period. The theory was that if the "national polity" is embodied in the emperor, then only the emperor, and those who serve him, can represent the entire nation. Thus, a small leadership elite group could keep power out of the hands of political parties while claiming to represent the nation. Still today, the goals of the nation and the state tend to be set by national leadership. This is not a national collectivity for action, but rather a national collectivity which calls for consensus from above for national decisions. There are few powerful national interest groups which spring from below.

The traditional collectivity of the national community, as expressed above, combines in postwar Japan with what we have described in the British context as the interventionist welfare state to form what Chalmers Johnson (1986) terms the developmental state. That is, Japan's economic growth in the postwar period has been planned and executed by an elite group of bureaucrats acting in the name of the national community. Their actions and their benevolence were accepted by both the Japanese people and the ruling party for many years, in part due to the traditions and behaviors discussed above.

As will be discussed in Chapter 7, acceptance of leadership of the bureaucracy, or of any group claiming the mantle of the national community, is no longer automatic because the importance of the individual vis-à-vis the group is increasing in Japan. But, relative to Britain and other Western democracies, the collectivity of the Japanese, both in their group orientation and in the power of the national community, as represented by an oligarchic elite, is still one of the most important factors of Japanese political culture.

We have said little about individualistic norms in Japan. Clearly there are and have been individuals and movements that have embraced Western libertarian values. Japan has an indigenous concept of equal rights, for example, the Freedom and Popular Rights movement and early Japanese socialism. The ideals of meritocracy and strengthening of personal ambition had taken root in prerestoration Japan (Ward 1965: 31). But individualism is a distinctly minority value. Despite this, libertarian values have been observed by many to be increasing in recent years, and we shall discuss this development below, as one of the manifestations of values change in Japan.

Harmony and Conflict

Politics is about both conflict and reconciliation, but political cultures exhibit the two in different proportions, and assign them different values. Japan and Britain are both societies, as we have seen, in which the social cleavages that have torn others asunder have either been largely absent (conflicting nationalism and class in Japan) or effectively managed (class in Britain). They are also both societies which, while exhibiting conflict, have placed a relatively high value on consensus. On the scale of harmony and conflict, Britain, and Japan to an even greater extent, should be placed toward the pole of harmony. The individualist/collectivist and harmony/conflict values dimensions are distinct, the former dealing with the relative ranking of individual and group needs and influence in the society, the latter dealing with the relations among the various political actors, individual, and group. Nevertheless, it is admittedly difficult at times to keep that distinction clear. Collectivist views of society imply a premium on social harmony. Indeed, in Japanese culture collectivity and harmony are nearly one in the same, and still to a large extent, strong individualism is viewed as discordant. At the same time, individualist values do not necessarily connote a conflictual society, as is demonstrated by British political culture.

Britain

Britain's history suggests that conflict is as much a tradition as deference. In the context of politics, and more especially industrial relations, it is even possible to say that a positive value is attached to confrontation. Both in the collectivist tradition of labor-management strife, and in the individualist tradition of defiance of authority, conflict is a legitimate means of defending rights. Indeed, recent observers have argued that more confrontational styles of politics are on the upswing. However, open confrontation and conflict are not the preferred norms of the political culture, even if they are on the rise. Quite to the contrary, the culture places a strong positive value on the harmonious resolution of disputes, especially at the elite level. As Edmund Burke said in calling for conciliation with America in 1775, "All government, indeed every human benefit and enjoyment, every virtue, and every prudent act, is founded on compromise and barter." Norton (1984: 30–31), whose consensualist optimism about Britain contrasts with the views of critics like Alan Marsh (1977), argues that "there is an almost instinctive distaste for conflict, both in personal relationships and in political life ... there is a penchant, almost, for resolving disputes by discussion, by sitting around a table and ironing out one's differences." This consensualism can be seen in public attitudes about appropriate means of protest—which to this day favor petition and orderly demonstration over more coercive means. It can be seen in conventions of government such as collective responsibility and confidentiality. It can be seen in the oft-noted moderation of the public's stands on policy questions. "A strong consensus on procedures for resolving differences is characteristic of the British" (Kavanagh 1980: 140). Conflict occurs within the context of consensus on basic laws and support for the parliamentary system (Rose 1986c: 142). Heath and Topf confirm this when they conclude that protest appears to be "directed *at* rather than *against* Parliament, and working *within* rather than *outside* the existing political system" (1987: 57).

At the elite level, one is also likely to find the coexistence of consensual and conflictual norms. Putnam's (1973: 150) study of political elites argues that Britain is an example of a polity where "integrative," "problem-solving" approaches eschew conflict in favor of "policies that meet the interests and desires of all the parties involved." This "cooperative problem solving," he finds, "is, in comparative perspective, quite remarkable" (1973: 151). Even where conflict exists, he concludes, it is essentially reconcilable (1973: 105). On the other hand, who could fail to observe the combat of adversarial politics as practiced in parliamentary debate and election campaigns. As Bagehot (1966: 262) observed in the 1860s, "we have ... inherited the traditions of conflict, and preserve them in the fullness of victory." Dore (1985: 208), who tends more than some to emphasize the normality of conflict in the British culture, has observed that "Britain substituted for martial warfare the verbal warfare of politics. Politics has been the sphere par excellence in which we have preserved the styles of leadership and domination appropriate to an aristocratic military society." Indeed, there is even evidence of erosion of elite consensus on the political rules of the game. Searing (1982: 240) argues that "politicians' attitudes towards the rules of the game are less consensual and are based on political values and partisan advantage more than traditional interpretations or recent democratic theory admit. . . . The present view is simply that the temptation has become greater during the postwar era, that administrative complexity has provided new opportunities for bending the rules, and that diminishing respect for authority has weakened normative constraints." Birch (1980: 14) would add that the replacement of party leaders from the traditional governing class by party leaders from grammar schools also contributed to the emergence of "a more abrasive style of party conflict." This style was certainly attributed to Mrs. Thatcher, who openly sought to replace the politics of consensus with the invariably more confrontational politics of conviction.

On balance, however, consensus has survived as a significant political norm. For one thing, insists Rose (1986c: 145), despite the acrimony of debate, "at the level of actions, not words, continuities are more substantial than differences." Kavanagh (1985a: 53) reminds us, too, that "The parties have been willing to compromise or, if not, then to abide by the results of a general election, hoping to reverse an objectionable policy at a future date. . . . But there has been general agreement among the major political parties about basic political procedures. Governments too have not wished to push policies to a point at which groups felt they were unfairly treated." Even Searing (1982: 256) concludes that "notwithstanding all the partisan prejudices . . . the Constitution's deliberative interpretation draws sufficient consensus that one could argue that perhaps Balfour was right [that the British people were 'so fundamentally at one that they can safely afford to bicker']—for a narrower range of rules of the game than has been assumed." There is a sense in which the balance between political conflict and harmony in Britain captures the *omote/ura* dimension of Japanese conflict, where adversarial politics represent the formal, "publicly legitimate, dramatized and dignified element," (*omote*); and where partisan compromise represents the "privately allowed, practical and efficient" element, (*ura*) (Ishida 1984: 21).

Support for consensus is buttressed by the legendary preference of what Kavanagh (1987: 17) calls this "rather immobilist society" for incrementalism and gradualism. "[O]ne great premise of English politics is that the past is assimilated by adapting rather than by abolishing ageing political institutions" (Rose 1986c: 23). Change is sought through increments within constitutional methods (Kavanagh 1985a: 53). "[I]nstinct, trial and error, and incremental change are the essence of the English approach to problem solving" (Norton 1984: 27). These preferences are strongly supported by survey data (Rose 1986c: Table IV.2, 125). The European Values System Survey in 1980 found "broad support right across the political spectrum for change through reform rather than revolution; for the rule of law rather than for drastic political solutions or methods" (Harding 1986: 108). As Table 1.1 suggests, with the exception of those on the political right, close to two-thirds or more of respondents prefer "gradual reform" to other means of change. Preference for reformism seems little affected by social class either, though the middle class does express a slightly greater

Table 1.1

Attitudes to Political Change of the Existing System by "Left-Right" Position (in percent)

	Left	Center Left	Center	Center Right	Right	All
Radical change	6	2	3	5	5	4
Gradual reform	64	82	71	66	49	66
Valiant defense	13	14	21	24	45	22
Don't know	16	1	4	5	2	8

Source: David Phillips, 1985. "Participation and Political Values." In *Values and Social Change in Britain,* ed. Mark Abrams et al.: Table 6.3, p. 161. London: Macmillan. © Mark Abrams, David Gerard, and Noel Timms. Used with permission of Macmillan Ltd.

preference than the working class (Phillips 1985: 163).

The revolutionary stance is not clearly linked to "left" or "right" positions, or to other beliefs (Phillips 1985: 164). Reformism does appear to be linked to age, however, with the youngest group, surprisingly, favoring gradual change more than the oldest group (Phillips 1985: 163). Even the unemployed are likely to believe that society should be gradually reformed, and to reject radical change by revolution. "The prevailing outlook, then, is one of broadly-based support for 'moderate' forms of change" (Phillips 1985: 162).

Variant ideas of social harmony are intrinsic to the major political and intellectual traditions of what are still the two major political parties in Britain—Labour and Conservative. In the socialist, or Labour vision of democracy, a fundamental dissensus is caused by capitalism and the class system, and this can only be remedied by placing government in the hands of "the people," embodied in the working class. Rule by the working class, through its "class" party, permits, for the first time, the creation of a harmonious polity rooted in the shared interest of all. This harmony is intrinsic to the collectivist conception of society, and extrinsic to the moral individualism of middle class liberalism. As Beer (1982b: 129) explains it, the "private will and personality would be merged in the comprehensive will of the community." In economic terms, "cooperation could take the place of the profit motive precisely because men could live in fellowship ... because they could be brought to identify their own individual good and gain with the common welfare" (Beer 1982b: 130). The Conservative legacy also includes a concept of social harmony, though one very different from the socialist. Generally speaking, harmony is perceived as the result of an organic, and hierarchically ordered society. Harmony is produced when the separate ranks of the corporate whole accept their place: the governing class to govern, the working classes to acquiesce. A more democratic variant of this vision of British social harmony was reflected in the *Civic Culture* model. Neither of these visions, of course, the socialist nor the Tory, represents the reality of British politics. They still do, however, form part of the party mythology of Britain, and they still inform political views and debate.

Japan

The importance of consensus as a social and political value in Japan and the consequent consensual nature of Japanese political culture is closely related to both the above-discussed collectivity of Japan and the importance of harmony. Whether one speaks of the Confucian Principle of the Mean, Taoist *yin* and *yang*, or Buddhist democratic equality, the concepts of balance and harmony have been the foundation of East Asian philosophy for thousands of years. Over 1,400 years ago, Prince Shotoku wrote words which still apply to Japanese society.

> Harmony is to be valued, and an avoidance of wanton opposition is to be honored. All men are influenced by partisanship, and there are few who are intelligent. Hence, there are some who disobey their lords and fathers, or who maintain feuds with the neighboring villages. But, when those above are harmonious and those below are friendly, and there is concord in the discussion of business, right views of things spontaneously gain acceptance. Then, what is there that cannot be accomplished?[3]

Of all the Japanese cultural influences upon the political process, perhaps the most commonly emphasized is the need for consensus. Maintaining harmony is the obligation of every Japanese citizen, and there is a variety of ways in which it is carried out. Intense pressures on the individual to conform to the group are transferred from individual norms of behavior to institutional norms of behavior. Japanese decision making is justifiably noted for its reliance on behavior that will bring about a unanimous, consensual decision. Contentious subjects that can create conflict are usually avoided in the formal decision-making setting. Instead, opinions are usually expressed in more informal settings, most commonly over an after-hours drink with co-workers, so that those who express the opinions do not have to be held to them (*ura*). At the same time, the participants can get an understanding of who supports which position and line up behind a forming majority. It is also outside the formal decision-making environment that superiors understand the need to go along with decisions agreed upon by subordinates and subordinates understand the need to conform to the rules of seniority. Proposals are widely distributed both horizontally and vertically so that everyone feels included in the process. By the time a formal meeting is held, the decision is often a foregone conclusion, and yet the consensus is reinforced one more time by having everyone in the group, down to the most junior member, included in the process by allowing them to state their position.

While most Japanese learn both the need to conform and the means of creating a consensus within their groups, the same consensus-building behavior is often attributed to interactions between groups as well. Consensus as the dominant theme in Japanese group relations is the foundation for the "ruling triad" or "Japan, Inc." models of Japanese policy making. However, at this level of policy making there cannot exist the unanimity that exists within the small group. For example, in the above models, public opinion, consumer groups, and any group outside the government that is not a "prime contractor" (to use Chalmers Johnson's terms) is going to have very little influence on policy (Johnson 1986: 51). But, given the pervasiveness of consensus in Japan, and the expectation of the citizenry that their leaders should rule with consensus, it still plays an important role in policy making at the institutional level.

The broadest and most general models of consensus formation in Japanese policy making are those with the least validity. It is easy to conjure up a picture of an overlapping elite from the political parties, the bureaucracy, and private enterprises meeting in geisha houses and other informal settings to reach a consensus on national policy. Certainly there are close ties among the members of these three elites, but there is no special cohesiveness in their social backgrounds (Muramatsu and Krauss 1984: 144), and the influence of private enterprise may be rather more limited than is commonly supposed (Muramatsu and Krauss 1984: 144; Johnson 1986: 52). There are many conflicts between the LDP and the bureaucracy, between the LDP and private enterprise, between private enterprise and the bureaucracy, and among factions within all three of these broader institutions (Muramatsu and Krauss 1984: 144; Pempel 1982: 26).

The concept of consensus is overused, often not rigorously defined, and has its greatest validity when applied on a more limited basis. The above-described need for group-belonging and the primacy of the group over the individual is the foundation for consensus in Japan. The need for consensus behavior derives from the homogeneity of the Japanese people and their societal values, the social pressures that channel behavior toward conformity with ubiquitous norms, and the positive value placed on conformity to the group over individual needs. Consensus is not only a goal, the attainment of unanimity by the group, it is also a societal norm that places pressure on each member of the group to conform to the perceived majority decision in order to maintain group harmony as a basis for the continued functioning of the group. Consensus is not created through a true agreement over what decision should be made, but through those who disagree with what is perceived as the majority decision submitting their will to the group. This act of submission will allow them greater power in the future to influence decisions made and will enhance their reputation as team players. In American political parlance, "You have to go along to get along." Although consensual and collective values are important to British politics, as we have seen, they do not have the same meaning as just described in the case of Japan.

When analyzing the role of consensus in Japanese politics it is also important to understand the level of interaction at which the consensus is to be formed, and the breadth of the consensus. The pressure to conform is most intense at the level of individual-group interaction. "Conspicuous idiosyncracy and dissension are avoided or suppressed, and acquiescence is upheld as a main mechanism for maintaining consensus ... The sense of identity anchored in group belonging-ness is thus sustained by going along with peers. This goes with the desirability of being accepted by peers, anxiety about being left out, and a competitive urge for always being 'in' " (Lebra 1976: 28–29). One's place in the group and the conformity that maintains it is daily reinforced through the language one uses and the almost ritualized forms of behavior one adopts toward other members of the group.

While this tendency to submit one's will to the group makes for much harmony and collectivity, the hallmarks of Japanese society, when the submission of one's will to others does not occur, the ability to communicate among the refusers and other members of the group usually ends. This creates a major problem in Japanese society. There is so much reliance on consensus in decision making that when the consensus breaks down there is no tradition of adversarial debate which allows parties in conflict to simultaneously maintain dialogue and conflict. Thus, Japanese politics tends to be defined either by those organizations that form the seamless whole that is called "Japan, Inc.," or the never-ending and violent conflicts symbolized by the struggle of the Sanrizuka and the state over Narita Airport.

We suggested above that the clear preference among all segments of the British population for gradual change was a further indication of the British preference for harmony. The Japanese adopt a similarly gradualist view, though in light of the brief life of the current Japanese polity, it is not possible to cite a historical pattern of reformism, as it is in the case of Britain. Ward (1965: 61) found, for example, that during the debate over constitutional revision in the 1950s, "despite the highly bitter and controversial nature of the struggle, very little of the agitation for major structural change is revolutionary in character." A plurality (40 percent) of Japanese in a 1981 cross-national survey agreed that "our society must be gradually improved by reforms" (Leisure Development Center 1981). This response was over twenty percentage points lower than the average for European countries surveyed. On the other hand, only 2 percent (one of the lowest rates compared to the European countries) favored radical change by revolutionary action.

Particularism/Universalism

This, the third of our dimensions, concerns the orientation toward universalistic (ideological) or particularistic (pragmatic) modes of thinking. Inglehart and Klingemann (1979: 205) define the ideological mode of thought as "a coherent world view, a comprehensive system of political beliefs in which political ideas are central ... a frame of reference, a taxonomy, that allows for a specific type of processing of politically relevant information." The ideological mode is not only a means of classifying information. It is a means of evaluating information as well. The more consistently people apply the "central elements" of such a world view—e.g., "common ownership of the means of production"—the more they may dichotomize political objects as desirable or undesirable, acceptable or unacceptable. The ideologue is likely not only to comprehend ideological concepts, but to hold strong convictions about what ought to be.

Conversely, we shall consider that the less consistently people apply such ideological models, the more they approach each situation, each new bit of information without reference to such a core of beliefs, the more "pragmatic," or "particularistic" they are. Pragmatists have a less cohesive view of political reality, are less committed to normative goals, and are therefore less inclined to impose a fixed standard when political choices must be made. Mayer (1989: 185) defines pragmatism as "the propensity to choose courses of action according to the criterion of whether they actually promote some end in view (i.e., they 'work'), irrespective of their consistency with any principle or of their logical consistency." In the 1979 Barnes and Kaase et al. study, nonideological modes of thinking were the norm in all the states, including Britain, where four-fifths of the population were found to use "nonideological modes of conceptualization of politics" (Klingemann 1979b: 224). Though Japan was not included in their study, other evidence overwhelmingly suggests the prevalence of particularism in Japanese political culture.

Britain

Ideology/Pragmatism

The nonideological, or pragmatic, approach to policy in Britain has been widely noted (Putnam 1973; Studlar and Welch 1981; Barnes et al. 1979; Rose 1986c). According to Norton (1984: 27), the empirical, or what we call particularistic, style "constitutes the most significant aspect of British culture." Conflicts are expected to be reconciled and a solution found, in the interest of getting on to the next problem. Pragmatism should not be understood to suggest the absence of values or the absence of conflict. As we saw above, a consensual tradition of politics coexists with an equally vigorous conflictual tradition.

The British disinclination to ideological thinking cannot be blamed on the unavailability of ideological models in the political culture. On the contrary, political ideology has been a component of British intellectual history far more than has been the case in Japan. Political theory has formed an important basis for political dialogue in Britain for centuries. The language of politics is derived from the writings of Locke, Burke, Spencer, Bentham, Carlisle, Mill, and the Webbs, among countless others. Contemporary political debates in Britain are often, though by no means exclusively, framed in terms of classical liberalism and socialism. Thatcher's call to abolish socialism in Britain certainly conveyed an ideological mode of thought, as do Labour's internal debates over "clause four" of its constitution. On the other hand, pluralism of ideologies in Britain is symptomatic of the failure of any one ideology to prevail. As Norton (1984: 28) has noted, "ideologies have been either discarded or else molded to fit with the experience of history."

The nonideological orientation among the British is confirmed when assessed according to the prevalent "left-right" and "liberal-conservative" dimensions that have predominated in Western cultures. By "left" we mean broadly the rejection of a hierarchical social order in favor of greater "uniformity of the social and political condition" and common ownership of the means of production. By "right" we mean conservation of a hierarchical social order and private owner-ship of the means of production (Inglehart and Klingemann 1979: 206). This dichotomy certainly exists in Britain, but it is very much muted.[4] Mass opinion is solidly moderate and has long tended to resist extremes, even in times of crisis. "The efforts of the extreme left and the extreme right to defy the law in the name of a self-proclaimed superior political morality," concludes Rose (1986c: 121), "is not accepted in England." The feeble efforts of the Communist Party and various right-wing parties suggest the abiding moderation of Britons.

Although recognition of the terms "left" and "right" is high in Britain as throughout Europe, understanding is not. Klingemann (1979b: 230–31) found the percentage of British respondents (11 percent) possessing an "ideological under-standing" of these terms to be the lowest among the five countries in the sample; in fact a larger percentage reversed the meanings of the two terms than under-stood them. Indeed, a very small percentage of Britons identify themselves on the far "right" or the far "left." This is true, despite a rather high degree of class polarization in Britain (see Chapter 2). In a 1986 survey, only 3 percent identify themselves as far left or right (Social Surveys Ltd. September 1986 cited in Hastings and Hastings 1988: 369). Phillips' analysis of the 1981 European Val-ues System Survey (EVSS) data strongly suggests moderation among the British. He found British self-identification slightly right compared to Europe as a whole, but not because of the weight of opinion on the far right. In the EVSS survey, 5 percent identified with the left, 8 percent with the right, 49 percent with the center, and 87 percent with center left to center right (Phillips 1985: Figure 6.1, 155). To the limited extent that left and right differ, however, they tend most to differ over "attitudes towards economic issues such as industrial control and confidence in the trade unions, and aspects of authority such as confidence in the armed forces and the police. There is, however, extensive agreement across the political spectrum on these and other issues, and so left-right orientation does not translate directly into alignment around specific political attitudes." Phillips (1985: 147) concludes "one looks in vain for evidence of sharpening divisions among the sample of respondents surveyed here. Indeed, the large majority of the population appear to share a broadly 'consensual' outlook on political affairs.

Attempts, using multivariate statistical techniques like cluster analysis, to identify groupings differing sharply in their political values, under headings such as 'Radical Left,' 'Militant Moderate,' 'New Right' and so on, were strikingly unsuccessful." The public has continued to eschew identification with either the left or the right, even as the two major parties have shown an upsurge of ideological battle during the 1970s and 1980s.

Such as it is, the left orientation in Britain is greater among the young and semi or nonskilled manual workers, while the right orientation is greater among the elderly, professionals, or managers (Phillips 1985: 157). Polarization also appears to be linked with other social value systems, such as moral traditionalism. Those who have more fixed ideas about good and evil tend to lean further to the right (Phillips 1985: 157). Ideological polarization is also linked to religiosity, and material and psychological satisfaction. Interestingly, though ideological polarization is associated to a degree with employment/unemployment, the slight association of the unemployed with the left does not translate into particularly radical views, in "their views either on society in general or on the organisation and management of work" (Fogarty 1985: 188).

Moral Absolutism/Relativism

Like other Western nations, Britain has inherited at the philosophical level an approach to understanding the political world that is highly dichotomized. Much of the philosophical and religious tradition of the West accepts the existence of truth and falsehood, good and evil, right and wrong. Increasingly with the decline of faith and the rise of secularism, it was accepted that science and reason were the tools for the discovery of the laws of society as well as the laws of nature. J. S. Mill wrote that "the collective series of social phenomena, in other words the course of history, is subject to general laws, which philosophy may possibly detect" (cited in Greenleaf 1983a: 238). Herbert Spencer deduced a "strictly scientific morality" consisting of "imperative ethical laws" (cited in Greenleaf 1983b: 63). In Western social psychology, this dichotomous perspective is reflected in the theory of cognitive consistency (Festinger 1957), which argues that people reject values and cognitions that fail to reinforce existing values or models of reality. While not ideological in their politics, Britons have been observed by some to be "markedly more moralistic" with respect to some attitudes than other Europeans (Harding 1985: 12). Heath and Topf (1987: 63) find in the data for the 1987 *British Social Attitudes* report that substantial majorities agreed with questions supporting "the prevailing moral order and the rule of law." The data presented in Table 1.2 suggest that Britons do indeed adopt an absolutist position more frequently than their European counterparts or the Japanese.

But one philosophical tradition (which in any case is one among many) and limited survey data do not define political culture. The existence of strong di-

Table 1.2

Guidelines for Good and Evil

Percentages agreeing with:	Britain	Japan	Europe
A. There are absolutely clear guidelines about what is good and evil. These always apply to everyone, whatever the circumstances	38	13	26
B. There can never be clear and absolute guidelines about what is good and evil. What is good and evil depends entirely upon the circumstances at the time	64	61	60

Source: Gordon Heald, 1982. "A Comparison between American, European and Japanese Values." Paper presented at The Annual Meeting of the World Association for Public Opinion Research, May 21: Table 12, p. 13.

chotomous traditions of thought does not mean that Britons take an entirely homogeneous and inflexible view of right and wrong, or are incapable of tolerating ambiguity. Johnston and Wood (1985: 121) point out that "many different conceptions of right and wrong co-exist in British society." Reviewing the EVSS data on ten countries, Harding and Phillips (1986: 15) find that on all three of the morality scales they identify, Britain showed levels of strictness and tolerance "which scarcely deviate from the European average."[5] As Table 1.2 shows, a clear majority of Europeans, British, and Japanese express agreement with a relativistic position.

Jowell and Topf (1988: 110) also confirm a relativist position in the public view that "Politicians are much more likely to be judged on their commitment to achieving results on behalf of their constituents, or on behalf of the nation—the ends or the motives, at least to an extent, justifying the means." This attitude has its counterpart in the Japanese notion of "sincerity," discussed below. Generally, the British are quite tolerant of nonconforming behavior. This may be linked to their strong preference for freedom of association and speech.

Contextualism/Legalism

Many Western states tend to be *rechstaats*, in which the laws of the state are interpreted very strictly and adhered to very closely. Contractual relations between individuals and between individuals and groups permeate Western society. The individual's obligations to others are explicit and contained within the confines of the contract. An employee's relationship with the company is defined by his or her contract, the relationship between husband and wife is defined by a prenuptial agreement, the relationship between banker and borrower is defined by the loan agreement, and the relationship between the state and the citizen is defined by constitutional and statutory law. Certainly with respect to business agreements and employment relationships, such a contractual view is the norm in Britain (Dore 1985: 213). In politics, the standard is somewhat different, however. In contrast to German society, for example, where the assumption is often made "that disagreements can be solved in a 'rational' and 'objective' manner by experts . . . the British are more likely to recognise that conflicts of interest and disputes involving value judgments do not allow such solutions: the centrality of politics is accepted" (Ridley 1984: 6). In many contexts pragmatism and administrative discretion are the rule. "[T]here are few published rules . . . defining the way officials must act in assessing a case," and "there is less inclination than in some countries to think of administrative decisions as the application of laws" (Ridley 1984: 4, 16). Instead, administrative decisions "are made in a pragmatic fashion with a wide element of discretion. . . such decisions involve the impressionistic assessment of facts, the application of value judgments and the search for compromise" (Ridley 1984: 6). Political struggle and compromise resolve differences, not law or constitution. The British penchant for minimizing conflict, noted above, may also help to deter legalistic, or zero-sum approaches. British civil servants have "no training in law whatsoever; in the words of one textbook author, "they work in an atmosphere far removed from legal influence . . . Their expertise lies in political and administrative sensitivity, and this shapes their approach in individual matters as well as to policy issues. They operate on the basis of 'feel' for the case rather than formalised procedures, and they search for a 'reasonable' rather than a rational solution' " (Ridley 1984: 7). In the case of tribunals, for example, while an effort is made to apply existing rules to a case, at base the process is to reconsider the case based on "what is reasonable within the framework of the ministry's rules," and what is appropriate, rather than what is legal (Ridley 1984: 13). "[T]he ideal of 'political' rather than 'legal' protection of citizens against administration is deeply imbedded in British political traditions and has imprinted itself on British ways of thought" (Ridley 1984: 4). The preeminence of politics is illustrated concretely by the low profile of the courts in political questions. While law is not the favored means of conflict resolution in either society, there are important differences in the motives for eschewing legalism in Japan and Britain. Both approaches are pragmatic and flexible. Both downplay implications of universalistic principles. In Britain, however, the preference for political over legal resolution does not imply that settlements depend upon personal ties or obligations among the participants. In Japan, such personalism is at the heart of the approach to conflict resolution.

Japan

One aspect of Japanese society long assumed to differentiate it from Western societies is its lack of adherence to universal principles. It is not that the Japanese have not attempted to introduce universal laws and principles—the above-mentioned Seventeen Article Constitution of the seventh century is proof that universal laws were applied very early in Japanese political history—rather it is that Japanese people tend to be much more pragmatic in their behavior and less concerned about consistency with any particular set of political or religious values. As Edwin Reischauer points out, "In the West the division was between good and evil, always in mortal combat with each other. In East Asia the division of *yang* and *yin* was between night and day, male and female, lightness and darkness, that is, between complementary forces which alternate with and balance each other" (Reischauer 1978: 139). Indeed, debate over the relationship between particularism and universalism was only debated in Japan by a few monastic scholars until the advent of Western learning (Nakamura 1967: 179). The particularism of the Japanese tends to make political behavior in Japan more pragmatic than ideological, more relative than absolute, more nondichotomous than dichotomous, more contextual than contractual, and more emotional than rational.

Ideology/Pragmatism

The Japanese are also well known for the pragmatic, nonideological nature of their political behavior. The lack of ideology in Japanese political relations stems from the egalitarian nature of Japanese society and the lack of concern with universal values. The Japanese perceive their society as being very equal and do not perceive the existence of class conflict. What class polarization that does exist tends to be an elite phenomenon and not a mass phenomenon (Flanagan 1978: 151). According to various survey data, including those carried out by the authors, Nippon Hoso Kyokai (NHK), and the Prime Minister's Office (PMO), generally about 90 percent put themselves in the middle class. As Ellis Krauss et al. (1984: 388) put it, even class groups "do not advocate an ideology based on class consciousness." Because of the homogeneous nature of Japanese society and the emphasis on harmony, Japanese people tend to stress the similarities among one another, and not the differences. This is reinforced by the structure of Japanese groups. Because each group is a discrete hierarchy, broader hierarchies consisting of nationwide mass, middle-class and elite are less common than in a country like Britain (Reischauer 1978: 160).

Wealth is shared fairly equally in Japan, relative to Britain and most Western states. There are few class differences in behavior or speech, and Japan is an efficiently operating meritocracy where almost all have a chance to succeed.

Both Marxism and, more successfully, democratic capitalism have taken root in Japan, but have not produced the same flowers as bloom in the West. Marxism has not been a truly popular ideology because of the lack of class consciousness and the success of democratic capitalism. Democracy, however, has succeeded, not for reasons of spiritual and intellectual commitment, but because it works.

This may sound cynical, but not if one takes the pragmatic, relativistic approach of Japanese political culture. "To grasp the essence of a political culture that does not recognize the possibility of transcendental truths demands an unusual intellectual effort for Westerners, an effort that is rarely made even in serious assessments of Japan" (van Wolferen 1990: 10). Ever since the American occupiers of Japan were loath to leave without a firm Japanese commitment to the values of democracy, there has been a hesitancy in the West to believe that the Japanese will remain a democratic state. Whether or not the Japanese have finally committed themselves to this particular ideology cannot be fully determined until its effectiveness is challenged, if ever. The question is whether a democratic political culture can be said to exist if it lacks the total and unwavering commitment to the universal values which comprise the ideology. To the universalistic mind-set the answer is "no," but to the particularistic mind-set the answer is "yes."

Moral Absolutism/Relativism

Students of Japan have often noted the prevalence of nondichotomous thought in that culture; the Japanese have a way of perceiving things that is highly tolerant of ambiguity (Wagatsuma 1984; Kyogoku 1987). Given the prominence of specific cultural explanations of relativistic, or nondichotomous thinking in the literature on Japan, it is somewhat surprising that the differences revealed in Table 1.2 between Europeans and Japanese are not greater. Yet significantly fewer Japanese agree that there are clear guidelines between good and evil, only 13 percent, while a full 26 percent either disagree with both positions or don't know. In all aspects of life there are irreconcilable ambiguities such as good and bad, positive and negative, true and false, real and unreal. In Japan, however, no one aspect need prevail over the other; no reconciliation of opposites is necessary. Because individual behavior in Japanese society operates under conditions of social relativism, there can be no absolutes and right and wrong. Good and bad can change according to circumstances, personality, environment, or a number of other conditional influences. Nothing, including political values, needs to be clear-cut.

In Japanese society, the ambiguities of nondichotomous thought are formalized in the two related concepts of *tatemae/honne* and *omote/ura* behavior. *Omote* (front) refers to that which is public, that which everyone can see, while *ura* (back) refers to that which is private, or hidden away from the sight of others. *Tatemae* (principle) is that to which one must agree outwardly, the standard accepted by most people in society. *Honne* (reality) is the inner reality or belief, that which is thought to be actually true. *Omote* and *ura* are often contradictory, as are *tatemae* and *honne*, but it is possible for these contradictions to exist without resolution. Indeed, the contradictions are encouraged for the harmonious functioning of society. Thus, for example, what one does or says in public (*omote*) will be accepted for what it is, even if it contradicts what is actually happening in private (*ura*). For example, during a public negotiating session between labor and management both sides may scowl, bang the table. and generally conduct themselves in a conflictual manner because that is the "face" that labor-management relations are assumed to have in that situation, but behind closed doors, and in a less formal setting, agreements may already have been made. When ex–Prime Minister Tanaka Kakuei was convicted of taking a bribe in the Lookheed scandal, the public, the opposition parties, and many members of the LDP demanded that he be removed as a member of the LDP. He was removed as a member of the party (*omote*), but he continued to be the most powerful influence on LDP politics (*ura*), until he was felled by a stroke. A classic example of *tatemae* and *honne*, and one we will return to later, concerns the role of the constitution in Japanese politics. The constitution of Japan is *tatemae*, that is, stated principle, and the Japanese know that as a democracy they must adhere to the principles embodied in the constitution. On the other hand, it is often quite inconvenient to act according to those principles and so the constitution becomes a *denka no hoto*, or sword handed down for many generations as a family treasure. It acts as a mighty symbol of the family, is revered and highly prized, but is never used (Kawashima 1967: 267). Of course, there is nothing unique about these behaviors, they exist in other societies as well, but there is a relative difference. They certainly seem to occur with much more frequency in Japanese society, they have been integrated into the very fabric of social behavior in Japan as social norms, and this type of behavior is not only tolerated but supported in many cases by the Japanese people.

Related to the concepts of *tatemae* and *honne* is Takie Sugiyama Lebra's concept of social relativism. The theory of social relativism explains Japanese particularism as being a function of the other-relatedness of the Japanese. As we saw in our discussion of Japanese collectivism, the Japanese are concerned above all else with their relationships with other people, and there is little belief in eternal life for the individual or universal religious principles (Kyogoku 1987: 44). Thus, behavior and actions are determined not by universal values or moral principles, but by the individual's perception of other's reactions to his or her behavior. Japanese behavior conforms more to situation ethics than to absolute principles (Lebra 1976: 1–21). This aspect of Japanese values has long caused problems between Japan and the West. Indeed, the continuing suspicion of whether Japan is really a democratic country stems in part from the reticence of the Japanese to adhere to any ideology. But there is also a positive aspect. Japanese society is quite tolerant in that the Japanese understand that there is good and bad in everyone and that no one is ever all one or the other. What is correct in one context may be wrong in another. Thus, one politician may be condemned for taking bribes if the money was to benefit him personally, but another politician's bribe taking may be treated more leniently if the money was to be used for the benefit of his faction. The sincerity of the wrongdoer may also excuse the transgression.

Contextualism/Legalism

In Japan, the context in which behavior takes place is more important than contract or law. There is a near absence of legalistic modes of thought and the enforcement of law depends upon various circumstances, including the relationship between the citizen and the official (Richardson and Flanagan 1984: 121, 181). When a Japanese employee enters into a contract with his or her company, that employee realizes that the contract is only a legalistic form of *tatemae*, but that the *honne* relationship is outside any contract. The *honne* relationship depends on understood conventions, the personal relationship between the employee and co-workers, and conditions of employment as they evolve. It is not written into the contract that the company may not fire the employee except under certain circumstances, but it is understood by both employer and employee that as long as the employee does his or her job at a minimal level, the employee will be retained until retirement. The contract may stipulate that the employee can have two weeks of vacation during the year, but if the office manager lets the employee know that his or her absence for two weeks would be a severe burden on the rest of the staff, then the vacation will not be taken.

This attitude is especially important when applied toward the relationship between statutory and constitutional laws and the polity. Laws, especially the constitution, become the *denka no hoto* described above, a *tatemae* principle which is revered but not necessarily obeyed. Other concerns, such as tradition or efficacy, may be more important than strict interpretation and enforcement of the law. Thus, "guidelines" issued by the administrative bureaucracy take precedence over law if they are thought more effective in dealing with the case at hand. Women may still be discriminated against in employment, even though it is in contradiction of constitutional and statutory law, because of the traditions of a male-dominated society.

In the West, there is assumed to be a tension between law and social practice, with the former controlling and evaluating the former. Japan, however, "does not have a tension between these two antitheses, but a continuum from one to the other, or, rather, a compromise between these two antitheses" (Kawashima 1967: 267). Thus, there is a tendency in Japan not to carry through with a law if it is contrary to traditional social behavior or is not effective. Take, for example, the American Volstead Act which prohibited the importation, sale, and consumption of alcoholic beverages. It could never have been effectively enforced because there was no desire to comply with the law among many citizens, but the state continued to try to force abstinent behavior on the society for over a decade. To use a Japanese example, when the Japanese government thought it proper to outlaw prostitution in order to appear modernized to the West, the Prostitution Surveillance Law was passed, but various forms of prostitution have been allowed to continue ever since. The state, recognizing the need for a law but also realizing that it could never be, and should not be, strictly enforced, has little trouble with the resulting ambiguity because both the "face" of the state and public harmony are maintained (Kawashima 1967: 267).

If Japanese political behavior depends much more on personalism and context than adherence to universal norms and laws, it is also the case that Japanese thought tends to be nonrational and nonlogical as we define those terms in the West. The Japanese thought process tends to be more intuitive, not tied to rational ordering, and not concerned with logical consequences (Nakamura 1967a: 143). The difference between Japanese and Western thought is summed up by Ellen Frost (1987: 85) as being the difference between "wet" Japan and the "dry" West. Japanese society frowns on any overt display of emotions because they are, by their very nature, disruptive both to the person expressing the emotions and those observing them. On the other hand, the Japanese are very emotional in their thought processes. They are very sensitive to nuances in behavior, and accordingly they place primary importance on interpersonal relationships.

Japanese language is a very good example of the "wetness" and contextualism of Japanese thought and behavior in that it is more a language of feel and intuition than logic. To the Westerner, the Japanese language is very imprecise. There is often no distinction used between singular and plural. Many words in a conversation, often very important words, are never spoken, but are implied. Japanese is a very indirect, nonverbal language that depends on the listener's understanding of the time, the place, and the conditions of the conversation, as much as the words that are being spoken. Verbs come at the end of the sentence, allowing the speaker to change the "feel" of the sentence as it is being spoken. Even the words of the language themselves have many definitions or nuances depending upon context (Suzuki 1984: 15–17). Westerners rarely become fluent in Japanese until they begin to understand that there is no logic, as they know it, just "feel," and a lot of memorization.

Organic/Nonorganic Development and Political Stability

The evolution of political values and orientations may be linked to the development of modern political institutions and to the process of mobilization of political support and participation. Stability may be linked in general to the development of both elite and societal consensus. The major contestants must emerge from the modernization process satisfied with the benefits and perceiving a stake in the institutions and rules of the polity. First, during *political institutionalization* (Huntington 1968), an elite consensus must emerge on political structures and the rules of the game. Second, during *cultural institutionalization*, the growth of popular participation must include socialization "of ever wider segments of the population into appropriate, supportive attitudinal orientations and participatory roles within the on-going structures and institutions of government" (Flanagan 1978: 136). These processes correspond to what Ashford (1980: 295) has called "elite consensus," which operates "*within* the institutions of the political system," and "societal consensus," which is *about* the political system." Societal consensus must accompany elite consensus to ensure high levels of support for the polity. According to Flanagan (1978: 133), stable democratic institutions will be facilitated where the transition from tradition to modernity is accomplished not by "breaking down and destroying traditional attitudes and orientations," but by the "fusing of old and new elements." We wish briefly to explore how one of the major contrasts between institution building in Britain and Japan may have affected the forming of a supportive political culture: the organic development of the British polity, and the nonorganic development of the Japanese. By organic we mean the development of political institutions and relationships as an integral part of a nation's history and culture. To what extent has the British political culture been shaped by the evolutionary, indigenous character of its constitution and formal governing institutions? To what extent has the Japanese political culture been affected by the "alien" character of its constitution and formal governing institutions? The answers will not be simple. The answer is not necessarily that the organic British system enjoys greater legitimacy than the nonorganic Japanese. However, there have been consequences of these two different developmental paths. In an important sense, both the Japanese and the British share strong social and cultural continuities. In the British case, cultural continuity has been accompanied by continuity of political institutions and rules as well. Political change occurred gradually and in tandem with social and cultural change. In the Japanese case, formal political institutions and rules are substantially imposed transplants, and represent considerable historical discontinuities. Yet many aspects of the culture survived political and economic modernization and contribute significantly to the rules of the political game in Japan. In a sense, these native and continuous aspects of the political culture (*honne/ura*) in some ways proceed parallel to, and in some ways incorporated, in the formal institutions and rules of politics (*tatemae/omote*).

Britain

We have already identified the prevalence of reformist, gradualist values in the British political culture. "One great premise," says Rose (1986c: 23), "of English politics is that the past is assimilated by adapting rather than by abolishing aging political institutions." These assimilative values certainly are reflected in the historical experience of the growth of British parliamentary democracy, in which new was grafted onto old. British political institutions are characterized by accretion and adaptation. They could never be derived, in toto, from "first principles" (Norton 1984: 28). Even the most radical of changes, the establishment of parliamentary supremacy, was not achieved by destroying the monarchy. The rise of the House of Commons was not achieved by the destruction of the House of Lords, or by the eclipse of aristocratic power. Other changes represented adaptations, often to significant social change, that nevertheless proceeded incrementally. For example, the expansion of the franchise covered nearly 150 years, and was achieved by several discreet acts of Parliament. Neither the introduction of the civil service nor the rise of mass parties proved especially disruptive. Elite consensus was created early in Britain around the struggle against the monarchy, and was accompanied and bolstered by on-going societal consensus (Ashford 1980: 14–15). The expansion of participation, including the incorporation of new economic classes, was achieved without crisis. "There was," concludes Ashford (1980: 14), "no crisis of legitimacy like those that forced leaders of other countries to demarcate the unalienable rights of citizens, the limits of executive and legislative powers, and the forms of redress, amendment, and political organization." The growth of democratic institutions and the expansion of participation were the product of social change and struggle, particularly the significant struggle for incorporation into society by rising new classes, first the middle class, then the working class. The successful incorporation of these new classes through political reform gave these classes a stake in the survival and success of the resulting institutions. The result of the ability of the British system over centuries to reconcile changing social realities and values to institutions has been a "high degree of elite and societal consensus" (Ashford 1980: 10).

Japan

In sharp contrast to Britain, democracy was grafted onto Japanese culture from "outside," in both the introduction of the Meiji constitution in 1889 and the MacArthur constitution in 1946. The former was given from above to the Japanese people by a ruling elite under pressure from abroad, and the latter was forced on Japan by its defeat in the Second World War (Flanagan 1978: 142). In neither case was political modernization contested. The roots of Japanese democracy are to be found in the Meiji period, but we are more concerned with the development of political culture after the imposition of the MacArthur constitution during the American occupation of Japan. Many of the fundamental values embodied in that constitution, such as the rights of the citizen vis-à-vis the state, women's rights, separation of church and state, decentralization of authority, separation of powers, and responsible party government have few and weak roots in the political and social history of Japan. These rights were not won through struggle or petition. In the Japanese case, modernization was not accompanied by intense internal struggle, either among elites or among classes. Both cultural considerations (an organic, corporate view of society) and international considerations (foreign threat or foreign occupation) inhibited aggressive assertion of class or group interests (Flanagan 1978: 143). In the case of prewar democratic institutions, this absence of conflict "forestalled the emergence of any strong class adherents to . . . democratic institutions" (Flanagan 1978: 143). More generally, "Because the major introductions of democratic rules incorporating broader segments of the populace into the political process were largely uncontested, there were no sharp societal contests between in-groups and out-groups, the privileged and the excluded. Without this kind of direct challenge, traditional submissive, conformist, and fatalistic orientations toward politics will not begin to be questioned and modified, and the development of modern, democratic norms will be slowed" (Richardson and Flanagan 1984: 169).

We have argued that the organic development of the British polity contributed, at least in the past, to its stability and widespread legitimacy. Yet in looking at the Japanese case, we cannot be so sure that the organic development of the political system is a necessary condition for what we referred to as political and cultural institutionalization. First, not all organically developed polities are democratic and stable. If the elite contestants and classes are not successfully incorporated into the polity, if there are losers who do not accept the legitimacy of the result, conflict may become chronic. The development of a postrevolutionary political culture in France created such conflict that the polity is just now, 200 years after the fact, beginning truly to unify. Still, there is the argument that a polity that does result from internal political struggles and compromises will enjoy generalized consent and legitimacy. Despite the absence of such a scenario in the Japanese case, we cannot argue that Japan has failed to become a truly democratic political system supported by the vast majority of the citizenry. As we shall see, there is substantial evidence that the Japanese lack enthusiasm for their polity, that they are acquiescent more than trusting. Nonetheless, in the few decades following the Second World War, Japan has begun to develop its own form of democratic political culture. If we cannot expect Japan to profit from the kind of support that is generated by an organically developed democracy, we may find that it has developed similar levels of support through its own organic processes subsequent to the introduction of democracy in 1946. An important part of our argument is that the Japanese have dealt with their alien polity in two ways. First, there is much of it that has been accepted. In many ways the functioning of Japanese parliamentary institutions are indistinguishable from their Western counterparts. Second, the Japanese have made "the political system less important to the society as a whole" (Ashford 1980: 295). In some ways, it is treated as the *tatemae* to the *honne* of more traditional and indigenous political and social norms and processes.

Values Change

John Gibbins (1989: 23) has remarked that "political culture, individual values and value priorities are going through a series of profound changes in the contemporary world," and that these changes are manifest in "the fragmentation of old cultures and the proliferation of new values, attitudes and attendant behavior, lifestyle and political movements in their place." Where a generation ago, political scientists were preoccupied with questions of stability, writes Topf (1989: 68), today, it is questions "about changes in value systems and ideologies, and related changes in political participation and political party support" that demand attention. In recent years, two major approaches to the question of values change have been advanced. The first, referred to as postmodernism, has been pursued by numerous scholars in a variety of fields. The second, referred to as postmaterialism, has been advanced for the most part by Ronald Inglehart and a few colleagues. Both theoretical approaches are seen as having a significant impact on political behavior and institutions (Gibbins 1989: 24).

Gibbins characterizes postmodernism as "the absence of unity and identity," a "picture of fragmentation, multidirectional change and a psychedelic collage of contemporary attitudes, values and beliefs." What unites the many disparate perspectives of the postmodernists is their belief that disenchantment with modern values will proceed eventually to "a transition to a postmodern age and society" rooted in "a radically new set of experiences, practices and life worlds for its inhabitants" (Gibbins 1989: 14). The essential characteristic of these new life worlds is diversity. Postmodernism has been defined as "a space ... where competing intentions, definitions, and effects, diverse social and intellectual tendencies and lines of force converge and clash" (Hebdige in Reimer 1989: 110–11). Changes in society associated with the spread of affluence and mobility create "a new sensibility" of "immediacy, spontaneity and sensation," while rejecting the values of order, rationality and discipline (Turner 1989: 203). People turn inward to "the body and the home," which become "the main theatres of pleasure" (Bordieu cited in Gibbins 1989: 19). Such a world will offer endless possibilities and choices of lifestyle that "make a nonsense of a moral or social order" (Gibbins 1989: 18), and relegate politics to ever less importance. "A postmodern politics and political culture would highlight a dissatisfaction with modern politics, its sameness, customary allegiances, its predictability, bureaucracy, discipline, authority and mechanical operation, and would stress the emergence of a politics featuring difference, dealignment and realignment, unpredictability, freedom, delegitimazation and distrust, power and spontaneity" (Gibbins 1989: 15–16). Indeed, says Turner (1989: 199), postmodern culture "tears away the vestiges of a general normative legitimacy for the polity." However, as the legitimacy of the old political culture erodes, the postmodern age will not be characterized by a new cultural hegemony, but rather by fragmentation, pluralism, and incommensurability. In its disjointedness, it is as likely to support neoconservatism as "antihierarchical and populist dimensions" (Turner 1989: 212).

In a major effort to study values change in advanced industrial societies, Ronald Inglehart has found that increased social affluence and education are associated with increased preference for "postmaterialist" values among those subject to this "formative affluence." With increased affluence comes a decreasing concern with physiological needs for safety and sustenance (materialism), and an increasing concern for social and self-actualizing needs, such as aesthetic and intellectual satisfaction, belonging and esteem. These include changes in both outcome and process values, specifically a decline of concern for economic and material security, a decline of political passivity, and a corresponding increase in the importance attributed to "quality of life" issues, social activism, and cooperative values (Inglehart 1977: 3–5, 12–14). These changes are compatible with the wider constellation of changes identified by the postmodernists (Inglehart 1989). From a political point of view, "postmaterialism"—with its weaker moral and social constraints and decreased emphasis on materialistic and authoritarian values—should translate into higher levels of participation and higher levels of contention (Flanagan 1982: 408). "Postmaterialists have a larger amount of psychic energy available for politics, they are less supportive of the established social order, and subjectively, they have less to lose from unconventional political action than Materialists" (Inglehart 1984: 567). Furthermore, their higher education levels have conferred on them increased political skills that permit them a more active role in affecting political decisions (Inglehart 1977: 363). To the extent, then, that postmaterialist values are present or increasing, one should expect among other things, less consensual, less reformist value orientations along with increased political participation.

How and to what extent have Japan and Britain been affected by values change? Is either becoming more or less individualistic or collectivist, more or less deferential or conflictual, more or less universalistic or particularistic?

Britain

In his 1977 study, Inglehart (1977: 364) observes that "the smallest amount of value change seems to have taken place" in Britain. He attributes this in part to Britain's relative prewar prosperity, Britain's escape from wartime occupation, and the relatively smaller gains in economic growth experienced by the British during the period under study (Inglehart 1977: 33–34; 1979: 323). Yet another factor affecting the growth of postmaterialism in Britain is the prevalence of pre-industrial antimaterialist attitudes among British elites (Wiener 1981a: 410).[6] However, data collected just a few years after Inglehart's initial survey suggested that a small increase in the proportion of postmaterialists had occurred by the end of the decade (Inglehart 1984: 572). In a survey conducted in the mid-1980s, the percentage of postmaterialists was found to be virtually identical to the average for the European Community countries as a whole, and the percentage of materialists somewhat lower (Inglehart 1989: Table 1, 252).

Still, as in most other European countries, combined materialists and postmaterialists comprise a minority of the population, and postmaterialism is less prevalent overall than materialism, except among the young.

In 1981, only 13 percent were postmaterialist and 25 percent materialist (Harding and Phillips 1986: 104). This proportion had changed little by the mid-1980s (Inglehart 1989: 252). In their 1988 study using a somewhat different set

Table 1.3

Distribution of Materialist (M) and Postmaterialist (PM) Value Types by Age Cohort in Britain (1986–1987), (in percent)

Age range in 1986	M	PM
15–20	12	19
21–30	18	19
31–40	22	16
41–50	18	15
51–60	23	11
61–70	29	9
71–80	34	11

Source: Ronald Inglehart, 1979. "Value Priorities and Socioeconomic Change." In *Political Action: Mass Participation in Five Western Democracies,* ed. Samuel Barnes et al: Table 1, p. 252. Beverly Hills: Sage. © Ronald Inglehart, 1989. Reprinted by permission of Sage Publications, Inc.

of questions, Heath and Evans (1988: 63) concluded, not surprisingly, that "it is the old agenda which is still central to working-class politics." On "new agenda" items such as the right to protest, however, they found the professional class (the salariat) to be more libertarian (Heath and Evans 1988: 55).

With regard to the impact of postmaterialist attitudes on political participation, Phillips observed that in Britain "Post-Materialists are more interested in politics than Materialists; they are more likely to be actively involved; they are more likely to consider taking part in political protest. Thus Post-Materialists tend to be more radical, more anti-traditional. Materialists are more conservative, more traditional" (Phillips 1985: 171). Heath and Topf (1987: 56–59) found a pronounced increase in the number of people agreeing that workers should be given more say in running the places where they work, as well as other evidence of increasingly participatory attitudes. From this evidence they conclude "that social changes—such as the expansion of higher education and the growth of the middle classes—are producing increased numbers of citizens with the self-confidence to participate in politics, with new political concerns and with a greater wish to be consulted in politics" (Heath and Topf 1987: 59). However, Inglehart himself found "no association between value orientation and conventional participation" and little more between value orientation and protest potential (cited in Topf 1989: 69).

Postmodernism constitutes the other dimension of values change in Britain, and some believe that like others, Britain has become a "fragmented postmodern culture," in which the new, affluent white-collar sector of the workforce has adopted postmodern lifestyles (Turner 1989: 210). As elsewhere, the rise of postmodern values has been associated with fundamental social and economic change. According to Turner (1989: 210), the old world of class politics "was changed fundamentally by the oil crisis of the 1970s, by changes in the structure of capitalism." Specifically, the decline of the traditional working class and the rise of a new middle-class "salariat," increased home ownership, mass consumption, and the prevalence of private transportation, are all seen as eroding older values and alignments, in short, creating the conditions for postmodernism. In the postmodernists' stress of the fluidity of mass values, opportunities have arisen in Britain as elsewhere for increased competition over the shaping of values. Through its control of government, the political right is seen as conducting a concerted effort to sustain the moral order through the inculcation of a new enterprise culture "aimed at transforming political attitudes, values and behaviour" (Gibbins 1989: 22). Likewise, from the left, the old Greater London Council attempted to create "hegemonic" populist culture, reconstructing "a socialist strategy upon postmodernist assumptions" (Gibbins 1989: 22).

From both the postmodernist and postmaterialist perspective, values change are underway in Britain. All in all, Phillips (1985: 172) concludes "The unexpected re-emergence of the Campaign for Nuclear Disarmament, the growth of the environmental movement and the more general adoption of conservationist goals may indeed point to an underlying shift in the focus of political values. The change is not dramatic or universal and whether one regards it as a move away from materialist, economic preoccupations towards postmaterialist concerns, or as some broader change in values is open to debate. It must also be viewed against the widespread agreement that exists for values such as personal freedom, patriotism, and general improvement through reform. Nevertheless, for significant numbers, particularly among those who have grown up since the Second World War, political concerns are in some sense different and involve new priorities." Girvin (1989: 32) warns that "too much emphasis on change understates the importance of countervailing features within each system." He remarks that even the disruptions to the political order in the 1960s and 1970s "can be interpreted as a normal feature of political evolution, when new values and ideas are absorbed, modified, or discarded by the society, rather than the portent of a fundamental realignment in political or social terms," and he points to the "continuing influence of liberal individualist values, the dominance of capitalist organization," among other factors conserving the political culture (1989: 31). The evidence presented throughout this study, while taking note of the evidence of postmaterialist and postmodernist change, tends to support this more cautious view.

Japan

In a critique of Inglehart, Scott Flanagan argues that the more relevant axis of change, in the Japanese case at least, has not been from materialist to postmaterialist, but from authoritarian and group-centered norms to libertarian values (Flanagan 1982). "[T]he shift toward libertarian values is associated with age in a pattern of intergenerational change, while the move toward nonacquisitive or nonmaterialist priorities conforms to a life cycle pattern of change" (Flanagan 1982: 412). Flanagan's theory is not far removed from Watanuki Joji's "cultural politics" theory in which the central values cleavage in Japan is not in terms of class values (class cleavage) but in terms of age and education (Watanuki 1980: 15). "[H]igher order nonmaterial issue priorities do not replace lower order material issue priorities in the same way that an older generation's austere, pietistic, collectivist, deferential value preferences are replaced by a younger generation's more self-indulgent, secular, independent, and self-assertive value orientations" (Flanagan 1982: 420).

Both Inglehart and Flanagan claim that their theories have broad application to Japanese and Western political cultures, even though the former's specialization has been in European politics while the latter's has been Japanese politics. However, it may be argued that postmaterialism in Japan presents a case especially distinct from that in the West because of Japan's retarded economic development and the nonorganic nature of Japanese political culture. Thus, attitudes that would be postmaterialist in the West, such as valuing cooperation and harmony, are in Japan prematerialist. "Industrialization, urbanization, the attainment of prosperity, and other aspects of modernization have taken place so recently and so rapidly that even while the rest of Japan is moving into the front rank of advanced industrial society, important segments of the population are still undergoing the retreat from preindustrial values. The transition from preindustrial to industrial values has been superimposed on the shift from materialism to Post-Materialist priorities. When they are lumped together, the former process can conceal the latter" (Inglehart 1982: 462). It should also be noted that all of the data used by both authors are well over a decade old and some more than twenty years old. Analysis supported by solid methodology will always be hampered with the time lag between the gathering and analysis of data, but it should be kept in mind that the development of political culture in Japan may have superseded some aspects of their debate.

Though there is disagreement about the direction and theoretical underpinnings for values change in Japan, there is widespread agreement that change has occurred, and that it represents more than life-cycle or period effects. Inglehart (1984: 566) examines evidence of change along several dimensions, including "a shift from Materialist to Post-Materialist priorities" and increased "emphasis on individuation and political participation." He concludes that "The time series data are unambiguous: from 1953 to 1978 there was an intergenerational shift away from Materialism among the Japanese public" (Inglehart 1984: 567). Much evidence has been mustered to suggest the rise, as in Britain, of less deferential and materialistic, more individualistic, more egalitarian, and more participatory values.[7] Krauss et al. (1984: 392) observe that "Particularly striking in recent years has been the extent to which egalitarian and democratic values have finally been accepted and internalized at the individual, grass-roots level, becoming intertwined with the problems of economic affluence and advanced industrialization."

Whether these changes are called postmaterialist or libertarian is of less concern than whether and to what extent changes are occurring. Japan began the 1980s with a smaller proportion of postmaterialists than in the West, and a far greater attachment to certain materialist values (Flanagan 1982; Inglehart 1982: 470). Inglehart (1982: 470) in general has found the Japanese "less Materialistic than most Westerners," but he attributes this in part to "the persistence of pre-industrial values more than the rise of Post-Materialism." In this influence of pre-industrial values opposed to materialism, we find a parallel with British experience. He nonetheless finds "a clear-cut shift away from Materialism" based on the same "Post-Materialist" forces that have been at work in the West (Inglehart 1982: 463). Indeed, Richardson and Flanagan (1984: 226; Inglehart 1982: 462) agree that "The traditional values of diligence, frugality, and striving for economic success ... have increasingly been supplanted by proclivities towards self-indulgence, immediate gratification, and a growing preoccupation with leisure activities." An important contrast to Western experience has been noted with respect to the increase of collectivist values normally associated with the rise of postmaterialism. According to Ike, "In Western culture, which has long stressed individualism, youth may seek a sense of belonging, whereas in Japanese culture, which has emphasized the group, youth may yearn for individuation and privatization" (cited in Inglehart 1982: 460). "For Japanese Post-Materialists, self-realization demands a wider margin of individual freedom from group constraints than the traditional society allowed" (Inglehart 1982: 461). Flanagan counters by arguing that hierarchic and deferential orientations are being superseded by egalitarian and self-assertive orientations (Richardson and Flanagan 1984: 225), "with the former falling from 53% to 18% and the latter rising from 14% to 61%" (Flanagan 1982: 426). Urbanization, the implanted constitution, increased education, and generational change have led to a shift from authority and conformity to equality, independence, and individualism as the "informed, sophisticated, and politically competent portion of the electorate" increased (Richardson and Flanagan 1984: 221, 227). Whatever the roots of change, increasing individuation or the rise of libertarian values among younger Japanese could be expected to have important implications for Japan's collectivist, consensualist, particularistic political culture.

Increased affluence is believed by most to have had a significant influence on values change. Flanagan argues that change is associated with national affluence and Inglehart believes that it is associated with individual affluence (Inglehart 1982: 471), but it seems reasonable to assume that both have had a significant effect. Although Inglehart and others have seen a decrease in materialist-related answers on self-report questionnaires, which leads them to believe that increased personal affluence has given the individual Japanese more time to reflect on the spiritual, to "stop and smell the roses" if you will, that does not always seem to be exhibited by individual behavior. The effects of affluence in Japan also appear to have worked in the opposite direction from that suggested by Inglehart.

Japan today is an increasingly materialist society, in some ways the epitome of what is called *narikin*, or a nouveau-riche society. Individual affluence has brought about a new consumer generation, the only generation in Japanese history that has assumed both personal affluence and national affluence. A widely used ephithetic description of the younger generation, *shinjinrui*, denotes a generation comprised of individuals attempting to differentiate themselves from others through consumption behavior and their willingness to risk incurring debt in order to do so. The *shinjinrui* are essentially materialists.

However, personal affluence does not necessarily mean a decreased need for harmonious human relations and the group ethic. Indeed, an increased desire for personal wealth and material goods can increase one's bond with the group, if one believes that it is only through the group that these ends can be achieved. In order to be successful in Japanese society, materially or otherwise, one must work through the group (Stronach 1980). Thus, affluence seeking does not have to mean increased individualism. As Fujioka Wakao, an expert on Japanese mass consumption, states "the increasingly subjective, aesthetic and emotionally oriented—in other words, the increasingly intuitive orientation—of people's needs and behavior is leading to the breakdown of the 'masses' into small groups of like-minded individuals, or micromasses" (*Japan Echo* Spring 1986: 31). After all, in what modern society do we find more than a negligible number of its members who are truly individuals?

The success of the Japanese economy, while creating greater affluence, micromasses, and greater political participation, has also created a greater pride in the Japanese about what are popularly believed to be traditional Japanese values (Curtis 1988: 230–32). The best-selling books in Japan of the 1980s have been those by both foreign and Japanese authors which credit "Confucian capitalism," "samurai capitalism," or some other form of "Japanized" capitalism as the key to Japan's success. On the other side of the coin, these books, especially those written by Japanese authors, tend to see the relative decline of the West as being due to the failures of Western values.

The turn to traditional Japanese values and lifestyles is due not only to the success of Japanese values in the development of Japan, it is also due to the need for younger Japanese to have some stability in their rapidly changing world. The success of the Japanese economy, the increased profile of the Japanese in the world, their increased interdependence and increased communication with the West has led to the intensification of a conundrum that has faced the Japanese ever since the Meiji restoration: Are we Asian or Western? As Japan becomes more Western and more modern, there will always be a need to turn back to tradition as a means of self-identification. This also brings up the question of participation. In Inglehart's terms, Japan does seem to be moving into a postmaterialist phase of political participation, but one which has not been inhibited by the increased national pride and emphasis on perceived traditional values.

Conclusions

It is our contention that the above-described norms concerning individual and group roles in the polity, authority relations, the degree of harmony and consensus that are desirable, and the appropriate role of ideology permeate the political systems of Japan and Britain. They may be subject to change. They influence and are influenced by the formal political institutions and processes, and they form the basis from which beliefs and attitudes about politics are derived. But at least with respect to the countries in this study, we agree with Girvin (1989: 46) that "The political culture internalizes development discreetly and . . . provides a bulwark against rapid change." The remainder of this book examines, in considerably more detail, both the mass basis of the political culture, and its specific application to elite policy making.

Notes

1. However, another survey suggested that the British would choose socialism over individualism by a margin of 64 percent to 26 percent (Hastings and Hastings 1982, cited in Dogan 1988: 34).

2. J. M. Robson, ed. *The Collected Works of John Stuart Mill*, pp. 219–20.

3. Prince Shotoku's "Seventeen Article Constitution" in Moore's *The Japanese Mind*, p. 7.

4. Ideological thinking certainly need not be grounded in left-right distinctions, as religious fundamentalism and the Green movement suggest. More to the point, we shall see that "left-right" conceptualization is even less common in Japan than in Britain.

5. Factor one, "personal-sexual morality," concerned interpersonal and sexual conduct, generally "related to religious orthodox views." Factor two, "self-interest morality," concerned "behaviours which involve an element of cheating or dishonesty," and factor three, "legal-illegal morality," concerned "behaviours whose nature casts them unmistakably beyond the law or in conflict with the state" (Harding and Phillips 1986: 11).

6. Such antimaterialist norms can be found in Cobden's nineteenth-century writings, and in Anthony Eden's famous oath that the Tory party was "not the party of cruel, unbridled capitalism." The nineteenth-century defeat of liberalism and its replacement by paternalistic, Disraelian conservatism, ensured the survival of premodern sentiments (Wiener 1981a: 411).

7. Inglehart 1982; Flanagan 1982.

2

The Mass Basis of Political Inputs: National Pride and Identity

One of the most important elements of political culture is the sense of identification with the nation (Verba 1967: 529). Since the early nineteenth century, the "irreducible core" of a political culture has been associated with "a strong sense of national identity which large numbers of individuals have been able to share" (Girvin 1989: 34). In order better to understand this concept, it will first be necessary to distinguish between the associated concepts of "state" and "nation." The concept of "the state" may be understood in one sense as the coercive and legal power of government and its institutions to command compliance from the population over which it rules. Quite a different concept is "the nation," which refers to "an emotional bond, a sense of belonging, which thereby creates a solidary relation with the group" (Beer and Ulam 1973: 36). There may be many groups other than the nation that establish and maintain solidary relations, for example, families, villages, trade unions, associations, and/or enterprises.[1] In Japan, especially, loyalty to such groups is another hallmark of the culture. In the case of the nation, however, unlike virtually all other solidaristic groups, this relationship is manifest in the desire for self-rule, for sovereignty. The concept of nation does not refer to the relationship between ruler and ruled, between government and citizen, but rather to the bonds among the people leading them to seek to govern their own affairs. Though the state is something apart from the nation, the nation has been of enormous importance to the state. For when the state can exploit the unity created by strong feelings of nation, the state benefits from increased legitimacy (Merkl 1988: 21). Both compliance and mobilization are more easily obtained, and thus a strong sense of national community can contribute to the power of the state. On the other hand, of course, a strong national community may pose significant and lasting problems for a government widely perceived as illegitimate, as was the case in Poland during the years of Communist governments. The state may also be undermined by conflicting nationalism within its borders, or aggressive nationalism without. Low levels of national solidarity may be reflected in political apathy, and may create impediments to mobilization. For these reasons, states have found it in their interests to try to transfer the loyalty inherent in the national community to the state. This may be attempted during the socialization process, through identification of the nation with state institutions and symbols. In this way, loyalty to the "tribe" or the "fatherland" may be commanded by the state as well.

Determining when and where a nation exists is a tricky business. No universal set of criteria has yet been agreed upon. We concur with Britain's Royal Commission on the Constitution (1973), however, that the national community can only be identified through the perceptions of its members. A nation exists where a people consider it to exist, where there is a perceived unity—nineteenth-century Poles or twentieth-century Palestinians for example—not just where a government and flag may be found. While this bond may be reinforced by attachment to political institutions and processes, it involves the more generalized commitment by the individual to the society and culture. Loyalty to the nation may be evoked by many things: common language, culture, history, ethnicity. One need not in fact support the current national polity at all to feel a strong sense of nationalism or patriotism. Revolutionaries and cynics alike may be quite patriotic, seeking no redrawing of boundaries, no separate state. We will argue that in postwar Japan, nationalism, the sense of community, has remained fairly strong, while the feelings of the people toward the government may have tended toward indifference. On the other hand, pride in the polity, while manifesting considerable ambiguity in some respects, has traditionally been one of the attributes of British nationalism.

The integrating force of an organically evolved polity was less evident in Japan, whose modern constitutional order was imposed and uncontested, than in Britain. As a result, the Japanese maintain a considerable distance between society, which did evolve organically, and polity, which did not. The relationship between individual and polity can be most clearly seen in the way both nations manifest pride in themselves. Not only does Japan by many measures have less pride in the nation than does Britain, but when that pride is expressed, the British, to a much greater extent, identify it in political terms. The ability to make a sharp distinction between the political and social system, and to remove oneself from the former, is aided by the traditional Japanese behavioral pattern of accepting ideas and situations which are seemingly incompatible, as discussed in the previous chapter. In a sense, the participatory aspects of democracy are accepted on a *tatemae* level by many Japanese, while the *honne* of their actual behavior is to participate as little as possible or in a symbolic way. In comparing Japan and Britain, we will look at four questions concerning national identity: (1) Who is included in the nation? (2) What is the source of the attachment? (3) How strong are the bonds of nationhood (how intense the commitment)? (4) What is the nature, intensity, and consequence of any competing community loyalties (class, local, regional, national, or international)? As noted, the degree and nature of the national community can significantly affect the operation of the polity. Britain and Japan share in many aspects of national identity the isolation and culturally xenophobic tendencies of an island people. Both are separated from continents historically shaken by political and military turmoil. However, compared to the British today, the Japanese are more nationalistic in terms of their reverence for the Japanese people, their belief in their own uniqueness, and their belief in the superiority of both nation and culture in comparison with the rest of the world. One source of this highly developed sense of identity is the homogeneity of the Japanese people. Japan is one of the few true nation-states, that is, almost everyone living in Japan is racially and ethnically Japanese, while relatively few Japanese live outside Japan. The United Kingdom not only embraces the four nations of English, Irish, Scottish, and Welsh, but a growing multi-ethnic, multiracial population as well. Britain is more homogeneous than most states, but less homogeneous than Japan.

In different ways and to different degrees, the insularity of both states is eroding. In the case of the United Kingdom, the principal agents of erosion are economic (and to an increasing degree political) integration into Europe, the pressures of global interdependence, and massive immigration of non-European citizens of Commonwealth countries as a legacy of the dissolution of the Empire. In the case of Japan, trade and its consequent economic and cultural integration are the paramount factors, though there is no comparable regional integration scheme to accelerate the dilution of Japan's nationalism. One must keep in mind, however, greater integration is not necessarily a predictor of declining national identity, as there are many factors in an interdependent world that can also stimulate feelings of national loyalty.

Defining the Nation: The Territorial Dimension

As implied in our definition, a nation need have no territorial dimension, since it exists in the aspirations and perceptions of "a nation" of people. However, both the Japanese and British nations occupy geographically distinct territories within, by and large, long-established boundaries. No doubt, the island character of both nations has contributed to their sense of identity and their views of their relations with other nations, and, combined with other factors, it has contributed to relative political stability.

The most obvious distinction between the territories of the United Kingdom and Japan is that the United Kingdom is composed of several national territories with long and distinctive histories, while in Japan only the Okinawan Islands can lay claim to a cultural and political heritage distinct from that of the main island group. The United Kingdom of Great Britain and Northern Ireland (the U.K.)—the state governing the British nation—has four component parts: England, Scotland, Wales, and Northern Ireland. Together, England, Scotland, and Wales comprise the island of Great Britain, while Northern Ireland is geographically a part of Ireland. England dominates territorially, in population, and in wealth—a factor of no small importance to both the evolution of the polity and present-day politics. England encompasses 50,000 square miles, or roughly half of the United Kingdom, and 83 percent of the population. Scotland has a total area of 30,000 square miles, but less than 10 percent of the population. Wales has an area of approximately 8,000 square miles and a population equal to 5 percent of the total. Northern Ireland, the smallest of the parts, has an area of 3,000 square miles, and a population equal to 3.5 percent of the total U.K. population.

Japan, with a population of 121 million, has a total area of 378,000 square kilometers (236,000 square miles), or about 2.4 times the size of the United Kingdom. It consists of four main island groups, Hokkaido to the north, the dominant, central island of Honshu, and Shikoku and Kyushu to the south. The fifth island group, the Ryukyu archipelago (Okinawa), stretches between Kyushu and Taiwan and is the only one that can be distinguished by a separate political tradition, culture, or history. Japan has a very high population density (319/km) and the highest concentrations of population are in the Kanto (Tokyo-Yokohama) and Kansai (Osaka-Kyoto) districts of eastern central Honshu.

The Cultural Dimension

Demographically, Britain and Japan are in some ways similar. The population of Japan, at 121 million, is roughly twice as large as that of Britain. Yet both populations can be characterized in global terms as middle-sized and stable. Both populations have supported industrialization on a massive scale, and propelled their countries, within memory, to world prominence. Both populations are, as noted, relatively homogeneous, with the Japanese being unusually so. A small percentage of the United Kingdom's population are descendants of peoples not already established in Britain by the twelfth century, and an even smaller percentage of Japanese have ancestors who arrived in the islands in the current millennium. In both countries, a common language and philosophical tradition is dominant.

These similarities are important, but there are also substantial differences that have been manifest in the evolution of the polity and in their contemporary political systems. Britain is a multinational, and now multiracial community, while Japan is more nearly homogeneous. The United Kingdom even faces problems in finding a name for its own nationality. There is in fact no U.K. nationality. But there is a British nationality. This is so despite the fact that Northern Ireland is not even part of Great Britain (the island comprised of England, Scotland, and Wales). Furthermore, the four parts of the United Kingdom each retain "a distinctive national identity, rooted in historically determined cultural differences" (Rose 1982: 6). Scottish and Welsh nationalism were subdued to permit union with England between the sixteenth and eighteenth centuries, but have revived in recent decades. Northern Ireland became part of the United Kingdom in 1920, and while it has proved "ungovernable," a majority of its citizens are, ironically, strong advocates of union. It is by no means clear that Northern Ireland has the basis for a separate national identity. By and large, the union have proved a successful one, creating an umbrella "British" nationality, while permitting the limited survival of distinct component nationalities. Because of the distinctive and anomalous position of Northern Ireland, the present study is concerned almost exclusively with the political culture of Britain, exclusive of Northern Ireland.

Despite these separate identities, identification of Britons with the country as a whole is slightly above other countries of Europe, though it is below that in Japan (Leisure Development Center [LDC] 1981 cited in Hastings and Hastings 1984: 552). The English, in particular, exhibit a "remarkably strong sense of national identity" (Rose 1964: 8). Though many English identify themselves primarily as British, at times, they may identify other Britons as English, to the displeasure of the non-English (Royal Commission on the Constitution 1973: 58). The sense of being British, while present outside of England, is weaker (Kavanagh 1980: 147). While finding considerable evidence of militant nationalism in Scotland and Wales, the Royal Commission on the Constitution found cause for optimism concerning the survival of the British nation. "Although," the commission noted, ". . . there remain within the United Kingdom some marked geographical differences in social and cultural characteristics and strongly held national and regional loyalties, there exist also, quite apart from the more tangible things we have mentioned as being held in common, innumerable close ties which result from centuries of intermingling and from shared language, experience, social institutions and attitudes to such fundamental matters as personal liberty and the rule of law" (Royal Commission on the Constitution 1973: 20). Support for the union has been high throughout the UK, but in recent years, as the commission and later surveys document, more assertive nationalism has revived, leading to sentiment for independence and devolution of powers from Parliament. Though Scottish voters rejected devolution by a substantial margin in the 1970s, many observers see a continuing threat to the constitutional arrangements that in the past governed relations between England, Scotland, and Wales (Kavanagh 1980: 147; Kellas 1990: 426). And indeed, results of more recent polls in Scotland, while ambiguous, suggest a continued potential for Scottish separatist sentiment. In a 1984 poll, 45 percent of Scots surveyed favored some form of autonomous Scottish parliament, while 25 percent favored independence (Market Opinion Research International [MORI] February 1984, cited in Hastings and Hastings 1985: 125). Since then sentiment for independence has, if anything, increased, with 35 percent in 1988 approving of complete independence (MORI April 1988, cited in Hastings and Hastings 1990: 295). Separatism is not the only threat to the British national identity. To resurgent nationalism has been added the problem of race. With the dissolution of the empire, Britain has experienced an influx of new citizens from commonwealth nations in Asia, the Caribbean, Africa, and the Middle East. These new citizens comprise about 4 percent of the population of the United Kingdom. This percentage, while small, represents a significant and rapid increase in the immigrant population of Britain, up from 0.2 percent in 1950. Unfortunately, until recently, race was a little studied subject of political inquiry (Welch and Studlar 1985). Small subsample size in national surveys makes reliable interpretation of the views of nonwhite Britons difficult. Though they enjoy full rights of citizenship, and while they appear as ready as other groups to consider themselves "British," they have confronted numerous problems of assimilation. While multiracial in fact, Britain is "not yet multiracial in political values" (Rose 1986c: 42). The British today believe that racial prejudice is even more prevalent than class discrimination, and take a relatively pessimistic view of the future of race relations (Airey 1984: 130). In a 1986 survey on what issues Britons considered important, 47 percent believed it "very" or "fairly" important that the government send colored immigrants back to their own country. On the other hand, the fact that this percent was smaller than on all but one of sixteen other issues in the survey may suggest a lower salience for issues of race than might first appear (SSLT November 1986, cited in Hastings and Hastings 1988: 153). Riots in largely immigrant areas in the 1980s, while not always clearly attributed to racial tensions, suggest the depth of immigrant frustration. Not until 1987 was a nonwhite Briton elected to Parliament. As the new Britons have no territorial base like the Scots, their political problems require different, and perhaps more complicated, solutions than simple devolution of power (Rose 1982: 19).

In comparison with the British, the Japanese are more nationalistic in terms of their reverence for the nation, their belief in their own uniqueness, and their belief in the superiority of both nation and culture in comparison with the rest of the world. The Japanese exhibit an intensely held in-group feeling, what Ward calls "the shared sense of uniqueness of being Japanese" (Ward 1978: 66). A larger proportion of Japanese than any other nationality, in an eleven-nation survey, indicated that they belonged "first of all" to their country as a whole as opposed to local, regional, or other entities (LDC 1981, cited in Hastings and Hastings 1984: 552). Homogeneity has made Japan one of the purest nation-states, in that non-Japanese residents and non-Japanese ethnic citizens combined account for less than 5 percent of the total population. Not only are almost all Japanese citizens racially and ethnically Japanese, but very few Japanese live outside Japan. The major Japanese expatriate communities are in the United

States and Brazil, but even these communities are small by any standard.

Unlike Britain, there exists no plausible threat to Japanese group identity. Though there are separate Japanese islands, these do not, by and large, constitute different ethnic or cultural traditions capable of challenging the majority. There is no distinct nation or territory analogous to Scotland or Wales, nor any minorities analogous to Welsh, Scottish, Caribbean, or Indian. The Japanese language has never had any indigenous competitors comparable to Welsh and Gaelic. There has been no need to create a "supranational" nationality, such as "British," to unite component nationalities. The Japanese have been a homogeneous people for well over 1,000 years. There had never been a successful invasion of the four main islands until 1945. Travel and trade to and from Japan (with minor exceptions) was forbidden from the 1630s to the 1850s, a period in which the roots of modern Japan were being nurtured. This foundation of homogeneity continues to be built upon today, as the socialization process assures commonly shared social values are disseminated throughout the country by a centralized media, bureaucracy, and educational system. A consequence of the strong group feeling of the Japanese has been a sense of separateness, even isolation. While national identity in both Britain and Japan is strong, the Japanese belief in national uniqueness separates them from not only Britain, but the West in general. To a far greater degree than citizens of any Western country, the Japanese are inclined to identify their culture as superior to that of any non-Japanese. One manifestation of the feeling of national separateness or distinctiveness is a concomitant sense of isolation and detachment from the outside world. Add to this the inner direction of Confucianism in its centering on family and village, and you have a strong impulse to insular attitudes. Only recently have the Japanese begun to move their frame of reference out into the larger world.

Even though economic development has led Japan to increase its interest in internationalization, it has been slow to change its attitudes toward racial and cultural distinctiveness. While the Japanese are ethnically more cohesive than the British, the homogeneity of the Japanese is much stronger in both perception and fact. The Japanese have long held to the uniqueness of their homogeneity of race and ethnicity, but in recent years the national concern over *nihonjinron* (the debate over the essence of being Japanese) may be due to an increased need for identity. The Japanese were forced to take a hard look at themselves after being shunned by the international community as a pariah from their invasion of China to their defeat in the Second World War. Indeed, war propaganda centered on the idea of the Japanese spirit being sufficient in and of itself to overcome the demographic and material advantages of the United States. The cultural identity of the nation has again been brought into question since Japan has reached the top tier of developed nations. Arrival as one of the world's foremost economic powers has created conditions that may seriously undermine Japan's homogeneity and perceived uniqueness, even if little change is evident thus far. Its economic growth has been export-driven and the consequent high level of economic interdependence has brought about pressure for greater cultural interdependence, especially through the movement of foreigners into Japan. The Japanese are, to a greater extent than ever before in their history, experiencing firsthand the outer world. The expansion of Japanese direct investment has sent a flood of Japanese businessmen, workers and managers to foreign markets. The rapid appreciation of the yen in both the mid-1970s and the mid-1980s led to a fivefold increase in the number of Japanese tourists abroad. Conversely, the lure of the Japanese economy has attracted many foreigners to Japan. Foreign professionals and businessmen either working for their firms in Japan or hired by Japanese companies demand that the old barriers separating foreigners and Japanese be torn down. The diversity of racial and ethnic groups in other countries to which the Japanese are tied economically has created a need for greater sensitivity toward these groups by the Japanese. Several comments by Japanese cabinet members disparaging American blacks have damaged the image of Japan in the United States. The Japanese are also now beginning to undergo a national debate over whether *gastarbeiters* should be allowed into the country.

The effect of the above has been to make the Japanese more outward looking than they have been in the past. In the 1976 JABISS study (Richardson and Flanagan 1984: 174–75), 41 percent of the respondents indicated that they were most interested in national politics, 45 percent indicated they were most interested in local politics, and only 5 percent indicated they were most interested in international politics. In our 1987 survey, however, 86 percent responded they were most interested in international politics as opposed to 35 percent in national and 19 percent in local.[2]

Other Significant Communal Loyalties

Identification with Social Class

Group solidarity may be manifest at other levels of society than the nation, and may actually compete with the nation for the loyalty of the individual. The extent of these loyalties and their impact on national loyalties are our concern here. Class remains a central concept in British political culture, though the impact of class on politics is quite different from what it was a century ago. A glance at the social backgrounds of government officials of both parties will suggest the much-reduced import of the old "upper classes." There is no longer a "governing class" consisting of the social aristocracy. Government is firmly in the hands of the upper middle class, however (Rose 1986c: 172). Nonetheless, political scientists have paid a great deal of attention to class and its impact on British politics, and despite recent studies that downgrade its importance, class remains a significant factor. At the mass level, a surprisingly small 20 percent of Britons conform exactly to the ideal-type criteria of "working" or "middle" class (Rose 1986c: 174). Class self-identification is another matter altogether, however. The concepts of middle and working class remain important to the British. According to the 1984 *British Social Attitudes Survey*, 70 percent thought that people are "very aware" or "quite aware of class," and Britons generally have a stronger sense of class identity (overwhelmingly working class) than the Japanese (see Table 2.1).[3] In the same survey, 23 percent identified with the upper working class and 46 percent with the working class, but only 24 percent identified with the middle class, and 2 percent or less with the upper middle class or the poor (Airey 1984: 131). Not only do Britons identify with a class, but they consider class an important influence in their lives. They do not view class as a benign influence, either. A large majority agree that there is a "class struggle" in Britain today (SSLT February 26–March 3 1986). And 68 percent think the Conservative party is "good for one class" (SSLT February 1987, cited in Hastings and Hastings 1988: 430). It is not always as clear, however, that people view that struggle, such as it is, in terms of the traditional classes. For example, while a surprising 76 percent in 1987 thought that conflict between the working class and the middle class was "not very strong" or that there were "no conflicts," 53 percent thought management-worker conflicts either "strong" or "very strong" (Jowell et al. 1988: 261), and 64 percent in 1986 thought social class affected opportunities in Britain a "great deal" or "quite a lot" (Jowell et al. 1987: 210). About half of Britons see class as a given feature of life now and in the future, and even more are "sceptical or pessimistic" that Britain can move toward a more nearly class-less society (Airey 1984: 130). Surveys have shown the public increasingly to see the country divided between the "haves" and the "have-nots," echoing Disraeli's image of "Two Britains" over a century earlier. Between 1984 and 1988, the percentage of Britons who thought of Britain as polarized between those two groups increased from 63 percent to 73 percent. Interestingly, however, while 37 percent consider themselves "have-nots," about as many see themselves as belonging to the "haves" as to the "have-nots" (SSLT March 23–29 1988). This perceived polarization in material wealth has not been reflected, as we have seen, in ideological polarization, and has not until recently threatened the British sense of national community. As we saw above, however, where class and region coincide, the potential exists for stress within the larger British community. For the Japanese, class is a minor consideration. On surveys, 90 percent regularly identify with the "middle class," despite the existence of a large percentage of "working-class" jobs in the economy (Flanagan 1978: 152). And as Table 2.1 shows, class identification is well below the figures for Britain.

Identification with Local Communities

In Britain, there is no sense in which association with a locality presents a threat to British national unity, though, as we have seen, loyalties to the component nations may pose such a threat. Rose (1982: 27) points out that "within each of the four nations of the U.K., inter-regional differences are diminishing." This is

Table 2.1

Class Awareness and Class Attitudes in Japan and Britain "Think of Self as Member of Social Class" (in percent)

	Japan	Britain
Yes	39	66
No	61	34

not to say that local identity is unimportant to Britons. A large number of Britons indicate that they identify primarily with their locality. But this may indicate only the greater salience of the locality to many people, not a higher claim of loyalty. In any case, the level of local identification is comparable to or slightly below the level of other European states (LDC 1981, cited in Hastings and Hastings 1984: 552).

In general, Japanese identification with their locality is strong. As we shall see, the Japanese "distrust and disdain" more distant political objects, while the trust of the proximate has strengthened local, community-based organizations (Richardson and Flanagan 1984: 175). The concept of congruent circles of group loyalty plays a major part in the sociology of Japan, and in politics, the village or comparable urban unit represents a crucial aspect of the polity. It may at first seem strange, then, that in one 1981 survey, a larger percentage of Japanese (42 percent) than citizens of any other industrial country surveyed said they belonged "first of all" to their country as a whole. A smaller percentage (33 percent) said they belonged primarily to "the locality or the town" where they lived (LDC 1981, cited in Hastings and Hastings 1984: 552). Part of the difficulty in interpreting these results may lie in what meaning "belonging 'first of all' " conveys. Does "first of all" refer to proximity, loyalty, or feelings of belonging? Respondents in different cultures may reach different conclusions. Perhaps more important, we have already seen that the sense of national identity in Japan is very high indeed. Nevertheless, local community loyalties appear to remain more important in Japan—where small-group social networks remain central to the election process— than in Britain, where local roots of candidates are often irrelevant to voting choices.

Identification with Supranational Communities of States

Both Japan and Britain are island states, and while neither has been able completely to remain isolated, the history and culture of each strongly reflects their insular identity. Richard Rose (1986c: 29) has written that "Insularity is one of the most striking characteristics" of the British, and it has become axiomatic to cite the strong group identity of the Japanese vis-à-vis the foreigner. How has the existence of strong national identity, reinforced by geographical separateness, affected the growth of identification with regional associations? England's international economic orientation has for hundreds of years, until recently, reflected its geographical and political distance from the continent. The Empire and later the Commonwealth long provided alternative trading partners.

At the same time, British international political relations have of necessity been partly oriented toward Europe. All but one of its principal historical rivals and enemies have been continental. Unlike Japan, Britain was not economically isolated or autarchic. Nor was Britain able to enjoy political or military isolation. Thus, while the attitudes of the British may have reflected insularity, the behavior of the British has been far from isolationist. Since World War II, the British public (though not always the leadership) has lagged behind most of its continental neighbors in its enthusiasm for various forms of union and cooperation among Europeans, as was indicated by its late entrance into the European Community. Even when Britain approved entry, that approval did not signal great enthusiasm. In 1973, only 37 percent were "very much for" or "for to some extent" West European unification. Even after Britain's narrow endorsement of European Economic Community membership in the 1973 referendum, the British public was slow to warm to the notion of European-ness. In the 1983 European parliamentary elections, the 32 percent British turnout was lower than any other electorate. In the European Values Systems Survey (EVSS) in 1981, only 7 percent of the respondents said they identified most with Europe, a far lower percentage than all but one other nation (Harding and Phillips 1986: 95). In 1986, when European Community members were asked if they thought of themselves not only as citizens of their country but also as citizens of Europe, the smallest percent of "often" (11 percent) and "sometimes" (21 percent) responses were British (European Economic Community-Gallup International Research Institute [EEC-GIRI] November 1986, cited in Hastings and Hastings 1988: 598). Some evidence even suggests that British interest is eroding, as between 1977 and 1986 the percentage of Britons who said they had seen or heard about the European Parliament dropped from 58 to 34 percent—about the same percent who had voted in 1983 (EEC-GIRI November 1986, cited in Hastings and Hastings 1988: 604). Perhaps Richard Rose (1986c: 37) was correct to observe that the greater the extent of international contacts, "the more insular public opinion has become."

Despite the evidence of continued British reticence to enter Europe, there is some contrary evidence that a significant change in British opinion has been under way for the past decade. Mrs. Thatcher's political demise was brought about in part by the strong pro-European sentiments of many in her party. Britain may have begun to catch up to other European states in its approval of European union. By 1986, British approval of West European unification had jumped to 69 percent, ahead of Denmark and Ireland (EEC-GIRI November 1986, cited in

Hastings and Hastings 1988: 608). At the same time, approval of a United States of Europe had jumped from 30 percent in 1970, to a majority (52 percent). *Eurobarometer* (March 1987: 28) was prompted to conclude, somewhat hopefully, that "the British disclose an impressive, steady evolution towards clearly 'pro European' positions. . . they have totally reversed the basic trend in their public opinion towards the Community." It seems safer to say that, while some measures of opinion toward association with Europe have become more positive, the evidence is still ambiguous, and insularity may still be the rule. As of 1988, the British were still the least likely of all European Community members to identify with Europe (EC-GIRI November 1988, cited in Hastings and Hastings 1990: 538). Resistance to union with Europe is not entirely spawned by insularity, for the British in modern times have always had a fairly large, internationalist population, albeit a minority, whose horizons are broader than Britain or Europe. In 1981, nine percent of Britons, a larger percentage than in any of the eleven survey countries but France and Italy, said they belonged "first of all" to the world as a whole (LDC 1981, cited in Hastings and Hastings 1984: 552). Such Britons might oppose a "1992" concept of Europe because its compass is too limited. Another manifestation of supranational identities among some British is the concept of Atlanticism, embodying the "special relationship" with the United States since the early part of this century.

Japan faces a very different regional context in the Pacific. Until the 1850s, its "regional" orientation was isolation. There was nothing in Japanese experience comparable to Europe's trading economies or rivalries. Since the Peace of Westphalia, Europe has had a system of relations based upon explicitly stated and implicitly understood principles that regulate a very high frequency of transactions. East Asian diplomatic tradition is rooted in the Chinese tributary system, in which a dominant, self-sufficient China was usually little concerned with seeking out relations with bordering "barbarian" nations. Japan's position as a tributary of China, in addition to its political isolation, limited Japan's impact on regional politics. This changed after Japan was forced to join the Western international relations system upon its "opening" by the United States. It soon dominated East Asia by defeating China in 1894 and Russia in 1905, respectively. These military victories allowed Japan to build a military and economic empire that by 1940 stretched from Taiwan, through coastal China, to the Russian-Manchurian border. Japan's prewar role in Asia supplanted and superseded that of China. It became the dominant state. Whereas China cared little for relations with other nations, however, Japan was hegemonic. Armed with a Pan-Asian ideology, economic power, and military coercion, it created the Greater East Asian Co-Prosperity Sphere.

Although Japan, South Korea, the Philippines, and Taiwan have been tied by trade and mutual alliances with the United States since the 1950s, no sense of regionalism has ever evolved, and given the disparity of economic and political systems in the region, there seems to be little chance that it will. Japan perceives itself more in global than regional terms, but there are regional problems they have to face. One is the question of Asian leadership. As Japan becomes economically more powerful, there are those inside and outside who call for greater Japanese leadership in Asia. The problem lies in traditional Asian distrust of the Japanese following their experiences in the Pacific war. Second, there is the competition between South Korea and Japan. Although they would seem to be natural allies, deep distrust, cultural antipathy, and economic competition keep them at arm's length. It was not until the mid-1980s that a Japanese prime minister visited South Korea. Feelings run so high that many Koreans believe the primary purpose for maintaining American forces in Japan should be to protect Korea from a Japanese military build up. Third, the three major powers of the region, Japan, the Soviet Union and China, have a long history of mutual suspicion and conflict. During the first four decades of the twentieth century, Japan and Russia were in conflict over Manchuria and northeast China, while all three were separated by ideology after the Second World War. Although nothing seems impossible in the post-cold war world, given the continuing differences among these three powers it is highly unlikely that they will form any regional association.

Under these conditions, there has never been, and will probably never be, an equivalent of "Western Europe"—a region including several proximate, equal, and interdependent powers. In short, while Britain has never been free of regional influences and pressures (however unsought), Japan was largely free of such influences. Whatever external pressures Japan's economy, society, and polity may have faced up to now to conform to supranational interests, they have not been regional. Possibly this state of affairs may change. Inasmuch as it reflected Japan's sense of dependence and vulnerability, however, Japan's aggression in East Asia during World War II implied a potential for a regional relationship, especially as countries like China, the Soviet Union, and even South Korea, emerge as important regional actors. Clearly, however, the dual legacies of the Second World War and Cold War divisions, remain a tremendous obstacle to Japanese regional diplomacy and the future of regionalism in the North Pacific.

As this work is being written, the international relations system is in a state of rapid change—Eastern European countries have broken away from the Soviet bloc, the Soviet Union appears to be disintegrating, and North America and the European Community are beginning to coalesce into highly integrated blocs. The events of 1989–1990 should have taught all scholars of political science and international relations never to say never, but it still appears as if true regional leadership for the Japanese, or any form of integrated bloc formation in East Asia, will be difficult, even though Japan would very much like to take on the role of regional political, as well as economic, power.

Pride in Country

Pride in country is a variable often cited in comparative political studies because higher levels of national pride are associated with other attitudes, such as trust and support. We should recognize at the outset, however, that "national pride" is no easy concept to isolate, or compare. This is partly due to the frequent disjunction we have already noted between "nation" and "state." Surveys on national pride do not always capture the difference, yet it is a distinction that helps to clarify the relatively high levels of national pride reflected in British surveys and the relatively low levels of pride reflected in Japanese surveys. As we have seen, the Japanese have a very strong and exclusionist sense of their national identity, a trait that we might expect to translate into equally strong feelings of patriotism. For their part, the British in recent years would seem to have less to be proud of than the Japanese in some ways, considering the relative economic decline of the past century and the loss of empire. The different levels and motivations of national pride in Japan and Britain have much to tell about the political cultures of the two nation-states.

Level of National Pride

The British remain a strongly patriotic people. In survey after survey, Britain remains near the top among European Community members in pride. They also express a greater willingness to fight for their country (61 percent) than their European Community associates (48 percent) (*Eurobarometer* December 1985: Table 9, 26). National pride is also remarkably consistent across the population (Rose 1984: 379). In 1985, 57 percent said they were "very proud," while the European Community average was 41 percent. Thirty-one percent said they were "quite proud," compared to 39 percent for the European Community as a whole (*Eurobarometer* December 1985: Table 8, 21). Pride among those identifying themselves as politically "left" (75 percent) was 21 percent lower than for "right" (96 percent), but still among the highest in Europe. Labour supporters tend to be less proud, but the proud still constitute a large majority. "Even among the small group on the far 'left' less than a quarter were 'not very' or 'not at all proud' to be British" (Phillips 1985: 160). Generational differences should be noted, however, with 18–24-year-olds in the EVSS showing the lowest levels in the "very proud" category (35 percent). In a 1988 Gallup poll, men aged 19–34 years of age indicated that they thought their generation was generally "less patriotic" than the older generation (Social Surveys Ltd. March 2–15, 1988), and another eleven-nation survey found British youth the least proud (Prime Minister's Office Spring 1988, cited in Hastings and Hastings 1990: 612). High levels of pride in nation go hand in hand with expressed willingness to fight for country—62 percent of respondents in one survey (Rose 1985: Table 5, 94). The British regularly emerge as among the most willing to take up the sword in defense of the country (Merkl 1988: Table 1.1, 52). The persistence of high levels of national pride are of potential political significance in mitigating what many writers have seen as an erosion of political stability in Britain over the past two decades. On the other hand, the generational decline of patriotism suggests caution in assuming the long-term operation of this effect.

By comparison with Britain and most other European citizens, the Japanese may appear less proud because Japanese pride in nation is both relatively defensive and manifests itself almost exclusively in nonpolitical symbols. In a 1985 study, Japan and Germany were identified as among the least proud of the fifteen countries surveyed (Rose 1985: 88). In 1981, 30 percent said they were "very proud," 32 percent "quite proud" (Heald 1982), whereas in 1987, 29 percent responded "proud" and 41 percent responded "quite proud" (Stronach 1988: 8). An as yet unpublished poll by the Dentsu Institute for Human Studies and the Leisure Development Center found that 62 percent of Japanese are proud of their country, whereas over 80 percent of respondents in each of the other countries surveyed—Nigeria, Chile, the United States, Spain, South Korea, Poland, Canada and Czechoslovakia—had pride in their countries. Japan was also lowest in those who said they would die for their country. Only ten percent of Japanese are willing to do so, while the next lowest nation was Spain at 47 percent (*Japan Times*, June 13, 1991–2). These figures are roughly comparable to Britain, but considerably lower than the United States, China, Korea, and Singapore.

One explanation offered for the lower levels of pride in Japan is the military defeat in 1945. (Germany exhibits similarly low levels.) Britain, as one of the victors in World War II, is able to look back at its wartime experience with pride, but the Japanese defeat stripped its military of all prestige, shamed the people of Japan, and laid them open to an occupation that attempted to remove all vehicles of nationalistic, militaristic, and patriotic socialization. The relative lack of patriotic pride in military/political institutions which this produced was enhanced by the imposition of a welcomed but alien democracy. While the LDP, the ruling conservative party, and other conservative institutions have periodically attempted to reassert national pride in political/military institutions, they have not met with much success. Although the Japanese people support the existence of the Self-Defense Forces (SDF) (Prime Minister's Office 1988), strong opposition during the 1990 Gulf Crisis to the government's attempt to pass a law allowing the SDF to join United Nations Peacekeeping Forces demonstrated the sensitivity of public opinion to any increase in the SDF's power or status. Indeed, when asked what they would do if Japan was invaded, only 7 percent of Japanese said they would join the SDF or put up guerrilla resistance, while 40 percent said that they would support the SDF "somehow." Nineteen percent said that they would resist by non-military means and 10 percent said that they would not resist at all (Prime Minister's Office 1988: 9).

The lack of success is manifested by the policies of the LDP. At various times from the 1960s to the mid-1980s, LDP policies included the three nonnuclear principles of not using, producing, or allowing nuclear weapons into the country, a strict policy of virtually banning the export of war materials, and a cap of one percent of GNP on the defense budget. Although the Nakasone government was successful in reversing the limits imposed on the military by the above policies, the military is still held in low esteem by the Japanese public. A career in the

Japanese military carries with it almost no prestige, and few people with high qualifications are willing to forego civilian life.

Only rarely does one see the national flag in Japan, or hear the national anthem. The American rites of playing the anthem before major sporting events and pledging allegiance to the flag in classrooms are seen by many Japanese as very reactionary. Japanese public school teachers and administrators have been hesitant to use the symbols of the Japanese state—as of the beginning of 1990 only about 30 percent of high schools flew the flag at graduation ceremonies and only about 2 percent sang the national anthem (*Japan Times* April 9–15, 1990: 7). In a move designed to increase patriotism, the Education Ministry began requiring all public elementary, middle, and high schools to raise the national flag and play the national anthem at entrance and graduation ceremonies, but in the first test of the new regulations, the spring 1990 entrance ceremonies, there appeared to have been a great deal of resistance (*Japan Times* April 23–29, 1990: 7).

However, the relatively low level of pride as expressed in some direct survey responses is somewhat deceiving. By some measures, patriotism approaches the levels of other industrial states, for example, 77 percent agreed or more or less agreed in 1981 that "patriotism and loyalty are the first and most important requirements of Japanese citizens" (NHK 1982: 71). And in a 1990 survey 52.9 percent responded that they have strong patriotic feelings—the highest in the twenty-one years the survey has been conducted (Prime Minister's Office 1990: 5).

To explain what has appeared to be relatively lower Japanese expression of "national pride," it may be necessary to distinguish between pride in the polity and institutions, and pride in the people and culture. The Japanese are not especially proud of their system of government, but they are quite proud of the Japanese people and their accomplishments. This explanation is borne out in survey evidence, as we shall see below, when we discuss sources of national pride. The strong in-group sense that foreigners observe in Japan suggests a strong sense of pride. Japanese, far more than other industrial states's populations, are likely to express a belief in their cultural superiority. In several polls, nearly 90 percent of respondents agreed that the Japanese were "by nature better than most other peoples" (NHK 1982: 69). By contrast, 47 percent of Americans considered themselves "better." However, it has been noted that the Japanese tend to experience swings of mood between inferiority and exaltation of the culture, therefore, some caution should be used in interpreting what appear to be self-congratulatory views (Ward 1965: 58).

Sources of National Pride

The differences between Japan and Britain with respect to national pride show up to a greater extent when we examine the motives for pride than when we look

Table 2.2

Sources of National Pride (in percent)

	Japan 1972	Japan 1987	Britain 1972
Political Institutions	5	7	46
Social Legislation	7	11	18
International Standing	11	25	11
Economics and Social Science	44	93	17
Arts, Culture, etc.	62	94	35

Sources: Scott C. Flanagan, 1978. "The Genesis of Variant Political Cultures: Contemporary Citizen Orientations in Japan, America, Britain, and Italy." In *The Citizen and Politics,* ed. Sidney Verba and Lucian W. Pye: Table 11, p. 153. Stamford, CT: Greylock; Bruce Stronach 1988. "Deference, Pride, and Political Culture: The Social Context of Japanese Political Participation in Comparison with Great Britain." Paper presented at the Annual Meeting of the Canadian Asian Studies Association, Windsor, Ontario, June.

only at the expressed level of pride. To examine this variable, we look at four sources: (1) abstractions such as land, people, culture, and symbols, (2) political institutions, (3) political outputs, such as economic and scientific achievements, social policy, and (4) international standing. The British exhibit a fairly clear notion of the sources of their pride that includes both cultural and political facets. The Japanese, on the other hand, still display some uncertainty over appropriate symbols of the nation. It has been characteristic of Japanese surveys in general that a large percentage of respondents answered "none" or "don't know." This pattern appears with respect to questions about reasons for pride as well. This apparent uncertainty may be changing, as the percentage of "none" or "don't know" responses dropped from 39 percent to 12 percent in some surveys conducted between 1971 and 1985. At the same time, percentages for each of the most cited reasons for pride increased (Prime Minister's Office 1986: 15).

Pride in Political Institutions

The most striking contrast between Japan and Britain is the degree to which pride in political institutions is a significant component of national pride in Britain, while it is quite minor in Japan (see Table 2.2). Britons are proud of past accomplishments, and especially the "maintenance of free representative government in peace and war" (Rose 1986c: 6). British reverence for at least some political institutions as a source of national pride is well documented. Flanagan's 1978 comparison found 46 percent of Britons ready to cite political institutions as an aspect of the nation in which they are proud (Flanagan 1978: 153). In survey after survey, Britain exceeds most other industrial states in expressed confidence in several institutions. In Britain, a lack of distinction between politics and society is characteristic of a polity that evolved as part of the total social fabric. In Britain, social, economic, political, and cultural change proceeded in complementary fashion. Nineteenth-century political reforms, for example, reflected the impact of industrialization and the changing social map of Britain. For the Japanese, the political system and its institutions remain somewhat detached from the essence of being Japanese. The Japanese are indeed proud, but that few cite political institutions as a source of pride (5 percent in the Nakamura 1972 study, 7 percent in the Stronach 1987 study) is an indication that pride in nation has not been fully transmitted to pride in the polity and its institutions (Richardson and Flanagan 1984; Stronach 1988: 9). It is worth considering that the generally lower level of pride is partially explained by different objects of national pride among the Japanese.

Pride in Political Symbols

As noted by Bagehot, symbols of nation are the "dignified part" of the British constitution. They "excite and preserve the reverence of the population." Apparently, they continue to do so in what is regarded as a far less deferential age. Reinforcing the notion of a confluence of pride in polity and pride in culture in Britain, even the symbols of British nationalism and pride are political. The mace, a symbol of central political power, is also a symbol of the unity of the British nation. The crown, of course, historically provided the bond that united the Welsh, Scottish, and English domains. Even today, Britons not only respect the monarchy, but consider it important. The 1984 *British Social Attitudes* survey found that 87 percent of respondents thought it very or quite important to have a monarchy (Young 1984: 30). Aside from the crown, national symbols do not play a prominent part in maintaining British national pride. As Rose (1986c: 117) has indicated, national pride in Britain is maintained without resort to manipulation of strongly emotional symbols.

In Japan, which is also a constitutional monarchy, the emperor continues to play a role in creating pride among Japanese. This is less so than in prewar Japan, when the doctrine of *kokutai* (emperor as spiritual, military, and political leader) prevailed. But even in postwar Japan, emperor and nation were an "important source of the spirit of sacrifice and the sense of discipline and the common good which explain so much of Japan's remarkable success" (Ward 1965: 60). In the late 1940s, support for the emperor exceeded 90 percent, and even today 84 percent think that the present emperor system should be maintained as it is, and another 5 percent wish to give the emperor more authority (*Mainichi Press* March 1987, cited in Hastings and Hastings 1989: 308). However, the events surrounding the death of Emperor Showa and the accession of Emperor Akihito would indicate that, as with the flag and the national anthem, there is little acceptance of the emperor as a patriotic symbol, but much acceptance of him as a symbol of the nation. It was feared that attempts by the government to enforce a national deathwatch during the long final illness of Emperor Showa and a period of mourning after his death would increase the patriotic symbolism of the Emperor Akihito, but the counterreaction of the public to those attempts, along with the actions taken by Akihito to divest himself of patriotic symbolism, seem to have decreased the political symbolism of the emperor. It seems safe to assume that as the memory of the last emperor who reigned under *kokutai* fades, so will the final remnants of political and patriotic symbolism in the emperor.

Pride in Land, Culture, People, and Religion

Many Britons take pride in their land, culture, people, and religion—35 percent in the 1978 Flanagan study. In a poll of sources of pride among the young (from which politics and political institutions were omitted), by far the most often cited source of pride—ahead of sports—was "history and cultural inheritance" (Prime Minister's Office 1988, cited in Hastings and Hastings 1990: 611). But this level of response, while second only to pride in institutions, is far below the level in Japan, where "culture" has proven a stronger bond than "politics." Flanagan found fully 62 percent of Japanese cited land, culture, people, and religion as a source of pride. Among the young as well, history and cultural inheritance held place of pride (Prime Minister's Office 1988, cited in Hastings and Hastings 1990: 611). Stronach found over 90 percent referring to arts and culture (Stronach 1988: 8). The 1986 *Public Opinion Survey on Society and State*, using different categories, also confirmed the importance of cultural aspects of nationhood in Japan, with 35 percent citing "industry and ability of the people" as the aspect of which they were the most proud, and 27 percent, "the beautiful natural scenery of the country" (another 19 percent cited "splendid culture and the arts"). The difference in the degree to which political institutions are a source of pride is one of the most clear-cut distinctions between Japanese and British political cultures.

Pride in Outputs

Some care must be used in interpreting pride in outputs as a factor in pride in nation. There is always the problem of sorting out support for the current governing party and policies, support for the polity, and pride in nation. In any case, both social and economic outputs may depend on ephemeral developments. Thus, the pride they instill may be distinguished from the "rain-or-shine commitment" that is usually associated with national pride (Verba 1967: 529). Be that as it may, social, scientific, and economic outputs are a major and growing source of pride in Japan, while they constitute a relatively smaller source of pride among Britons. In the 1978 Flanagan study, 18 percent of Britons reported pride in social legislation, and 17 percent cited economic and scientific achievements (Flanagan 1978: 153). This combined 35 percent is not low. It is equal to the percentage in Britain citing "land, culture, people, and religion." But it is much lower than the figure for Japan (44 percent for economic and scientific achievement, 7 percent for social legislation according to the 1978 Flanagan study). The 1986 Prime Minister's Office Survey, using different categories, also found high levels of pride in "outputs"—"well-maintained law and order," 27 percent; "the high level of education," 20 percent; "economic prosperity," 19 percent; "splendid culture and the arts," 20 percent. There is some evidence that the level of support for outputs, particularly economic success, is growing. By 1987, over 90 percent of Japanese cited "the economy and science" as a source of pride (Stronach 1988: 8). Certainly the contrasting economic performances of Japan and Britain must be considered as one explanation for the relative difference in levels of pride in the economic and scientific spheres. But it may also be that in Britain skepticism with regard to applied science and industrial entrepreneurship may have inhibited the growth of such pride, at least in the pre-Thatcher years.

International Standing

In the past, Britain's imperial responsibilities and achievements may have had a role in cementing national solidarity and instilling pride. Pride in British history, political institutions, and military exploits continued up to and into the 1950s. But while some pride in these past accomplishments may have survived the liquidation of British overseas possessions, overall, global power is neither an expectation nor a goal of most Britons. In 1978, 11 percent cited international standing as a source of pride (Flanagan 1978: 153). By 1983, 53 percent of Britons indicated that they wanted to emulate small neutral states, not great powers (Rose 1986c: 37). "Little Britain" represents a great adjustment in the expectations of Britons, but it represents a source of pride nonetheless. It is significant that even though the Falklands war called forth outpourings of national pride, most Britons (53 percent), within a year after the war concluded that holding on to the islands was not worth the money (Rose 1986c: 33).

One might expect that, for different reasons, international standing might enjoy a similarly low profile in Japan during the postwar period. The compulsory loss of empire and the constraints imposed by the new constitution provided reasons for lowered expectations. Indeed, in 1972, only 11 percent of the sample associated pride with Japan's international standing (Nakamura 1975: 11). However, we must consider that a part of Japanese pride in economic achievements may have reflected a pride in the international status of the Japanese economy. Furthermore, it is interesting to note that recent findings confirm that growing numbers of Japanese are prepared for Japan to resume a more assertive international role. By 1987, 25 percent cited international standing as a source of pride, apart from economic achievements (Stronach 1988: 8).

Summary and Conclusions

The levels of pride that the British and Japanese feel toward their respective nations differ as a result of the distinctly different histories of political development in the two countries. While the peoples of both countries exhibit high levels of national pride, the British are proud of political institutions as well as history and cultural heritage. The merging of British culture with the development of its domestic political institutions over the past two centuries, in combination with a history of international military and political successes over the same period of time, have created a well of patriotism which seems to have supported the British through decolonization and the economic reverses which followed it, though feelings of national pride among the young do appear to have declined.

Japan's ignominious defeat in World War II and forced acceptance of a foreign political system has reinforced a separation between nation and state which had existed up until the Meiji period. Thus, Japanese pride is directed toward the people and culture of the nation, their traditions, and their economic and scientific successes during the period of postwar recovery. Political institutions have yet to serve as an inspiration of pride.

Notes

1. Gamson (1968: 34–35) uses "solidary groups" in a more restricted sense, to refer to psychological groups, bound together emotionally. These groups are "collections of individuals who think in terms of the effect of political decisions on the aggregate and feel that they are in some way personally affected by what happens to the aggregate." Interest groups, which we consider in Chapter 7, "are formal organizations which represent the demands of such solidary groups in the political system."

2. In the 1976 JABISS survey respondents were allowed only one choice, but were allowed multiple choices in the 1987 Stronach survey.

3. Not everyone agrees that class identification is high. Rose (1986: 171) reports, based on the 1983 Election Survey, that "only 32 percent say they think of themselves as working class, and 21 percent as middle class. Half do not think of themselves as belonging to a particular class." Rose sees the issue of class as less pervasive. "Class differences," he notes, "have been considered important because they are the only substantial division within English society" (Rose 1986: 173). "Class differences have not translated into political differences to the degree implied by much social theory and political rhetoric." (Rose 1986: 173). This certainly seemed true a generation ago, when "Butler and Stokes found that less than one-tenth of the electorate overall see politics in terms of opposing class interests" (Rose 1986: 171).

3

Political Efficacy
and Trust

National identity and national pride are concepts that deal with the attitudes of people at the most abstract level toward their nation and the state. We turn in Chapter 3 to another aspect of the political culture, citizen attitudes toward the political system itself, specifically their sense of efficacy, or sense of political competence, and trust or belief in the honesty and responsiveness of politicians and political institutions. These attitudes are major components of political culture, and are closely linked to the degree of popular support accorded to the regime.

An important measure of political attitudes is "political efficacy." Political efficacy (sometimes referred to as internal efficacy) is the self-perceived capacity to understand politics, to express demands and effect positive political change. Efficacy expresses the attitudes of the individual toward his or her own competence as subject and citizen. Since it relates to the interest-articulation stage of the political process, efficacy may be considered part of the "input" dimension of political attitudes (Marsh 1977: 116).[1] In short, it is about self-confidence. When combined with political trust (or external efficacy)—belief in the honesty and the responsiveness of political authorities to expressed demands and needs—efficacy is believed to help determine the participant orientation of citizens. Indeed, many believe that efficacy is the more important of the two variables, and is in itself sufficient to motivate citizen activism.

A wide array of survey questions have been devised to elicit responses about efficacy and trust. A number of these have been used regularly in survey research over the past twenty-five years, including surveys in Japan and Britain. These questions, therefore, provide direct comparability between the two countries, and will constitute the core of our discussion of political trust and efficacy. This is not to claim that they are perfect measures. There is still disagreement about defining trust and efficacy, and about which questions best measure them. Barnes, Kaase et al. (1979: 574–75), for example, propose a third set of attitudes— their "system responsiveness index"—which attempts to distinguish between the honesty of politicians (intrinsic trust), and their willingness to listen to citizen demands (system responsiveness). Admittedly, as Marsh (1977: 258) has pointed out, there is some difficulty in attempting to separate the question of the citizen's feelings of competence from other feelings of trust in politicians or institutions, since the two are likely to influence each other. For example, a person's belief that he or she can "influence government" may be a reflection of skill and self-confidence, or of the concern and responsiveness of politicians. Notwithstanding these caveats, we elect to work with the two traditional categories of affect—efficacy and trust—to simplify the task of making comparative judgments about Britain and Japan.

Personal Efficacy

Political efficacy may be distinguished from *personal* efficacy, which refers to the individual's confidence to deal with family, friends, peers, and supervisors at work. While we are principally concerned with political efficacy, the possibility that personal efficacy may be related to political efficacy leads us to look briefly at this variable as well. The British exhibit a mixture of attitudes about their personal efficacy. They are as confident as most other Europeans that they can exercise control over their lives, but take significantly more pride in their work (Halsey 1985: 13).

The percentage of Britons who feel free to complain about a decision with which they disagree strongly within the family (63 percent) and on the job (89 percent) are high in absolute terms, but relative to Japan, the difference becomes striking (Table 3.1). To the extent that the British do feel more personally efficacious, one explanation that has been offered is that many more Britons are likely to feel more of a sense of control over their lives "in the private [rather] than in the public domain" (Marshall et al. 1985: 273).

However, other evidence would suggest that the British feel less personally efficacious and that they might be "exceptionally likely to back off from changes which might involve strong and prolonged controversy" (Fogarty 1985: 180). Willingness to complain at work may reflect a "grumbling appendix" rather than real desire to effect change (Fogarty 1985: 180). In a 1989 Gallup poll, 63 percent agreed with the statement that "what you think doesn't count much any more" (Social Surveys Ltd. [SSLT] August 1989, cited in *World Opinion Update* 1989: 118). Furthermore, the British are less likely than the European average to set out to persuade others on matters on which they hold a strong view. In 1987, 11 percent said that when they held an opinion strongly, they would try to persuade friends or fellow workers to adopt this opinion "often," 28 percent said "from time to time," and 60 percent said "rarely" or "never" (SSLT July 3–7 1987).[2] Fogarty (1985: 180) found from the European Values System Survey

Table 3.1

Percentage Who Feel Free to Complain About a Decision with Which They Disagree

	Japan	U.K.
In family	30	63
On job	38	89

Source: Scott C. Flanagan, 1978. "The Genesis of Variant Political Cultures: Contemporary Citizen Orientations in Japan, America, Britain and Italy." In *The Citizen and Politics*, ed. Sidney Verba and Lucian W. Pye: Table 13, p. 155.

data that the British take a largely uncritical attitude toward work, and lack by and large "a dynamic drive for change." These relatively passive orientations may be indicative of low levels of efficacy per se, but there are other possible explanations, however, such as a relatively high degree of satisfaction with personal life, low levels of trust (producing alienation), or even high levels of trust (producing deference). But before we examine the question of trust, we shall tentatively suggest that though the evidence is mixed, the British sense of personal efficacy is lower than found elsewhere in Europe. As we shall see, however, it also appears to be higher than that found among the Japanese.

Personal efficacy has been low throughout the postwar period in Japan. For example, as we saw in Table 3.1 above, the Japanese have been found to be quite reluctant to complain about decisions they disagreed with both at home and at work. But evidence points to a potentially dramatic increase of efficacy, at least with regard to family relations, that may place it on a par with Europe. In Nakamura's 1972 survey (Nakamura 1975: 18–19), only 30 percent of respondents said they felt free to complain about decisions in the family with which they disagreed strongly, but by 1987 that figure had risen to 71 percent. One area where personal efficacy seems not to have increased is on the job. In the Nakamura study, 38 percent were willing to speak up on the job (Nakamura 1975: 18–19), whereas only 30 percent similarly responded in 1987. The reluctance to complain about a decision at work they disagreed with would seem to suggest low personal efficacy, but it may also reflect the consensual style of the Japanese culture, in which an individual's feelings are taken into account before a decision is made.

Political Efficacy

Political efficacy refers to the confidence the citizen has to influence the political environment, just as personal efficacy refers to influence over the social and work environment. Almond and Verba's civic culture model had assumed what Topf (1989: 61) has called the "myth of civic competence," whereby the British believed themselves capable of having influence in the political process. Yet,

Table 3.2

Political Efficacy (as indicated by the percentage of respondents who agree with the following statements)

	U.K.	Japan
Sometimes politics and government are too complicated for someone like me to understand.	74	76
People like me don't have any say in what the government does.	61	67
Voting is the only way people like me can have any say about how the government runs things.	74	62

Sources: NHK 1982:6568; Alan Marsh, 1977. *Protest and Political Consciousness* (Beverly Hills: Sage): Table 5.4, p. 115. © Alan Marsh, 1977. Reprinted by permission of Sage Publications, Inc.

Topf's (1989: 61) and other data suggest that in reality "citizens suffer from no such delusion." The British display low political efficacy, though on a level comparable to Western Europe as a whole and to Japan. Paralleling their sense of low personal efficacy, a large majority do not see "people like themselves" as having a say in government, nor do they generally view politics as comprehensible to people like themselves. However, significantly larger percentages—in some cases a plurality—believe they could take some specific action to affect a local or national law which they think harmful. This response is consistent with people's belief that they are free to complain about decisions in the home or workplace. If we look more closely at the survey questions commonly used to measure efficacy, we will see these general impressions confirmed.

There is some evidence of an increase in political efficacy in Britain, though it is not conclusive. Two decades ago, the Royal Commission on the Constitution noted increased efficacy among a significant minority of Britons, coupled with high levels of cynicism and rejection of traditional democratic politics. Young (1984: 11, 22), while observing the continued "prevalence of acquiescence" in Britain, notes "some evidence of the very transformation in the level of citizen assertiveness that has been mentioned by recent commentators." Heath and Topf (1987: 56–58) find evidence that "confidence in one's own ability to affect the political process" is now "much more evident than at the time of the 1959 Almond and Verba study." Still others, however, point to a decline of subjective competence and growing apathy, and to a turning away from politics (Kavanagh 1980: 150; Wright 1987: 53; Royal Commission on the Constitution 1973: 124). Marshall et al. (1985: 72) claim that "the apparent intractability of Britain's economic problems has led to increasing fatalism about their solution." In fact, both trends could well be under way. Some Britons turn away from politics, some to activism and protest. We shall consider below, in Chapter 5, the case for the appearance of growing political activism.

Observers tend to be more united and more emphatic on the low political efficacy to be found in Japan than we have seen to be the case in Britain. "One concludes," writes Ward (1965: 68), "that there is a good deal of political apathy combined with negative or low estimations of the role of self as political actor to be found in both rural and urban Japan. There is small indication in many contexts that the citizen approaches government with the expectation of receiving courteous, prompt, and efficient service as a matter of right. In fact his attitude is apt to be compounded more of elements of servility, resignation, and supplication. The feeling that bureaucrats are superior beings with favors to be bestowed—which, incidentally, is to a very appreciable extent shared by the bureaucracy itself—is an aspect of the traditional political culture which dies hard in Japan." More recent commentary confirms this analysis. Flanagan (1978: 154) observes that "politics is not only an external activity but also a difficult one as well, for the Japanese citizen tends to lack the confidence in his ability to exercise any influence over political affairs." Despite the apparent consensus among scholars that efficacy in Japan is low, there is some evidence of increased efficacy during the postwar period. Ward noted as early as 1965 that the growth of interest groups shows "more positive attitudes toward efficacy of popular participation" (Ward 1965: 69).

We now turn to a comparison of responses to specific survey questions related to efficacy.

Politics Too Complicated

A large majority of the British tend to agree that politics is "too complicated" for people like themselves to understand. Marsh (1977: Table 5.4, 115) found that 74 percent "agreed strongly" or "agreed" with the statement, while 23 percent "disagreed strongly" or "disagreed." In 1986, 69 percent agreed (Topf 1989: Table 1, 56). The Royal Commission on the Constitution attributed these high levels of perplexity to the fact that "ordinary people tend to be confused by the wide range of government institutions, and are said to have difficulty in discovering, let alone defending, their rights" (Royal Commission on the Constitution 1973: 99). Ridley (1984: 4) attributes the British disdain for litigation at least in part to this confusion, and its effect in deterring ordinary people from seeking redress. British agreement on this item is on a par with Japan, where 76 percent agree (Nippon Hoso Kyoka [NHK] 1982: 67). "Politics," notes Flanagan (1978: 152), "does not lie within the domain of the average citizen," and accordingly, has not become involved.

People Like Me Have No Say in Government

Surveys invariably find that respondents, when asked to rank the influence of various groups in society, place "people like yourself" near the bottom (Kavanagh 1980: 150). Asked how much say people like themselves have on their country's future, 8 percent in one British survey said "a lot," 38 percent

said "a little," and 50 percent said "none at all" (behind all other named influences on government in both the "a lot" and the "none at all" categories) (SSLT
November 4–9, 1987). When asked in the 1974 Marsh (1977: Table 5.4, 115) survey
whether they agreed that "people like me have no say in what government does," 14
percent agreed strongly, 47 percent agreed, 32 percent disagreed, and 2 percent
disagreed strongly. Sixty-one percent in 1986 agreed with the statement that "people
like me are powerless to change things in this country" (Market Opinion Research
International [MORI] August 1986, cited in Hastings and Hastings 1988: 488).
These levels of response are quite similar to those found in Japanese surveys. A high
percentage of Japanese feel that they have little say in government. Sixty-seven
percent agreed or more or less agreed that "people like me have no say," compared
with 61 percent in Britain, 66 percent in West Germany, 59 percent in the United
States (NHK 1982: 65; American Institute for Public Opinion [AIPO] December
1980; Institut GmbH & Co. [EMNID] December 1981, in Hastings and Hastings,
1982: 517; Marsh 1977: 115). Similar percentages for Japan are confirmed in the
1987 Stronach survey, in which 62 percent agreed, 37 percent disagreed, and 1
percent could not say (Stronach 1988: 7). In the most recent Prime Minister's Office
survey, only 33 percent of respondents thought that their will was reflected in
national policy, while 59 percent did not (Prime Minister's Office 1990: 5).

Voting Only Effective Means of Participation

Another measure of efficacy frequently used is the feelings of people that their
sphere of political input is limited to voting. Britons overwhelmingly adopt this
view, though the responses leave unclear whether people think their input *should*
be so limited. In the Marsh (1977: Table 5.4, 115) survey, 15 percent indicated
"agree strongly," 59 percent "agree," 19 percent "disagree," and 1 percent "disagree strongly." We shall see that this response is largely reflected in the
expressed lack of either intention to participate or actual participation beyond
voting. In Japan, 62 percent agreed that voting is the only way people like
themselves can have any say about how the government runs things (40 percent
agree, and 22 percent more or less agree), compared with Britain, and with the
United States, where 66 percent agreed (NHK 1982: 66; AIPO December 1980,
cited in Hastings and Hastings 1982: 517; Marsh 1977: 115).

Allowing for differences in the timing of the surveys and wording of questions, on none of the three standard questions on political efficacy used above
does a very large difference emerge between Britain and Japan. By these measures, the sense of political efficacy in both countries is low.

National and Local Competence

Generally, it appears that Britons' sense of competence to change a specific law
at either the local or national level is higher than the abstract sense of political

Table 3.3

Local and National Competence

Could Do Something about an Unjust Local Regulation or National Law:

Local		National	
Britain	Japan	Britain	Japan
78	58	62	42

Source: Scott C. Flanagan, 1978. "The Genesis of Variant Political Cultures: Contemporary Citizen Orientations in Japan, America, Britain and Italy." In *The Citizen and Politics*, ed. Sidney Verba and Lucian W. Pye: Table 17, p. 156. Stamford, CT: Greylock, 1978.

competence we have just examined. Levels of national and local competence are higher than would be expected in the light of respondents' feelings of powerlessness "to change things in this country." One explanation for this inconsistency between the more abstract questions on efficacy and the more specific questions on competence to change a law is that the abstract questions tap beliefs about what is true at the moment, and the local and national competence question taps the individual's beliefs about his potential future effectiveness, what he could do (Kavanagh 1980: 149). The attitude expressed may be something like "I don't have much say most of the time, but I could if I wanted to."

Several surveys have found majorities who express competence to affect local and national legislation. Heath and Topf (1987: 56) conclude that "confidence in one's ability to affect the political process" has become "much more evident" in Britain. With respect to both local and national competence, Britain scores higher than Japan, though the difference appears to be greater with respect to national competence.

Asked what specific actions they would take to try to influence government if an unjust or unfair national law were passed, 65 percent said in 1986 they would sign a petition, 52 percent that they would contact their member of Parliament (MP), and eleven percent that they would protest or demonstrate. Compared with 1959, when 34 percent said they would do nothing, only 10 percent so indicated in 1986 (Topf 1989: Table 2, 60). In both the 1959 Almond and Verba survey and the 1974 Marsh survey, differences in national and local competence appeared. Significantly larger percentages at the national level indicated that they would do nothing, on the one hand, and significantly smaller percentages indicated that they would organize an ad hoc protest group (Kavanagh 1980: Table V.5, 150). Based on the 1984 *British Social Attitudes* data, Young (1984: 21) found that, of the minority of respondents (31 percent) who thought unjust national laws had been passed, only about half would take any action. Forty-six percent would contact an MP, 54 percent would sign a petition. Curiously, only three-quarters of those who would contact an MP thought that action most effective; only one-fifth who would sign a petition thought that action most effective. Apparently for some, expected failure is no deterrent to contemplating action. These results, though derived from a small sample, suggest a somewhat fatalistic view of political actions, at least for some Britons, and are consistent with low efficacy. Topf (1989: 67) notes the same dissonance between willingness to act and expectation of success in his 1989 study of British political culture.

Compared to the British, the Japanese lack confidence in their ability to exercise influence over political affairs or to do anything about an unjust law, at either the national or local level (Richardson and Flanagan 1984: 180). Twenty percentage points separate the British from the Japanese at both levels (see Table 3.3 above). The sense of competence, as in Britain, is greater concerning local laws. More than is the case in Britain, national politics seems remote to the Japanese. As Flanagan (1978: 153) has observed, "to the average Japanese citizen, national politics remains a rather distant play." This greater sense of local efficacy is also reflected, in Japan at least, in higher trust in local political institutions (see White 1981: 378).

Relying on the traditional measures of efficacy, the differences between Britain and Japan may be less than would be apparent from the literature, though still significant. In both countries, majorities consider politics complicated and beyond their influence. And more Japanese and Britons express confidence in their ability to affect a specific law with which they disagree, than would seem likely based on their more abstract expressions of passivity.

At the more abstract level, the Japanese sense of efficacy is comparable to the British. On the more concrete level tapped by the national and local competence questions, the Japanese emerge less efficacious. The lower local and national competence, especially when combined with the relatively low levels of personal satisfaction, happiness, and optimism for the future, would suggest that efficacy really is lower in Japan than in Britain. Low efficacy may be related to fatalism in Japanese culture. However, lack of a sense of efficacy in the usual sense may also mask the effectiveness of the Japanese in working within their own group-centered norms to get what they, individually, want. In a system where decisions emerge, rather than being the product of open choice, individual "efficacy" may lack the relevance it has in the West, where decisions tend more to be the product of open discussion and argument among individuals, often sealed with a vote that confirms the importance of the individual in the decision.

Variables Affecting Efficacy

In Britain, education levels are a poor predictor of efficacy. The evidence presented in *The Civic Culture* "suggested that education was not strongly related to subject or citizen competence" (Heath and Topf 1986: 551). In his examination of the Almond and Verba data, Kavanagh (1980: 135) found "perceived high levels of political and subject competence among the less educated British voters."

This is explained by replacement of formal education by other institutions. In Britain, such long-established organizations as trade unions, cooperative societies, and the Labour Party have made explicit appeals to the working class and mobilized them into comparatively high levels of political activity (Kavanagh 1980: 135). As we would expect from this finding, efficacy does not necessarily increase with higher class standing. On the contrary,

> On a number of tests, including subjective competence, sense of obligation to take part in political activities, and perceived freedom to protest at work, the British workers show a more participant outlook than those of other nations, including the United States. Moreover, the difference in political competence tends to be quite marked in favour of the British worker. Similar findings emerge from a sophisticated secondary analysis of this data; regardless of the level of voluntary organizational involvement low-status Britons perform better on elaborate tests of political participation than those from other nations.[3]

These findings give little indication, however, that attitudes among the working class are any more or less efficacious than those among the British population as a whole.

In Japan, like Britain, efficacy is less correlated with the level of education than would normally be expected. Flanagan (1978: 157) finds only a "weak" association, efficacy increasing with education to a far less extent than in the United States (see White 1981; 378). Lower efficacy is shown in urban areas, where personal networks are harder to establish, than in rural areas. "In the rural areas, over a half of the respondents felt they could approach an official directly" (Richardson and Flanagan 1984: 180). White (1981: 388) finds moderately strong efficacy in his Tokyo sample.

Trust/Cynicism

Unlike efficacy, which concerns the image of self as competent, trust concerns the perception that others are honest and responsive, and hence, that personal involvement with them is worthwhile. Social trust refers to confidence in peers in a social or economic context. Political trust refers to confidence in political officeholders and political institutions. Those who are high in trust are considered "trusting," those who are low in trust are considered "cynical." Efficacy and trust in combination produce different orientations to political participation. Generally, we could expect to find citizens who (1) feel effective and trusting, (2) feel effective but not trusting, (3) feel ineffective but trusting, and (4) feel ineffective and not trusting. Political scientists have attached different names to these four variants to indicate their correlation with different degrees and types of participation. We shall turn again to them when we consider in Chapter 5 their significance for political behavior.

In this study, we define trust as the attitude that others are honest and responsive. Trust is closely related to another attitude that has assumed considerable importance in the discussion of Japanese and British political culture: deference. Flanagan (1978: 134) defines deference as attitudes of "respect, delegation and compliance vis-à-vis sanctioned political offices and authorities and identification with and conservatism towards the symbols and institutions of the state." Deference is the attitude that "I trust those in authority enough to let them make decisions affecting my welfare." Often trust and deference are used interchangeably, but we think a distinction important. Deference strongly implies behavior, namely a passive orientation toward participation in decisions in the workplace or in politics. It is possible to trust without being deferent, but true deference is impossible without trust. In both Britain and Japan, political behavior that appears deferent, and which was long assumed to be deferent, may not be so. Politically passive or acquiescent attitudes and behavior are still diagnostic of Japan and Britain, but less and less can they be explained by traditional deference. We shall have more to say on this subject in Chapter 4.

Social Trust

To some observers, trust has been a hallmark of the British. In his 1964 study, Rose finds it "pervasive" (1964: 43). Twenty years later, Norton (1984: 31) writes that "trust in one's fellow countrymen remains a significant feature of contemporary British society." Whether trust is pervasive or not, it does appear by some measures to be higher in Britain than elsewhere. The 1981 European Values System Survey found that a greater proportion of British were likely to believe that most people can be trusted (43 percent) than the European sample as a whole (30 percent) and that Britain and Ireland were found to have the highest levels of trust (Harding and Phillips 1986: Table 6.6, 204–5). Still, levels of trust are not impressive. In every country surveyed but Denmark, more lacked trust than expressed it (Harding and Phillips 1986: Table 6.6, 204–205). Trust may be more prevalent in Britain because of the relative lack of polarization (e.g. religious or ideological conflict), and possibly the fact that there is no British equivalent of national betrayal to a foreign power such as the case of Vichy France (see Fogarty 1985: Table 7.7). Comparatively, the British show more trust in management, and are thus closer to the Japanese than to other Europeans. Half the British respondents, reports Fogarty, "compared to 35 percent across Europe, express outright support for capitalist ownership and management," and "their confidence in major companies is above the European average" (Fogarty 1985: 176).

There are important qualifications, however, to this picture of social trust. In 1989, 64 percent of British respondents felt that "most people with power try to take advantage of people like yourself" (SSLT August 1989, cited in *World Opinion Update* 1989: 118). The EVSS bears this out for the workplace, where a larger percentage of Britons (64 percent) than in the European sample as a whole (53 percent) said that they "often" or "sometimes" feel exploited or taken advantage of at work (Fogarty 1985: Table 7.4, 177). Nearly half of all British respondents, and more than half of those under twenty-five, do *not* think that orders should be carried out without first being convinced of their appropriateness (Fogarty 1985: Table 7.3, 177). Dore is quite emphatic about the relative absence of trust—either in the competence of management or in its good intentions—in the British workplace, and traces this low trust to a deeply ingrained suspicion of power in Britain (Dore 1985: 203–8). Among the unemployed in Britain, trust is much lower than for others. "Nor," found Fogarty, "was the low confidence of the unemployed in political and economic institutions offset by any high level of confidence in their fellow-citizens generally. The unemployed were exceptionally likely to say that most people cannot be trusted and that people are less willing to help each other than in the past, and doubted as strongly as anyone else whether other people's moral standards were as high as their own" (Fogarty 1985: 191).

All in all, while social trust appears low by many measures in Britain, it is higher than in most European countries. It shows up in greater obedience to superiors and in greater acquiescence in the capitalist order generally. This somewhat higher level of trust may be related to high levels of job satisfaction, overall satisfaction with life, and happiness. In contrast to this trusting subculture, we should be quick to add, is the far more skeptical and militant subculture found among many labor union members, where traditional distrust of management belies the image of the trusting British.

Compared with the British, the Japanese lack significant trust in each other. In the 1987 Stronach survey, approximately 70 percent of respondents said that most people would take advantage of them if given the chance (1988: 8). In a 1980 NHK survey, 64 percent took the same position. In the same survey, 68 percent thought that people do not try to be helpful, but rather are looking out for themselves, and 53 percent agreed that you can't be too careful since most people cannot be trusted (NHK 1982: 32–34). Although these results are somewhat surprising, given the contemporary image of Japan as a cooperative, harmonious nation, cooperation and harmony do not necessarily rely upon a foundation of trust. Although the Japanese do not express trust for others in the abstract, trust for other group members in the particular tends to be high. Significantly, trust is relatively high between managers and subordinates, which may be based on the Confucian expectation of benevolence (Dore 1985: 209). Unlike Britain, this trust is usually not diminished by membership in most labor unions.

Political Trust

By most measures, neither the Japanese nor the British today are very trusting of their politicians. In the case of Britain, this view tends to be at odds with the long-accepted conclusion that the British are especially trusting. Birch finds that the British public places a relatively high degree of trust in public servants, and generally considers them "honest, considerate, trustworthy, and willing to re-spond to public pressure" (Birch 1980: 15). Historically, the absence of constitu-tional restraints on governmental power may itself be regarded as evidence of trust (Kavanagh 1980: 156). As Rose (1986c: 128) notes, in the absence of explicit constitutional protections, citizens have had to trust the government not to "go 'too far' in the use of power." In a similar vein, the legal and "strong cultural sanctions upholding the value of privacy in governmental deliberations" imply a high degree of citizen trust (Rose 1964: 43). Secrecy has been given a wide degree of tolerance, and government has been much freer of suspicion than, for example, in the United States. This trust is captured by the conclusions of the Royal Commission on the Constitution on government secrecy. While acknowl-edging that "too much government is carried on in secret," the commission conceded "delicate problems of diplomacy and practical administration which cannot simply be ignored in the interests of more open government" (Royal Commission on the Constitution 1973: 99).

The survey evidence pertaining to political trust does little to confirm the existence of a trusting electorate, though, as we shall see, some evidence bears out a high degree of trust in selected institutions. Britons do not appear to believe either that politicians are truthful, or that they are very effective in performing what they see as the principal representative function. Marsh's 1977 study indi-cated that 57 percent of respondents trusted the government in Westminster "to do what is right" only some of the time, or almost never (Marsh 1977: 118). This lack of confidence is confirmed by overall government approval ratings, which have been consistently under 50 percent for decades (Butler and Butler 1986: 254–64). A 1987 poll, taken three months before the election, found majorities or pluralities disapproving of the government's handling of thirteen of fourteen major policy questions (SSLT February 1987, cited in Hastings and Hastings 1988: 174). Recent pressure to formalize constitutional guarantees of civil rights, calls for proportional elections, and continued pressures for national autonomy outside of England suggest that trust is less widespread than formerly. Further-more, if tolerance for government secrecy is to be interpreted as a sign of trust, it may be significant that in a mid-1980s poll, a majority of Britons (58 percent) indicated that they would feel more confident in the British democratic system if there were a freedom of information act (SSLT December 17–23, 1986). A number of studies have claimed indeed that trust has declined precipitously in Britain (Royal Commission on the Constitution 1973: 123–24; Marsh 1977: 119; Beer 1982a: 213). Even Norton, who generally stresses stability and continuity in British political culture, admits that "with a decline in resources available to government in the 1960s and 1970s, the degree of trust has declined," albeit relatively. "Indeed," he says, recovering his optimism, "what is remarkable . . . is that the decline in trust has not been greater" (Norton 1984: 363). Many observ-ers reject the idea of declining trust, and caution that low levels of trust have long been the norm (Dore 1984: 204; Held 1987: 233; Kavanagh 1980: 153;

Topf 1989: 72). Heath and Topf (1987: 55) conclude that "cynicism about politics and politicians is not a novel phenomenon brought about by the failures of
recent governments to solve Britain's economic and social problems. Rather it is
a long-standing feature of British political culture, which goes back at least as far
as the 1950s when Britain was regarded as an exemplary stable democracy—and
perhaps much further back than that." The British, like citizens of most industrial
democracies, are skeptical of politicians. In the end, Britain provides a mixed
picture of cynicism and contentment.

High levels of dissatisfaction are to be expected vis-à-vis a constitution of
"alien authorship," and Japan is no exception (Ward 1965: 60). A large proportion of Japanese do not believe their politicians are an honest lot. Richardson and
Flanagan (1984: 240) point out that "On a number of indicators of political trust
and system support, the Japanese mass public has scored unusually low," and it
appears that such low levels characterize the postwar period. In fact, the lack of
trust in politicians started in the prewar years and continues today. "Typically it
has been found that large majorities feel that government leaders do not understand the people's wishes, are unresponsive to their needs, and run the government for the benefit of big business and other special interests" (Richardson and
Flanagan 1984: 240). Of those in a 1989 Prime Minister's Office survey who
responded that they do not think government policy reflects the popular will (63
percent), a third blamed it on politicians who "should listen more closely to what
people have to say" (Prime Minister's Office 1989a: 11). White (1981: 372)
claims that "some Japanese data suggest that not only is distrust, or political
cynicism, deeper and more enduring in Japan than in, for example, the United
States, but even that 'political cynicism' may be approaching a new level of
intensity in Japan." White's Tokyo survey also revealed a low "sense of trust"
among the Japanese, while Stronach's 1987 survey found 63 percent of respondents had little or no trust (Stronach 1988: 8).

At this point, we turn to a more detailed examination of political trust in
Britain and Japan. Trust in politics and politicians may be seen as comprised of
four facets: (1) intrinsic trust, or confidence in the honesty and public spirited-
ness of politicians, (2) trust in the responsiveness of politicians, or confidence
that they listen, (3) pragmatic trust, or confidence that politicians will carry out
their promises, and (4) trust in the competency of specific institutions.

Trust in the Integrity and Public-Spiritedness of Politicians

Britons are not very confident in the integrity of their public officials. In one
survey, 57 percent agreed that "British government of any party cannot be
trusted to place needs of country above interests of [their] own political party"
(Topf 1989: Table 1, 56). When asked if most politicians are sincere and want to
serve the community, 44 percent of Britons disagree, compared to 33 percent
who agree (MORI August 1986, cited in Hastings and Hastings 1988: 488).

Marsh found that 70 percent of respondents thought that "when people in politics speak on television or to the newspapers, or in Parliament," they tell the truth "only some of the time" or "never" (Marsh 1977: 115). On the other hand, public officials are generally held to a higher standard of conduct than officials in the private sector (Johnston and Wood 1985: 129). To some extent, the lower trust may be a reflection of that higher standard. If there is cynicism about officials, there is less likely to be an expectation of corruption than in Japan. It is indeed striking how seldom, compared with Japan, contemporary public corruption is dealt with in surveys or the political science literature. Certainly the corrupting influence of money on politics is far less visible in Britain than in Japan, though the Poulson affair in the 1970s offered dramatic evidence of it (Doig 1983: 319–20). And charges of police corruption have contributed to the erosion of public trust. Most of the political scandals that have been front-page news have concerned sex, espionage, and intrigue, but less often bribery, graft and influence peddling. (See, for example, Butler and Butler. 1986: 280–81.)

Japanese regard for both politicians and political institutions is low, but public images of politicians and their activities are uncommonly negative from a comparative perspective (Richardson and Flanagan 1984: 240–41). In a specific comparison between images held by British and Japanese students, the Japanese were found to identify politicians, in order of frequency, with the terms "rich, shifty, dishonest, overbearing, and aged," while their British counterparts listed "ambitious, intelligent, shrewd, persuasive, and manipulative" (Richardson and Flanagan 1984: 241). The practice of bribery, frequent disregard of electoral laws, and regular falsification of reported financing information reinforce the view that "politics is a dirty, dishonest activity" (Richardson and Flanagan 1984: 189–90). On the question "With regard to freedom from corruption, what mark would you give our governmental system as a whole," considerably more Japanese than Americans and West Germans gave their government the lowest five marks, and 62 percent gave the lowest three marks (compared to 41 percent for West Germany, and 37 percent for the United States) (NHK 1982: 62; EMNID December 1981 and AIPO December 1980, cited in Hastings and Hastings 1982: 516). Even in 1987, a relatively scandal-free year, the Japanese gave their government a "4" on a 1–10 (most corrupt–least corrupt) scale of freedom from corruption (Stronach 1988: 8). Ever since its founding over thirty years ago, the LDP has been constantly surrounded with scandals and controversy concerning dirty politics. The Recruit scandal of 1988 is only the latest (at this writing) in a series of LDP "dirty money" and campaign-financing scandals that date back through the tenure of ex–Prime Minister Tanaka Kakuei to the very beginning of the LDP.

The Japanese people expect their politicians and elected officials to be distant and corrupt and yet, given the low levels of efficacy we have already seen, do not feel especially competent to intervene, even to the extent of changing their vote. A goodly amount of corruption and conniving is more or less taken for granted, but it is balanced by a feeling that the government is ultimately responsible for the well-being of the country and people and that things cannot be allowed to get too far out of hand (Ward 1965: 71). The Japanese are reluctant to punish political corruption because they are beneficiaries. For example, many people accepted, or even supported, Kakuei Tanaka's bribe taking while prime minister because it was not done for personal gain, but to increase the monies available for the support of his faction. Indeed, he received the highest vote total in his home district in the election of 1983, two months after having been convicted of taking bribes from Lockheed. Under postwar circumstances, distrust, however widespread, has seldom reached a critical level (Ward 1965: 71; White 1981: 373).

Responsiveness

A majority of Britons see the principal role of their MPs as representing their constituents. This is true for all classes and parties (Young 1984: Tables 2.4 and 2.5, 40). Yet they do not, in the abstract at least, seem to trust politicians to listen to them or represent them in practice. Marsh (1977: 115) concludes that a majority view exists in Britain "that politics is [a] remote and an unresponsive system run by cynical and aloof politicians." In 1972, a plurality—38 percent—believed that "politicians are out for themselves," 22 percent that "politicians are out for their party," and 28 percent that "politicians do what is best for the country" (Kavanagh 1980: Table V.6, 153–54). In 1989, 57 percent believed that "the people running the government don't really care about what happens to you," while 37 percent did not so believe (SSLT August 1989, cited in *World Opinion Update* 1989: 118). Sixty-five percent of respondents in the Marsh survey agreed strongly or agreed that "I don't think that public officials care much about what people like me think" and 67 percent agreed strongly or agreed that "Generally speaking, those we elect to Parliament lose touch with the people pretty quickly" (Marsh 1977: Table 5.4, 115). The results were little changed by the mid-1980s (Heath and Topf 1987: 54). A large plurality (48 percent) agree that "generally speaking, this country is run by a few big interests concerned only for themselves," and not "for the benefit of the people" (37 percent) (Marsh 1977: Table 5.5., 118). In 1988, the fact that 65 percent of Britons not only felt that the present government did not listen, but that it actually "enforces important decisions against the will of the people" reflected an extraordinary degree of disenchantment (SSLT January 14–19, 1988). As we shall see, however, many British are disposed to participate in politics despite their belief that their actions are ineffective (Topf 1989: 61).

Despite what appears to be overwhelming skepticism regarding the responsiveness of government politicians and officials, there is contradictory survey evidence on this point. High percentages of respondents in the 1978 Flanagan survey thought they would be given equal treatment by a government office (83 percent) or the police (89 percent). And in stark contrast to the abstract feeling of

Britons that government doesn't care what people like them think, 60 percent think their point of view would be given serious consideration by a government office, and 73 percent would expect such consideration from the police (Flanagan 1978: Table 15, 156). People seem more optimistic about specific offices with which they might have to deal than with "government" as an abstraction. Heath and Topf (1987: 55) explain this result by suggesting that "while perceived fairness of public officials may well be an important feature of British political culture, it is not to be confused with deference to politicians."

As noted above, many Japanese believe that government leaders are not only untrustworthy, but are unresponsive to their needs as well. In Ward's (1965: 68) description of the Japanese attitude, "There is small indication in many contexts that the citizen approaches government with the expectation of receiving courteous, prompt, and efficient service as a matter of right. In fact his attitude is apt to be compounded more of elements of servility, resignation, and supplication. The feeling that bureaucrats are superior beings with favors to be bestowed—which, incidentally, is to a very appreciable extent shared by the bureaucracy itself—is an aspect of the traditional political culture which dies hard in Japan." According to Richardson and Flanagan (1984: 180), "Only a quarter to a third of the Japanese compared to over 80 percent of the Americans report that they would expect to receive equal treatment if they had to go to a government office or the police about some problem." The Japanese do not regard their institutions as effectively representative and responsive. As we have seen in the 1990 Prime Minister's Office survey, only 32 percent believed that "the people's will is well reflected in national policy" (continuing a small annual upward trend since 1982), while 59 percent believed it was not (Prime Minister's Office 1986, Fig. 7.9). Attitudes toward whether the policies and actions of the party in power would ever endanger the country's welfare are comparable in Britain and Japan (Flanagan in Verba and Pye 1978: 151). The LDP's tendency to force bills through the legislature in an undemocratic and nonconsensual manner adds to the public's perception that politicians and political parties cannot be trusted. This particular phenomenon will be discussed more thoroughly in later chapters.

The aphorism "officials esteemed; the people disdained" (kanson-mimpi) is still widely accepted as true (Flanagan 1978: Tables 15, 16, 155; Ward 1965: 35). During the prewar years when the modern bureaucracy was first formed, the bureaucracy was under the direct command of the emperor and his advisors, and civil servants were seen as the minions of the emperor, not the employees of the nation. This supported the concept of a superior, elitist bureaucracy commanding a servile citizenry. Although this is a phrase from the prewar period, 50.7 percent of respondents in the 1987 Stronach survey agreed that it still holds true today. This is not surprising, as 64.8 percent of the same respondents felt that they would be handicapped in getting assistance from a government office without personal connections (Stronach 1988: 8). In keeping with the centrality of personalism to social relations, trust in local representatives offsets the generally negative attitude adopted toward politicians in general (Richardson and Flanagan 1984: 244; White 1981: 378). Half of White's (1981: 378) rural sample were confident that they could approach officials directly.

Pragmatic Trust

Vivien Hart defines political distrust as "perception of a discrepancy between the ideals and realities of the political process," and "frustration at the practical failure of this political process to meet the expectations and demands of citizens" (Hart 1978: 1). For some time, the British have been dissatisfied with the ability of specific governments to fulfill their promises to the electorate. In the months prior to the national electoral victory of the Tories in 1987, only 25 percent thought that the Conservative Party had kept its promises, while 69 percent thought that the party had "failed to solve Britain's more important problems" (SSLT January 1987, cited in Hastings and Hastings 1988: 430). Indeed "overload," or the excess of promises over delivery, has been cited by critics as a prime cause of Britain's political decline (Brittan 1975; King 1977; Beer 1982; Birch 1984). This cynicism could be interpreted as a threat to system legitimacy, but, as Kavanagh (1980: 153) has noted, it "may simply indicate appropriately modest expectations of what governments and politicians can achieve."

Such trust as there is in Japan has a largely pragmatic quality. Whatever else may be said, the present system is accepted in part because the LDP has been so successful in producing outputs that satisfy the vast majority of Japanese. Although they are the conservative party, they have maintained an extensive social welfare system, created (over the objections of their right wing) what in the West would be seen as very liberal military and foreign policies, and have ruled without coercion and with much consensus. Most importantly, they have guided Japan's economy through the biggest boom in modern world history, a boom which has brought both evenly distributed material gains and a level of international prestige perhaps superior to any other era of Japanese history. There are, as in any democracy, many groups within Japanese society that feel that their needs are not being met as well as they could be, but, on the whole, most are content with what has been provided since 1955. The long rule of the LDP and its integral ties to both private enterprise and the bureaucracy have created the perception that it is the only party capable of ruling. Some Japanese appear to have doubts about the appropriateness of government outputs. However the expectation that politicians are serving their constituents seems to explain some of their reluctance to prosecute corruption.

Effectiveness of Specific Institutions

We noted above the view that in Britain trust in government has long been lower than traditional assumptions would lead us to believe. A partial exception to this

Table 3.4

Confidence in Institutions (positive responses)

	Britain		Japan	Europe
	1981	1987	1981	1981
Police	86	(79)	67	71
The Armed Forces	81	(83)	37	60
The Legal System	66	(45)	68	57
The Education System	60	(33)	51	55
Parliament	40	(44)	30	43
The Civil Service	48	(45)	31	40

Sources: Poll sponsored by Leisure Development Center 1981, cited in Elizabeth Hann Hastings and Philip K. Hastings,eds., *Index to International Public Opinion, 1982–1983*, 1984. Westport: Greenwood Press, used with permission; British figures in parentheses are from Social Surveys Ltd., *Gallup Political Index*, London, November 19–24, 1987.

concerns some of the specific institutions of government. Despite low levels of trust in politicians, Britons demonstrate quite positive attitudes toward the effectiveness and fairness of at least some institutions of government. Trust in institutions of government has long been, and remains, higher than in many other countries, including Japan. This was not always so. As Greenleaf has pointed out, after the damaging loss of the American colonies in the 1780s, "the whole structure of government was called into question" (Greenleaf 1983a: 230). Yet after several decades of reforms—including electoral reforms and extension of the franchise, establishment of the responsibility of ministers to Parliament, civil service reform, and enforcement of greater honesty in government—*The Times* could proclaim that "Government work is better done than any other work" (cited in Greenleaf 1983a: 231). Ample survey evidence corroborates the view of the trusting Briton—at least for some institutions. Among the most trusting responses can be found in the 1984 *British Social Attitudes Survey*, which revealed that a remarkable 69 percent of respondents claimed never even to have considered a parliamentary law unjust or harmful (Young 1985: 21). This is true even though Parliament as an institution enjoys only modest confidence. More trust is accorded public, not private, institutions.

As Table 3.4 shows, trust in specific institutions is highest for those (police and army) that constitute the core of state power, and that lie the furthest from public control (Rose 1986c: 135). In 1981, 81 percent expressed a great deal or quite a lot of confidence in the armed forces, 86 percent in the police, and 66 percent in the legal system. Britons had somewhat lower confidence in Parliament (40 percent) and the civil service (48 percent). Confidence in national institutions has generally been found to be correlated with high levels of patriotism, and this certainly appears to be the case with respect to Britain (Harding and Phillips 1986: 96).

Table 3.5

The Unemployed: Orthodoxy, Reform, and Radicalism

		Whole Population		
	Unemployed	18–24	Semi and Unskilled	All
Confidence in Political Institutions (a great deal/quite a lot)				
Armed Forces	70	75	82	81
Police	72	79	85	86
Legal System	51	60	57	66
Parliament	28	31	35	40
Civil Service	44	40	51	48

Source: Michael Fogerty, 1985. ''British Attitudes to Work.'' In *Values and Social Change in Britain,* ed. Mark Abrams et al.: Table 7.13, p. 189. London: Macmillan. © Mark Abrams, David Gerard, and Noel Timms, 1985. Used with permission of Macmillan Ltd.

Recent survey data, however, suggest that trust in institutions has indeed declined during the recent decade, especially among the young. Confidence in the police, while still relatively high (75 percent), has declined (MORI April 1989, cited in *World Opinion Update* 1989: 72; Young 1984: 193).[4] More dramatically, Gallup data for 1987 show that since 1980 confidence in the legal system has dropped twenty-one percentage points, and confidence in the education system twenty-seven points over the same period (SSLT November 1987, cited in Hastings and Hastings 1989: 299–300).

Erosion of trust is not limited to the formal governing institutions. In fact, the most notable decline of trust has been in Britain's political parties. Both party identification and trust in parties and their leaders have declined substantially since the early 1960s (Kavanagh 1980: 141). Butler and Stokes found "an increase during the 1960s in those who doubted the ability of those institutions [parties] to make the government responsive to public opinion" (Kavanagh 1980: 149–46). Negative attitudes toward parties appear in a wide range of survey questions. In 1986, majorities thought neither the Labour Party (53 percent) nor the Conservative Party (72 percent) was representative of the views of the general public as a whole (SSLT January 29–February 2, 1986). These views are reflected in the voting figures (though the Conservative Party manages to get reelected despite its perceived unrepresentativeness). This is not to say Britons view parties as dangerous. Flanagan found in 1978 that only about a sixth of British respondents thought that "the policies and activities of the party in power would ever seriously endanger the country's welfare" (Flanagan 1978: 151). This figure was quite a bit higher than in the United States (4 percent), but far lower than in Italy (60 percent).

As might be expected in light of lower confidence in the major parties, the election system itself has not fared well either. Since the 1960s, calls for a proportional system of representation have been voiced, and about half of Britons surveyed in 1986 indicate that a system of proportional representation would increase their confidence in the British democratic system (SSLT December 17–23, 1986). The "first-past-the-post" electoral system and alternation of government have been part of the bedrock of the British parliamentary system, so that any fundamental change in public attitudes toward those features could be significant. However, despite all the interest in proportional representation as a means of creating a more responsive system, a majority still reject the proposition that "we should change the voting system to allow smaller political parties to get a fairer share of MPs" (SSLT January 14–18, 1988).

Despite all that has been written about governmental paralysis in the 1970s, and despite the regularly low ratings people give the sitting governments of the past two decades for their efforts to solve major problems, a majority nevertheless believe that the government has the capacity to act effectively. According to one survey, more than 60 percent of Britons believed the government could do "quite a bit" to change things, with regard to prices, unemployment, taxes, standard of living, health services, wage and salary increases, and crime, with a somewhat smaller majority (56 percent) believing the government could prevent strikes (SSLT September 1986, cited in Hastings and Hastings 1988: 163). Surveys also suggest that people still want strong government. For all the complaints about overzealous government, a majority believe that coalition government "would not last long in Britain because it could not provide strong leadership and would get little done" (SSLT January 14–19, 1988). These results suggest that people distinguish between the abstract "system" of parliamentary government—in which they have some confidence—and the concrete reality of specific leaders, parties, and governments—in which they have less confidence. "Government," in the former sense, is still seen as effective. But in the latter sense, "the government" is often seen as ineffective. Surveys that show lack of trust in specific institutions should, perhaps, be understood "as references to the people who run them" (Merkl 1988: 26).

In comparison with Britain, Japan exhibits lower levels of confidence in public institutions. Asked "What mark would you give our governmental system as a whole when it comes to efficiency in handling the problems that face us," 30 percent graded the government from six to ten (with ten the highest rank), a figure similar to results from West Germany (29 percent) and the United States (38 percent) (NHK 1982: 60). As can be seen by table 3.4, the Japanese have less respect for those institutions which exercise authority than the British. In stark contrast to Britain, only 37 percent have either a great deal or quite a lot of confidence in the military. This should not be surprising in light of Article 9 of the MacArthur constitution and the legacy of the Second World War. Sixty-seven percent have either a great deal or quite a lot of confidence in the police, but this is also below levels in Britain. Japanese trust in Parliament is also low as demonstrated in a 1981 survey that ranked it the lowest of eleven nations (Table 3.4).

Trust in the civil service is likewise considerably below that in Britain and Europe. This result is somewhat surprising in light of the high reputation attributed by Westerners to the Japanese civil service meritocracy, and there are two somewhat contradictory attitudes held by the Japanese toward their civil service. During the prewar years when the modern bureaucracy was first formed, the first government officials tended to be recruited from the *samurai*, thereby giving them social status backed by the power of a centralized autocratic government. The civil service in the Meiji constitution was under the direct command of the emperor and his advisors, and they acted as his representatives. Civil servants were seen as the minions of the emperor, not the employees of the nation (Tsuji 1984: 3–4). The concept of a superior, elitist bureaucracy commanding a servile citizenry is a result of prewar conditions but, as mentioned previously, many Japanese believe that *kanson mimpi* still holds true today. Contemporary Japanese still view their civil service as an elite group comprised of the best and the brightest Japan has to offer, recruiting only the top students from the most prestigious universities in Japan. Civil servants are expected to be both capable and dedicated, but they, in turn, expect to be allowed significant control over state policy making as well as administration. (This is especially true of the "big three" ministries—the Ministry of International Trade and Industry, the Ministry of Foreign Affairs, and the Ministry of Finance.) The resulting perception is of a civil service which is capable but haughty and dedicated to the welfare of the nation, but less than concerned with the individual citizen. Given the above perception, it is not surprising that 65 percent of Stronach's 1987 survey respondents felt that they would be handicapped in getting assistance from a government office without personal connections (Stronach 1988: 8).

As in the case of trust in individual politicians, trust in institutions appears to increase for local political institutions. Among those Japanese wishing to affect changes in politics, local politics provides an area of trust, in which elites do not dominate and which are seen as more responsive. The 1976 JABISS study confirmed a significant higher trust in local politics than national (Richardson and Flanagan 1984: 245). Because of his parochial orientation, the Japanese "distrusts or disdains" more distant objects, while trust of the proximate has strengthened local, community-based organizations. Local elections have been seen as reflecting the national will more than national elections (White 1981: 378). These attitudes have potentially important consequences for policy, for as Richardson and Flanagan (1984: 175) have noted, "distrust of the distant and unfamiliar has impeded the horizontal mobilization of socio-economic strata and interests." Thus, for the group-oriented Japanese, parochialism blunts their potential to aggregate their interests nationally.

Summary and Conclusions

An examination of efficacy data over the last twenty-five years makes amply clear that responses indicating low efficacy are common throughout the industrial world. Large majorities in most countries where cross-national comparisons have been made feel that people like them don't understand politics, can't have a political impact on their country's future, and are limited to voting as an input. We are left then with the task of comparing polities in which low efficacy is the norm. What variation there is appears at the low end of the scale. As long as this is kept in mind, it is possible to point to differences between Japan and Britain, particularly as regards ability to affect a specific law. The Japanese do indeed tend to have unusually low confidence in their ability in this regard, though it is still in both cases close to or over 50 percent. We have seen that the British exhibit in their social relations a reluctance to attempt to effect change, either by persuading others to accept their beliefs, or by taking actions to bring about change. Even when the British do indicate that they would consider taking action, it is interesting that they, like the Japanese, do not always feel that their chosen action would be very effective. This evidence of low efficacy must be weighed against other evidence, such as that presented by Heath and Topf, of increased feelings of efficacy among the British.

Evidence of trust is ambiguous, but, at least by many survey measures, only a minority of Britons are trusting of politicians and government. On balance, however, the British remain modestly more trusting than others, including the Japanese, in a world where trust in government is not normally high. This is true particularly of British attitudes in the workplace and toward a few specific political institutions and officials. This conclusion is compatible with the findings cited above that pride in institutions (more generalized to include their historical development and performance) is an important source of pride in nation for the British. We may speculate that the relatively higher levels of trust found in Britain may be traced to the highly positive attitudes toward government that emerged during the last half of the nineteenth century, to perceived high levels of performance during most of the present century, and to the absence in modern British history of foreign occupation and the attendant appearance of Quislings or Lavals to create deep hostilities and suspicions. The "track record" of the government respecting liberties—the chief concern of the British—in the absence of constitutional guarantees, may also have contributed in the past to the British trust in institutions and high levels of national pride. Finally, the relatively small percentage of Britons receiving higher education may have contributed to overall levels of trust in the same way that it may have boosted national pride in the past.

Though political trust in Britain may have been low for a long period of time, evidence does point to some erosion of levels of trust. Whether that erosion is related to growing authoritarianism, as some would claim, to the progressive weakening of government in the face of "overload," or to other factors, is unclear. But it may in part be related to the growing size and complexity of government. What trust there is, is not evenly shared across all sectors of the population.

The evidence of trust in Japan is less problematical in that there are clear signs of relatively low levels of trust in politicians and institutions. The Japanese do not so much trust their government and political institutions as accept their right to rule. What we see is closer to consent than legitimacy, and may not be too dissimilar to Hart's (1978: 45) view of the British attitude as "more pragmatic acceptance of inevitabilities than a normative commitment." There is little pride in political institutions, there is a feeling of separation between the citizenry and the bureaucracy, and there is a constant suspicion of corruption. Again, however, the separation theme is dominant. The above factors may distance the citizenry from the political system, but there is little evidence that the citizenry wants to get actively involved to change matters. Therefore, even though there may be a lack of intrinsic trust, people "trust" the government and political institutions to get on with the job of governing and running the economy. If the British are concerned that big government no longer takes their individual feelings into account, that has rarely, if ever, been a concern in Japan.

Some have expressed concern over the low levels of trust in Japan. As early as 1965 Ward (1965: 60) found many Japanese youth to be ideologically alienated. While agreeing that trust is very low, White challenges the view that low trust is a threat to stable polity. He believes that a number of factors attenuate the impact of low trust on regime stability, including contentment with other social relations, higher trust in "participatory" or "input" political institutions than in output-oriented institutions, greater trust in local politics and citizens' movements, a general growth in individual economic and political freedom, increased pragmatic trust, and a localization of protest and dispersion of "protestors" throughout the society. After all is said and done, levels of cynicism in Japan are comparable to those in Western societies.

Notes

1. A slightly different variant is offered by William Gamson, who sees in efficacy a combination of citizen self-assurance and responsiveness of politicians. As Marsh describes this approach, "efficacy requires the basic self-assurance that the authority system is democratically responsive to the active demands (i.e. the inputs) of the citizenry" (1977: 116–17). We choose to confine "efficacy" to the aspect of self-confidence, assigning the question of responsiveness (which is characteristic of output) to "trust."

2. Men are more likely than women to attempt to persuade others. Fifty percent of men and only 33 percent of women "often" or "sometimes" argue and attempt to persuade others when they have a strong view (Fogarty 1985: Table 7.16, 195). With respect to freedom to make decisions in work, the difference between men and women in mean scores on a ten-point scale was 1.26 (Fogarty 1985: Table 7.15, 193). But this difference very likely reflects differences in the kinds of jobs men and women hold, and may not constitute evidence of different levels of efficacy.

3. Dennis Kavanagh, "The Deferential English," pp. 357–58. Heath and Topf suggest "that social changes—such as the expansion of higher education and the growth of the middle classes—are producing increased numbers of citizens with self-confidence to participate in politics" (1987: 59).

4. A large plurality now believes that "When it comes to crime, there is one law for

the public and another for the police" (MORI April 1989, cited in *World Opinion Update* 1989: 72). The tendency of the Thatcher government to use the police as a tool of social control, cited by Budge and McKay, may be one possible factor for this decline of trust (Budge and McKay 1988: viii). It should be noted that despite the overall decline in expressed trust, 81 percent of respondents in one survey agreed that "there should be more police on the 'beat' in this area (MORI April 1989).

4

Political Support I: Compliant/Subject Support

In Chapter 4, we move to the consideration of another important attitudinal component of the political culture—support for the polity. The concept is generally used to express citizens' positive feelings about, and their allegiance to, the political system and rules, but there is much less agreement on its precise operational meaning. The problem is made no easier by the difficulties of measuring people's attitudes about such abstractions as "support," for they are bound to be complex. Allegiance to the system and gratification with the performance of specific politicians, institutions, and governments are bound to intermingle. Furthermore, as Heath and Topf (1987: 110) comment, people will be ambivalent; "they will be proud *and* ashamed, respectful *and* contemptuous, affectionate *and* despairing, in varying measures."

David Easton's (1965: 124–25) distinction between "diffuse" and "specific" support clears up some, but not all, of the difficulties. In his formulation, diffuse support is the generalized, reflexive support for the political system as a whole and for its rules, and it is granted by citizens in such a way that "regardless of what happens the members will continue to be bound to it by strong ties of loyalty and affection." In this characteristic display of constancy, diffuse support is analogous to national pride, and indeed, it has been argued that the legitimizing power of nationalism or patriotism may be an important contributor to support (Merkl 1988: 21). Diffuse support reflects the concession of normative legitimacy—a belief in the fairness, the rightness of political authority. Diffuse support is as important for what it is not as for what it is. It is not defined solely by satisfaction with government outputs. It is not influenced by changes of incumbent or policy, nor by cyclical or transient political and economic phenomena. Therefore it is not conditional or volatile. There is widespread agreement that some degree of support is necessary for regime stability, effectiveness in policy making and administration, and even for survival. Like strong nationalism, diffuse support is a reserve upon which a government may draw to mobilize the population to some important national task, as in time of war or economic crisis (Easton 1965: 125). Specific support, on the other hand, is the support given by citizens to a particular set of incumbents, in response to particular governmental outputs or behavior. It is conditional; it is volatile. It is quite susceptible to short-term phenomena, and it is normally not expected to affect diffuse support, unless, perhaps, it is withdrawn for a prolonged period.

Useful as the specific/diffuse dichotomy is, however, it is not always easy to make, either for the survey respondent, or for the researcher. As Marsh (1977: 153) points out, "experience has shown that it is extremely difficult to ask questions about the 'political system' and specifically about its performance and ability to meet individual material demands without thoroughly implicating the government of the day and thereby arousing all the partisanship associated with such a judgment." More important, the concept of diffuse support, linked as it is to "legitimacy," "loyalty," and "affection," excludes an attitude which we find quite prevalent in both Britain and Japan, namely, support that is generalized, stable, but not necessarily normative. In the case of Japan, for example, democracy seems to have been able to operate quite effectively and stably without a great reservoir of classically defined diffuse support. The case of Japan alerts us to the possibility that diffuse support—implying full, normative legitimacy—may not be essential for system stability. Even with respect to the British parliamentary democracy, which is often assumed to enjoy widespread diffuse support, much evidence points to support which is sustained and pervasive, but normative only in part. We suggest that the motives for support are diverse, spilling over beyond the specific/diffuse dimension, and that such a mixture of motives, even without a strong normative component, provides, at least in the cases examined, a fairly broad, and acceptable, base of support for democratic government.

We will define support as a constellation of attitudinal dimensions encompassing: (1) holding of positive feelings about the institutions and ground rules of the polity, (2) willingness voluntarily to *comply* with the law, (3) willingness voluntarily to *acquiesce* in the exercise of political authority, and (4) willingness voluntarily to *participate* in the political life of the country. These attitudinal dimensions are indicative of support, but we would emphasize that they may be present in variable degrees, and that we cannot make any firm judgment about what degree or combination of these attitudes is necessary or even desirable. With respect to the first of these attitudes, "the acceptance of the legal and constitutional order as a source of legitimacy can ... be measured through polls about popular satisfaction with democracy" (Merkl 1988: 22). Accordingly, we shall again begin with a comparison of Japanese and British responses to questions frequently asked in cross-cultural surveys about satisfaction with democracy. Such measures provide a broad initial impression of people's loyalty to the system, as well as provide a fairly wide comparative base, but they tell us little of people's dispositions toward performance of their own political roles. It is through positive attitudes toward these roles, and performance of these roles, that people most directly indicate whether they support or do not support the political system.

The remaining three attitudes go beyond people's generalized confidence in their democracy to attitudes about their own involvement. The second attitude focuses on people's willingness voluntarily to comply with laws and decisions that apply to them. Compliance implies obedience to authority, and a belief that others should be obedient. The third attitude encompasses people's willingness to acquiesce in the decision-making powers of the authorities. It is not a matter of obedience to, but of tolerance of, governmental action. This acquiescence implies voluntary consent to authority, the withholding or tempering of a claim to a share in decision making (Kaase 1988: 125). Though Rose (1986c: 116) has argued that compliance with basic laws and support for the regime are distinct, we suggest that positive attitudes toward compliance and acquiescence may both be important indicators of support for the regime. Together, they represent fairly passive components of support. When positive, they reflect Almond and Verba's "subject competence." In order better to relate these attitudes to our schema of "support," we shall refer to compliance and acquiescence together as compliant/subject support. People may render this kind of support for a variety of reasons, ranging from custom, to pragmatism, to normative agreement.

The main point, and one to which we shall return, is that "trust" is not a necessary precondition for either compliance or acquiescence, and that therefore acquiescence is not identical to deference—the trusting concession of decision authority to government officials. We deliberately choose to focus on "acquiescent" rather than "deferent" attitudes because "acquiescence," or passive acceptance, is a more accurate characterization of the weakly participant attitudes of the Japanese and British today than is deference. As we have already seen, overall levels of trust are low, even if the British still emerge as more trusting than many other citizens in some respects. The distinction is all the more important to make because of the enormous attention that has been heaped upon the concept of "deference" and its decline, particularly in the case of Britain. In both Britain and Japan, the sort of deference to authority often associated with traditional societies is much less common than has often been assumed. The basic thrust of our argument in this chapter is that in both Japan and Britain compliant/subject support remains based on the persistence of acquiescent, rather than deferent, attitudes toward political authority, though citizens of both countries appear to have become less acquiescent in recent decades.[1] Beyond this, we find that support in the two countries is in little danger of unraveling, and that differences in motives for this facet of support can largely be traced to contrasting historical paths to the present political order, and to contrasting opportunities for the state to offer economic rewards.

The fourth measure of support that we propose consists of positive attitudes toward, and performance of, an active citizen role as articulator of interests and participant in politics. This set of attitudes, comprising what we refer to as participant/citizen support, reflects Almond and Verba's "citizen competence." Popular support may be visible in either the compliant or participant manifestations, or both. As Almond and Verba (1963: 479) have pointed out, while a considerable degree of citizen acquiescence is a condition for stability, a considerable degree of citizen participation—what we call participant/citizen support—is required for the system to work effectively. Critical examination of policy and active debate are part of the citizen role, and assist the government in recognition of national problems and the search for their solution. Even protest behavior may not in fact imply absence of system support. It may be diagnostic of a properly functioning polity (Kaase 1988: 125). Still, there is much disagreement over what constitutes an optimal "balance" between subject and citizen behavior. It is not our intention here to attempt to resolve that disagreement.

In the present chapter, we will confine our investigation to those dimensions suggestive of "compliant/subject" support. To introduce the subject, we shall review the overall levels of political support in Britain and Japan. We shall then turn to the evidence of positive feelings about political institutions and ground rules: are citizens satisfied in general with the way democracy works in their country? Finally, we consider the two central attributes of compliant/subject support: are citizens disposed to be compliant with authority, and are they inclined willingly to acquiesce in elite control of decision making? We will defer consideration of participant/citizen support until Chapter 5.

Overall Level of Support

During the 1950s and early 1960s, observers considered Britain a paradigm of democratic stability. In Almond and Verba's classic model, presented in *The Civic Culture* (1963), British subjects were found to combine the ideal mix of deferent and participant attitudes, accepting of political leadership but committed to the expression of their views through the ballot box. In their words, the citizen "must be active, yet passive; involved, yet not too involved; influential, yet deferential" (Almond and Verba 1963: 479). For two decades, a debate has continued over the contemporary (if not original) validity for Britain of the *Civic Culture* model, with some seeing in place of a civic culture, a crisis in state authority in Britain. At the time Almond and Verba's work was published, admirers of Britain believed they were witnessing the "end of ideology" and an emergence of "shared values." Britain was widely believed to enjoy a consensus, not only on national policy, but in an approach to the conduct of politics that was both collectivist and civil. Putnam (1973) found these consensual attitudes to pervade the British political elite, and Nordlinger (1967) revealed the extent of their penetration into the working class. Richard Rose's (1964: 399) study concluded "England is outstanding for its durable representative institutions and the allegiance that its citizens give to political authority." Critics, on the contrary, believed the model to be a straitjacket that relegated the British people to a choice of what lot of politicians would tell them what to do (Marsh 1977: 31). Some saw a "one-dimensional" society, "ideological domination," "hegemony," and "false consciousness," in which elites successfully imposed their views of politics and order on the working class.

To these critics, the social, economic, and political crises of the 1960s abruptly changed the focus from political solidarity to disintegration of the political culture. Within a few years of the appearance of the *Civic Culture*'s analysis, a series of crises in a succession of British governments prompted many observers, both friendly and critical, to revise their views of the British paradigm. An astonishing output of works focused on the decline of Britain. Some analysts warned of "breakdown," and "overload" (King 1975; Birch 1984), "adversarial politics" (Finer 1975), "pluralist stagnation" (Beer 1982a), or "legitimation crisis" (Habermas 1975). Broadly speaking, one school attributed the crisis to rising public demands on government and an attendant loss of governmental competence or will to resolve public debate. Another identified the increasingly polarized behavior of the party system. Marxists saw a "legitimation crisis"—an inevitable product of government's efforts to placate its capitalist allies and at the same time, the electorate, sufficiently to ensure reelection. Samuel Beer, once an uncritical admirer of Britain's consensual and collectivist polity, asserted that "it is no exaggeration to speak of the decline in the civic culture as a 'collapse' " (Beer 1982a: 119). Beer believed Britain had become gripped by "pluralistic stagnation," as interests that no longer trusted other interests to exercise restraint bombarded a government with demands it could no longer meet. "As doubt of the legitimacy and effectiveness of established authority rises," said Beer (1982a: 108), "the polity loses its capacity to mobilize consent and to act in concert." The collapse of the deferent working-class attitudes that were a mainstay of the civic culture, he concluded, "affected both the hierarchic and the organic values embodied in the traditionalism of Britain's unique political culture" (Beer 1982a: 110). Mine workers' union leader Arthur Scargill's remark that "we have no intention of abiding by laws either civil or criminal which restrict our ability as a trade union to fight for the rights of our members," is put forward as an example of the extent to which support has eroded (Rose 1986c: 122). The trade unions' decision in 1926 to forego violence in the general strike, cited as evidence of past working-class deference, offers an interesting comparison. Elites as well as the working class are also seen as victims of the decline of the civic culture. Both Kavanagh (1980: 156) and Searing (1982: 240) find, contrary to Putnam's earlier observations, that agreement among elites on the political rules of the game has eroded.

Not all critics see such an acute crisis. Some writers, including some who themselves have offered strong criticisms of the British political system, see the state surviving and maintaining public support. Some assert that support, while diminished, is still relatively strong. Dennis Kavanagh's views, put forth in his insightful critique of Almond and Verba's *The Civic Culture*, are instructive in this regard. Kavanagh (1980: 156) judges that the principal change in the political culture has been a *"decline* of deference," not a collapse [emphasis added]. He finds "many indicators of public dissatisfaction with politicians, institutions, and policies, but not out-and-out rejection of the political system" (Kavanagh 1985: 48). He argues that dissatisfaction with democracy in Britain at the moment is largely "specific," though a possibility exists that if prolonged, specific dissatisfaction might lead to a "cumulative effect," and a loss of diffuse support (Kavanagh 1980: 153; see also Gamble 1982: 35). Wright (1987: 53) argues that despite a "turning away from the political system," there has been no breakdown. Rose (1986c: 124) adds that while a large fraction of the British are not satisfied that democracy works, people are not revolutionary. The 1987 *British Social Attitudes* survey data also confirms that despite distrust of politicians and increasing efficacy, there was no evidence "that either phenomenon implies any loss of respect for democratic procedures" (Heath and Topf 1987: 58). Topf (1989: 73) concludes that despite cynicism and distrust, "there is little evidence indeed of a collapsing moral order of the civic culture." All in all, while these observers find that levels of support in Britain are not very compatible with the optimistic assessments in *The Civic Culture*, they are ready to concede a persistence of support sufficient to allay concern for the future of the polity. Concludes Topf (1989: 73), "there is little evidence indeed of a collapsing moral order of the civic culture."

An intriguing argument for continuity and stability is made by David Held (1987: 231), who insists "there is no clear empirical evidence to support the claim of a progressively worsening crisis of the state's authority or legitimacy." At the same time, however, he finds that the British system of government enjoys little normative support from the populace—or at least from a large segment of it. He believes in fact that diffuse, mass support has never been very extensive in Britain. Nor has legitimacy extended very far down the social and political hierarchy. Held's assessment confirms the claim we examined in Chapter 3 that trust is low, and has long been so. Perhaps, Held says, the explanation for the changes that occurred between the era of "consensus" and the era of "breakdown" is "not so much that the authority of the state is suddenly in decline because demands have become excessive, or that legitimacy is now undermined, rather it is that the cynicism, scepticism, detachment of many people today failed sometimes to be offset by sufficient comforts and/or the promise of future benefits as the economy and successive governments run into seemingly ever worse problems" (Held 1987: 233). When the instrumental rewards underpinning specific support declined, the system was left with no visible means of support.

Having said this much, however, Held goes on to argue that such widespread, normative support is unnecessary. The progressive withdrawal of instrumental rewards for millions of Britons did not shake the foundations of the state. The state, he says, has been able to retain its authority by ensuring "the acquiescence and support of those collectivities which are crucial for the continuity of the existing order" (Held 1987: 234). Government can pursue a strategy of simultaneously shifting the burden of adjustment to the least organized groups in society, lowering mass expectations of government, and channeling rewards to "crucial" collectivities (Held 1987: 234). Young (1984: 20) puts the same proposition this way: "The logic of overloaded government is clear: enhance the capacity to deliver or depress popular expectations. The strategy of lowering expectations has been pursued in Britain for almost four years by the present administration." Others corroborate "a revolution of declining expectations," and a drop in public generosity in relieving the pressure of "overload" on government (Wright 1987: 44; Alt 1979: 249). Bulpitt (1986: 27–33) has argued that government, as part of its strategy of lowering expectations, sought to refocus the perceived sphere of government onto traditional Tory "high politics," through its privatization programs, monetarist strategies, and active foreign policy.

It is also implicit in Held's writing—and this is very important—that support can be conferred, even by those who have neither been recent beneficiaries of the system nor have shared a sense of normative agreement with the system. Support for the regime, he seems to suggest, may be at quite a sufficient level without the mass legitimacy that has long been the focus of democratic theory. Held applies his ideas to Britain, but they should be as interesting when applied to Japan, where "legitimacy" is even more widely held to be absent. Vivien Hart (1978: 36) has written of a British government that is characterized by "an elite which comprehends and endorses democracy, sustains democratic government with the assent but not the commitment of the majority."

In Japan, the debate over support does not start, as it does in the case of Britain, with the presumption that support for the system was once exemplary. The issue has focused more on why support for the postwar regime has consistently appeared so low, and whether it is declining even further. Over twenty years ago, Ward noticed something akin to "pluralistic stagnation" in Japan when he observed that because of the proliferation of groups and factions, there was "a significant degree of instability and a good deal of dissatisfaction." "In general," he continued, "in a complex, modern, output-oriented society practically everyone is more or less seriously dissatisfied with some aspects of government output and performance. Few if any get all they want or feel they deserve. Again, then, the practical question becomes what is the critical mass of dissatisfaction both in particular cases and for the political system as a whole" (Ward 1965: 65). Few have claimed that such a "critical mass" has been reached, but many have expressed their concern. Flanagan and Richardson (cited in White

1981: 342) wrote in 1980 that "analysis of political disaffection in Japan would suggest that there is a high and perhaps rising potential for civil disobedience and political instability in Japan."

It appears to be true that disaffection is on the rise. However, despite some cause for uneasiness about the future, democracy in Japan is not seriously threatened (Flanagan 1978: 245). Disaffection does not necessarily cause instability, nor does it necessarily suggest a rejection of regime legitimacy. As White (1981: 391) argues, "healthily functioning democracy is compatible with considerable popular political dissatisfaction." Furthermore, just as public dissatisfaction in Britain during the 1960s and 1970s was attributed by some to rising economic expectations, dissatisfaction in Japan could be a product of increased expectations in the wake of Japan's enormous economic success. In a society where outputs have multiplied and political sophistication increased, a theory of rising expectations would lead us to expect increased and more complex demands, all of which could not possibly be met even in an expanding economy.

But more fundamentally, while the democratic political system in Japan has taken root and become extremely fruitful, it is still an alien, Western system applied by fiat on a Confucian-Buddhist society. Democracy has brought economic success and political stability, and the Japanese understand that their very place in the international community is defined by being a democratic, capitalist—almost "Western"—nation. But in spite of all that, democracy can still be more *tatemae* than *honne*. That is to say, the rules and forms of behavior that comprise a democratic political system are understood and followed, but involvement in and commitment to the system are not as integral as they are in a system like Britain's. This behavior is in keeping with the perception of Japan as having a spectator political culture, but, as will be discussed in Chapter 5, this view seems more and more open to question, as evidence mounts of both increasing efficacy and increasing participation among the Japanese.

Now we are ready to return to the three questions that we raised at the outset of the chapter: Are citizens satisfied in general with the way their system works? Are they disposed to be compliant with authority? And are they inclined willingly to acquiesce to elite control of decision making?

Satisfaction with How Democracy Is Working

Overall satisfaction with democracy is a natural extension of the concept of "trust," which we applied to politicians and specific institutions in Chapter 3. At first blush, the level of public satisfaction with British democracy is not impressive. In 1988, only 10 percent said they were very satisfied and another 47 percent that they were fairly satisfied, while 38 percent expressed some level of dissatisfaction. However, Britons' "satisfied" responses were average for the European Community as a whole (EEC/GIRI April 1988, cited in Hastings and Hastings 1990: 524). This majority, while not large, suggests that respondents are able, at least to a degree, to separate their evaluations of specific government performance, which are normally quite low, from their feelings about the system in general. Other evidence, however, indicates that satisfaction with democracy is quite susceptible to short-run political phenomena, and indeed satisfaction with democracy peaked after the successful Falklands/Malvinas war (Widmaier: 1988: 149). Other survey evidence tends to reinforce the impression of higher levels of confidence in British democracy. Ninety-four percent support government by elected representatives as "good" or "fairly good" (Rose 1986c: 125). Positive responses are found when Britons are asked how well private and public institutions work, or how well their leaders (in general) are doing their jobs.

As noted above, the British combined relatively high confidence in those political institutions central to the exercise of state power with relatively high levels of national pride, when compared with other industrial democracies, including Japan. A relatively low level of confidence in Parliament (40 percent) might seem more significant for overall system support if it were not in line with similar or lower levels of confidence in legislatures found elsewhere, including Japan, and if Parliament were in reality a more powerful political actor. A problem remains in that the "confidence-in-institutions question" may evoke declarations of specific support or dissatisfaction. Reactions to elective institutions such as Parliament may be more likely to tap feelings about the policies of the current majority party in Parliament—a question of specific support—than questions about the police, the army, or the legal system. Or they may tap into what we have seen to be the low esteem in which politicians and parties in general are held. Expressed dislike of "politics"—understood on the level of unsavory dealings and exercise of influence—which is widespread virtually everywhere, need not necessarily raise concern about system stability. The finding cited above that 69 percent of Britons did not believe Parliament had ever passed a harmful law is striking testimony to continued British approval of their system of government, even if it is difficult to corroborate. This finding is even more extraordinary when we consider the low levels of intrinsic trust, and the perception that government is not effective in providing desired outputs. The democratic whole definitely appears to be greater than the sum of its parts.

The statistical evidence as to how the Japanese feel about democracy is also somewhat mixed. In an NHK survey conducted in 1980, 52 percent of Japanese indicated that they were either very satisfied (only 3 percent) or fairly satisfied (49 percent) with the way democracy works in their country, with 43 percent expressing some level of dissatisfaction (NHK 1982: 73). These results are quite similar overall to those found in Britain, though the percentage of those "very satisfied" is among the lowest among the industrial democracies. Even this modest level of satisfaction is not confirmed, however, in other surveys. Both the 1972 Nakamura survey and the 1987 Stronach survey found that only 40 percent of respondents were satisfied with the way democracy was working in Japan. The level of those dissatisfied rose to almost 50 percent in 1987. Fully a third of

Table 4.1

The Business and Industrial Framework of Respect for Authority
(in percent)

	Britain	Japan	Ten European Countries
Orders at work should be followed even when not fully agreeing with them	49	51	32
Only if first convinced/it depends	48	44	64

Sources: For Britain and Europe, Michael Fogarty, 1985. "British Attitudes to Work." In *Values and Social Change in Britain*, ed. Mark Abrams et al.: Table 7.3, p. 177. London: Macmillan. © Mark Abrams, David Gerard, and Noel Timms. Used with permission of Macmillan Ltd.

the respondents in a 1987 NHK survey wanted to change the political system, as opposed to 20 percent who were satisfied with the present system (Wakiya 1987: 23).

Flanagan (1978: 152–53) says of Japan that "we find very low levels of identification with political institutions and with most other national political objects, such as parties, party leaders and national issues." Confidence in specific governmental institutions, as we have seen, is below, in some cases far below, that in Britain, and in all but one case (the legal system) below European averages.

Attitudes toward Compliance with Authority

We have defined compliant/subject support as (1) voluntary compliance with basic political laws, and (2) willingness to consent to the exercise of authority. Because noncompliance carries with it so many potential penalties for the individual, we should not expect it to be widespread even in countries where support for the system is very low. Compliant behavior may mask the wish not to comply or signal approval of noncompliance. Therefore, it is important to examine people's attitudes toward compliance with authority in order better to gauge how voluntary it is.

Britons are ambivalent about authority. They are deeply mistrustful of it and any extension of it that limits their personal liberty. Yet they are obedient, and somewhat more willing than other peoples to accept extensions of certain uses of state power—for example, in law enforcement. As we saw in Chapter 2, the British are among the most willing to take up arms to defend the nation. Table 4.1 suggests that this ambivalence is shared, at least in the workplace, by both the British and the Japanese, in comparison with the more-defiant Europeans. It may be true that many British feel free to complain about a problem at work, but far fewer appear prepared to resist an order.

Topf (1989: 69–70) has concluded that "the predominant British disposition in the 1980s must be regarded as authoritarian." A majority of Britons in 1987 thought that declining respect for authority had gone "much too far" (35 percent) or "a little too far" (24 percent). By the same token, the authors of *Values and Social Change in Britain* observe that the British are more approving of any future increase in respect for authority than their European counterparts (Halsey 1985: 12). This observation is born out by the 1984 and 1985 *British Social Attitudes* surveys. In the 1985 survey, 57 percent of respondents believed that others should "obey the law without exception," while 42 percent said that they should "follow their conscience on occasion." They were even stricter about their own behavior, with 63 percent saying that there were no circumstances in which they might break a law to which they were opposed (Young 1985: 15). As noted, the British place more confidence in the police than do Europeans or Japanese. British workers are less likely than other Europeans to believe fighting the police could "ever be justified" (Fogarty 1985: 179). Further, the British also seem more prepared to endorse police use of force against illegal protesters. Marsh uses the concept of "super-orthodox political behavior," or "repression potential," to measure the tolerance of Britons for strict law enforcement against political protesters or strikers. Repression potential refers to the willingness to see authorities use force against lawbreakers. From his data, he concludes that "these estimates of repression potential seem to rehabilitate the 'deference theory' of British behavior" (Marsh, 1977: 61). Marsh and Kaase (1979b: 87–89) also find a higher "repression potential" in Britain than in other countries in the Marsh study. The percentage of British approval of courts giving severe sentences (77 percent) was higher than in the Netherlands, the United States, West Germany, or Austria, and approval of police using force against demonstrators (68 percent) higher than all of those states except the United States, which approved to an equal degree (Barnes, Kaase et al. 1979: Table TA.5, 556). More recent evidence bears out this image of the law-abiding Briton, who wishes his liberties protected, but is not tolerant of actions outside the law and wishes to see such actions punished.[2] Some Britons were likely, in this view, to support some of the Thatcher government's tough law-and-order policies despite the threat they posed to civil liberties.

Complementary to the respect for authority among Britons is their attraction for strong leaders (Dore 1985: 204). What could better demonstrate this fact than British attitudes about Margaret Thatcher? Though her party only received 43 percent of the vote in the 1987 election, this represented a larger plurality than the proportion who expressed agreement with Conservative policies. The negative ratings the Conservatives got on policy questions often seemed quite high for a thrice-elected government. Despite this fact, and despite generally strong dislike expressed for Mrs. Thatcher herself, the prime minister and her party were given very high ratings for toughness and leadership. We do not mean to say that this respect explains the Conservative victories, only that many Britons admire strength and authority even in those whose policies they may oppose.

From a different perspective, Dore (1985: 204) claims that strong leadership is needed "precisely because the impulse to defy has so commonly to be reckoned with." He takes the position that in Britain "authority is generally much more problematic than in Japan; its legitimacy is always closer to being questioned." He has pointed out that British political tradition has kept alive "distrust of all those who exercise authority" (Dore 1985: 203, 205). Union strikers, CND demonstrators and antitax rioters have at times embodied what he calls the spirit of heroic defiance.

Britons may value respect for the law, and they may value strong, decisive leadership, but as we have seen, they are still very jealous of their individual liberties, or what Barry (1970, cited in Heath and Topf 1987: 52) calls "sturdy independence." While the British do support fairly permissive stop-and-search rules for police and want stiffer penalties for criminals, for example, large majorities oppose questioning suspects before they have been allowed to consult a lawyer or detaining suspects for more than twenty-four hours without charges being brought (Social Surveys Ltd. [SSLT] December 10–15, 1987). Rose appears to be correct when he concludes that "insofar as people do trust government, they show confidence that the governors of the day will not go 'too far' in the use of power" (Rose 1986c: 128). Taking note of this fact, the Royal Commission on the Constitution (1973: 123) expressed concern over growing government restrictions on personal liberty, and the possibility that if carried too far, they could lead Britons to conclude that government was no longer their agent, but "their master." Of the one-third of Britons surveyed who could envision breaking a law which they strongly opposed somewhat less than a third cited "protection of existing rights and liberties" as a legitimate reason (Young 1985: 17).

Although the Japanese have a reputation, arising out of the past, for authoritarian attitudes, Japanese willingness to comply with authority is quite relativistic. As discussed in Chapter 1, personalism, *tatemae/honne* behavior, and nondichotomous modes of analysis all reinforce such a relativistic approach to the law and civil authority among the Japanese. Respect for the law in Japan, accordingly, lacks the universalistic basis which we find in Britain. Among politicians, campaign laws are widely ignored, and dishonesty in reporting campaign contributions is widespread. Lawbreaking and even violence may be considered justified where a law does not meet a situation, or where the lawbreaker demonstrates sincerity (Richardson and Flanagan 1984: 122). Although this tendency was most notoriously evident during the prewar ultranationalist trials, it still exists today. It is also still common practice for citizens to approach police officers who are new to the community with favors to help assure sympathetic treatment. This is not at all to say that the Japanese are a society of scoff-laws, or worse, cynics who are contemptuous of law and governmental authority. The police, for example, enjoy considerably more scope for judgment and action than in either Britain or the United States. Rather, it is to say that unlike the Americans, and the British to a lesser extent (because of the importance of political means to resolve disputes), the Japanese do not consider law the arbiter in social relations that it is considered in those countries. If we consider that, as in the case of Britain, willingness to fight for country is an index of compliant attitudes toward authority, then the relatively low Japanese ranking might be interpreted as suggesting potential "incivism" in society (Merkl 1988: 41).

Acquiescence and Deference

The second component of attitudes of compliant/subject support is *acquiescence* in elite control of political decisions. We have already noted our preference for the term "acquiescence" over the term "deference." For while both the British and the Japanese exhibit relatively passive and acquiescent attitudes when it comes to influencing policy, it is no longer very widely thought that true "deference"—the trusting concession of decision authority—is very widespread either in Britain or in Japan. Both in Britain and Japan, we may see behaviors that appear deferent—lack of participation in politics, passive acceptance of government action—but which represent quite different sets of motives. Acquiescence is the act of withholding self-assertion or participation in favor of government responsibility for decision. Deference is acquiescence motivated by trust, by the willingness of citizens to write a "blank check"(Gamson 1968) to the authorities "on the assumption of government responsiveness" (Kaase and Marsh 1979b: 40). The concept of "acquiescence" allows for the fact that citizens may assent to the exercise of authority out of a variety of motives: custom, pragmatism, or true deference. We shall attempt to show that with the decline of deference and the rise of more participant orientations, acquiescent and passive attitudes and behaviors, albeit less reinforced by trust, continue to distinguish both societies.

Deference

Both social deference (deference to those of ascribed higher status in the workplace) and political deference (deference to political authorities) continue to play a role in both Japanese and British political culture, but it is a role that is smaller than has often been assumed, and appears to be declining. In the British context, deference was usually associated with the class system. Members of the working class were thought to act deferentially to members of the upper classes. This social deference was translated into political deference to the ruling elite (itself dominated by the upper classes), based on the assumption of their superior qualifications to govern (Nordlinger 1967). The "civic culture" was thought to be based partly on elite perceptions of self-competence to rule and working-class acceptance of the claims of the "natural" rulers. Upper-class norms were assimilated by the working classes. In his 1967 study, *The Working Class Tories*, Nordlinger (1967: 82) writes that "The unmistakable conclusion ... is that the

Table 4.2

Qualities Important for Children to Learn (percent favorable)

	Britain	West Germany	Ten European Countries
"Passive" qualities: (good manners, politeness, neatness, honesty, patience, tolerance/respect for others, self-control, unselfishness, obedience, loyalty)	44	30	36
"Dynamic" qualities: (independence, hard work, responsibility, imagination, leadership, thrift, determination/ perseverance)	15	39	23
Net dynamism score (passive minus dynamic)	−29	+9	−13

Source: Michael Fogarty, 1985. "British Attitudes to Work." In *Values and Social Change in Britain,* ed. Mark Abrams et al.: Table 7.7, p. 181. London: Macmillan. © Mark Abrams, David Gerard, and Noel Timms, 1985. Used by permission of Macmillan Ltd.

marked upper class and aristocratic strains in the English political culture are strongly infused in the working class political culture." In Chapter 3, we found some evidence of levels of trust that would support deferential attitudes in certain conditions. Despite "a greater interest in information and explanation as a basis for authority," a higher proportion of Britons support capitalist ownership than elsewhere in Europe. Far more Britons (50 percent) than Europeans (35 percent) as a whole are willing to agree that owners should control and appoint managers (Fogarty 1985: Table 7.3, 177). Attitudes toward which personal qualities are desirable may also cast some light on the survival of social passivity, if not outright deference. Flanagan's 1978 study showed that the British admired "dynamic-competent" qualities more than "passive-deferential" qualities by a margin of 29 percent to 14 percent, leading him to perceive "a conscious rejection of the traditional model of the good British subject" (Flanagan 1978: 155). However, 49 percent in Flanagan's own survey said they admired "generous-considerate" qualities more than either dynamic or passive qualities—hardly a clear mandate for individual assertiveness (Flanagan 1978: Table 14, 155).[3] In addition, studies have shown that the British put less emphasis than the European average, and much less than the Germans, on developing dynamic qualities in their own children (see Table 4.2). The proportions of British choosing tolerance and respect, good manners, unselfishness, and obedience were higher than for any of the countries outside the United Kingdom. (Northern Ireland scored higher on both good manners and obedience.)

Potentially deferential attitudes such as those described above must be highly qualified. Despite relatively high levels of approval for capitalism, and majority agreement that business and industry have either "the right amount" or "too little power," the belief that "workers should be given more say in running the places where they work" increased dramatically in recent decades, from 56 percent agreement in 1964 to 80 percent agreement in 1986 (Heath and Topf 1987: 58).

If the evidence on deference in the social context is somewhat ambiguous, leaving room for the belief in a residuum of deferential attitudes, the same cannot be said for political deference. The data on trust that we examined in Chapter 3 would seem to exclude deference to politicians. In his reappraisal of *The Civic Culture*, Kavanagh (1980: 157–59, 170) argues that class-based deference has all but disappeared with the growth of instrumental voting among workers, the shrinking of the old governing class, the loosening of the bonds of British nationalism, and the undermining of governmental authority in the 1960s and 1970s. Marsh asserts that the widespread cynicism revealed by his data should completely dispose of the "myth" of "people deferent towards political authority" (Marsh 1977: 119). As Moorhouse and Chamberlain found, attitudes among the working class toward property "differed sharply from the normative expectations attached to the deference theory," and the British lower class observes "radical *traditions* and holds radical *attitudes*" (cited in Marsh 1977: 36). Heath and Topf (1987: 54) conclude that the 1987 *British Social Attitudes* data "certainly dispel any notion that British voters are generally deferential towards and trusting of political leaders." Jowell and Topf (1988: 121) confirmed a year later that "the British electorate is far from being compliant or deferential."

The prevailing concept of representation and parliamentary accountability in Britain today also casts doubt that there is room in British attitudes for deference. The trustee is "out" and the delegate is "in." As we have seen, the view is widespread in all social classes in Britain today that MPs should represent the views of their constituencies. This is true across party, social class, education, region, and occupation (Young 1984: 18–19). The view of MP as trustee is more common in Japan. The British stress on accountability obviously qualifies the meaning of "deferent" in an important way. For even if the relationship between MP and constituent does not require much more of the constituent than good subject behavior, neither does it relinquish or abdicate decisions to the judgment of the MP. Though the British may expect their MPs to represent them, they also believe, overwhelmingly, that "those we elect as MPs lose touch with the people pretty quickly" (Heath and Topf 1987: 54).

Despite all the evidence that has been offered that deference is dead, it is a myth that dies hard. Our explanation is that passive and acquiescent attitudes, which may appear indistinguishable from trusting, deferential attitudes, remain an important component of the British and the Japanese political cultures. Though survey evidence shows a decided ambivalence about authority, much of it continues to show an electorate that is tolerant of government and acquiescent to it—but not trusting. Heath and Topf (1988: 120) suggest that "governments of any party can rely on a generally rather compliant electorate when it comes to implementing unpopular policies." While pointing to "a decline of political passivity," Young (1985: 11) notes that "passivity is still more characteristic than protest." He even goes so far as to say that "the values of civility which were celebrated by Almond and Verba in 1963 . . . seem to be alive and well. The 'old restraints of hierarchy and deference' may indeed have waned but the civic culture is better founded on the spirit of pragmatism and tolerance for which there is ample evidence in our findings" (Young 1985: 31). He concludes that "in all, reports of the death of the civic culture . . . appear to have been premature" (Young 1985: 17). Norton (1984: 362–64) argues for "the continuing strength of the political culture," and the effect of its "orientation to cooperation" to provide to government "a breathing space" in its efforts to resolve the nation's problems. When we examine British political behavior in Chapter 5, we shall see that, despite evidence of considerable decline of public acquiescence, low levels of interest and participation in politics remain the norm in Britain.

Acquiescent political attitudes are as pervasive in Japan as they are in Britain, and much of the literature on political culture also considers the role of deference. Though deference in Japan has not been associated with class, as it has in the past in Britain, it is possible to speak of a socially based deference, if it is understood that personalistic and holistic norms rather than class are the basis for this "deferential" behavior. Deference occurs within a group cemented by mutual obligations and clearly delineated hierarchical relations, not between members of different social classes. The consensus thus becomes assumed and enforced by the group over the individual. The resulting conformity leads to a much higher level of social deference than is found in Britain.

The generally compliant attitude toward authority in the workplace—an environment where the expected networks of *giri* are to be found—is born out by an NHK Public Opinion Research Institute survey that asked, as in the EVSS survey, whether people should follow their superior's instructions even if they do not agree with them, or whether there is no need to follow those instructions unless one is convinced that the instructions are correct (see Table 4.1). Respondents chose to follow superiors' instructions by a margin of 51 percent to 44 percent (NHK 1982: 20). These results are comparable to the British responses. What may be surprising is that a larger percentage of Japanese is not ready to obey orders at work. But it is possible that in a country where many employees expect to be consulted in advance about decisions in the workplace, respondents would look unfavorably upon "orders" from their bosses.

When we turn to the question of preferences for different character traits, we find some other surprising comparisons between Britain and Japan. At first, the British and Japanese both appear to favor passive qualities. For example, Flanagan (1982: Table 14, 155) reports a relatively strong Japanese preference (59 percent) for passive-deferential personality traits. In a direct comparison with Britain and other European countries on the importance of instilling certain qualities in children, a 1981 survey (LDC 1981, cited in Hastings and Hastings 1984: 545) found the Japanese were as likely as the British to consider good manners important but, with respect to other values favored by the British, the Japanese responses were quite different. While the proportion of British favoring tolerance and respect for others was the highest in the eleven-nation survey (62 percent), the proportion of Japanese favoring the same qualities was the lowest (39 percent). The proportion who thought unselfishness important was fourteen percentage points lower than the British, and on a par with the rest of West Europe. These data do not seem to support the idea that the Japanese are especially prone to social deference.

Indeed, it would seem both survey data and observation indicate that social deference, as in Britain, is decreasing. When asked in the 1972 Nakamura survey whether they would feel free to complain about a decision about which they felt strongly, only 30 percent of respondents said they would, but that increased to 71 percent when the same question was asked in the 1987 Stronach survey. Likewise, when asked in the 1976 JABISS survey whether it was more important to do what was right or to follow custom, if they were in conflict, 31 percent said to do what is right, 44 percent said to follow custom and 25 percent said that it depends. Between 1953 and 1983 those who follow custom have actually increased from 35 percent to 40 percent, while those who go ahead and do what they want have decreased from 40 percent to 30 percent and those who reply that it depends on the circumstances have increased from 20 percent to 30 percent (Hayashi 1988: 8). Statistician and social observer, Hayashi Chikio, points out that an increasing number of young people are given neither to mindless individualism nor to the mindless following of custom, but make their decisions based upon the circumstances of the moment. This, he believes, demonstrates that they have effectively escaped beyond the traditions of Japanese behavioral patterns (Hayashi 1988).

Decreased social deference can also be inferred through the way in which Japanese people respond to political questions that they feel are sensitive or intrusive. Past multination surveys typically elicited a very high percentage of "don't know" and "no answer" responses, especially on controversial questions, but as opinion holding has increased, so has the percentage of DK/NA responses decreased drastically in the 1980s. When we compare the 1987 survey responses to surveys in the 1970s, we find a much lower percentage of DK and NA responses. In Nakamura's 1972 survey (Nakamura 1975: 6, 15, 18, 19) on the questions of social deference, satisfaction with democracy, and interest in politics, there is an aggregate 79 percent DK and NA, as opposed to 35 percent for the 1987 survey. The difference is even more striking when the 1976 JABISS survey is compared to the 1987 survey. The aggregate DK and NA for the JABISS survey on the questions of whether those in leadership positions ought to have their opinions respected because they are outstanding people and whether people like the respondents have any say in government was 60 percent, whereas the same total was 5 percent in 1987. If inability or unwillingness to respond to survey questions is a sign of deference, then to the extent that people are more likely to express their opinions, social deference has decreased.

Surprisingly, acquiescence to the authority of the state seems to persist despite the above-described waning of social deference. The Japanese, in contrast to the British, continue to see political leaders as trustees to whom the running of the political system should be handed over. The Japanese literally defer to politicians and bureaucrats when it comes to taking responsibility for the political system and for political action. Japanese see it as "quite appropriate to delegate responsibility for politics to elected leaders rather than personally involving themselves in politics in any way" (Richardson and Flanagan 1984: 177).

Logically, we should expect citizens to exhibit some congruence between deference to social and to political superiors. Richardson and Flanagan (1984:177) state that deference toward social and economic superiors "strongly conditions one's attitudes towards political authority figures." And one could hypothesize that a decrease in social deference would be accompanied by a corresponding decrease in political deference. However, other data do not seem to show this expected relationship. As in Britain, political attitudes and behaviors that at least appear deferent have outlasted the waning of socially deferential attitudes. Though we can observe change since 1972 with respect to some deferential attitudes—protest a decision at home, follow custom—we do not find this change reflected in attitudes toward government (Stronach 1988: 3, 4). On the most directly related question, we found that only 38 percent of respondents would be willing to speak up against government decisions about which they felt strongly opposed, that is, only a small percentage above those willing to speak up on the job and a little more than half those willing to speak up against their own families. There were no similar questions on previous surveys to which our results could be compared. The lack of transference of decreased social deference to political deference is supported by continued findings of both high political deference and a low sense of efficacy in Japan. It is possible that this incongruence reflects no more than a lag between declining social deference and an eventual decline of political deference, but the explanation may lie in the nature of motives for political acquiescence among the Japanese.

Motives for Compliant/Subject Support

A comparison of British and Japanese support for their respective political regimes hinges on the motives for their support. Why do they hold the attitudes they do toward the functioning of democracy in their countries? Why are they willing or not willing to comply with laws and norms and to acquiesce in the exercise of authority by the elites?[4] We have chosen to stress not a binary classification between diffuse and specific support, but to use instead the more differentiated scale of motives for support suggested by David Held (1987: 232–

33).[5] Held presents a typology of seven "different grounds for obeying a command, complying with a rule, agreeing or consenting to something":

1. There is no choice in the matter (following orders, or coercion).
2. No thought has ever been given to it and we do it as it has always been done (tradition).
3. We cannot be bothered one way or another (apathy).
4. Although we do not like the situation—it is not satisfactory and far from ideal—we cannot imagine things being really different and so we "shrug our shoulders" and accept what seems like fate (pragmatic acquiescence).
5. We are dissatisfied with things as they are but nevertheless go along with them in order to secure an end; we acquiesce because it is in the long-run to our advantage (instrumental acceptance or conditional agreement/consent).
6. In the circumstances before us, and with the information available to us at the moment, we conclude it is "right," "correct," "proper" for us as an individual or member of a collectivity: it is what we genuinely should do or ought to do (normative agreement).
7. It is what in ideal circumstances—with, for instance, all the knowledge we would like, all the opportunity to discover the circumstances and requirements of others—we would have agreed to do (ideal normative agreement).

Wright (1976) had already questioned whether a broad public consensus was required for support (cited in Kaase 1988: 125). Held's classification scheme makes clear that compliance and consent may be given for a variety of reasons, and without normative agreement, without full legitimacy. The disadvantage of the scheme is that it excludes sets of motivations that we have already seen to be important in the Japanese and British political cultures. Held does not specifically acknowledge deference as a motive for compliance and acquiescence, but it could reasonably be subsumed under normative agreement (notwithstanding deference's associations with tradition). One important source of normative support that we find in Japan but not in Britain is the set of norms that include personalism, holism and particularism. We include a separate discussion of the role of these group factors in maintaining support in Japan.

Generally, Britons cite a number of reasons for compliance (Rose 1986c: 128–29), and the same might be said of acquiescence in the exercise of authority as well. But observers disagree quite strongly over which reasons predominate. We would venture to say, however, that pragmatic, if not traditional, motives prevail, in part because they best reflect the fact that people are unlikely to have thought very much about the question of support. It appears, however, that there is a reservoir of diffuse, or normative, support (perhaps the cumulative effect of instrumental rewards in the past?) that has remained high throughout the period of economic decline, the period of government "u-turns," and more recently the unpopularity of many of the policies of the Conservative government. Instrumental reasons appear to be the least influential.

It may seem surprising that despite such low trust in politicians and negative feelings about politics, the Japanese are prepared to acquiesce in their rule, not to mention return the ruling government to power in election after election despite major scandals. As in Britain, the basis for these attitudes is mixed, though on balance it tends even more toward abdication than among even the politically inactive British. The major difference between Japan and Britain lies in the dominant role of personalism in compliance and acquiescence. The roots of these attitudes lie in the feudal structure of old Japan, and are fed by traditional, pragmatic, or instrumental motives, rather than by trust or normative agreement. The Japanese only began to consider the adoption of a democratic political system about 120 years ago, and participation in its most developed form was not allowed until the postwar period. The origins of the modern Japanese bureaucratic system exalted the bureaucracy above the people, and today the hierarchical nature of Confucian society reinforces a diffidence toward those in authority. The lack of trust in government institutions and political leaders in Japan does not necessarily mean instability or lack of support for the political system. This is so, first, because the individual has traditionally been outside the system, second, because the outputs of the system are satisfactory, and third, because the norms of social behavior include an acceptance of incompatibility between *tatemae* and *honne*. There is some evidence for increased normative support, but on balance the picture remains unchanged throughout the postwar period.

Coercion

Rose (1989: 146) argues that support for authority is not the result of "carefully calculated policies pursued by politicians," let alone coercive policies. Yet the argument is made by critics on the left not that force is used to maintain authority in Britain, but that other means available to the state are being employed to enforce a hegemony of values. They find that integration or consensus is achieved by means of a dominant value system, so pervasive that it reconciles a substantial proportion of the working class to the contemporary social and political order and attenuates a radical subculture (Birch 1984: 143; and see Miliband 1982). "Real conflicts of interest and inequalities," according to this view, "are muffled over by 'false consciousness' " (Kavanagh 1980: 128–29). Citizens of all classes have been coopted into political combat played out on the terms set by the ruling class, and a "one-dimensional" society has been created. Postmodernism, as we saw above, would seem to argue for the collapse of any such one-dimensional society in Britain, but postmodernism incorporates as part of the values fragmentation the strong defense by the Thatcher government of the traditional moral order against just such disintegrative forces of postmodernism (Gibbins 1989: 22).

For some Britons, no doubt, compliance is the result of coercion or the fear of coercion. Noting the accumulated evidence of declining trust in Britain, Cotgrove (1982: 77) gives the example of working class rent-strikers in London who called off their strike and paid the rent increase, not out of respect for the law, "but because they saw no alternative and feared the consequences." Certainly during the Conservatives' recent tenure, many have pointed to an increased coercive role for the "strong state." The changing role of the police is often cited as an example (Savage 1987: 232; Alderson 1987: 319). The police have become more intrusive, and sometimes violent, most notably in Northern Ireland, but also in dealing with crime and civic disorder in Great Britain (Norton 1984: 320–22). These changes in some ways reflect legislative efforts to modernize and make more effective the machinery of law enforcement. The 1984 miners' strike called attention to police (and union) violence, and urban rioting evoked tactics hitherto confined to Northern Ireland (Peel 1988: 168). These negative images have been reinforced by perceived politicization of the police and by tales of corruption. But while there may be stirrings of a more coercive state, the evidence is still overwhelming that support is not the result of coercion.

State coercion in Japan is of little significance today in maintenance of compliance, but the memories of coercion still remain vivid in the collective Japanese memory. The democratic system that exists today originated in part by coercion—the occupation of Japan by the United States. The left has always been concerned that those who donned the democratic mantle after the war were those who participated in the highly coercive governments that preceded the occupation. The first three LDP prime ministers, Hatoyama Ichiro, Kishi Nobusuke, and Ishibushi Tanzan were purged from politics by SCAP and did not return to active politics until after the occupation.

Tradition

Tradition, in Held's sense, may play a role, albeit a minor one, in maintaining support. Traditional symbols continue to extract allegiance. We have already seen the high regard in which the monarchy is held, and its role in solidifying the sense of a British nation. Kavanagh (1980: 142–43) notes that "There is some evidence that the monarchy still adds something to the authority and legitimacy of the system. A study of attitudes to monarchy found that pro-monarchists are more likely than anti-monarchists to support the regime and comply with its basic political laws." The unusually strong sense of national pride that we noted in Chapter 2 may also qualify as a traditional, and fairly important motive for support (Merkl 1988: 27). This allegiance to the nation, while not necessarily transferable to the state, should bolster a political system whose development is so entwined with the history of the nation. As Rose observes, national pride can provide support at the primitive level (diffuse) even if instrumental support is threatened by economic crisis (Rose 1985: 91). But we should be careful about adding to the list of traditions reinforcing support. Tradition may play a role, but as Rose makes clear, regicide and popular revolt are also British traditions, and they are not so likely to reinforce support (Rose 1989: 146). And while public ceremony may act as reinforcements, many of the "traditions" often associated with the British political system are little more ancient than the ubiquitous ploughman's lunch served in pubs.

In the case of Japan, we could not reasonably expect tradition to play more than an indirect role in contributing to support for a political system not yet fifty years old. The institution of the emperor may be an exception. The authoritarian nature of Japanese politics and lack of democratic political values prior to 1946, and the continued importance of authoritarian hierarchies in Japanese social and economic groups may still contribute to the acquiescent attitudes of many Japanese, even after over forty years of democracy. Such attitudes remain highest in rural communities and among the elderly, and is still strong, relative to other developed democratic countries, in both urban areas and among the young. Government is accepted as part of the order of things. National pride, which is potentially a significant contributor to support in Britain, is much less of a factor in Japan. Japan may be a good example of how factors that may seem to be significant contributors to support in one polity, may not be essential in another.

Pragmatism

People are more likely to comply with authority for pragmatic reasons than tradition. "It may be deduced," writes Hart, "that, while the British still give more support to representative government than direct democracy by comparison with the Americans, this may be more pragmatic acceptance of inevitabilities than a normative commitment" (Hart 1978: 45). "When surveys ask English people to evaluate reasons for giving allegiance to authority," says Rose, "the reason most often endorsed is pragmatic: 77 percent believe 'it's the best form of government we know.' A majority of Britons (65 percent) recognizes the inevitability of government: 'We've got to accept it whatever we think' " (Rose 1986c: 128–29). "Such a judgment does not regard authority as perfect or even trouble-free. Government is regarded as good enough, or simply as the least of many possible evils" (Rose 1986c: 128). This basis of support would be consistent with the large percentages of Britons who are only somewhat satisfied, or not satisfied with the way democracy works in Britain, with the large percentage who see many flaws in British society, and with the "grumbling appendix" Fogarty identifies in British workers. People may not be very enthusiastic about government, but they see no likely alternative.

In Japan, evidence of pragmatic acceptance may be found in the attitude taken toward the constitution itself, which, after forty years, is accepted for lack of a realistic alternative. Ward finds that "Despite the adaptations which have subsequently been made there is bound to be considerable dissatisfaction with a political structure of this sort—if only on the grounds of its alien authorship" (Ward 1965: 60). Ward wrote the above twenty-seven years ago, and yet there has been no apparent move to rid Japan of its alien political system or to amend the constitution, even though there have been calls for just such actions, especially from the far right. Although there has always been support on the fringes for a change in the constitution, it has never succeeded and success is not on the horizon. This is most clearly demonstrated by the role of the constitution, the embodiment of a democratic political system, in Japanese political culture. One would suspect that if such a call were to be heeded, it would be in the near future as Japan increases its self-esteem and, at the same time, sees the United States, the author of the system, as falling into decline and disrepute. We would argue, however, that Japan now defines itself as a member of the Western world and the Western political/military/economic bloc. As such, it accepts democracy as part of that identity.

Instrumentalism

The major difficulty in assessing instrumental motives for system support is that with these motives, more than the others, the distinction between support for the system and support for the government of the day becomes blurred. Be that as it may, several authors' explanations for the British system's resiliency in the face of change and crisis revolve around an interpretation of system support that is highly instrumental. As Kavanagh (1980: 133) puts it, "we are suggesting that the political culture substantially depends on the performance of political institutions over time." The decline of partisanship in voters has made support for party and government more instrumental (Kavanagh 1980: 156). The decline in government approval ratings since the 1950s indicates a decline in specific support. And throughout much of the 1980s, a majority of Britons has expressed disapproval of the government's record and its ability to solve Britain's problems, as well as of the government's handling of specific issues such as prices, employment, education, the health service, housing, and taxation, among others. As far as their own instrumental rewards from government are concerned, 60 percent in one survey disagreed that the Thatcher government "has new policies which will help people like me" (SSLT October 1986, cited in Hastings and Hastings 1988: 173). In light of this prolonged drop in public confidence in the government of the day, one would hope that system support is not very closely tied to specific support. Specific support is, by definition, transitory, and could change with a new election or a different political climate. In the short run, lower normative agreement with the policy decisions of the government of the day, and less expectation of benefit from those policies, may create the appearance of a shift from normative and instrumental, toward pragmatic or traditional support. Continued confidence in institutions of state authority, through times of economic and political crisis, has long been one of the strongest indicators of diffuse public support in Britain. But if Widmaier (1988: 148) is correct, "to deplete the stock of legitimacy severely, persistent and strong negative trends in government popularity have to occur," any prolonged decline in confidence bears watching, and the decline has already been evident for a generation.

But even if levels of specific support are low, the consequences may not be as dire as some fear, if, as Rose argues, instrumentalism is of some, but not primary importance in system support. He finds that 49 percent consider "the effectiveness of government in providing the right things for people" a good reason for accepting authority, but that "Contrary to the argument sometimes offered by economic determinists, popular allegiance is not bought by providing public benefits" (Rose 1986c: 129). Even if popular allegiance is more instrumental than Rose contends, Alt and others have observed potentially important mitigating factors. Alt finds a clear decline of material expectations among the British during the 1970s. This conclusion does not necessarily mean that instrumentalism has declined, just that the standard for measuring performance by the government has been relaxed. With declining expectations, the prospect of dissatisfaction recedes. Despite the perceived contraction of rewards in recent times, and the perception of a growing number of "have-nots," there remains some evidence of instrumental satisfaction among a substantial number of Britons. First, there is the continuing flow of rewards to "crucial collectivities" to which Held (1987: 33–34) alludes. Even more interesting, we noted above that even among the public at large, a plurality of the British considered that they were the very "haves" that the Thatcher government was perceived to have benefited. Finally, other factors in motivating support should cushion the impact of poor instrumental performance.

There is clearly an instrumental component to Japanese support (Richardson and Flanagan 1984: 214). The Japanese believe that the role of the state is a paternalistic one—to take care of them. The British have been more ambivalent about the state as caretaker, approving of social programs but fearful of the effects of dependency on welfare. The Japanese ask not what they can do for the state, but what the state can do for them. When asked in a Prime Minister's Office survey whether "they wanted the country to do something for them, or if they wanted to do something for the country," 44 percent of respondents chose the former and 14 percent chose the latter, while a third said it should be about even (Prime Minister's Office 1989a: 9). According to White, "Apparently the conviction that one can influence or get what one wants out of government is more important in goading one to try than whether or not one likes the system or those who staff it" (White 1981: 380). They expect favorable outputs from governments officials. In Japan, constituents adopt a critical attitude toward stingy officials. Instrumental support has been strongest in recent years as the rewards of economic growth became more apparent. Continued acquiescence is in many ways related to the perennial rule of the leading governmental institution, the Liberal Democratic Party. The long rule of the LDP and its integral ties to both private enterprise and the bureaucracy have created the perception that it is the only party capable of ruling. Although its popular vote never goes higher than a plurality, with each electoral victory the perception of inevitability of victory in subsequent elections is reinforced. The present system is accepted in part because the LDP has been so successful in producing outputs that satisfy the vast majority of Japanese. Although they are the conservative party, they have maintained an extensive social welfare system and have guided Japan's economy through what is arguably the biggest peacetime boom in modern world history, a boom which has brought both evenly distributed material gains and a level of international prestige superior to any other era of Japanese history. Even at the beginning of Japan's present boom, Ward (1965: 63–64) could observe that "Most political observers would grant that a very large share of the present government's hold on political power in Japan is attributable to the popular credit and support it has acquired as the self-proclaimed creator and sustainer of a boom economy . . . . The people now look to government as a normal means of producing or ensuring a vast variety of goods and services ranging from peace and order through transportation and communications to a broad range of welfare and social security measures, as well as serving as a planning and regulatory mechanism for the maintenance of general and increasing economic prosperity throughout the society. . . . The Japanese view of their political system has in this sense become output oriented." There are, as in any democracy, many groups within Japanese society who feel that their needs are not being met as well as they could be, but on the whole, most are content with what has been provided since 1955. This is demonstrated in polls taken annually since 1958. A majority of those polled have always felt more satisfied than dissatisfied with their lives, and the level of satisfaction at the time of this writing is as high as it was during the economic boom years (Prime Minister's Office 1989b: 4).

Normative/Ideal Normative

Much of the evidence of declining trust we examined in Chapter 3 would suggest a diminished capacity for normative support among the British. However, some observers conclude that system support in Britain is decidedly normative, reflecting the consensualist and gradualist norms we examined in Chapter 1. It is not derived from tradition, or symbols, or competence, or provision of benefits (Rose 1986c: 127–29). The "commitment of the English people to lawful political action," declares Rose, "reflects values about how people ought to act, and not simply calculations about what will work" (Rose 1986c: 123, 142). He says further that government's respect for one of the fundamental norms of society—individual liberty—is a source of support. "Avoiding the abuse of power, rather than effectiveness in its use, is the cornerstone of support for government in England" (Rose 1989: 147). Norton (1984: 33–34) asserts that normative support represents the accumulation over time of satisfied instrumental satisfaction. "[T]he civic culture remains," he says, because past capacity to meet expectations built up "a body of diffuse support . . . that now exists independently of particular failures to meet demands."

Deference can be an expression of normative support, but while it is normative, it is based on a belief in the virtue and merit of the authorities, rather than
on a judgment of the legitimacy of their specific actions. Among the educated
populations of the industrial democracies, we would expect normative agreement
to focus on the content and ideological basis of government actions. We have
seen that at one time deference may have been a significant factor inducing
support among major segments of the working class. Working-class deference
has all but disappeared, though, as we have seen, surveys suggest that deferential
attitudes survive among a significant minority of Britons. Overall, however, as
our earlier discussion of deference suggested, we should not look to deference as
an explanation for political support in Britain.

While some argue that normative support is prevalent, others argue for its
scarcity. Held (1987: 233), for example, considers that normative support for
British institutions has been low throughout the postwar period. Such normative
support as it exists, he says, has been class-related, but with the working class
much less likely to extend it. We saw in Chapter 3 that by many measures,
working-class respondents were less trusting than the middle classes. Certainly
the breakdown of order in Northern Ireland and the nationalist challenges from
Scotland and Wales clearly point to a serious deterioration in whatever normative support may have existed in those regions. If Rose is right that normative
support is rooted in the belief that government will not go too far in the abuse of
power, people's belief that the Thatcher government sometimes implemented
policies against the will of the people comes close to the heart of normative
support in Britain. While such a view appears to reflect loss of support for the
incumbent government (specific support), there is some risk of some decline in
diffuse support as well. On the other hand, it is well to keep in mind, as Heath
and Topf (1987: 55) suggest, that "lack of trust in politicians might lead to a
willingness to strengthen constitutional checks on their power, rather than to disillusionment with constitutional procedures." For this reason, we would argue that even
the movement for a written bill of rights, given momentum by a number of Conservative policies in the 1980s, suggests strong support for the constitutional order, in
opposition to the government's perceived undermining of that order.

Most Japan specialists would argue that instrumental/conditional forces are
the strongest motive for compliance, but that is not to say that normative forces
do not also come into play. There is little normative support in the sense we saw
in Britain, that is, individual concurrence with the values embodied in government policies and practices. One interesting piece of evidence for increasing
support of this type, however, is the apparent small increase between 1982 and
1989 in the percentage of respondents who agree that the will of the people is
reflected in national policy.

Even if normative support is rooted neither in deference nor in agreement
with the government's values and policies, there is normative support if we take
into account the role of group norms. Held's usage of normative compliance, i.e.,

Table 4.3

Personal Happiness (percentage who consider themselves happy)

	Great Britain	Japan	Europe
Very happy	38	15	21
Quite happy	57	62	64
Not very happy	4	14	11
Not at all happy	0	1	1
Don't know	0	7	3

Source: Gordon Heald, 1982."A Comparison between American, European and Japanese Values." Paper presented at the Annual Meeting of the World Association for Public Opinion Research, May 21.

"we conclude that it is 'right', 'correct', and 'proper' for us as an individual member of a collectivity; it is what we genuinely should or ought to do (normative agreement)," allows for inclusion of the social nature of normative support in Japan. However, this aspect of Japanese political culture is so different from what we have seen with respect to Britain, that we consider it separately here.

Group Norms

The greatest contrast between support in Britain and support in Japan may be seen in the centrality of group norms in dictating authority relations. In Japan, people comply because it is expected of the group. One complies with laws and regulations of government institutions because it is socially right and proper. One complies because it is socially improper not to respect authority, to go against the grain. One complies not because there is a need for people in a democratic society to live up to ideal political norms, rather it is done for the necessity of living up to ideal social norms. The homogeneity of the society and its consequent shared social values of compliance and harmony reinforce acquiescence to the authority of the government and state (Ward 1965: 60). The collective and particularist natures of Japanese political culture as discussed in Chapter 1 are also important in reinforcing acquiescence.

Variables Affecting Support

There are factors affecting the degree of compliant/subject support that have little to do with anything the government does. Ironically, one of these is the belief that government does not affect people's lives very much. The other is that, regardless of what government does, people are happy in their day-to-day lives, and hence not inclined to feelings of alienation or noncompliance.

In Britain, cynicism about government can be attenuated by satisfaction with

Table 4.4

Britain: Psychological Well-Being in Relation to Political Values

	Society needs			Terrorism Justified		Fight for Country	
	Change	Reform	Defense	Some-times	Never	Yes	No
Degree of happiness (percent)							
Very happy	31	38	42	33	39	40	36
Quite happy	64	57	54	61	56	56	58
Not very/at all happy	5	4	4	4	6	6	4
Satisfaction with life (average on 1—10 scale)	7.2	7.7	7.9	7.4	7.7	7.7	7.6

Source: Stephen Harding, 1985. "Values and the Nature of Psychological Well-being." In *Values and Social Change in Britain,* ed. Mark Abrams et al. London: Macmillan. © Mark Abrams, David Gerard, and Noel Timms, 1985. Used by permission of Macmillan Ltd.

personal life and face-to-face relations (Kavanagh 1980:154; Rose 1989: 147). Some surveys have shown Britons personally more satisfied and happier than most European Community citizens (Kavanagh 1985a: 48), and others that they are at least on a par with other citizens (Commission in the European Community/Gallup International Research Institute [EEC-GIRI] April 1988, cited in Hastings and Hastings 1990: 523). In one multinational study, the Danes rated their satisfaction highest at 8.21 on a scale of ten, Britons 7.67, and Japanese the lowest, 6.39 (Heald 1982: 15, 16).

The same results are obtained when Britons are asked about how happy they are, with a remarkable 95 percent indicating that they are "very" (38 percent) or "quite" (57 percent) happy, compared with 85 percent of Europeans and 77 percent of Japanese (see Table 4.3). Table 4.4 above suggests the relationship between personal satisfaction and political support. As Harding (1985: 233–34) describes it, "The data demonstrate that reported well-being is related both to political and religious values. In each case a more anti-traditional or radical values stance was associated with lower well-being, when compared with those respondents who expressed more traditional or conservative values ... those expressing the conservative stance emerged with the highest average levels of well-being across all three measures." Other observers are less sure that personal happiness is relevant to legitimacy (Merkl 1988: 24).

Another factor that may attenuate cynicism is the belief by many people that

Table 4.5

Impact of Government (percentage of respondents who felt the activities and laws passed by government have a great effect on day-to-day life)

	Japan	U.S.	U.K.
National	46	41	33
Local	43	35	23

Source: Scott C. Flanagan, 1978. ''The Genesis of Variant Politcal Cultures: Contemporary Citizen Orientations in Japan, America, Britain and Italy.'' In *The Citizen and Politics*, ed. Sidney Verba and Lucian W. Pye: Table 2, p. 147. Stamford, CT: Greylock.

government does not greatly affect their lives. This belief is rather remarkable in light of the pervasiveness of public services in the lives of a majority of Britons. When asked whether they think the actions of government have helped to make their position better or worse than it might have been, the most frequent response (47 percent) is that it has not had much effect; 11 percent say better in some and worse in others. Eighteen percent see government as making their lives worse, 24 percent better (Rose 1986c: 127–28). Table 4.5 shows that only a minority of respondents in Japan, the United States, and Britain feel that either national or local government has a great effect on their lives. The percentage of British people who feel so is far lower with respect to both national and local government activities, and smallest among the three countries surveyed. This result is compatible with the impact of localism in Japanese politics, but is somewhat surprising given the general view that it is the Japanese who feel the greatest distance from national political objects.

White argues that in Japan, as in Britain, satisfaction with aspects of personal life attenuates the impact of low levels of trust. This may be true, but based on survey evidence, the Japanese have a more modest reservoir of personal satisfaction on which to rely than the British. The 1980 NHK survey found that about 10 percent of respondents were very satisfied with their present life and 56 percent were fairly satisfied, while 32 percent were not very satisfied and 2 percent were not at all satisfied (NHK 1982: 72). Japanese are less likely than British to admit to personal happiness (Turner 1989: 190). A far lower percentage than either Britons or Europeans indicate that they are very happy—15 percent in Table 4.3. When Gallup asked respondents in thirty-eight countries, "so far as you are concerned do you think that 1988 will be better or worse than 1987?" one of the largest percentages indicated "better" in Britain—49 percent—and one of the smallest indicated "better"—24 percent—in Japan (SSLT December 1987, cited in Hastings and Hastings 1989: 576–77). The fatalism associated with Japanese culture may affect their response and counteract what appears to outsiders to be the benefits of a prosperous and growing economy.

Summary and Conclusions

We have made the argument that support and legitimacy are less directly linked than is often believed. We are not arguing, however, that the British or Japanese systems of government lack legitimacy, only that they both enjoy fairly widespread support based not only on citizen perceptions of normative legitimacy, but on a host of other considerations: tradition, satisfaction with material outputs, pragmatic resignation, and, in the case of Japan, group pressure.

The Kilbrandon Commission, while reporting a decline in support compared with twenty years earlier, "found no evidence of seething discontent throughout the land." Instead, "although the people of Britain have less attachment to their system of government than in the past, in our opinion it cannot be said that they are seriously dissatisfied with it" (Royal Commission on the Constitution 1973: 100). This conclusion seems largely to have held up over the ensuing twenty years. Support in Britain has been made more stable by dependence on a variety of citizen motivations, especially pragmatic and traditional, and less so, instrumental. Increasingly modest expectations over the years about what government can do may themselves have contributed to the stability of support. Perhaps, as Jowell and Topf (1988: 122) conclude, "the surest protection against disillusionment with public figures and powerful institutions is to avoid developing illusions about them in the first place."

Does support in Japan rest more on traditional, pragmatic, instrumental, or normative elements? We find neither the same diffuse pride in nation, respect for institutions, nor agreement on compliance with basic political laws as in Britain. We do find evidence of pragmatic acceptance of government as "part of the order of things." More important, the opportunities for instrumental, conditional support have been greater in Japan for many years. Japan, unlike Britain, has not faced an "overload" crisis on anything like the scale that some observers have perceived in Britain in the 1970s. Nor, to put it mildly, has it faced economic decline, either absolute or relative. We would expect to find, then, sustained levels of instrumental and conditional support, even before we consider factors particular to the Japanese political culture. It is that culture that has shaped the distinctive normative component of compliant/subject support in Japan. Such support, in contrast to Britain, rests on group norms of harmony, personalism, and particularism. It is not that the Japanese share in the ideals, values, and motives of officials. It is that group pressures encourage acquiescence.

Despite instrumental rewards and pressures to conform, we have seen an increasing propensity of the Japanese to express dissatisfaction with the way democracy works. This dissatisfaction could be caused by Japan's very success. In a society where outputs have multiplied and political sophistication increased, a theory of rising expectations would lead us to expect higher and more complex demands, and all of them could not possibly be met. But more fundamentally, while the democratic political system has taken root and become extremely fruitful, it is still an alien, Western system applied by force on a Confucian-Buddhist society. Democracy has brought economic success and political stability, and the Japanese understand that their very place in the international community is defined by being a democratic, capitalist, almost a "Western," nation. But in spite of all that, democracy can still be more *tatemae* than *honne*. That is to say, the rules and forms of behavior that comprise a democratic political system are understood and followed, the involvement and participation in the system are not as integral as they are in a system like Britain's.

Dissatisfaction may also be a result of values change. Richardson and Flanagan (1984: 245) assert that "the younger generations and those with libertarian and other modern values exhibit the lowest levels of system support." This is significant in light of Flanagan's argument that libertarian values are replacing authoritarian values in postindustrial Japan. If he is correct, "Demographic and social change are replacing the most supportive elements with the most cynical and disaffected elements" (Richardson and Flanagan 1984: 245). But is there any evidence of decline in system support or political deference? One would assume that as libertarian values and cynicism have replaced authoritarian values, and as tradition, apathy, and pragmatic acquiescence have declined, instrumental support has increased.

Finally, we return to the idea that the Japanese polity, unlike the British, did not evolve gradually, organically. As an imposed polity, whether under the Meiji constitution or the MacArthur constitution, it has not yet succeeded in stimulating any great degree of emotional attachment. Although there has been no attempt to replace or amend the constitution, this may be due more to instrumental reasons of success and the perceived need to retain the superficial institutions of democracy, as opposed to a true "rooting" of the constitution in the polity.

Despite different cultural bases for compliant/subject support, Britain and Japan are more similar than normally thought. Neither enjoys particularly widespread normative support for the polity, certainly not based on deferential norms. Both depend on pragmatic, traditional, and instrumental support. The difference is that Britain has been unable for some time to offer instrumental rewards to the extent that Japan has. Instrumental support remains at the top of the list of motives for support in Japan. In Britain, it has moved far down the list. If a country is dependent on instrumental support alone, it is clearly in trouble if, like Britain, the government loses its capacity to deliver. Instrumentally motivated support may have declined in Britain, with the decline of expectations, but with the declining expectations comes a decline in the importance of instrumental support within the constellation of factors contributing to support. On the other hand, Japan has yet to experience a withdrawal of instrumental rewards. This may be changing as resentment builds over prices and the scarcity of affordable land, but, so far, instrumentally based support still seems alive and well. Even if it should erode, the strong group values of harmony and consensus should mitigate rising dissatisfaction.

Notes

1. Hence we argue against Kaase's use of "trust" and "support" as synonymous (Kaase 1988: 125). People may acquiesce in government power to make certain decisions "without prior consultation," but this acceptance may or may not be a product of trust.

2. A 1987 Gallup poll found that majorities felt that the police should have the power to "fingerprint everyone in an area where a serious crime has been committed," "stop and search anyone they think is suspicious," and "use plastic bullets, water cannon and tear gas to disperse potentially violent demonstrators"(SSLT December 10–15, 1987).

3. Though British admiration for unselfishness may be higher than elsewhere, Alt has contended that a decline of public generosity has occurred in the wake of the economic decline of the 1970s (Alt 1979: vii, 249; Wright 1987: 44).

4. We shall defer until Chapter 5 consideration of motives for specific types of *participant* behavior, such as voting and protest. In our consideration of motives for support, we have eliminated "apathy" on the grounds that we could not find a way satisfactorily to distinguish it from either traditional or pragmatic acceptance.

5. It should be noted that Held's classifications include both "specific" reasons for support (instrumental) and "diffuse" reasons (traditional, normative, ideal normative), but they are not limited to those two forms of support.

Part II

Political Participation

Compliant/subject support is one manifestation of popular support for a political system. People comply with or acquiesce in the decisions of political authorities and thereby indicate at least their consent, if not allegiance, to state power. But compliance is only one aspect of the behavior through which the individual can express support for the polity. Indeed, obeying authority and acquiescing in its exercise may not be enough to ensure the degree of mobilization required by a political regime. In Part II, therefore, we shift our attention from compliant/subject support to participant/citizen support.

There is a myriad of ways in which citizens can participate. The problem is getting political scientists to agree upon what should be included, and what should be excluded, from the definition of "political participation." Participation, Verba and Nie have observed, "refers to those activities by private citizens that are more or less directly aimed at influencing the selection of governmental personnel and/or the actions they take" (Verba and Nie 1972: 2). That influence may be brought to bear on agenda setting, formulation, passage, or implementation (Higgins and Richardson 1976: 6). It may even be argued that a large number of participatory acts are not directed at influence, for example, when citizens are mobilized to implement or legitimize government actions, or when participation is largely expressive. Participation may be individual or collective, local or national, verbal or written, violent or nonviolent, casual or intense (Conge 1988: 246–47).

We exclude simple cognizance of politics and attitudes about behavior from the definition of participation *per se*, but deal in Part II with both attitudes about behavior and behavior itself in order to emphasize their interrelatedness. Participation is a potentially significant manifestation of support. Its basis is the desire and willingness of citizens to perform their roles as articulators of interests, legitimizers, electors, and in some instances, as policy makers and policy im-

123

plementers, or as protesters. Government interest in citizen mobilization, of course, is not confined to democratic states. But as Kaase and Marsh (1979b: 38) have put it, "democratic societies, at the very least, guarantee individual citizens or social groups the chance to influence decisions by political authorities." The authoritarian state will concentrate more on socializing, legitimizing, and implementing activities on the part of citizens. The democratic state will also be concerned with these activities, but it seeks to mobilize citizens to varying degrees in the exercise of influence, and its role in mobilization is generally noncoercive.

There is no reason why individuals cannot comfortably fill both the compliant/subject and participant/citizen roles. Indeed, as noted, Almond and Verba, echoing earlier ideas of "balanced" government put forward by Mill and Bagehot, posit the view in *The Civic Culture* that the good subject is also likely to be the good citizen. They suggest that a balance between subject and citizen roles may be ideal. From this perspective, at least those people who trust government enough to accord it normative compliance may be expected to trust its responsiveness enough to participate. On the other hand, our examination of support in the previous chapter should make it apparent that compliant subjects may not be efficacious citizens. Although strong compliant/subject support may reinforce strong participant/citizen support, it may have a different effect. Acquiescence–the willingness to let others decide—still characterizes the attitudes of many people in Japan and Britain. For them, compliant attitudes, whether based on tradition, pragmatic acceptance, or even normative acceptance, may be equally likely to inhibit participation or to channel it into ritualistic forms.

Much of the political science literature of the past two decades has focused on whether or not direct participation, and protest behavior in particular, has been increasing in the industrial democracies. Many have pointed to the rise of populist politics in conjunction with "postmaterialist" democratic values (Inglehart 1977). Whether or not such a change has occurred, we can start with the proposition that high levels of citizen activism are rarely to be found anywhere. The majority of citizens in most political systems do not even exhibit much interest in politics, let alone participate actively. Voting is the limit of many people's participation. As we have seen in our discussion of efficacy and trust, politics frequently lacks the saliency of other concerns. This state of affairs seems to have remained largely true despite increases in levels of interest in politics that are associated with economic development, the spread of education, and the communications explosion. Kaase and Marsh (1979b: 36–37) do note "the increasing political involvement of the citizenry," in the industrial West, and a possible shift to less conventional behavior in light of these factors. While there is a growing body of evidence to support the existence of increased conventional participation in Britain and Japan, the evidence concerning increased protest and support is much less clear. In any case, disinterest and weak participation still prevail in the two countries. Realistically, the more active roles are assumed by a minority of citizens, even if that minority is expanding, and these activists exhibit participation along a wide range, from less to more active, conventional to protest behavior. Nevertheless, there seems very little question that changes are occurring in the ways that significant numbers of Japanese and British view political participation. The British, in particular, seem more and more willing to approach government about their individual concerns and interests, but it is not as clear that the British have become increasingly mobilized to influence national politics.

In Part II, we shall look both at attitudes towards political participation, and at the types and extent of participation in Britain and Japan. The distinction is important, because people's attitudes may not, for a variety of reasons, be a very good predictor of behavior. This is especially true of attitudes about the more active forms of behavior, where holding an opinion is easier than taking action. Political action carries with it certain costs, and the greater the involvement, the greater the costs. Some activities require more sophistication and effort, and may entail more opportunity costs than others (Dalton 1988: 36; Verba et al. 1978: 55). Because people may hold, but not act on, impulses to protest, some students of the more active forms of participation have focused on what they call "protest potential," or favorable disposition to protest, rather than on protest activity itself (Marsh 1977; Barnes and Kaase 1979). In considering popular *attitudes* toward participation, we shall be asking, how do people define their obligations and participant roles? What are their motives for participation? And in which activities are they willing to participate? Chapter 5 will provide an overview of the full range of participant/citizen activities in Britain and Japan. Chapter 6 will return for a closer look at the motives and outcomes of voting behavior.

5

Support II:
Participant/
Citizen Support

This chapter examines the gamut of what Parry (1972) calls "taking part" in politics, from levels of interest in politics, to types and intensities of participation, to general motives for participation. We shall look first at the levels of interest in and knowledge about politics in Japan and Britain. Then, we shall consider attitudes toward participation and actual levels and intensities of participation in various forms of political activity. In doing so, we shall focus on the distinction commonly made in the literature between *conventional* behavior—such as voting and campaign work, attending political meetings, and discussing politics—and *unconventional* political behaviors—such as signing petitions, attending demonstrations, participating in boycotts, and committing acts of violent protest, and upon the distinction between individual and collective modes of participation. Finally, we shall examine and compare motives for participation. This question is of special interest in light of the evidence presented in Chapter 3, qualified as it is, of low trust and efficacy in Japan and Britain.

Interest in Politics

Interest in and knowledge of politics are not in themselves "political participation," but they are normally considered prerequisites of participation. People who are interested in, knowledgeable about, and who follow politics, should be the most likely to pay attention to a campaign, to vote, and to engage in other conventional forms of political participation. By same token, however, the informed and interested citizen may be more likely to possess the knowledge and political skills to disagree and to protest. We might expect that levels of political interest and participation would increase with the general level of education, and recent evidence points to this conclusion (Topf 1989: 63; Heath and Topf 1986: 565). Britons are no more interested in following politics than citizens of many other developed states, including the United States. In the case of Japan, we shall see a pattern of relatively high expressed interest in and knowledge about politics, but levels of participation similar to those found in Britain, and even higher with respect to certain activities.

The 1981 European Values Systems Survey found that in Britain "the broad majority of the population do not appear to take a great deal of interest in politics," but that this result was typical of that found for Europe as a whole (Phillips 1985: 148). Likewise the 1981 Leisure Development Center (LDC) Survey found that the 39 percent of Britons expressing interest in politics (5 percent active interest, 34 percent nonactive interest) was considerably below the 63 percent and 57 percent figures for France and Japan, respectively, though considerably above levels of interest found in Ireland, Belgium, Spain, and Italy (LDC 1981 cited in Hastings and Hastings 1984: 545). The figures in a July 1987 Gallup survey were comparable. A later EEC/GIRI poll (June 1989, cited in Hastings and Hastings 1990: 555) yielded somewhat different results, however. The 60 percent expressing some extent or a great deal of interest was exceeded to any significant degree by Denmark alone. If confirmed, these results would suggest the need to revise the view of the British as disinterested in politics.[1] Interest in local politics is especially low. The qualifications of local councillors is often held suspect, and aside from the question of local taxes, or rates, people consider local government to be concerned with minor issues (Punnett 1988: 440).[2] Rising concern for planning and land use may be modifying this position, however, and as we shall see, a rising proportion of citizen contacts with officials concern local and personal issues.

Despite the modest interest in politics, opportunities for exposure to politics in the media are abundant. In comparison with most countries, except the Japanese, the British are avid newspaper readers (Norton 1984: 329). There are over 100 daily and Sunday newspapers in Britain, with a circulation over 30 million (Banks 1989). About four-fifths of British households read a national daily. Two papers, *News of the World* (circulation 4.9 million), and *The Sun* (4 million), are among the leaders in circulation worldwide (Punnett 1988: 10–11; Banks 1989). A recent innovation, made possible by new print technology, has been the locally distributed "free sheets" which have often been independent, at least up to now (Newton 1988: 317). Although television appears to have outstripped newspapers as a source of political information for people (Harrop 1988: 45–46), a large majority indicate that newspapers remain one of their top two sources of news (Dunleavy 1987: 87). Most newspapers are openly partisan, and Conservative at that, although it may be argued that editorial policy is not a particularly strong influence on voting.[3] But the press can play an important investigative role, as it did in digging out the facts and pressing for an inquiry in the Poulson case in the 1970s.

As of 1987, there were 19 million television sets in Britain, and most people cite television as their primary source of news. After the 1983 election, 63 percent indicated that it was their primary source of political information. Viewers have a choice between the government-owned British Broadcasting Corporation (BBC) channels, and the channels operated under the Independent Broadcasting Authority, both of which tend to be dominated by national programming, though regional programs have been expanded (Newton 1988: 318). In 1991, the sixteen independent stations were each auctioned off to private interests. The typical Briton watched between twenty-five and thirty hours of television per week in 1987, with lower social classes viewing considerably more (*Social Trends 18* 1988: 159). Television coverage of political news in terms of hours of broadcast time—about 25 percent—is less than Japan, France, or West Germany (Dalton 1988: 21). There is no equivalent to Japan's Nippon Hoso Kyokai–General (NHK-G) that devotes a large percentage of air time to news. Partisanship is far less evident in the broadcast media, which are regulated by their charters, than in the print media. But broadcasters are not passive. They present investigative pieces on government in programs like the BBC's *Panorama*, but are ambivalent about reacting strongly to perceived governmental interference. The media complained loudly over police raids at BBC offices in Scotland in 1987, but chose to take no legal action (in any case successful litigation would have been unlikely) against the government's edict forbidding broadcast interviews with IRA members or supporters. The media is also mindful that the government can exercise prior censorship (as in the 1990 case of a film about the controversial author Salman Rushdie), and it can always take punitive actions through its powers of broadcast regulation.

It remains difficult to prove what political effects television has, though it is generally recognized that it tends to reinforce rather than create predispositions. It is not in doubt that the government recognizes the potential impact of television news on governing. As official publicity during the Falklands war showed, the government is careful to manage the flow of televised information to minimize constraints on its freedom of action (Norton 1984: 334). The 1988 ban on broadcast interviews with IRA supporters and members, referred to above, only underscored the perceived political significance of the electronic media.

Subscription, readership, and viewership figures do not necessarily imply that political information is sought or absorbed. In most British media, political coverage is modest, though it has increased (Newton 1988: 318). On the other hand, increased emphasis on human interest stories tends to work against political coverage. But of course, this emphasis reflects a market in which, as we have seen, interest in politics is modest. One survey showed more readers to be interested in their horoscopes than national or international political news (Norton 1984: 333).

Table 5.1

Interest in Politics

Average percent that report interest in three dimensions of involvement:

	Highly involved		Uninvolved	
	Japan	U.K.	Japan	U.K.
Interest in government and political affairs				
Follow national election campaign	25	23	17	31
Discuss politics with friends				

Source: Scott C. Flanagan. 1978. "The Genesis of Variant Political Cultures: Contemporary Citizen Orientations in Japan, America, Britain, and Italy." In *The Citizen and Politics*, ed. Sidney Verba and Lucian W. Pye: Table 2, p. 145. Stamford, CT: Greylock.

The Japanese, in contrast to the British, admit to one of the highest levels of interest in politics in the industrial democracies—57 percent in one multination survey (LDC 1981, cited in Hastings and Hastings 1984: 545)—and far higher levels in others. There are indications that interest in politics is increasing. In a 1972 survey (Nakamura 1975: 6), 22 percent responded that they were interested, 61 percent that they were somewhat interested, and 7 percent that they were not at all interested, while in 1987, 29 percent were interested, 60 percent were somewhat interested, and 3 percent were not at all interested (Stronach 1988:7). The Japan Election Study (JES) of the 1983 election (see Chapter 6) reported that 15 percent of respondents were interested in politics all the time, 34 percent were sometimes interested, and 36 percent were occasionally interested (Watanuki et al. 1986: 196). Other comparative data also suggest a somewhat higher level of interest in politics among the Japanese than the British, with a higher percentage of Britons than Japanese admitting to be "uninvolved" in politics (Table 5.1). Despite high newspaper circulation, and the wide availability of television, the British are not as avid consumers of media as the Japanese, as table 5.2 shows. There is no doubt that the Japanese people are both exposed to (amount of information disseminated by the mass media consumed) and have access to (amount of information available from the mass media) a very large amount of political information through print and broadcast media (Frey 1973: 361). Exposure to both print and broadcast media is significantly higher than that of the British or Americans (Flanagan 1978: 147), though we cannot necessarily infer from that the extent of their interest in politics *per se*. As of 1985 Japan

Table 5.2

Exposure to the Mass Media

Percentages of respondents who report viewing or reading the following kinds of media once a week or more:

	Japan	U.K.
TV or Radio	81	36
Newspapers	64	43
Magazines	29	6

Source: Adapted from Scott C. Flanagan. 1978. "The Genesis of Variant Political Cultures: Contemporary Citizen Orientations in Japan, America, Britain, and Italy." In *The Citizen and Politics*, ed. Sidney Verba and Lucian W. Pye: Table 1, p. 147. Stamford, CT: Greylock.

Table 5.3

Political Information

Percentage of respondents giving correct names for:

	Japan	U.S.	U.K.
National Party Leaders			
• four or more correct names	48	65	43
• no correct names	23	17	20
District representatives			
• one or more names	67	42	—

Source: Adapted from Scott C. Flanagan. 1978. "The Genesis of Variant Political Cultures: Contemporary Citizen Orientations in Japan, America, Britain, and Italy." In *The Citizen and Politics*, ed. Sidney Verba and Lucian W. Pye: Table 2, p. 147. Stamford, CT: Greylock.

published 154 newspapers, with a combined daily circulation of 68,142,000—a little more than one newspaper for every two people in the country. In the same year, there were a total of 3.8 billion copies of about 150 magazines published. Almost all Japanese households have televisions and at least one of the stations that all households nationwide can receive, NHK-G, spent 42 percent of its air time broadcasting news (Foreign Press Center 1989: 97). Of course, it is very difficult to assess the impact of that exposure on opinion formation, though the Japanese appear to exhibit a level of political knowledge similar to that found in the United States and Britain. Table 5.3 also confirms the greater interest by the Japanese in local rather than national affairs, just the opposite of the British case.

That political knowledge in Japan should only be on a par with, or somewhat less than, that found in the United States and Britain, seems inconsistent with high expressed interest and uniquely high exposure to the news. Modest, or even low, levels of political interest and knowledge would seem more consistent with a culture that is low on political trust and efficacy, and characterized by feelings of distance from politics. This anomaly may seem less puzzling when we note that reported active interest in Japan (4 percent) is comparable to the levels reported in European states including Britain in the 1981 LDC poll. Fifty-three percent said they were interested, but did not take an active interest.

Participation Typology and General Orientations

A number of studies have attempted to identify a typology of political behaviors engaged in or supported that may be used for cross-national comparisons (Almond and Verba 1963; Marsh 1977; Barnes and Kaase 1979). These approaches generally distinguish whether the activity occurs within the conventional framework of electoral politics and contacts with officials or outside, through unconventional or protest activity. Conventional activities consist of such things as working on community problems, contacting politicians and public officials, membership in organizations, convincing friends to vote as one's self, participating in an election campaign, attending political meetings, and voting. Protest may include petitions, boycotts, strikes, demonstrations, and acts of violence. But these by no means exhaust the possibilities. Other studies relate the extent of participation in these behaviors to subjective attitudinal dispositions toward participation (Flanagan 1978; White 1981). Based on these studies, we can identify four general classifications of political activism: *inactives, passive-subject* participants, *conventionally active* participants, and *potential protesters*. Inactives are indifferent to or reject politics. They are unlikely to participate. The passive-subject participants could also be called "deferentials" or "entrusters." They are our compliant subjects when it comes to their attitudes towards authority. Though they may engage in a very narrow range of conventional activities, often confined to voting, they are inclined by and large to leave governing to officials. The conventionally active citizens do more than just vote, and may engage in a wide range of behaviors, including legal protest. They are likely to exhibit what Almond and Verba call "citizen" orientations. Almond and Verba (1963: 481) conclude that "the subjectively competent citizen" is more likely to have attempted to influence government "than is the citizen who does not consider himself competent." Finally, the potential protesters reject confinement to conventional politics and as a result are likely to rely on unconventional, even illegal, avenues of political action. A relationship between trust and efficacy and levels and types of participation is often hypothesized (see Table 5.4), but some researchers on Japanese and British politics have not always been able to confirm the expected relationship for all types of behavior.[4]

In order to stress that citizen behaviors are often a mixture of conventional

Table 5.4

Participant Attitudes in Britain and Japan

	Japan	Britain
Alienates / inactive (low trust and efficacy)	29	30
Entrusters / passive subjects (high trust, low efficacy)	19	15
Active conformists / conventionally active (High trust and efficacy)	28	32.1*
Potential protesters (low trust, high efficacy)	23	22.4

Source: Adapted from James W. White, 1981. "Civic Attitudes, Poltical Participation and System Stability in Japan." *Comparative Political Studies*: 14: 382; Max Kaase and Alan Marsh, 1979. "Political Action Repertory: Charge over Time and a New Typology." In *Political Action: Mass Participation in Five Western Democracies*, ed. Samuel Barnes et al.: Table 5.5, p. 155. Beverly Hills: Sage. (Italicized terms are White's.)
*Combines Barnes and Kaase's reformers and activists.

and unconventional, Kaase and Marsh identify "reformers" and "activists," who participate in both types of behavior. In their view, conventional and unconventional behaviors are not necessarily dichotomous, with unconventional behaviors being somehow "outside" participant politics and conventional behaviors "inside." Conventional and unconventional (protest) behaviors represent a continuum of activities comprising the citizen's political action repertory (Kaase and Marsh 1979a: 149–60). This perspective, which has been borne out by survey research, is important because it forces us to question the assumption that system stability is necessarily placed at risk by the observed increase of "potential" and actual protesters in many societies, including Britain and Japan.

What we have then is a typology of participant attitudes, in which both inactives and passive subjects are unlikely to want to participate very much, if at all, and in which conventionally active types and potential protesters are likely to want to participate, albeit in different ways. Of course the suggested typologies are imprecise, and have a way of getting confounded when applied to individual cases. And behaviors that in one society may indicate "protest" may in another indicate conventional activity. Accordingly, this classification scheme should only be taken as indicative of the range of possibilities for participation.

As we have seen, neither the British nor the Japanese exhibit a very active interest in politics, though the Japanese express in general far higher levels of moderate interest than the British. In Britain, however, levels of interest are consistent with levels of participation. Both the level of interest and the level of involvement are low, though possibly on the rise. If there is a puzzle in the British case, it is that given pride in the polity and its history, and higher than average trust in several of its institutions, interest and involvement are not higher. The case of Japan is different. For the Japanese, there has tended to be a decided contrast between high levels of political awareness, and low levels of involvement (Richardson and Flanagan 1984: 235). As we have noted, one explanation is that their passive interest in politics reflects their "spectator" orientation (Shupe 1979: 244–46; Flanagan 1978: 146). As we shall see, however, there is contradictory evidence on this point, and Japanese participation is in some cases greater than that in Britain.

Overall Levels of Participation

The British have a reputation as law-abiding people who display a low level of political involvement, and who eschew protest behavior (Phillips 1985: 150). Those who do participate are, in our typology, conventionally active. Three-quarters of the British limit their participation to voting (Dalton 1988: 48). Kaase and Marsh (1979a: 155) find Britain to have one of the highest percentages of inactives (30 percent) in the sample, and an average percentage of conformists (15 percent). In a comparative study with three other industrial democracies, Britain had the smallest percentage (8 percent) who participated in all three modes examined in the study (Dalton 1988: 48). Low levels of conventional participation in Britain are consistent with low interest in politics and with a centralized political system that minimizes the independence of the MP, denies voters input into the choice of party leaders, rigorously maintains secrecy, and limits the scope of local government.

Despite the persistence of acquiescent attitudes, a very large number of Britons vote, and there is evidence that a smaller but growing number participate in other ways. According to Young (1984: 22), the 1984 *British Social Attitudes* data "provide some evidence of the very transformation in the level of citizen assertiveness that has been mentioned by recent commentators." Subsequent *British Social Attitudes* surveys confirm increased citizen activism, or at least the potential for increased activism. The percentages of people indicating that they would take action in response to an unjust or unfair law, and the percentages saying they had taken action, had increased substantially since surveys conducted in 1959 and 1974 (Topf 1989: Table 2, 60; Heath and Topf 1987: 58). The numbers and memberships of politically active groups has also increased substantially (Moran 1987: 181). There can be little question that new forms of conventional participation are available and are being used. Participation in local planning, new means of bringing grievances against authorities, increased memberships in environmental and other public interest groups, participation in European parliamentary elections and referenda have given Britons far greater scope for participation than formerly. Yet there is also evidence that such increases in participation as have occurred have largely been confined to signing a petition and contacting an MP (Topf 1989: 61), while participation in such traditional modes as voting and campaigning have stagnated or even declined (Dalton 1988: Table 3.3, 44, 56). Even after the increases of the past few decades have been noted, it is still a small minority who are politically active.

Interest in politics in Japan is high; information about politics is ubiquitous and is readily consumed, and the Japanese even theoretically approve of various forms of political participation. Yet the Japanese—like the British—are more noted for their subject than their citizen behavior. Most scholars agree with Richardson and Flanagan (1984: 176) that politics for the Japanese is a distant, difficult, and alien activity. It would seem that the Japanese still have difficulty perceiving themselves as active participants in the political system, even though they are highly educated, affluent, and much more interested in national and international politics. As noted above, data show that there has been an increase in interest in politics and opinion holding, both of which have been demonstrated elsewhere to be highly correlated with greater participation. However, in the case of Japan, this expected correlation does not materialize. The Japanese are interested principally as spectators. Indeed, there are indications that voting participation in national elections, as in Britain, has declined. And like the British and Europeans, Japanese participate in few political activities beyond voting. Many factors lead the Japanese to be subject entrusters who remove themselves from the political system, becoming involved only when absolutely necessary. On the other hand, however, there is much evidence to suggest that the Japanese actually have a much higher level of conventional participation than the British, at least with respect to certain activities.

Specifically, what forms of political participation do citizens in the two countries consider appropriate, and in which do they engage? To help further compare Japanese and British perspectives on participation, we shall take our definition of political participation and apply it from two perspectives: (1) Barnes et al.'s "political action repertory" of citizens, ranging from conventional behaviors such as voting or working for a party, to unconventional behaviors, such as protests or violence, and (2) the degree of group-oriented versus individual political action.

Conventional Political Behavior

In surveys, conventional political behavior is often defined by seven behaviors: reading about politics in the papers, discussing politics with friends, working on community problems, contacting politicians and public officials, convincing friends to vote as one's self, participating in an election campaign, and attending political meetings. But these by no means exhaust the possibilities, and arguably reading about and even discussing politics might better be included under the rubric of interest in politics. Other activities, of course, could and should also be included. Voting is regarded as the classic participant role. Party and other organizational memberships, officeholding in public or private organizations, political speech making, and many other activities might be indicative of conventional participation. We would argue that citizens seeking redress from government are participating, too. In fact, since such activities normally require a high degree of motivation, information, and political skills, they might well be classified as a relatively high order of political activity though they are seldom given attention in the literature on participation. Our discussion below is deliberately eclectic, seeking to apply a broad and inclusive definition of participation. We consider specifically and in a degree of detail, participation through party membership and identification, and through voting, and, in less detail, other forms of participation.

Partisan Identification and Party Membership

Party membership and identification constitute a major form of participation in many countries. Particularly at early stages of the evolution of modern democratic development, parties were critical engines of political mobilization, acting as intermediaries between elites and voters. The electorate generally lacked education and political skills. As Inglehart and Klingemann (1979: 207) put it, parties and other "elite-directed" institutions such as church and union "were effective in bringing large numbers of newly enfranchised citizens to the polls in an era when universal compulsory education had just taken root." "Political participation," they wrote, "remained relatively dependent on permanently established organizations as long as most people lacked organizational skills." According to them, however, rising levels of education and political skills in the twentieth century have created conditions for a second path to mobilization—an "elite challenging mode." It is this mode that has been identified as the "new politics" of direct action. In this more populist style of politics, "ad hoc organizations can be brought into being in response to any current political issue because the public has an unprecedentedly large leavening of potential counter-elites. Effective boycotts, demonstrations, and similar activities can be organized and publicized by skilled amateurs, acting outside established channels" (Inglehart and Klingemann 1979: 208). Dalton's "mass mobilization typology" further distinguishes between these two principal, but different sources of mobilization to political action: the first, he calls "partisan" and the second "cognitive." Partisan mobilization occurs when parties provide political cues to citizens. Cognitive mobilization occurs when citizens develop the necessary skills "to orient themselves to politics without depending on party labels." Like Inglehart and Klingemann, Dalton (1984: 271) associates cognitive mobilization (their "elite challenging participation") with the generally rising levels of education and political sophistication in industrial countries, and with a psychological involvement in politics that is absent in the case of partisan mobilization. "When citizens of these countries [that are low in cognitive mobilization] become mobilized into politics, it is largely through partisan channels" (Dalton 1984: 271; and see Inglehart 1970).

Dalton himself (1988: 18) finds "a dramatic transformation" toward cognitive mobilization in the West, including Britain, as education levels, media exposure and political sophistication have increased. As early as 1973, the Royal Commission on the Constitution (1973: 124) stated "the volume of active interest in party politics now bears no comparison with that of twenty years ago." If more people today indicate their willingness to act to correct an injustice, apparently fewer would do so through their traditional parties (Topf 1989: 73). Yet in a comparative context, Britain appears to lag. Party identification has, until recently, been very high, though evidence now suggests a significant decline in strong partisan identification. Dalton's (1988: Table 9.2, 183) own study suggests the continuation of relatively higher party identification than in other industrial democracies. It remains to be seen whether the decline in partisan identification during the postwar period, to which we turn in greater detail in Chapter 6, represents an increase in "cognitive mobilization" among the British.

Party membership, defined by dues paying, is not large in Britain, although Labour retains a far larger membership through its trade union affiliations than either the Conservatives or the other parties. Overall, fewer than eight million Britons are party members, and a large number of these confine their participation to the annual paying of dues (Rose 1986c: 187–88). While party membership is not large, partisan identification is relatively widespread, though declining. As we shall see in Chapter 6, partisan identification has played an important role in motivation for voting choice over the years.

Party membership in Japan is extremely low. Membership in all parties totals only about 4 to 7 percent of the population (Hrebenar 1986: 20). Japan is also relatively low, in comparison to most democracies, including Britain, in any form of attachment to or support of political parties, and in party identification. In Chapter 6, however, evidence of increasing party identification will be discussed.

Voting

A common measure of democratic participation is voter turnout. How do British and Japanese turnouts compare? What do these levels tell us? What factors affect turnout? Here we are concerned only with the decision to vote, not with the choice of candidate or party.

Levels of Voter Turnout. In Britain, the franchise is normally open to all British subjects, including Commonwealth citizens, who are over eighteen years of age and residing in the United Kingdom on October 10 preceding the election. Registration is accomplished through a system requiring each head of household to enter the names of all eligible residents on a form provided by the registration officer. A registration list is then compiled from the forms. About 93 percent of eligible voters actually do register. The registration rates for Asians and Afro-Caribbeans were much lower than for whites in the early 1970s. Even in 1981, 31 percent of new Commonwealth citizens were unregistered (Husbands 1988:

Table 5.5

Japanese and British Voter Turnout in National Elections since 1945

	Number of elections	Mean turnout	Rank out of 28
Japan	13	73.1	17
Britain	11	76.9	14

Source: Ivor Crewe, 1981. "Electoral Participation." In *Democracy at the Polls: A Comparison Study of Competitive National Elections*, ed. David Butler, et al.: Table 10.3, p. 235. Washington, D.C.: American Enterprise Institute. Reprinted with permission of The American Enterprise Institute for Public Policy Research, Washington, D.C.

300). But even at that, by 1983, registration by Asians and Afro-Caribbeans had increased markedly. According to Charlot (1985: 143), the Asian registration rate was virtually the same as that for whites.

Postwar voter turnout for national elections in Britain, officially at about 75 percent today, is much higher than in the United States and somewhat higher than in Japan, but lower than in most of Europe. As Table 5.5 shows, for the postwar period as a whole, British voter turnout for parliamentary elections has averaged approximately 77 percent. Since the 1950s, the percentage has dropped modestly to its present level. This compares with a 73 percent turnout for national elections in Japan over the same period. Neither Britain nor Japan ranks especially high in voter turnout among twenty-eight democracies examined by Ivor Crewe (1981).

Britain's lack of interest in politics is more dramatically reflected in the low voter turnout for council elections—usually about 40 percent, but sometimes as low as 10 percent. Richard Rose (1986c: 184) has observed that "the proportion working for local authorities—about one in eight of the total labour force in Britain—is almost as numerous, and certainly more immediately influential, than those who regularly vote to elect the councils to which local employees are meant to be responsible."

Because of inefficiencies in the British register, however, "electoral turnout is effectively seven or eight percent higher than the reported figure" (Kavanagh 1985a: 101). For example, while official figures for the elections in the 1970s showed considerable fluctuation between a low of 73 percent and a high of 78 percent, adjusted figures indicate stability at around 79 percent (Crewe 1981: 233). It is difficult to evaluate the effect of registration inaccuracies in comparative terms, but their existence would counsel caution in overinterpreting small fluctuations and differences (Crewe 1981: 233). In the case of Britain, at any rate, the result of upward adjustments in the voting turnout would seem to minimize further the significance of the non-voting proportion in Britain. Whichever set of figures is used, however, Britain is one of the few industrial democracies, along with the United States, to witness a decline of voter turnout over the past forty years. Turnout today is five to ten points lower than three decades ago (Alt 1984: 302).

Table 5.6

Voting in Japan and Britain

	Type of constituency	Mode of election	Franchise	Election holiday
Japan	Multiple member	Plurality	Citizens over 20	Yes
Britain	Single member	Plurality	Citizens over 18	No

	Postal voting	Proxy voting	Advance voting	Ballot
Japan	None	Appointed proxies for illiterate or ill	Yes	Handwritten
Britain	None	For most absences by application	No	Machine

Source: Ivor Crewe, 1981. "Electoral Participation." In *Democracy at the Polls,* ed. David Butler et al.: Table 10.4, pp. 244–45. Washington, D.C.: American Enterprise Institute, reprinted with permission; P. Norton, *The British Polity*: Table 5.1, pp. 76–77. White Plains: Longman.

At present, voting participation in national elections in Japan approximates that in Britain. On the whole, the voting rate in national elections has been dropping since the 1950s, when it reached its peak (77 percent) in the election of 1958. Since that time there has been a gradual decline—with fluctuations bringing it as low as 68 percent in the 1969 and 1983 elections and as high as 74 percent in the 1967, 1976, and 1980 elections. The trend toward fluctuation is most striking in the three elections of the 1980s with the 1980 election attaining a 74.5 percent voting rate which then dropped to 67.9 percent in the 1983 elections, rose again to 71.4 percent in 1986 and remained steady at 68 percent in the 1990 election. As has been pointed out previously, a major difference in voting rates between Japan and Britain is that in Japan there is much higher turnout in local elections than in national elections. This has been especially true in most rural and low-density political districts (Ward 1978: 118–19).

Factors in Voter Turnout

The turnout is affected both by the elector's environment and by his or her attitudes and attributes. Environmental factors may include the legal and administrative framework of elections, the degree of institutional mobilization of the vote, for example, through parties and other organizations, and factors such as competitiveness of the election (Crewe 1981: 239).

One set of factors that may affect turnout is the legal and administrative arrangements for voting. Registration requirements and procedures, access to polling places, complexity of the ballot, and provisions for mail and proxy voting can all affect turnout. Table 5.6 compares selected aspects of the Japanese and British electoral systems.

Voting in a parliamentary election in Britain is a simple matter. Although election day is not a holiday, voting places are numerous and accessible. At the time of parliamentary elections, there are no other local or national offices for which to vote, no referenda questions to be decided. Not only is there only one office for which to vote, but the ballot itself is simple and direct. For each parliamentary constituency, the names of candidates and their party affiliations are listed. The voter checks a box next to the preferred candidate.

The simplicity of the ballot could work two ways on voter turnout. On the one hand, it could increase turnout by avoiding any deterrent effect associated with a complex or difficult ballot. Furthermore, the paucity of national elective offices for which the voter can express a choice may actually help turnout, as voters recognize that "casting a vote for one candidate for one seat in the House of Commons is the only chance there is to participate in a nationwide ballot" (Rose 1986c: 186). On the other hand, the lack of diversity of choices on the ballot could reduce voter interest. As Crewe (1981: 231) suggests, "electors in a categorical-ballot, simple-majority, single-member electoral system such as Britain's could claim with reason that one of their votes involved a more limited form of choice of representatives than the vote of a Frenchman or an Irishman." In the end, however, we should not make too much of the value of ballot simplicity, as a comparable proportion of Japanese vote, despite a ballot that would intimidate most Western voters.

As Crewe's criticism also implies, the single-member constituency system leaves little incentive for supporters of third parties to cast their ballots. While proxy and postal voting do make it easier for some people to vote, the impact on turnout is not large. For example, the postal vote in Britain is estimated to account for only 1.5 to 2 percent of the vote (Crewe 1981: 249). All in all, the impact of administrative arrangements in Britain and Japan, as in most democracies, is not very great.

As elsewhere, Britons are socialized to vote, and they perceive voting as a matter of simple civic duty (Jessop, 1971: 7). One might expect that the act of voting might be related to a strong degree of partisanship. Indeed, party loyalty does seem to "get out the vote" (Kavanagh 1985a: 69), and this is consistent with the mobilizing role generally credited to political parties. As Crewe (1981: 251) notes, "an obvious possible source of national differences in turnout rates is the relative intensity of the efforts made by parties and affiliated organizations such as trade unions and churches to get citizens to the polls." While this may be true, it is worth noting that voter turnout, despite some volatility over the past thirty years, has declined much less than strong partisan identity. The latter has weakened considerably, but people still vote. One explanation is that identification need not be strong in order to motivate people to vote. Finally, as Dalton (1984) has suggested, perhaps other factors, such as rising levels of education, have begun to take over some of the motivating role for voting.

As we might anticipate, nonvoters tend to be less interested in and informed about politics, less attached to a party, and less concerned about the election outcome than voters (Kavanagh 1985a: 69). Even given the attitudinal differences between voters and nonvoters, though, the fact is that a good deal of nonvoting is explained not by apathy or cynicism, but by such mundane reasons as illness and absence from the constituency. A rather small percent of nonvoters say they "couldn't be bothered" to vote (Heath and Topf 1986: 553). To the extent that nonvoting reflects a turning away from politics, however, apathy, rather than cynicism, seems more often to characterize nonvoters. Nonvoters are generally not so disinterested that they become chronic nonvoters. Only 1 percent of all voters in one survey claimed not to have voted in any election between 1966 and 1974 (Kavanagh 1985a: 69). While people abstain for political reasons or out of apathy, the percentage who do so is not large. Most nonvoters stay away from the polls for mundane reasons (Rose 1986c: 186). Race is a factor, with Afro-Caribbeans least likely to vote (Husbands 1988: 301). However, education affects turnout less than would normally be expected (Heath and Topf 1986: 553).

In evaluating voter turnout in Britain, we have a question of "half empty, or half full?" Whether or not the British have a problem mobilizing their citizens to vote depends largely on whether one chooses to focus on the aggregate level of voting, which is respectably high, and the increasing turnout among nonwhite Britons, or the decline in turnout since the 1950s. The turnout in Britain is impressive, though, considering that there is no national leader for whom the voter can cast a ballot, and normally no opportunity to vote on referenda.

The Japanese turn out to vote for many of the same reasons as the British: social pressure and duty, and to a lesser extent, voting regulations. All Japanese twenty or older are enfranchised, and their registration is automatic. A neighborhood census is taken yearly and the voter registration list is compiled from that census. This list is updated before every national election, and when one moves from one neighborhood to another, the move is registered at the local police box and the change will be forwarded to the voting rolls. Certainly the automatic nature of registration in Japan has much to do with why registration rates are so much higher than in countries like the United States, where the onus of registration is on the citizen. As election day is on Sunday, work is no excuse for nonvoting, and those who are ill can vote by proxy. There is no mail-in ballot, but advance voting is permitted. The fact that voters must write in the name of the candidate they favor would seem to be a deterrent to voting, but this does not appear to be so. All in all, as in Britain and most other democracies, the impact of administrative arrangements on voter turnout is not very great.

It would appear that socioeconomic status does not have a direct relationship to voting participation in Japan. Indeed, people of higher socioeconomic status seem to have lower rates of voting participation than those of lower socioeconomic status (Auh 1978: 67). Singling out the component factors of socioeconomic status, it has been found that education is positively correlated with voting rates, but that income and occupation are not. The higher one's income, the more likely he or she should be to vote, but those in the higher income and occupational brackets have lower rates of voting participation (Auh 1978: 71). The most likely explanation for this is that those with higher incomes and occupations tend to be urban dwellers, and urban rates of voting participation are lower than rural rates of voting participation. Gerald Curtis (1988: 201–2) has also found that the "new independents" who tend to have lower voting rates are urban, educated, salaried workers.

As we have seen, social pressures account for a considerable amount of Japanese participation. This relationship holds true for voting as well. "In Japan, however, high levels of voting participation are not necessarily indicative of high political involvement, as is evident from the fact that turnout levels are highest in Japan's rural areas where they usually exceed 80 percent in national elections and attain even higher rates in local elections. These high rates are an expression of mobilized participation on the basis of social obligations and community solidarity and do not necessarily reflect much interest in national politics. . . . Moreover, their participation in them [election meetings] may in many cases reflect considerations of social obligations more than political interest" (Richardson and Flanagan 1984: 233–34). White (1982: 199) also finds that those who participate more in urban areas tend to come from those neighborhoods that are more tightly organized, unified, and cohesive.

Even if three-quarters of Britons and two-thirds of Japanese admit, as we have seen, that politics is too complicated for people like them to understand, about the same proportion apparently do not find the process of voting to be so complicated that they stay home on election day.

Other Forms of Conventional Participation

In the deferential model of English politics, the principal role of the citizen is to vote. The willingness of citizens to so restrict their political activities is seen as a good thing, conducive to stability and efficiency. But critics have accused Almond and Verba of advocating too deferential a citizen role. The Britain of Almond and Verba, insists Marsh (1977: 31), limits the public to "infrequent and possibly accidental changes in the set of politicians by whom the majority prefer to be told what to do." Whether or not such a condition is "patronizing" and "wrong," as Marsh contends, it would still appear that most Britons (like citizens elsewhere) do confine their participation to voting.

For many forms of activity, Britons have been found to be less likely to participate than Americans and even the Japanese. We saw earlier how the

Table 5.7

Frequency of Conventional Participation in Britain

Percentage that engages in selected conventional activities:

	Often	Sometimes
Read about politics in papers	36	30
Discuss politics with friends	16	30
Convince friends to vote as self	3	6
Work to solve community problems	4	13
Attend political meetings	2	7
Contact officials or politicians	2	9
Campaign for candidate	1	3

Source: Samuel A. Barnes, Max Kaase et al., eds., 1979. *Political Action: Mass Participation in Five Western Democracies*: Table TA.1, p. 541. Beverly Hills: Sage. © Samuel H. Barnes and Max Kaase, 1979. Reprinted by permission of Sage Publications, Inc.

British expressed strong preference for fairly passive, conventional strategies for influencing a law which they thought harmful, and this is borne out by their actual political behavior, which overwhelmingly opts for conventional political activities (Topf 1989: 61). Table 5.7, which reviews a spectrum of activities, confirms this impression. We would argue that the most common activity, reading about politics, is really a measure of interest, not participation. The percentages of British respondents who indicate that they discuss politics "sometimes" or "often," 46 percent, is similar to the Japanese response. But like reading the newspaper, discussing politics with friends would seem a passive (though sometimes contentious) form of activity. Though other sources indicate somewhat higher rates of participation than those shown in Table 5.7 (Phillips 1985: Table 6.1, 153; Parry, Moyser, and Day cited in Budge and McKay 1988: 86), activities beyond discussing politics remain decidedly the province of a small minority. Dalton (1988: Table 3.3, 44) notes that for a number of campaign-related activities where time series are available, such as canvassing, working for a party or candidate, or attending meetings, British participation declined or stayed the same from the early 1960s to the late 1970s or early 1980s.

Arguably the most active participants are those who are "in politics"—the officeholders—and those outside applying pressure and organizing others to apply pressure. It is very difficult to estimate total numbers of the politically active given difficulties in settling on a satisfactory definition. But in any case, the total number of elected MPs, county, district, borough, parish, and community councillors is approximately 100,000—a large number but a small percentage of the population. If we were to include unsuccessful candidates for office, the number would, of course, be much larger. The Royal Commission on the Constitution (1973: 97) found in its survey perhaps 20 percent or more of Britons "who consider that they have the basic ability to play some part in government."

And Rose (1986c: 185) notes that about 5 percent of Britons claim to have considered running for local office. "Activists," defined as people who engage in at least half of the most common political behaviors, number nearly three million (Rose 1986c: 188). Activists are difficult to distinguish demographically from nonactivists. Education seems to have little effect. They are, however, more likely to be male and from a higher class background (Worcester 1976: 202–3).

Most people who do participate, of course, do so from the outside, as members of interest groups and as ordinary citizens. Citizens need not be members of politically oriented interest groups or parties to gain a hearing in government. Indeed, most citizens interact with government—be it inquiries, requests, or complaints—on an occasional basis, and through a wide variety of channels. This kind of participation may be aimed either at appealing a decision already taken, or at having an impact on the decision (Ridley 1984: 27–28). Many British government texts, argues Ridley (1984: 27), misleadingly "look at the picture from the top down rather than from the bottom up and do not begin to describe how most citizens behave most of the time when they seek to protect their interests against public authorities." As we note above, it is the desire to alleviate personal or local problems that motivates a great many people to participate in politics. Citizens contact government to deal with personal questions, from taxes to pensions to health care to land use.[5] This contact suggests, if anything, a parochial orientation toward government and a predilection for individual rather than collective interest articulation.

The growing caseload of MPs is a good example of growth in this aspect of participation. In contrast with the Parry and Moyser findings cited above, indicating that people are more likely to contact local councillors than their MPs, James Marsh (1985: 80–81) concludes that between MPs and local councillors, "most individuals choose to use the services of their Member of Parliament," and that "MPs are still the more active of the two representatives." He finds the importance of the MP in constituency service to be growing. In Britain the traditional remedy for individual grievances against government has been Parliament. And indeed, parliamentary intercession is an important means of citizen redress, even if its place in the hierarchy of government-citizen channels is in dispute. Control of government has constitutionally rested with the minister-in-parliament, and accordingly the development of other systematized controls has been resisted (Ridley 1984: 3). This fact may account for many people's tendency still to think of their MP when they are asked whom they would contact about a local or national problem, as well as for the slowness of the British to create alternate channels of political communication. Furthermore, people may see their MP as having the necessary connections, moral authority, enthusiasm, and necessary electoral stake to provide effective help (J. Marsh 1985: 81). It may also be that people's preference for dealing with their MP reflects alternatives which are "so ineffective, expensive or intimidating that the constituent may feel that the odds are too greatly stacked against him" (J. Marsh 1985: 71).

By contacting the MP, a citizen is indicating the expectation that the MP will use his or her good offices on behalf of the citizen, not to "lobby" the MP to affect legislation. The fact that MPs may subsequently apply what they "learn" from their constituents to policy matters does not in any way prove that the citizen's intent is to affect policy. Given the minor role of MPs in shaping legislation, it makes sense that citizens would go to their MP for help in raising grievances only in the ex post facto application of a law in their individual case.

Despite the continuing importance of elected MPs and councillors, a significant number of other formal and informal means of citizen appeals exist, and are used by Britons: the ordinary courts, specialized tribunals, ombudsmen, inquiries by ministry inspectors, legal advice centers, and various voluntary organizations (Ridley 1984: 2). The caseload of these institutions is considerable. For example, the General Commissioners of Income Tax heard nearly 800,000 cases in 1985–86 (*Social Trends* 18 1988: 177). An overwhelming number of citizen contacts are with local, often informal, organizations (Moran 1987: 184). For our purposes, it is important to note the tremendous increase in this type of participation. During the 1970s a host of local organizations were created to assist citizens in dealing with their problems with both the public and private sectors. "The number of advice centres and counselling services is growing," comments Ridley (1984: 27), "and such bodies are playing an increasing role as intermediaries between the citizen and the administration." Citizens Advice Bureaux alone, providing information about a great range of matters, served over seven million people in 1986, up from a few hundred in 1971. The growing importance of local, private, and voluntary organizations to assist citizens with grievances against government, indicating a collectivist tradition, has prompted Ridley to conclude, in contrast to James Marsh, that "The focus is shifting to community organisations as the channels for the expression of popular will and the defence of citizen interests. . . . We may increasingly expect citizens to turn not to their elected representatives, not to Ombudsmen or the courts, but to their own organisations for help in obtaining redress of grievances and for that redress to be obtained through pressure on decision-making authorities" (Ridley 1984: 321).

Though people may be most likely to participate as individuals protecting their interests, many do associate with organized interest groups, again reflecting the British collective tradition. Membership in politically oriented organizations gives us another measure of participation. "Britain," says Ridley (1984: 30, 31), "is a country of associations," and "the strength of voluntary organisations and the role they play in public life is a feature of British society not always reflected in other European states." Although a large majority of Britons (60 percent of the electorate) are organization members, only about 20 percent claim to belong to organizations concerned with public issues, and a large proportion of these are trade union members (Rose 1986c: 187). Furthermore, many association members remain largely inactive (Higgins and Richardson 1976: 14). Nevertheless, memberships in certain types of organizations, particularly environmental groups, have been increasing rapidly in the past twenty years. Community interests have increasingly found representation in tenants associations and neighborhood councils (Higgins and Richardson 1976: 18). Moran (1987: 180) concludes that "there is little doubt that in the last two decades there has been an explosive growth in both the numbers of pressure groups and in their membership.... Local groups are now so numerous that the exact size of the pressure group world is literally incalculable." Total membership in the National Trust, the Royal Society for Nature Conservation, the World Wildlife Fund, and the Royal Society for the Protection of Birds increased nearly five-fold from 452,000 in 1971 to 2,208,000 in 1986 (*Social Trends* 18, 1988: table 11.4, 169). By 1987, the Campaign for Nuclear Disarmament claimed 100,000 members (Moran 1987: 180).

Since protection of citizens has traditionally been the province of political institutions, it is not surprising that the courts have played a smaller role than in other countries and that informal, "political" means are preferred (Ridley 1984: 4). Their diminished role is further enhanced by the difficulty for most people of access to the courts, by high costs, delays, and "almost incomprehensible procedures" and by laws themselves (Ridley 1984: 4).

In addition to the changes in the internal means of participation, British membership in the European Community has opened up several new means for citizen participation. Elections to the European Parliament involve millions of Britons in a new electoral arena, and the European Human Rights Commission has become available to Britons with grievances against their government. Appeals by British nationals to this body are infrequent, only 103 in 1986, but somewhat ahead of appeals from either France or Germany. Nevertheless, the availability of such an avenue of redress is a significant exception to parliamentary supremacy.

The low level of active interest in politics in Japan is reflected by the relatively small amount of interpersonal conversation about politics. Though the lack of comparability of survey questions presents a considerable obstacle to comparison, it appears that the Japanese, like the British, do not discuss politics frequently, only 6 percent "everyday" and 33 percent "at least once a week" (Stronach 1988: 7; Nakamura 1975). When respondents were asked in 1972 (Nakamura 1975: 7) how often they discussed politics and national affairs, 12 percent said a lot, 29 percent said some, and 48 percent said never. When asked the same question in 1987, 6 percent said everyday, 33 percent said at least once a week, 52 percent said rarely, and 8 percent said never. Though there is a gender gap in discussing politics in both Britain and Japan, the gap is twice as large in Japan, and the percentage of women discussing politics was the lowest in a twenty-nation comparison (Inglehart 1990: Table 10–3, 348). According to Flanagan, Japanese interest in discussing politics is lower than for other passive forms of interest such as following elections or following politics in general (Flanagan 1978: 146). The Japanese appear no less prone to try to convince

Table 5.8

Nonvoting Conventional Participation in Japan

	None	1–3	3–10	>10
Watch TV broadcasts on candidates	16	34	37	13
Read newspaper articles on candidates	16	32	34	18
Discuss election with friends, etc.	15	34	36	14

	Yes	No
Try to persuade friends to vote as self	12.9	87.1
Member of *koenkai*	28.6	68

Have you participated in any of the following in the last five years?

	1–2 times	>3 times	No
Citizens' or residents' movement	4.7	3.5	90.5
Self-government association	9.5	6.5	81.9
Contact local official or politician because you needed something	9.4	2.9	92.6
Contact a national official or politician because you needed something	2.7	2.9	92.6
Petition local government office	4.2	2.5	92.6
Attend demonstration	2.3	2.1	94.4
Attend political meetings, rallies	19.6	8.5	70.0
Work for campaign	11.8	5.3	81.4
Donate money to campaign	4.9	1.8	91.3

Source: Joji Watanuki et al. 1986. *Electoral Behavior in the 1983 Japanese Elections.* Tokyo: Institute for International Relations, Sophia University

others than the British. Although there are no statistics to support this contention, there is much anecdotal evidence to support the hypothesis that discussions of politics often concern the specific and "interesting" or "scandalous" aspects of daily politics, such as that reported in the columns on factional politics and reporting of the reigning scandal of the day.

It would seem from a comparison of the data in Table 5.8 with the data in Table 5.7 that the Japanese are actually more likely to participate in some types of conventional, nonvoting political behavior than the British.[6] More, for example, indicate that they have worked for a campaign. Even keeping in mind that the collection of the data immediately after an election might have boosted the participatory responses, this might seem somewhat surprising. However, the data do not differ significantly from other studies that have found Japanese participation in both voting and nonvoting conventional behavior to be higher than that in the United States and some West European countries (Richardson and Flanagan 1984: 231–34).[7] Another example of relatively high participation is membership in politicians' political support groups, or *koenkai*, in Japan. Twenty-nine percent of Japanese belong to *koenkai*, a large number when we consider the generally low levels of participation in most countries, and when we consider that it is a relatively active form of participation, requiring considerable commitment from the member. *Koenkai* membership is much higher than party membership. Japanese associate with these groups for social as much as for political motives, and they are one of the most popular forms of participation. For many individuals, membership in such a localized group structures his or her participation to a considerable degree. Constituency party organizations in Britain perform a role which is only marginally analogous.

Given the reluctance of the Japanese to participate, it should also be somewhat surprising that those forms of behavior that are generally higher in Japan than in the West are precisely those that could be seen as having the highest opportunity costs—either financially (e.g., campaign contributions) or in terms of time and effort (e.g., attending meetings). As demonstrated in Table 5.8, *koenkai* membership is, aside from voting, one of the most frequent forms of high-opportunity–cost-conventional participation. Higher levels of participation in those behaviors that have the greatest opportunity costs for a people that are notoriously conservative with their money and have little leisure time implies that their participation must be highly motivated. Another explanation may be that for the Japanese, there is a higher emotional cost associated with outgoing behaviors that are more prevalent in at least some Western countries.

The group orientation of the Japanese does not translate directly into high levels of membership in politically oriented organizations. Taking as examples the organizations given in Table 5.9, we can see that the highest rates of membership are in community associations, womens', youth, and senior citizens' associations, the PTA, and hobby and sports clubs. These particular groups are essentially social in nature and their political impact would be limited to the local, even neighborhood, level. This is especially true of the neighborhood associations and the PTA. Membership in these organizations is often obligatory. Although one can refuse to join a neighborhood association or the PTA (if one has a child in school), such a refusal may lead to ostracism or shunning. These organizations are, however, active in transmitting demands to local government.

Other than overtly political organizations such as political parties and candidate support groups, the next layer of organizations are essentially occupational. These organizations do have a great deal of impact as transmitters of public opinion on political decisionmaking, as will be discussed in Chapter 7. The leadership of these organizations has the greatest political impact, but the rank-and-file membership, especially of unions and agricultural cooperatives does

Table 5.9

Organizational Membership—Japan (in percent)

Labor union member   9.8

	Affiliated	Nonaffiliated
Commercial association	14.3	82.4
Agricultural cooperative	21.8	75.5
Community association	61.4	36.5
Women's, youth, or senior citizen club or association	34	63.6
PTA	29.5	68.6
Citizens', residents', or women's movement	6.4	91.3
Political association	16.1	81.3
Hobby or sports club	27.7	70.2
Religious association	9.8	87.3

Source: Joji Watanuki et al. 1986. *Electoral Behavior in the 1983 Japanese Elections*, pp. 141–43. Tokyo: Institute for International Relations, Sophia University.

participate in various types of political activities including campaign support and demonstrations.

There are a number of private consumer movements in Japan, but the membership is rather limited and the consumer movement in general is rather weak. There is no Japanese version of Common Cause or Ralph Nader. Similar groups and individuals exist, are applauded and are praised, but they are not joined or actively supported by many. Take, for example, the Japanese national co-op movement (*Nihon Seikatsu Kyodo Kumiai*). The co-op members are housewives in most communities around Japan who use their organization to buy low cost, organically grown food. While they have an impact on the food retailers in the areas where they have strong organizations, they have minimal impact on national policies. Quite a few environmental organizations have emerged in recent years, in part because of the failure of traditional occupational organizations to tackle the problems of pollution, and in part because of increased interest in local autonomy (Ishida 1984: 32).

Unconventional Participation/ Protest Behavior

Beyond conventional behavior lies a range of behaviors referred to as "unconventional," because they lie outside the normal, officially sanctioned institutional channels for citizen input available in a democratic society: elections, parties, contacts with officials. Such behaviors are often referred to as "protest" behaviors. Though confined to a relatively small minority of citizens in the industrial democracies, protest is an important element of political participation and constitutes an important part of the "political action repertory" of citizens. The following political actions are often considered "unconventional": signing petitions, joining boycotts, attending lawful demonstrations, joining unofficial strikes, occupying buildings and factories, damaging things, using violence. Most of these behaviors, while not conventional, are fully legal, nonviolent, and may even reflect unquestioning support for the political system, if not always confidence in official channels or officeholders. Petitions, certainly, and demonstrations on occasion, may be of this type.

As we have noted, conventional and protest behavior are not discontinuous. Unconventional behavior is not necessarily an alternative to conventional action, undertaken by those who have lost faith in "the system." Protest may actually be a sign of a healthy polity. Even the more extreme forms of protest may be less "unconventional" than we would normally assume. Protest behavior and violence may certainly signal withdrawal of support from a regime, and even if they do not, they may undermine the authority of a regime. We could hardly call Northern Ireland's chronic violence, or assassination attempts in Japan, examples of fulfillment of the "citizen" role. Nevertheless, while it is easy to assume that illegal or violent protest indicates nonsupport for the system, we should avoid reaching that conclusion prematurely. Such forms of protest may themselves be ritualized within the system, regarded by political activists as an effective option within the system "to teach the government and the majority supporting it a painful lesson," but not to overthrow the existing political framework (Merkl 1988: 42).

In the popular image of Britain prior to the 1970s, perceived values of "consensus, pragmatism, gradualism, tolerance, limited partisanship, and deference" (Kavanagh 1980: 127) were believed to explain the British disdain for violence and lawbreaking. Yet many in recent years have become convinced that protest, and the potential for protest, are on the rise in Britain. In his well-known study of protest behavior among the British, Alan Marsh (1977: 39) argues that "protest behavior, far from being the occasional outbursts of a hopelessly alienated minority . . . is an integral part of the British political consciousness and is viewed, under a variety of circumstances, as a legitimate pathway of political redress by widely differing sections of the community." Support by over a fifth of his sample for "the full gamut of aggressive protest against the authorities," he argues, is solid proof of this view, as opposed to the "established position that the British have an exaggerated respect for political authority" (Marsh 1977: 51).

In Britain, as early as 1970, there was evidence of growing dissatisfaction and a turning to unconventional political activity. The Royal Commission on the Constitution identified "a substantial minority, confident in their own ability to judge what government should do and feeling unable to register their views effectively through their elected representatives or through membership of a political party, have been turning to other methods. Among all sections of society there has been a growth of demonstrations and other forms of direct action designed to by-pass the formal democratic process" (Royal Commission on the Constitution 1973: 124). Kaase and Marsh (1979b: 40–41) speculate that "it is now reasonable to predict that there will be an increasing tendency for citizens with particular demands to organize themselves outside the established political institutions in general and outside the existing parties in particular." The 1981 EVSS results suggest that in Britain "Although few have actually participated, there does indeed appear to be greater readiness to contemplate more lawful types of protest. Almost one-third of the sample say they 'might' be prepared to take part in demonstrations and political boycotts" (Phillips 1985: 166–67). And Young (1984: 11) concludes, "Foremost among other changes in popular orientations to politics are indicators of a decline in political passivity in the face of unwelcome government actions. Compared with evidence of two decades ago, today's electors are more active; in particular, the propensity to combine with others in political dissent appears to have increased, as has the propensity to register an individual protest."

But there are good reasons for withholding judgment about the magnitude of change in either protest attitudes or behavior. In general, we lack reliable time series, certainly going back more than two or at the most three decades, on which to base such judgments. Any claims of increased protest potential and its significance must be judged against modern British history, even twentieth-century history. "Bearing in mind the extent of public disorder in the early part of this century," concludes Norton (1984: 362), "[the Barnes and Kaase data] if anything, supports my argument as to the continuing strength of the political culture, not its erosion." There is mounting evidence of increased conventional participation. Such evidence as exists seems to show that while protest potential and activity may have increased slightly over the last thirty years, they have been in the direction of the most law-abiding forms. As Phillips (1985: 169) concludes, "Levels of support for political protest are generally low and even among those who view it most favourably, support for protest exists much more at the level of ideas than action." Young (1984: 11), whose finding of increased propensity to protest we have noted, still concludes "passivity is still more common than protest." Even Marsh (cited in Kavanagh 1980: 150), whose work purported to show a precipitous decline of political trust, finds relatively little change in preferred forms of political action, despite a small shift to forms "of more direct action." In Europe as a whole, including Britain, the 1981 EVSS found that "There is little evidence of support on any broad scale for 'protest' and less orthodox forms of political activity, although demonstrations are increasingly accepted as a legitimate means of political expression" (Harding and Phillips 1986: 108). Heath and Topf (1987: 58) conclude in their study of political culture in Britain that "there are very high levels of support for orderly and conventional forms of protest, but support falls off sharply as we move down the list to forms of direct or violent action." "The protests our respondents had in mind seem therefore to be of a rather orderly kind, directed *at* rather than *against* Parliament, and working *within* rather than *outside* the existing political system" (Heath and Topf 1987: 57).

Legal Forms of Protest

Table 5.10 confirms the strong gradation of support for and participation in unconventional behavior that Heath and Topf suggest above. Clearly, the British are not out of the mainstream of the industrial democracies when it comes to their participation in or attitudes toward unconventional political activity. Minuscule proportions have committed, or approved of, illegal acts of protest. The most marked characteristic of British protest behavior is the strength of the tradition of petition. In 1981 a far larger percentage of Britons had signed petitions than the citizens of any European Community member nation or Japan, and while other surveys do not indicate quite so large a proportion of petition signers, petitions are clearly the preferred method of protest (Heath and Topf 1987: 56). This should not be surprising, since petition as a method of political communication has ancient roots in Britain. What may be surprising is that petitions are classified as unconventional behavior at all. Not only are they conventional, but to some extent they are derived from paternalistic concepts of government.

Neither the Japanese nor the British show much inclination to go beyond petitioning, though approval of boycotts and lawful demonstrations is also higher than for more controversial actions. Nor does either appear any more prone to damage property or commit political acts of violence than European citizens. But, compared with other industrial democracies, the British and the Japanese are the least likely to have attended a lawful demonstration. However, notably higher percentages of Japanese (40 percent) would consider joining a boycott than citizens in Britain or Europe. Notwithstanding this exception, however, overall the Japanese are even less likely than the British to consider those unconventional political acts listed on the survey.

Even where Japanese approval of political action is relatively high, approval is not likely to be transmitted beyond passive recognition into active behavior. While there are more local exceptions, on the national level mainstream Japanese do not participate in protest activities. When they do engage in them, they have a highly expressive character. "Even opposition movements, labor strikes and political demonstrations tend to resemble highly orchestrated pageants or morality plays, which the Japanese population periodically views with a kind of sympathetic understanding. But nothing happens, nothing changes" (Flanagan 1978: 157).

Though less frequent than in the other industrial democracies, participation in demonstrations in Japan is second behind petitions as the most-favored form of protest, and it is by far the most obvious form of nonconventional political behavior. Demonstrations in Japan can be categorized as "permanent," those that have been conducted by the same parties over the same issues for many years, and "transient," those that are concerned with issues that have a relatively short life. Examples of the former are rightist demonstrations calling for the full restoration of the emperor system and leftist demonstrations calling for the ouster of American troops from Japan. An example of the latter were the demonstrations

Table 5.10

Unconventional Political Behaviors

Percentage of respondents who have done, might do, or would never, under any circumstances, do the following:

	Japan	Britain	Europe
Signing a petition			
• have done	43	62	41
• might do	27	27	32
• would never do	15	9	20
• don't know	15	2	6
Joining in boycotts			
• have done	2	6	7
• might do	40	29	28
• would never do	33	60	57
• don't know	25	5	9
Attending lawful demonstrations			
• have done	7	9	17
• might do	20	32	29
• would never do	48	57	49
• don't know	25	2	6
Joining unofficial strikes			
• have done	2	8	5
• might do	10	16	14
• would never do	65	74	74
• don't know	23	2	6
Occupying buildings or factories			
• have done	—	2	3
• might do	4	10	13
• would never do	74	85	78
• don't know	22	3	6
Damaging things like breaking windows			
• have done	—	2	1
• might do	3	1	2
• would never do	82	96	93
• don't know	15	1	4
Using violence like fighting with other demonstrators			
• have done	—	1	1
• might do	3	3	4
• would never do	83	95	91
• don't know	14	1	4

Sources: Japanese and British data from Leisure Development Center Survey, 1981, cited in E. Hastings and P. Hastings, eds., 1984. *Index to International Opinion, 1982–1983.* Westport: Greenwood Press, pp. 545–46. Used with permission. European data from European Values System Survey, 1981, cited in S. Harding and D. Phillips, eds., 1986, *Contrasting Values in Western Europe: Unity, Diversity and Change.* London: Macmillan, appendix.

against a Japanese agreement reducing agricultural quotas on beef and oranges or the demonstrations against the tax reform policy of the LDP. The distinction between permanent and transient demonstrations may be blurred as transient demonstrations are often reactions to particular events in the context of a long-term problem. An example of this case would be a particular community's grievance against specific actions by American forces in that community.

Demonstrations are centered around well-defined cohesive groups. The typical demonstrations and protests in Japan over the past twenty years have concerned Japanese support for the American war in Vietnam, student rebellions, the building, and later expansion, of the new Tokyo International Airport in Narita, expansion of the *shinkansen* (bullet train), the stationing of the nuclear-powered freighter at Mutsu, demonstrations against the treatment of *burakumin*, agricultural protests against the importation of American agricultural products, protests concerning a range of issues that arise from the stationing of U.S. armed forces personnel in Japan, including the expansion of bases and night take-off-and-landing training in populated areas, and a wide range of environmental issues and events.

The most formalized and regular of the permanent protests come from the reactionary organizations of the far right. These organizations have mutual support links with both the LDP and out-groups such as the *yakuza*. They often have small paramilitary youth groups recruited from bike and car gangs and the "punk" (*chimpira*) levels of the yakuza. These groups carry out regular protests everyday throughout Japan, centered around the issues of reinstating the imperial way, supporting the military, and regaining the northern territories lost to the Soviet Union at the end of World War II via the Yalta Agreements. Their daily protests most often consist of driving around sound trucks that blast out martial music and exhortations at very high volume, stopping occasionally so that a member can give a speech from the roof of the van. They do occasionally mass for other demonstrations, especially the harassment of leftist labor unions when they hold their annual meetings. The permanent demonstrations of the left tend to be held less frequently, but also seem never to change. The most typical of these are marches on the Diet building or the American embassy, calling for the removal of American forces from Japan, and the *shunto* (spring wage struggle). The ritual, formalized, and permanent nature of these protests is in itself an indication of the low impact that such demonstrations have had on the political process. They have become a regular part of the political landscape, they are accepted as legitimate, and rarely involve violence on either side of the line, but they have not had an impact on policy.

It is much less typical to have a protest movement created by an individual or a group of individuals bound by no associational ties other than the protest group itself and their orientation toward the operative issue. Housewives may venture out once a year to wave their rice ladles at the Ministry of Agriculture, when the rice price supports are being negotiated, but specific actions through consumer groups is relatively rare. As we have seen, consumer interests are poorly organized, and in any case, rarely push issues through unconventional means, even demonstrations. There has been no powerful consumer backlash even though inflation has drastically reduced the purchasing power of the middle class, and government tariff barriers and agricultural subsidies have pushed the price of even essential commodities to levels many times higher than the world price. Anyone going door to door with a political petition in any Japanese city or village, or anyone trying to start a spontaneous demonstration in Kasumigaseki, the government district in Tokyo, would soon despair of success. There are few cases that one can compare to Howard Jarvis's Proposition 13 movement in California, and few grass-roots groups that can compare to the American womens' groups that boycotted sugar, coffee, and beef following drastic price rises in the 1970s. Even when the Japanese do protest, the attitude is "nothing happens, nothing changes" (Flanagan 1978: 157). These passive orientations are changing somewhat. As a result of value changes taking place in Japan toward greater libertarianism, we are likely to find more positive attitudes toward participation (Richardson and Flanagan 1984: 227).

Illegal Protest

As we have already seen, a fairly large minority of British consider it, in theory, defensible on occasion to break an unjust law (Young 1984: 26). Nearly a third in some surveys say there are circumstances in which they would break a law with which they strongly disagreed (Kaase and Marsh 1979a: Table 5.5, 155; Young 1984: 27). But this attitude has been rarely reported as actualized, and most survey evidence points to a strong reluctance to condone lawbreaking for political ends. The EVSS data suggest very small percentages of respondents are willing to engage in certain types of illegal protests themselves. Rose (1986c: 123) also finds "very little support for political action outside the law." Whatever widespread protest potential that existed "was rarely directed against the regime: few of the latent rebels had in mind the overthrow of capitalism or the government. They were more concerned to defend what they regarded as their 'normal' rights, such as their civil liberties, protecting their homes against threat of eviction, resisting threats to living standards, and using industrial action to protect free wage bargaining" (Kavanagh 1980: 151; and see Kaase and Marsh 1979a: Table 5.8, 162). We should be careful about concluding from protest behavior that the protestors have ceased to give diffuse support to the political system. Protests can be employed in any society to call attention to the need to conform to what the protestors view as the true constitutional order. Consider the example of the United States civil rights movement that sought inclusion for blacks in the constitutional scheme, or Charter 88's call for a codified British bill of rights. There is little to suggest that most political action on behalf of Commonwealth minorities in Britain is undertaken for any other goal than inclusion. Some critics of the British system see the heart of the political problem in the success of the hegemonial class in dictating the terms of debate for dissenters. "In no other major capitalist country," writes Miliband (1982: 2), has the containment and reduction of popular pressure been achieved "quite so smoothly and effectively."

In Japan, protest does not connote illegality; even violence may be approved in light of the motives (or sincerity) of the actor (White 1981: 381; Ward 1965: 63). "This type of sincerity is of the greatest importance in Japanese politics. If one acts sincerely, that is, through pure and personally disinterested motives, and if one is willing to pay an appropriate price for such action—such as suicide or execution in more serious cases—there is in Japan a traditional inclination to approve, or at least to 'understand,' both the actor and his act. . . . The violence of numerous 'demonstrations' by opposition elements both in the streets and on the floor of the National Diet would seem to indicate that it is still alive. 'Sincerity' continues to excuse a great deal in Japanese politics" (Ward 1978: 71). This, again, is an example of how the context can take precedence over the law in Japan.

Such a concept is nowhere near as prevalent in Britain as in Japan, though something like it is reflected in the concept of sympathy for the act of conscience: civil disobedience. The image of the defiant antinuclearist Bertrand Russell in the 1950s successfully captures British admiration for principled defiance of authority. In the Western concept of civil disobedience, however, the cause must be just and the act nonviolent to receive sympathy. In the Japanese concept of sincerity, the subjective dedication of the activist, not the worth of his cause, is the criterion for sympathy.

Japan's homogeneity has removed one of the major causes of protest and violence found elsewhere in the world—the assimilation of minority groups. But even that may be changing as illegal protests have been recently conducted by the minorities of Japan—ethnic Koreans, ethnic Chinese and, to a much lesser extent, Western foreigners resident in Japan. A growing number in the Korean and Chinese ethnic communities have refused to be fingerprinted for their alien registration cards as a protest against the Japanese treatment of minority groups within Japan. But, again, in these cases the protests to date have been very low-key, passive, and nonviolent.

Violent Protest

Politically motivated lawbreaking and violence are far from unknown in British history. Levelers and Luddites in other eras, and some mine workers' union members and Committee for Nuclear Disarmament activists, not to mention the antagonists in Northern Ireland in more recent times have shown this in varying degrees. And indeed, political violence and support for violence may still be found among the British: 27 percent agreed that "the use of violence is sometimes justified in bringing about political change" (Market Opinion Research

International [MORI] August 1986, cited in Hastings and Hastings 1988: 488). The London tax riots in 1990 certainly demonstrated this attitude in action. However, most of the data pertaining to citizens' political action repertoires continue to show that in all the industrial democracies, including Britain and Japan, support for violent protest is very low, and willingness to engage in it even lower; 95 percent of Britons surveyed say they would never use violence, and less than 2 percent say they have committed violent political acts (see Table 5.10). Eighty-four percent of Britons see no circumstances in which terrorism would be justified, a figure higher than every country surveyed in Europe but one (LDC 1981, cited in Hastings and Hastings 1984: 552).

The Japanese appear neither more nor less prone to violent protest than the British. According to Table 5.10, they are even less likely than the British to have occupied a building, damaged property, or used violence against others, though somewhat fewer are prepared to rule out those acts (in part as a result of the high percentage of "don't know" responses). "Looked at cross-nationally," notes White, "Japan is less protest-wracked than many introspective Japanese might imagine." The 14 percent of Tokyoites surveyed by White who would not rule out violence "is more nearly comparable to the 15 percent of Marsh's (1977: 204) British sample which was unprepared to rule out the use of violence. Looked at thus, today's Tokyoites appear neither more protest-prone nor accepting of political violence than citizens in societies whose political stability is seldom questioned" (White 1981: 371–75).

That is not to say that radicals are not alive and active in Japan. In recent years Red Army members have been implicated in numerous acts of violence within and outside Japan. Firebombs have been thrown at police boxes and stations. Homemade rockets were launched at the site of the 1986 economic summit in Tokyo. Railway stations have been bombed. Radical groups such as the student activist faction, the Chukkaha, and left union factions have combined with more mainstream citizen action groups to oppose specific policies. However, they do not seem to have been successful in attaining support or any other goal. The enthronement of Emperor Akihito was a self-proclaimed occasion for a major show of force by Japanese radicals, but even though 36 separate incidents of arson and mortar attacks were reported on that day, none caused much damage and all were well away from the ceremonies (*Japan Times*, November 14, 1990: 2).

Violence in the political process is not a recent phenomenon. The Tokugawa period (1615–1868) put an end to both the internecine feudal wars that racked Japan for much of its history and foreign wars, but the entire period was marked by peasant uprisings brought on by the declining standard of living, volatility of rice prices, increasing taxes, and government mismanagement. The latter part of the nineteenth century was marked by the upheavals of modernization including samurai rebellions and anti-Westernization backlashes. The first half of the twentieth century was marked by state violence against socialists, unions, antiwar protestors and dissidents in general, and the "politics of assassination" by ultra-nationalist societies.

In the postwar era, there have been a few highly publicized attacks reminiscent of political violence in the 1930s, such as the stabbings of Socialist Party Chairman Asanuma and American Ambassador Reischauer, and the attempted kamikaze attack against ultranationalist chieftain Kodama Yoshio. Political violence on the right often takes place within the context of political intimidation of "politics through assassination." Anyone of public stature who dares to speak out against these reactionary groups is often physically attacked by them. At least one journalist who dared to oppose them and their policies was assassinated, and an assassination attempt was made against the mayor of Nagasaki when he raised in public the possible war guilt of Emperor Showa. Political violence on the left tends more toward massive confrontation with the state, either through direct conflict, such as the riots at the Narita Airport, or terrorist activities, such as the launching of homemade rockets during the enthronement ceremonies.

Collective versus Individual Action

Collective forms of participation, including petitions, demonstrations, boycotts, and the like, have long been available to complement individual acts such as voting and contacting officials. It is well established, however, that collective political organization pays great dividends, especially in the light of the tremendous impact of mass media and communications. Both Britain and Japan, as we have seen, have strong collectivist traditions, and we should therefore expect that political activism should manifest itself collectively more so than in countries, as France, where the collectivist tradition is less notable.

Many collective avenues of influence exist within the British system, and as we shall see in Chapter 7, many of these are accorded a prominent place, and exert significant influence on political decisions. In the 1970s, it was quite fashionable to characterize Britain as "neocorporatist" or "collectivist," though time and the Thatcher years have led to a reassessment of that view. But to what extent does the tradition of collective action affect mass behavior in the choice between individual, and collective avenues? The institutions and rules of politics that emerged in the nineteenth century stressed collective, rather than individual mobilization and expression of demands. Political parties arose as mediating bodies between citizen and government, and class shaped the creation of political parties. Indeed Labour arose as an explicitly working-class party.

The data in Table 5.11 suggest that, by 1983, Britons were considerably more likely to take either personal (contact MP, contact influential person, contact government department, contact press or TV) or collective (sign petition, raise issue in organization, form a group of like-minded demonstrators, or protest) action than they had been twenty-five years earlier. Young (1984: 22) observes that the increase was greatest with respect to collective actions. But at the same

Table 5.11

Personal and Collective Political Action (Britain)

Faced with the prospect of an unjust or "harmful law" respondent would (in percent):

	1960	1983
Take personal action	47	77
Take collective action	23	77
Do nothing	32	14
Don't know	6	1

Source: K. Young, 1984. "Political Affairs." In *British Social Attitudes: The 1984 Report*, ed. R. Jowell and C. Airey: p. 22. Brookfield, VT: Gower. Used with permission.

time there was evidence of an increase in individual initiatives.

Ridley's study of citizen approaches to redress of grievances confirms a growing resort to collective action among Britons. He cites the growth of "community organizations," directed at such goals as "defence groups against the police, the housing authorities and other representatives of power" as well as providing services to various community groups. And he concludes that in the future, Britons are likely, to an increasing degree, to turn "to their own organizations for help" (Ridley 1984: 31–32). The Royal Commission on the Constitution (1973: 124) commented upon the growing willingness of people to form protest groups "almost as a first resort." "They have discovered that group action works and for some groups physical protest, often for reasons of publicity, is coming to be a regular part of the pattern" (see Moran 1987: 181). The political uses of the courts, such as they are, also tend to suggest the collectivist orientation (see Chapter 1).

As noted above, however, the highest levels of participation among Britons, aside from voting, involve individual contacts with officials. We have noted, in fact, evidence of a decrease of collective perspective and organization, in favor of a general "retreat into the privatized world within home and family" (Marshall et al. 1985: 274). As a consequence, "even the various forms of militant collective action may only be so many collective means to individual ends; that is, the improvement of the position of separate individuals, rather than of the class as a whole" (Marshall et al. 1985: 273). Indeed, as we have seen, the most spectacular increases in citizen activism in Britain have been in the arena of individual appeals, albeit assisted by or mediated through groups. Certainly the declining influence of industrial labor unions over the past ten years suggests that in that historically important arena for collective action, the trend is negative. Perhaps dealignment from the Conservative and Labour parties is another indicator of the shift from collectivist to individual orientations toward the polity. We cannot rule out that "cognitive" mobilization may indeed be on the rise.

Britain was collectivist in building a consensus in support of the modern political system, but remained individualistic in its view of freedom from state authority. As a result, self-reliance, defiance of authority, and individualism are an integral part of a society that is also collective. While Britons are more likely than the Japanese to take individual initiative in their dealings with government, they, like the Japanese, have many collective forms of participation available. All this would tend to support the conclusions of *The Civic Culture* concerning Britain's mixed polity.

As should be clear by now, given the group nature of Japanese society, there is little individual unconventional, or even conventional, political participation. The overriding value in Japan is the reduction of conflict and the maintenance of harmony, thus there is a double barrier to individual action in Japan. The first is the resistance to recognizing an individual unless the individual is a member of a group and is acting with and for the group. Secondly, any action that creates conflict in the society is going to create an initial negative reaction, not because of the intrinsic value of the issue for which the action is initiated, but because the creation of a disturbance itself is a negative act. Thus, those who have what might be defined as a legitimate protest, such as equal treatment for women, are curbed by the necessity to conduct their protests in as nondisruptive a manner as possible. Those individuals outside of the political mainstream who conduct high-profile political protests tend to be ridiculed. Examples that come to mind are Ms. Enoki, leader of the radical feminist faction Chupiren, Okuzaki Kozo, whose activism against the emperor for causing the death of his comrades during the Second World War was made famous by the documentary film, *The Emperor's Naked Army Marches On*, and the late "soapbox" orator of the Ginza, Akao Bin. All of these people have been generally treated by the press and the public as either laughably comic or literally insane. The hackneyed phrase, "the nail that sticks up gets hammered down," should in the modern political context be changed to "the person who stands out gets shunned."

Explaining Participation

People participate in politics for a variety of reasons: sense of obligation, social pressure or custom, the desire for personal benefit, and coercion, among others. Where rational considerations prevail, people are said to act out of *instrumental* motives. Participation is affected, however, by many other factors than conscious motivations, however, such as class and education. We will attempt to identify a number of these *expressive* factors as well. Reasons will vary from activity to activity, from circumstance to circumstance, and from individual to individual. As in the case of most motives, reasons for participation may often be mixed, or imperfectly perceived. Nevertheless, researchers have attempted to delineate some of these reasons, and to suggest how they may differ from one polity to another. We shall have to live with the fact that, as in so much else, the one thing students of political culture and participation are likely to agree upon is that our understanding of contemporary participation is limited. So much of the literature on behavior concerns voting that we shall consider motives for voting choice separately, and in far greater detail, in Chapter 6.

Britain

Several explanations may be offered for the level and modes of participation in Britain. From a historical perspective, the struggles for inclusion by emerging new social classes in the nineteenth century were a force both for participation, and once successful, for legitimacy and stability (Flanagan 1978: 138). These struggles tended to create a wider repertory of participant orientations, at an earlier date than in Japan, where modern democratic politics developed along a very different, and later, path. Yet the long-term impact of this process was mixed. On one hand, the historical process engendered qualities of protest and defiance of authority, in both individualist and collectivist forms. On the other hand, the result of the open struggles over incorporation was the establishment of democratic institutions and processes accepted by the various parties as legitimate. Despite the contested but ultimately successful incorporations that cemented agreement on the political rules of the game, the British continue to participate in politics at no greater a rate than the Japanese, whose political system did not emerge in the same way. This may be in part due to the fact that the rules that emerged during the contests for incorporation were not populist, and retained much that was traditional about the exercise of power in Britain. The absence of a doctrine of popular sovereignty, and the substitution of the convention of parliamentary supremacy certainly gave intellectual reinforcement to the idea that it is for the government to decide. The successful political struggle for inclusion, first by the middle class and later by the working class, seems to have preserved traditional norms of trust, support, and deference at least for a time. While the emergence of democracy entailed new values and processes, it did not replace Tory paternalism and the preference for strong government, each of which shaped views of what participation was appropriate.

As we noted above, conventional participation is often associated with strong feelings of trust and efficacy. Marsh (1977: 123) speaks of the conventionally oriented "voters, joiners, and do-ers who . . . remain reasonably confident that their role as citizens still counts," and Young (1984: 24) notes "strong associations between orientations to the political system and a sense of political efficacy." It may be also argued that people participate because they expect benefit or wish to defend their interests. Almond and Verba (1963: 184) suggest that people are more likely to try to influence government where they perceive "that an activity of the government is threatening." Some political scientists have indeed argued that participation is "the key instrumental political action" (Verba et al. 1978: 301). Kaase and Marsh (1979b: 38) hypothesize that when the system is perceived as responsive, citizens will engage in conventional, institutionalized forms of participation. Those who express a willingness to do something about an unjust national law would seem to be thinking instrumentally. In Chapter 3, we saw that personal issues had the highest salience among Britons. So it is not surprising that Britons' conventional contacts with officials tend to deal with personal and family problems, and indeed, even protest activities are often motivated by concern for "local and environmental problems" (Budge and McKay 1988: 86–87). Expectation of benefit is at least one motivation in these cases. As we shall see in Chapter 6, however, the prospects for individual benefit tend not to be a very strong consideration in voting behavior. The dwindling of economic resources available to society over the past generation, and the deliberate efforts of the Thatcher government to contract the sphere of government, may have contradictory effects on participation. On the one hand, it is likely to constrain participation, as prospects for instrumental gain from participation decline. On the other, it may encourage it, as people participate more actively to protect their shares or to protest their losses.

Some claim that normative, not instrumental, motives, are a more important stimulus to participation or nonparticipation among the British. This is true both in the sense that people regard voting as a duty, and in the sense that the norms of strong government militate against acceptance of "direct popular participation in government" (Jessop 1971: 7). The traditional norm of "tolerance of elitism in government" may "result in even the critical Briton being less vocal and less assertive than his American counterpart" (Hart 1978: 35). Certainly social concerns are not absent from the motivations for participation. Even if personal and family concerns predominate, Britons have organized in the past and continue to organize politically to support various causes, from antislavery in the nineteenth century to environmental causes and antinuclearism in recent years. As we shall see, the argument is made that social justice is said by at least some observers to be a significant factor in voting choice (Heath et al. 1985: 166). While we cannot exclude that many people support such movements out of concern for personal welfare, movement objectives are framed in terms of wider issues and impact, and organization is collective.

Topf (1989) has found cause in the *British Social Attitudes* survey data to question the prevalence of instrumentalism. If, as we saw in Chapter 3, most British do not think they have much say over what government does, how would instrumental expectations explain their participation? Considering this point, Topf rejects a strongly instrumental interpretation of political participation, and finds that people participate in spite of low efficacy. He argues that Britons increasingly participate "as a moral good," in spite of their belief that their specific actions are often ineffective (Topf 1989: Table 4, 64, 75; and see Young 1984: 21–22).

In much of the literature on participation, rising levels of education are associated with increased participation. But Marsh and Kaase (1979a: 112) find that "young people—by far the best educated generation the country has yet produced—noticeably shun conventional participation." There are a variety of reasons why education might be less of a factor, at least in conventional participation, in Britain than in Europe or Japan. Even if education were strongly correlated with participation, the percentages of the population attaining advanced degrees is relatively low. Only about 5 percent of the electorate hold degrees (Heath and Topf 1986: 344), and only 19 percent of Britons in the relevant age group are enrolled in institutions of higher education, as compared to 32 percent in Japan, 28 percent in France, and 31 percent in West Germany (Foreign Press Center 1989: 92). This is true despite significant growth in university enrollments from the 1950s to the 1970s, which lagged somewhat behind those in West Germany and France (Dalton 1988: 18). A common view has been that, compared with other industrial democracies, there is less of a relationship between levels of education and participation levels or types (Kavanagh 1980: 134). Heath and Topf (1986: 553–55) observe that a majority at all levels of education are alike in their willingness to vote, to engage in other conventional activities, and to engage in unconventional protest. They conclude, in contrast to Dalton's major hypothesis, that there is little evidence that "educational expansion will have major implications for political participation," at least in Britain. Almond (1980: 23–24) also tends to downplay the role of education. He concludes that, "Higher education did not as significantly affect attitudes towards civic obligation and other democratic values. . . . Here, national historical experiences tended to create special patterns in which education seemed to have relatively little influence." A more recent and dissenting voice has been raised by Topf (1989: 64) who finds that those with better education "are more likely to say they would engage in political activities within conventional norms, and are more likely to say they have in practice done so on more than one occasion." Other evidence that confirms the education-participation relationship may be found in the fact that British participation seems channeled more into contacts with MPs over personal matters and into group memberships than into voting or campaign activity. As Dalton (Dalton 1988: 57) argues, "rising sophistication levels may be more important in changing the *nature* of participation. . . . An increasingly sophisticated and cognitively mobilized electorate is not likely to rely on voting and campaign activity as the primary means of expanding its involvement in politics."

Because protest behavior is so often considered as a special form of behavior, we should briefly comment on factors that affect this class of behavior. Potential protesters confirm the ideal type presented at the beginning of the chapter. They have been found to be high on efficacy if not trust (Marsh 1977: 123, 127). Evidence for Britain more firmly supports a positive relationship between higher levels of education and protest potential than we saw to be the case for conventional behavior (Marsh 1977: 72; Phillips 1985: 167,169; Topf 1989: 63; Young 1984: 11). However, Waterman (1988: 406) finds that "while there has been some protest among the most highly educated, students in general are not very different from their elders in a country in which the political generation gap is among the smallest." Perhaps surprisingly, it is not the disadvantaged who seem most inclined to protest (Marsh and Kaase 1979a: 127), nor is it the working class (Marsh 1977: 72–73). While class and economic conditions appear to be poor predictors of protest behavior, trade unionism remains an influential variable (Marsh and Kaase 1979a: 130; Phillips 1985: 167). Protest potential has also been found to increase with higher levels of ideological conceptualization. If so, this fact has important implications for protest in Britain which has among the lowest proportions of respondents with a high level of ideological conceptualization, and among the lowest proportions showing "ideological potential" (Klingemann 1979b: 245).

Throughout our study, one of the variables with which we have been most concerned is how greatly different levels of gross economic performance in Britain and Japan effect political attitudes and behavior in the two countries. It is tempting to hypothesize that the relative dynamism of the Japanese economy would have a positive impact on conventional participation, while the relative stagnation in Britain would provoke protest and demands for a better life. Yet we have already seen that Britons are relatively content with their personal lives despite all the bad economic news. Marsh's research bears out the conclusion that individually, Britons remain fairly isolated from their country's relative decline, and hence, are no more likely to protest than the relatively prosperous Japanese. "Very few people feel their rate of relative gratification to be in decline ... in Britain, the traditional view of the effect of economic and social threat, in the form of increased relative deprivation, upon popular militancy is not merely unfounded, it is strongly reversed" (Marsh 1977: 147, 163) suggests that such complacency may be encouraged by the personal security provided by the welfare state, as well as by a tendency to rationalization. The sense of personal well-being to be found among the British can also help to explain a relatively modest level of protest behavior amidst economic circumstances that could reasonably have been expected to generate more protest than has occurred. British avoidance of protest may be neither greater nor less than elsewhere in Europe. But when viewed against the backdrop of Britain's relatively poor economic performance and the economic crises of the 1970s, it may be worthy of note that protest is not viewed even more sympathetically than it is.

We should not ignore the possibility that there are structural factors at work in "containing" protest potential in Britain. As Kavanagh has noted, "the political-party parliamentary arena of leadership has left little scope for populism in British politics. The absence, until very recently, of referendums and of the election of party leaders by party members, the virtually assured renomination of sitting MPs by their constituency parties, and the continued refusal to allow television coverage of parliamentary debates all reinforce the traditional insulation of the elite from the electorate" (Kavanagh 1985a: 63). Vivien Hart has argued that, in effect, the dominant British political culture has imposed a strait-jacket that has inhibited Britons from even conceiving of any other, more popu-list paths to political behavior. "Both structural and cultural inhibitions may contribute to the difference between holding attitudes, expressing them openly and acting upon them. . . . There are less immediately coercive limitations, such as the political education of citizens into the perception of a limited number of legitimate modes of political action, and the actual availability of channels for expression and action, including the accessibility of organisations, institutions, personnel and the media. . . . Internalised language and norms may provide pow-erful inhibitions against the articulation of vaguely felt discontent. . . . Knowing 'how we do things' here is not enough if you want to do them differently" (Hart 1978: 34–35). The legal system is particularly unsuited for use against the gov-ernment, both for constitutional reasons and because of idiosyncracies of the litigation process that discourage citizens from going to court.

Japan

Participation in prewar Japan was very limited. Democracy was never really trusted by the ruling elite, the fledgling socialist/populist movements of the turn of the century were ruthlessly put down by the state and even when democratic political values began to take hold in the 1920s they were depreciated by the military's ability to manipulate the government. In the days of the Meiji constitu-tion, participation was not perceived as a right of the individual, but, at best, as a gift to be given or rescinded by the emperor, the only true embodiment of the will of the people.

The occupation reforms, though not organic, released a flood of pent-up par-ticipation. More female members of the Diet were elected in the very first elec-tion that granted female suffrage, April 1946, than at any time since, and union membership and labor disputes skyrocketed, but eventually the enthusiasm di-minished. SCAP's policy during the occupation was to democratize Japan and increase political participation. However, the long-term effect of the occupation may have been to limit the potential for participation. It is true that the occupa-tion reforms went a long way to institutionalize democracy in Japan. But, in order to create the conditions for democracy, the occupation also had to employ a highly centralized, autocratic bureaucracy that used coercive measures, such as censorship of the press, to rule Japan. Some would argue that the lesson learned by the Japanese was that participation in a democratic government would be infinitely safer, but only relatively more effective, than participation in the pre-war militaristic political system.

We saw in Chapter 2 that the distance between individual and polity can be clearly seen in the way both nations manifest pride in themselves. Japan has a great deal of pride in the nation but little pride in the state. The ability of the Japanese to make a sharp distinction between the political and social system, and remove themselves from the former, is aided by the traditional Japanese non-dichotomous behavioral pattern discussed in Chapter 1. In a sense, the participatory aspects of democracy are accepted on a *tatemae* level by many Japanese, while the *honne* of their actual behavior is to participate as little as possible. An example of the individual's psychological removal from the political system may be found in the passive acceptance that underlies the uncontested dominance of the LDP as the government party since 1955.

Group norms, as we have seen previously, play a greater and different role in Japanese behavior than British. These norms both inhibit and encourage participation. The spectator nature of the political culture tends to work against participation. Political activism requires community support, and "dependency on one's group and weak sense of autonomy means that Japanese citizens frequently lack the self assurance to involve themselves individually in active participatory roles" (Richardson and Flanagan 1984: 193). For example, as the citizen moves out of the local group environment, he or she may encounter difficulty in establishing necessary personal relations and networks. This problem is especially acute for issues that cut across traditional groups—such as environmental or consumer issues. Horizontal mobilization, therefore, can present a problem for the Japanese (Richardson and Flanagan 1984: 175).

Factors of which we have spoken before, namely low efficacy, low trust, and traditional acceptance of authority may combine with these norms of social behavior to reinforce the spectator approach to politics. Japan shares with Britain a low sense of efficacy as a possible motive for nonparticipation, which may be related to the dependency factor just discussed. There is little confidence in the individual's ability to change a bad law and there is little desire to become involved to the point of increasing one's ability. Since 1973, Japanese surveys actually show a steady decline in those who believe voting, demonstrations, or petitions have at least a "somewhat strong" influence on national government. Accordingly, many Japanese may feel no incentive to participate, since problems are "beyond the reach of individuals" (Richardson and Flanagan 1984: 195). The Japanese reluctance to become participants is also reinforced by the lack of trust in Japanese political institutions and by their perceived corruption and unresponsiveness (see Chapter 3). It should be noted, however, that there are significant differences among age groups. Youths are more likely to believe that their views are not reflected in policy, and the only age group in which a near majority (50 percent) believed that their views were reflected was men aged 50–70 years of age (Prime Minister's Office 1986: 9). The low trust in politicians we saw in Chapter 3, in particular, as expressed in the elite power game of factional politics, "further inhibits popular participation in politics and ill serves the public interest" (Richardson and Flanagan 1984: 182). Without a sense of efficacy, and without a trust in the responsiveness of institutions, there seems little incentive to attempt through politics to change those institutions. If politicians are perceived as corrupt and dirty, that is even more reason for not getting involved.

Richardson and Flanagan describe two types of Japanese "spectators," the traditional/rural spectator whose noninvolvement derives from deferential, personalistic and parochial orientations and the modern/urban spectator whose noninvolvement derives from disillusionment and cynicism. As Japan undergoes a wide range of value changes, from greater affluence to changing socialization patterns, more spectators move from the former group to the latter. Thus, they argue, the context and motives for noninvolvement may vary but the spectator culture continues (Richardson and Flanagan 1984: 224–35).

The view of the Japanese as "spectators" is not, however, universally shared. There are those who see Japan more in the mainstream of industrial democracies when it comes to behavior. White (1982: 173), in his study of the effect of migration on three Tokyo neighborhoods, finds that "Tokyo residents are politically quite active, despite occasional assertions that participation in Japan is low and limited to 'spectator' rather than actively participant forms." White then goes on to report survey data that show levels of nonvoting conventional participation equal to or higher than that reported above. According to Ward (1978: 70), "[v]estiges of the older practices and traditional relationships frequently appear in certain contexts, but basically the Japanese both vote and participate in interest groups to a degree comparable to that in the West. They also profess in polls and elsewhere to have a sense of their own political efficacy—that is, of the collective importance of their votes and of the influence of the electorate on government. . . . Japan now has a vastly more participant political system than was the case before the war, and in general, this degree of popular participation has produced consequences comparable to those that took place earlier in the West." In a 1983 survey, 68 percent thought that the general public should not leave politics to the politicians after elections (*Asahi Shimbun*). We have already examined, above, evidence of greater, rather than lesser, Japanese activism in certain spheres.

It is also arguable that as cynicism and apathy replace traditional motives for nonparticipation, the distinct concept of "spectator" may lose its significance. Nonparticipants in Japan, Britain, and other countries would all share a common outlook and motivation, unrelated to any distinctive characteristics of the culture. It becomes important in this regard to determine whether the "urban/spectators" retain the strong interest and knowledge of politics that is characteristic of the spectator model, or whether, like cynics and apathetics in the West, they lack even interest.

If Japan is to continue to be classified as an essentially nonparticipatory, spectator society, the seeming contradiction between a "spectator" explanation of Japanese political culture and some areas of higher participation levels must be reconciled. As we have seen, social as well as political motives stimulate participation. In Japan, the need to maintain close relations with and conformity to the group, in conjunction with the understanding that Japanese society is kept harmonious by maintaining bonds of personal obligation and loyalty to others, is

Table 5.12

Contribution to Society by Age and Sex, Japan (in percent)

Age	Sex	Want to be of use	Don't want to be of use
20–24	male	30	59
20–24	female	28	62
40–45	male	58	35
40–45	female	49	42
65–69	male	65	30
65–69	female	38	48

Source: Prime Minister's Office, 1986. *Public Opinion Survey on Society and State*: p. 5. Tokyo: Foreign Press Center.

one of the most important factors in motivating behavior—including political behavior. Indeed, Japanese participation is highest in those activities with the highest social component. This may explain why Japanese participation is higher than expected, given feelings of inefficacy, mistrust, and distance from politics. But it does not explain how, in a society where participation is driven by the desire for conformity, participation is not as high as societies in which the strength of group norms is lacking.

Many Japanese do not have a generalized sense of obligation to society as a whole, and this may further inhibit political participation. When one looks at whether the general Japanese population is oriented toward society or toward themselves as individuals, those who are society-oriented (38.3 percent) only outweigh those who are individual-oriented (35.6 percent) by a small margin. This situation also seems to be relatively stable since the early 1970s (Prime Minister's Office 1989a: 8). The Prime Minister's Office regularly conducts a survey asking people whether they want to be of use to society or whether they do not want to be of use to society. Those who answered that they want to be of use to society have increased from 45 percent to 47 percent from 1977 to 1985, and those who responded that they did not want to be of use decreased from 48 percent to 44 percent over the same period. This represents still an especially large number of people who specifically state that they do not want to be of use to society (Prime Minister's Office 1986: 8). This lack of concern with public service is even more startling when broken down by age and sex. Table 5.12 indicates that youth are the least motivated to be involved in conventional participation and public service, and that there are significant differences in participation between men and women. Among the public, especially youths and women, there is actually a much diminished sense of national service.

With so many arguments against participation, why do the Japanese participate at all? As in Britain, efficacy seems substantially linked to participation while the impact of trust is debated (White 1982: 372, 380). White finds that while widespread in Japan, cynicism has little impact on behavior, and is "almost a ritualistic affectation" (White 1982: 391). Despite a generalized lack of confidence in politics and politicians, it appears that instrumental considerations are an important motive in Japanese participation. "Apparently," concludes White, "the conviction that one can influence or get what one wants out of government is more important in goading one to try than whether or not one likes the system or those who staff it" (White 1981: 380). Ironically, citizens are even reluctant to have political wrongdoers punished because of their perceptions that, to a degree, they may share in the fruits of corruption (Richardson and Flanagan 1984: 183, 380). Although there was a strong public outcry following the Recruit scandal of the late 1980s, of the sixteen most important politicians implicated in the scandal to run for reelection in the February 1990 lower-house elections, fourteen were successful (*Mainichi Daily News* February 20, 1990: n.p.).

Another factor encouraging participation, ironically, lies in the same group orientation that we have seen inhibiting participation. One assumes that in a developed democratic society, motives for participation are expressly political— e.g., partisanship, ideological preference, issue orientation, personal gain, efficacy, or civic duty. It may be, however, that along with these political motives, we may find social motives that are also important stimuli for participation. In this case, social motivation for political participation is essentially the affiliation motive, that is, the need to maintain close relations and conformity with the group. In more concrete terms, Japanese people may feel the need to participate less for the above "political" reasons, but because they feel the pressure from their neighborhood, work, or union groups to do so. In the same context, they may vote for a particular candidate because of personal ties. The voter may come from the same town or village, may be personally obliged to someone who supports the candidate, or may have a friend or relative in the candidate's *koenkai*. Voting is an act of seeking group solidarity, not a result of "a positive orientation towards the self as a political actor" (Ward 1965: 59).

The importance of social motives for political participation may be especially dependent upon context. We saw above in Chapter 3 that in Japan efficacy is higher at the local than the national level. It should come as no surprise, then, that participation is higher on the local than the national level as well. Social motives are likely to be more important in rural, more traditional areas of Japan where the traditions of interpersonal bonds of obligation and loyalty are stronger between members of the community and nonconformity to the group brings greater punishments than in the urban areas. While most scholars seem to agree that participation on the local level is higher than that on the national level (Nakamura 1975; Richardson and Flanagan 1984; Ward 1978; Auh 1978), there is disagreement as to whether participation is higher in urban or rural areas. White implies that participation is higher in metropolitan districts as compared to rural districts (1982: 173), while Richardson and Flanagan (1984: 234) argue the opposite.

Little sense of national service inhibits participation among a majority of young Japanese, but its presence reinforces participation among many others. Particularly among elites, there is a sense of national service, which, while not precluding corruption, has always been present in modern times. It is not surprising that those who are most society-oriented, men over forty years of age, are also those who have both the greatest impact on society and the largest stake in it.

While Japanese political participation is highly motivated (including protest behavior), it is the motives for participation that most separate Japanese from Western political participation, and is most crucial to the understanding of differences between political cultures. Participation in Japan is directly related to one's obligations to the group and possible coercive measures for those who do not follow the group (Kyogoku 1987: 160). With the exception of the early student protests, most demonstrations have been centered around well-organized groups that expect their members to attend. Union members are expected to be active in the yearly spring wage struggles (*shunto*), members of the national agricultural association, Nokkyo, are expected by their peers to attend rallies and demonstrations opposing imports of American agricultural goods, and a great many of the demonstrations pit local communities—Narita, Zushi, Mutsu—against the national government.

Japan is a rapidly changing country, and one cannot assume the accepted truths about political behavior in Japan ten years ago still hold true today. There have been since the early 1960s a number of important population shifts in Japan from the countryside to the larger urban areas, from the large urban areas to suburban areas, and from the countryside to smaller and medium-sized communities. These migrations have depopulated many villages, and raised the status of others to small or medium-sized cities (Fukutake 1982: 72). There are few traditional small farms left in Japan. Most farms in Japan are part-time farms, meaning that they only depend on farming for some of their income (Calder 1989: 21). Farmers are no longer the poor country cousins, as they have higher levels of consumption, more living space and better living conditions (Fukutake 1982: 55). This means that the rural village as the traditional community is disintegrating. Today, it is less accurate to speak of a rural Japan than it is to speak instead of a regional Japan.[8] The communal, holistic nature of the traditional rural village has disappeared under the burden of greater affluence, an influx of commuting urbanites in the case of suburban communities, the growth of industrial and population centers in the case of regional city centers, and depopulation in the deserted remote communities. All of these shifts combine to bring Japan somewhat more in line with Britain, where urban/rural differences have long lacked significance as predictors of attitudes or political behavior. Although the political development theories of Lerner, Milbrath, Almond and Verba, and Inkeles do not have the same credibility that they had in the 1960s, we assume the migrations taking place in Japan should have some effect on political participation in that we assume social mobility, social modernization, and urbanization to be associated with greater opinion holding and political participation. However, White found in his study *Migration in Metropolitan Japan* that migration had no effect at all on either participation or politicization. The next question should be whether the above-described migrations will have an effect on the motives for participation.

It is difficult to tell the extent to which the "greening" and urbanization of Japan will alter political behavior. At the moment, the answers remain highly speculative. It may be the case that the traditional social motivation for Japanese conventional participation may change to a lesser degree than expected. This may be the case because although *koenkai* are generally thought to be a product of more traditional, rural areas, there is evidence to show that *koenkai* now have the highest levels of support in small- and medium-sized cities, as opposed to the towns and villages (Watanuki et al. 1986: 7). In addition, the patterns of interpersonal behavior that reinforce social motivation of political participation, e.g., personalism, and loyalty/obligation bonds, exist not only in rural villages and small towns, but also exist in many contexts within the highly modern urban environment, such as urban neighborhoods, large corporations, the bureaucracy, and unions. One might say that Japanese society has built its reputation on maintaining these traditional patterns of interpersonal behavior while modernizing. There seems to be no reason to believe that this pattern will change in the near future.

Summary and Conclusions

We have found little persuasive evidence that participation, in the most familiar conventional or unconventional modes, has increased in any fundamental way in Britain. It is undeniable that fewer Britons turn out to vote than forty years ago, a trend uncharacteristic of most democratic states. But the change has been gradual, and no convincing explanation has been offered for it. People are no more inclined to campaign or to attend demonstrations than they were in the past, despite the resurrection of a "third force" in party politics during the 1980s. Strong partisan identification and party membership are down—suggesting a decline in the mobilizing role of parties. However, interest group formation and group memberships, and individually initiated contacts with officials are up— perhaps suggesting an increased role for "cognitive mobilization." Those forms of participation that do show an increase tend, interestingly, to be in those areas that require greater effort and political sophistication. Certainly, however, there is nothing to indicate a clear move in the direction of participatory democracy. If participatory democracy is understood to imply significant direct citizen input into the formulation of policy, that is not the direction Britain is going. The British increasingly participate in ways that defend their own personal or family interests. When it comes to public policy, the traditions of representative government die hard, and the impact of conventions and traditions are carried on in old structures, procedures, and even the "cognitive maps" and language of politics in Britain. The evidence we have examined tends to suggest the prevalence of conventional activities such as petitions and contacts with MPs. The impact of traditional values on contemporary political practice and change probably receives more attention in analyses of Japan, but it has been important in Britain as well.

Undeniably, however, recent survey and other evidence point to change. There does appear to be an increased willingness to approach government, at least in conventional ways, and this attitudinal change has been reflected in a greater frequency of citizen contacts. Some of the increased pressure for participation has been institutionalized by widening the scope of consultation to include new interest groups, and by providing new avenues for grievances. The landscape of mass politics has changed most clearly when it comes to the opening up of new channels for citizens to raise their individual problems and grievances with government. The increased intervention of the state in individual welfare matters, land use, and transportation has manifested itself not only in increased citizen reliance on MPs, but in the appearance of new channels such as the parliamentary ombudsman, the European Human Rights Commission, and, most important, the myriad of local citizens' aid organizations and in increased emphasis by MPs on constituency services. There is no doubt that citizens are voicing more complaints through a greater number of channels than before. Local participatory organizations may replace (but have not yet) some of the traditional importance of the MP as the conduit from citizen to government. However, an important qualification is that increased contacts between citizens and government, whether mediated or not, seem to reflect individual concerns rather than an effort to influence policy making.

Britain faces a number of challenges to its constitutional order—not revolutionary ones, but evolutionary ones, brought about by changes in the internal and international environment. What our review shows is that changes in mass behavior are not the most urgent among these challenges. Political dissent, protest, and violence is not new to Britain. An increase would not be unprecedented, nor should it necessarily give rise to fears for the system. As we noted in Chapter 4, Britain enjoys a diverse and extensive amount of support from its citizens, and this remains true both in the face of low levels of participation, and occasional outbursts of protest.

Japanese political behavior, too, is changing as the society urbanizes, democracy becomes accepted as a native tradition, and modern values impinge upon traditional values. As a result of these changes, participant orientations are more prevalent than in the past, and some observers have questioned the continued validity of the "spectator" model of Japanese behavior. But, in a comparative perspective, the authors believe that Japan still lags behind the United States and many European countries other than Britain in participant orientation. There seems to be little doubt that in some conventional forms—voting, membership in koenkai, campaign donations—political participation in Japan is often higher than in the West, and is consistently higher than or roughly equal to political participation in Britain. The apparent contradiction between the "spectator" model and the reality of areas of relatively high rates of participation may lie in the high social component in motives for participation.

There is considerable academic debate over whether increased protest behavior, reflecting the high levels of alienation, is likely in Japan, and whether increased protest threatens to destabilize the young Japanese democracy. Richardson and Flanagan (1984: 19, 27) conclude that "analysis of political disaffection in Japan would suggest that there is a high and perhaps rising potential for civil disobedience and political instability in Japan." White argues, to the contrary, that protest behavior does not appear to constitute a destabilizing force in Japanese politics. "If the cynics are widely dispersed in society," he says, "or located in social groups which for one or another reason are very unlikely to indulge in radical behavior, then even high levels of alienation may be little cause for worry" (White 1981: 375, 387). White (1981: 387) considers that in Japan the greater threat is from inactive alienates, not potential protestors. It is the absence of serious internal conflict in modern Japanese history, not its presence, that has disruptive potential for democracy in Japan. In order to judge the potential threat to stability from protest, two additional factors need to be kept in mind. The first is the ritualistic character of much of Japanese protest. Such protest may not undermine stability at all. On the other hand, should protest break out of its ritual context, it is possible that disorder may be more threatening to Japan than similar levels of disorder would be in Britain.

What comparisons can be made? In the end it would appear that the levels of both conventional and nonconventional participation are not so dissimilar in Britain and Japan, although one polity may be more inclined to participate in certain forms than the other. What does differentiate the two are the traditions of participation from which the contemporary habits of participation are drawn. Tradition and the inertia of passive citizen orientations may have contributed to the slow growth of participatory democracy in both Britain and Japan. But where democratic ideas, norms, and institutions grew up indigenously in Britain, Japan has had to approach the implementation of democratic practices from the "outside." This is true both in the sense that norms of political openness and democratic politics are relatively new to Japan, and in the sense that they are in a sense imposed. When the "alien" constitution is considered, Japan's adjustment to democratic norms and institutions is really quite impressive.

The levels of interest in politics, often, but not necessarily, a prerequisite for participation, are actually higher in Japan than in Britain, though in contrast to Britain, interest in local affairs exceeds interest in national affairs. Both the Japanese and the British are avid consumers of information, but the Japanese interest in politics does not drive them to participate at levels that might seem indicated. For the Japanese, there is a decided contrast between high levels of political awareness, and low levels of involvement, leading to the characterization of "spectator." In contrast to Japan, British levels of interest are consistent with levels of participation. If there is a seeming contradiction in the British case, it is that low interest and involvement in politics are found together with pride in polity and history, and somewhat higher than average trust in at least several of its institutions.

Somewhat surprisingly, in view of the "spectator" model, Japanese participation is in some cases greater than that in Britain. Both Japan and Britain have relatively high-to-moderate voting rates, participate less frequently than citizens in many other industrial democracies in other forms of participation, and exhibit a low propensity to political violence. A few differences emerge, however. The Japanese are more active than the British in attending meetings, working in a campaign, and in supporting boycotts; and the British are more active than the Japanese in signing petitions, attending demonstrations, and as we have seen, in making individual approaches to officials. If we concentrate on group memberships, and activity within those groups, the British are more likely to belong to horizontal, voluntary groups that are issue-specific such as ban the bomb or environmental groups, and to be spurred spontaneously to political activity by events around them. The Japanese, on the other hand, are more likely to belong to enterprise-based organizations or to nonpolitical organizations, and to engage in ritual protest behavior in a variety of institutionalized demonstrations, such as the annual *shunto*. Thus, to a limited degree, there may be a higher potential in Britain for participation that is intended to influence political outcomes than in Japan. The hierarchical nature of holistic norms in Japan have made horizontal citizen mobilization more difficult than in Britain.

Within the range of conventional activities, Flanagan observes, the differences that do emerge between Japan and Britain tend to reflect both the stronger Japanese preference for group activities, and the less-developed tradition of accountability of elected officials. While politically active Britons will rely more on individual initiatives such as writing elected representatives or the press, their Japanese counterparts strongly prefer to act through a "formal, organized group" (Flanagan 1978: 157). Those British who participate prefer informal group activities such as organizing petitions, writing letters, or attending meetings. Where the British might write their MP, the Japanese will be more likely to contact bureaucrats. The frequency of Japanese membership in *koenkai* represents a distinct area of participation which could be interpreted as making the Japanese more participant than the British.

In both countries those who protest are those who have a higher sense of efficacy than the general public, but it seems that, given the relatively low levels of efficacy in both countries, protest behavior should not be extensive. The relatively low level of protest activity may have been abetted by the lack of institutions designed to transmit discontent. Take, for example, the legal system. Compared to the United States, the institutions available to be used by Japanese and British citizens to bring litigation against the government are relatively few, rules for using the courts complex and confusing, and the political and social support for that litigation relatively weak. Finally, there should be no underestimating the pull of inertia. In both Britain and Japan, traditional ideas, assumptions and procedures for doing things also make it difficult for individuals to conceive doing things in a new way with which they lack experience.

As we saw in Chapter 1, an important difference between Britain and Japan is the rich legacy of political philosophy in Britain—a tradition that includes collectivist and individualist (if not populist) elements—and its near absence in Japan. Spencer's and Mill's liberalism provide ample justification for individual resistance to state encroachments, and the tradition of individual civil disobedience and protest is still much more prevalent than in Japan. Japan is a perfect anti-Millian society, where there are almost no traditional social or philosophic values that support the strong individual who wants to row against the tide. Political protest behavior is perceived as legitimate in both Britain and Japan, but only in Britain is it a part of the intellectual and political consciousness. It is possible that the absence of an intellectual grounding for protest behavior might make it more difficult to control, suggesting that perhaps the ritualization of protest is a means of social control in the absence of intellectual rules of the game for protest.

If motives for either compliant or participant support are instrumental, at least in part, then the ability of the state to offer rewards should affect the levels of support. Yet so far, at least, there has been little evidence that Britain's relatively weak international economic performance, or Japan's relatively strong performance, have affected the levels and modes of political participation. What is striking is that when we look at questions of trust, efficacy, and most important, support, Britain comes out better, or no worse than Japan. It would appear that Britain has been able to sustain support through hard times and declining instrumental rewards. In view of what many see as a steady, long-term economic decline, extending back to the nineteenth century, the ability of Britain to maintain relatively stable levels of both compliant and participant support is striking. Conversely, if the Japanese exhibit comparatively lower levels of citizen support for the political system during the very best of times, what are the implications for any future economic crisis? It is possible that Japan could face its own "legitimation crisis," as instrumental rewards stagnate or are perceived either to fall or to be unfairly distributed. But to the extent that present legitimacy is traditional, pragmatic, or normative, rather than instrumental, that support could remain stable.

The apparently negligible impact of economic factors on British and Japanese participation rates gives rise to a final comparison. An extraordinary thing about the Japanese and British is that they participate in politics despite demonstrably low levels of trust and efficacy. A consistently large proportion of citizens of both countries express a lack of confidence in their ability to be heard or to influence government, and yet, as we have seen, they vote and, increasingly, participate in other forms of conventional political activity. As Topf's analysis of Britain shows, there are far more people willing to attempt to influence government than there are people who think their efforts will do any good. This phenomenon can be explained if we consider the importance of expressive, rather than instrumental, explanations for participation. This is not so surprising in the case of Japan, where group norms have played such a central role in motivating participation. In the past, "partisan mobilization" might have supplied an analogous motivator in Britain. But with such low levels of trust, the decline of partisan identification, and the putative rise of "cognitive mobilization," it is a bit puzzling why citizens should be increasingly disposed toward participation—especially conventional participation.

Notes

1. As Klingemann points out, responses concerning interest in politics may be difficult to interpret because responses are "situation bound," and may vary widely over time and circumstances (1979a: 264). Nonetheless, reported levels of political interest among Britons have generally remained quite stable.

2. Before the poll tax replaced the property-based tax in 1990.

3. Patrick Dunleavy has argued, on the contrary, that "the current one-sidedness of Fleet Street is a major force undermining the fabric of democratic politics in Britain" (1985: 86).

4. White has found links between trust, efficacy, and behavior are weak in Japan (White 1981: 376), but efficacy is more important than trust, instrumentalism is more important than normative considerations; and trust and efficacy in combination is the key determinant of participation (White 1981: 380). For Britain, Topf (1989: 72–73) has argued that longstanding political cynicism does not imply a "behavioural disposition" in either direction, either toward apathy or toward political action.

5. Literally millions of cases are heard each year by various agencies and offices, and as many of the issues are private, and have little to so with citizen-government relations except the fact that a public agency has been sought out for assistance, only a portion could truly be considered political participation. Citizens seeking help in their marriage, or for drug or alcohol problems are no more political participants than members of social organizations.

6. This, and much of the data in the following section, is taken from Watanuki et al. *Electoral Behavior in the 1983 Japanese Elections*. Institute of International Relations, Sophia University: 1986. The book is an analysis of the Japanese election Study of 1983 and includes the responses of three sections of a panel survey, the first taken following the July 1983 House of Councillors election, the second taken before the December 1983 House of Representatives election, and the third taken after the December 1983 House of Representatives election. Each panel consisted of a sample of approximately 1700 respondents.

7. The Watanuki study found, however, that the election campaign had little effect in stimulating interest in politics.

8. William Kelly in a paper entitled "Rice and Ritual: Cultural Politics and Agricultural Policies in New Middle Class Japan," delivered to the Association of Asian Studies 1989 annual meeting.

6

Electoral Choice

In Chapter 5, we considered the gamut of political participation in Britain and Japan, including the factors that led people in Britain and Japan to participate, or not to participate, in voting. Chapter 6 turns to what is arguably a more important question, and most certainly a more studied one—why people vote for one candidate or party over another. It is in voting that most citizens find their voice in determining the character of national leadership, though this act alone usually has quite minimal effect in communicating voter opinion about the political agenda.

Many theories, often in conflict, have been put forward to explain voter choice within Britain and within Japan. This fact makes reliable voting analysis a daunting task, but it renders comparison even more daunting. As in the case of other aspects of political culture, we must take into account the further consideration that the different traditions and vocabulary of Japanologists and Europeanists may contribute to the confusion. Notwithstanding these caveats, we hope to cast light on the similarities and differences in Japanese and British voting behavior. Some comparisons are fairly clear-cut. For example, territorial voting patterns have become quite prominent in Britain but remain insignificant in Japan, and while class still lies close to the heart of British voting, it is of much less salience in the case of Japan.

Most important, however, are the contrasting roles of group processes in influencing the vote in Britain and Japan. Although the dominant British voting model has stressed the impact of occupational class and socialization upon individual party identification and voting choice, in fact, very little is explained about how groups influence their members' voting choices—"who says what to whom with what electoral effects" (Harrop 1988: 41, 58). Japanese voting theories, on the other hand, place the impact of group norms and personal obligations at the center of voting behavior, and in Japan other group memberships than social class have played a far more prominent and direct role in explaining voting behavior than is the case in Britain. The groups that influence voting are both more numerous and more varied than in Britain. And in Japan the nexus between the group context and individual voter's choice is quite direct and personalistic. For many Japanese, the choice of candidate represents the conscious discharge of personal obligation, not necessarily to the candidate, but to a relative, local influential, co-worker, or a friend with links to the candidate. While explanations of Japanese voting behavior often focus on the nature and mechanism of group influence, in the case of Britain, they do so far less frequently.

There are important similarities as well as differences in the voting behavior of the two countries. For example, in neither the dominant British voting models nor the dominant Japanese models has issue voting played a very large part. At the same time, observers point to an increase in issue voting in both countries in recent years. Even where differences between Japanese and British voting behavior appear wide, we must be careful not to make too much of the dichotomy or to attribute them exclusively to cultural differences. Even with respect to the group effects in Japan, it is clear that analogous, if less-well-understood effects operate in Britain. In both the traditional "class" or "union-membership" voting models, and the more recent "social milieu," "contagion," and "neighbourhood" voting models, a mechanism of "face-to-face" group influence is believed to be at work. We cannot yet be sure whether the British "social milieu" models, superficially similar as they are in some respects to Japanese voting models, represent the appearance of a new voting choice mechanism in Britain, or merely the revelation of a traditional pattern.

In this chapter, we will continue the idea, discussed in the case of general participation, that both "instrumental" and "expressive" factors may account for many aspects of behavior. This is by no means the only distinction that can be offered, but it helps to capture much of the academic debate in the West over voting behavior, and it is a useful starting point for a discussion of Japanese voting behavior. Expressive theories—based on class, social-cleavage, or social-psychological factors—stress the decisive impact on voting behavior of social environment, and in particular early, adult, or cumulative lifelong socialization experiences (Rose 1989: 169). Individual characteristics such as class attributes, and group processes such as pressures for conformity from parents, friends, and workmates, reinforce each other to root party preference firmly in the individual psyche (Heath et al. 1985: 8). Once formed, party identification is believed to be increasingly durable. Individual election issue preferences are an effect of class, or as Budge and McKay (1988: 99) put it in the British case, class plays the role of " 'fixating' most electors on certain policy areas by rendering these of prime importance for the individual and his family." Electoral choice is viewed as fairly deterministic, allowing the individual voter only limited scope to change his or her vote in response to short-term considerations of interest. Voting from this perspective is a reflexive act. Expressive factors are more likely to stabilize voting patterns, as individuals repeat their voting choice in election after election. In Britain, the key group referents are the traditional working and middle classes, while in Japan, traditional occupational classes have been accorded little weight. Those other group affiliations that cut across traditional class lines may be more important. The candidate support groups, or *koenkai*, to which we referred earlier, territorially oriented groups, like the *jiban*, or the workplace may be more influential in Japan than Britain.

Some theorists now entertain the notion that new production and consumption cleavages have replaced the old occupational class cleavages as the relevant variables (Dunleavy and Husbands 1985). In these latter models, manual/non-manual occupational classifications are replaced by a scheme dividing interests according to "market situation" or degree of "control over working conditions," and the resulting "differing degrees of support for government intervention and free enterprise" (Heath et al. 1985: 14–19). These theories have been applied to Britain, but have received little attention in Japanese voting studies. How important these new cleavages are in determining voting behavior still remains to be seen. In any case, the occupational and social structure in both Britain and Japan is changing, and these changes should be expected to have some impact on expressive voting behaviors.

Instrumental—or rational—models, on the other hand, stress the role of calculations of individual self-interest and issue preferences on electoral choice. Voter choice is conscious and deliberate, not reflexive or deterministic. Voting is a means by which the individual attempts to maximize his or her utility. Rational or instrumental models stress the ability of voters to gauge candidates, party positions or images in terms of their own self-interest. These theories hold that voting is "analogous to other consumer choices and involves deliberate comparisons between the competing qualities of the various packages on offer" (Heath et al. 1985: 9; see Himmelweit et al. 1981). In this model, issue positions, performance, and perceived leaders' abilities, as well as the media's communication of information and values, affect voting behavior. The precise mechanism by which voters exercise their rationality is elusive. It is unclear what salience the individual voter gives to his or her evaluation of comparative past performance of parties or candidates, personal or national economic well-being, issue positions, ideology, or calculation of expected future benefits. It is likely that to the extent voters are rational, their behavior combines these different considerations. While expressive voting is said to be conducive to stability, instrumental voting is said to produce volatility, as the factors that influence individual voter choice will vary considerably from election to election. Where expressive factors are strong, there should be less scope for instrumental factors. Where expressive factors are weak, there should be relatively greater scope for instrumental factors.

It is most probable that voting behavior in both Japan and Britain represents a hybrid of expressive and rational voting models in three senses: (1) the individual voter may act out of mixed motives in variable proportions from election to election, (2) different voters may act out of different motives, and (3) what is perceived as rational for the individual may be strongly shaped by class circumstances and associated lifestyle. Voters are neither fully independent of, nor prisoners of, their socialization or the groups to which they belong. Speaking of Britain, Heath et al. (1985: 10) observe that:

> Any act of voting must involve both expressive and instrumental elements, and we very much doubt whether the balance between these two elements has changed much in the course of this century.... On the one hand, social class, housing, education and other aspects of social structure constitute the sources of group interests. These interests provide a potential for political action. On the other hand, the political parties may help to shape group values and foster an awareness of their interests. They can influence the extent to which the potentials are realized. It is the interaction between the social and the political that determines how people vote.

Expressive factors represent underlying causes that operate over the long term, while instrumental factors represent short-term, or proximate causes (Kavanagh 1985a: 105). For example, socialization experiences may predispose a voter toward the Labour Party in Britain or the LDP in Japan, but issues can reinforce, or, should they be important enough, counteract that predisposition. Whiteley's "inertia-shock" model, which captures the interplay of expressive and instrumental voting forces, is one example of a mixed voting model.[1] Voters normally will not override their sociologically conditioned "inertia of party loyalty." But major events and issues can bring about significant volatility. According to the "inertia-shock" model, "public opinion is a relatively inert system which changes in response to innovations or shocks ... such as the split in the Labour Party in 1981, and the Falklands War of 1982" (Whiteley 1986: 57). Such "shocks" may occur as part of the election campaign and the build-up to it. The "inertia-shock" model, unlike the earlier "swing" model, concedes more scope for change to even loyal party supporters, if the issue shock is sufficient. Dealignment, or a weakening of the "inertia" factor, correspondingly increases the potential influence of short-term factors in voting choice (Kavanagh 1985a: 109). In Japan, voting patterns following major scandals may suggest something like the inertia-shock model in operation.

The dichotomy between expressive and instrumental voting is challenged specifically in the Japanese case. The "social network" model described by Richardson and Flanagan, Watanuki, and others suggests that many Japanese voters' decision to vote in response to considerations of group loyalty is both expressive and rational. While it may be true that politicians manipulate personal relationships, rather than issues, to gain votes, it is hard to fit such behavior very precisely into an "expressive" straitjacket. Such voting appears to be quite different from the automatic voting attributed to Labour and Conservative loyalists in

Britain. Another factor militating against interpreting Japanese voting through the lens of "expressive" models is the relatively recent appearance of the main Japanese parties. It would seem unlikely that childhood socialization could have played a very direct role in shaping party preference, at least for millions of older Japanese (though some effect from socialization into identification with conservative prewar antecedents is possible).

In Britain the act of voting in national elections involves a choice between parties, rather than individuals. The candidate's name does appear on the ballot, but the vote is usually cast for his or her party. The 1969 change in the electoral law permitting a candidate's party affiliation to appear on the ballot only recognized the de facto centrality of party to voter choice (Norton 1984: 82). There is little room for the maverick MP, free to tailor electoral promises, or parliamentary votes, to his or her constituency. While voters express an abstract preference for candidates who will be familiar with and defend local interests, and while parties tend to consider how well a candidate will represent constituency interests (J. Marsh 1985: 77, 84), residency requirements for candidate MPs have been notable for their absence. Thus, as we look at motives for voting in Britain, we will be principally concerned with the voter's "party" vote.

In Japan, by contrast, the act of voting in national elections depends upon an individual's ties to the candidates as much as, if not more than, his or her attitudes toward the parties. Voters must be able to write the name of the candidate of their choice on the ballot. Thus name recognition, if not familiarity, are critical factors, and tend to emphasize local connections and the local campaign. Although Diet members are no more free than their British counterparts to establish individual policy positions that may favor their constituents, they are expected to a far greater degree to develop personal ties to their constituents and even to deliver favors.

Electoral Structure and the Vote

Before turning to the debate about the motives for choice, we should briefly look at the ways in which the electoral system itself can structure voter choice. Although the two systems have similarities, Britain's first-past-the-post, single-member district system affects electoral behavior quite differently from Japan's single nontransferable vote (SNTV) system. Britain's winner-take-all system has been quite effective in manufacturing parliamentary majorities over the years, and has encouraged party voting. On the other hand, it has tended to discourage the emergence of competitive new parties, which have trouble gaining a foothold (footholds count for nothing where the majority rules) in Parliament. Even with their excellent showing at the polls in both the 1983 and 1987 elections, the Alliance parties proved unable to win seats on anything like a proportional basis. Despite coming in second in 1983 in more constituencies than Labour and proving to have appeal in all regions, the plurality election system ensured that parties with stronger regional concentrations would perform better at winning seats. Persistent inability to win tends to undermine third party claims to be a real governing alternative. This phenomenon certainly contributed to the decline of the Liberal and Social Democratic parties after the 1987 elections. Party discipline, a necessary correlate of government by responsible majority, also tends to influence the vote by reducing the power of individual MPs to offer rewards to their constituents. The personal vote, quite important in Japan, is of minor but growing importance in Britain.

The SNTV system has quite different effects. In the Japanese House of Representatives multiple-member district system, voters cast but one vote, however many seats are being contested. Though not a decisive factor in voting, the electoral system does tend to reinforce the existing social patterns whose more substantial impact we examine below (Stockwin 1983: 222). Multiple seat constituencies have a low "threshold of inclusion," and candidates may win seats with far lower voting percentages than the Alliance parties in Britain garnered in the 1980s (Lijphart 1984: 210). Much of the effect of the system on voting is indirect, in that it influences party nominating strategies. In multiple-member districts, seats may be lost either by nominating too many candidates, who split the vote and allow smaller parties to win, or by nominating too popular a candidate, who siphons off too much of the party vote. Parties thus seek to optimalize their chances of winning seats by nominating fewer candidates than the maximum the constituency might allow, and by nominating candidates who will produce a relatively balanced party vote. This conservatism reduces the chances of spreading the party vote too thinly, but it also tends to have a limiting affect on voter choice (Lijphart et al. 1986: 161). Particularly for the LDP, which is the party most capable of capturing multiple seats, the election is as much intraparty as interparty. The result is to reinforce a more candidate-centered electoral process than in party-centered Britain, and a more decentralized campaign (Stockwin 1983: 220–21).

At the time of this writing, the LDP had introduced sweeping electoral reforms which would reduce the number of seats in the House of Representatives from 512 to 471, and replace the multiple member district system with 300 seats from single member districts and 171 seats to be allocated by proportional representation. The final reform package, the timing of the reforms, and their ultimate success may not be determined for some time, however, as both the opposition parties and some members of the LDP are opposed to the reforms. The introduction of single member districts will undoubtedly favor the LDP, but the seats of individual LDP members may be lost through redistricting.

Expressive Factors

For both Britain and Japan, it has generally been considered that issues, or instrumental considerations, have not been the principal driving force behind individual voting decisions. Instead, what we have called expressive factors, conditioned by social environment, tend to be of primary importance. These factors, however, differ between Britain and Japan. We shall examine those that have been most often identified with voting behavior in either or both of the two countries, namely: social class, party identification, group process (or personalism), regional and local influences, housing tenancy, race, gender, and age.

Social Class and Party Identification

While not denying that individual voters consider and weigh issues and performance when they vote, the dominant schools of British electoral studies have largely relegated voter choice to the position of artifact of the social environment. Expressive theories of voting have long held the field (Butler and Stokes 1969, 1974; Heath et al. 1985), and among these, class has been the star variable. Most voting behavior is explained in terms of social or occupational class.

The predominant view until quite recently was that "class is the basis of British party politics" (Pulzer 1967: 98), with middle and working class Britons casting their vote for their "natural" class party, either Conservative or Labour, in a two-party, two-class system. Congruence between Labour and the manual occupations of the working class, and the Conservatives and the nonmanual occupations of the middle class, characterized a system of class/party alignment. In the elections of the 1960s, two-thirds of voters on the manual and nonmanual occupational classifications voted for their "natural" party (Scarbrough 1987: 219). In this environment, the "swing" model held that a large majority of voters cast their ballots for their class party in election after election. Relatively few voters switched, and most of those who did engaged in cautious one-step shifts from one of the major parties to nonvoting, or to a third party, or from non-voting to a new party, rather than from one major party to the other. Election outcomes were determined by these "floating" voters in the middle, not the great blocs of loyal Conservative and Labour voters. Thus most voters were seen as shaped by their socialization into a class pattern of voting. Issues were not without importance, but voters' issue preferences reflected class.

Budge and McKay (1988: 99) explain the relationship between class and voting as a process by which class fixates "most electors on certain policy areas by rendering these of prime importance for the individual and his family." "For example," they point out, "an unskilled labourer in the North of England hovering on the fringe of the poverty line, is likely to be concerned with welfare benefits to the exclusion of all else. Unswayed by any issues coming up in a particular election, such a person votes Labour consistently, since in all conceivable circumstances Labour will extend welfare more than the Conservatives, and this is crucial to the well-being both of himself and his family." As long as voting decisions were tied to relatively inert class identities, voting patterns in Britain were remarkably stable. Such movements as occurred were viewed as

Table 6.1

Changing Profiles of British Voters, 1974–1983 (in percent)

	1974	1979	1983	Change 1979–1983
Sex				
Male	48	51	48	−3
Female	52	49	52	+3
Age				
18–24	11	12	13	+1
25–34	16	21	21	0
35–54	35	31	32	+1
55+	38	36	34	−2
Class				
ABC (middle class; white collar and professional)	35	35	40	+5
C2 (skilled working class)	32	33	31	−2
DE (unskilled working class)	33	32	29	−3
Trade Union membership				
Yes	28	30	25	−5
No	72	70	75	+5
Area				
North (incl. Scotland)	—	37	35	−2
Midlands (incl. Wales)	—	24	24	0
South	—	39	41	+2
Housing				
Owner occupier	50	52	58	+6
Council (local authority)	53 (*sic*)	35	29	−6

Source: Robert Worcester, 1984. "The Polls: Britain at the Polls, 1945–83." *Public Opinion Quarterly* 48: Table 2, p. 826. © The University of Chicago Press. Used with permission.

generational shifts, reflecting changed socializing environments. The fact that upwards of a third of working-class people voted Tory was seen in the 1960s as a phenomenon of great interest, in that it departed from the expected class mold. "Class" was not an adequate explanation for the votes of these "working class Tories" (McAllister and Mughan 1987: 48), but it was accepted for most other voters. For this simple model however, it would be important that, as Table 6.1 shows, the proportion of working class Britons has been falling, while the proportion of middle-class Britons has been rising. If class were equivalent to vote, that would seem to be bad news for the Labour Party. As we shall see, however, changes in class composition have been accompanied by a greater volatility and complexity in party identification and voting patterns.

"Because party allegiance is often learnt in the home and is thus in a social class milieu," writes Kavanagh (1985a: 107), "it is difficult to separate the influence of class and partisanship" on voting. Nevertheless, party identification is usually viewed as an important influence on voter choice in Britain. Party identification refers to the voter's feelings of loyalty to a particular party, not to his or her decision to vote for that party in a particular election. Traditionally, however, party vote and party identification have been highly congruent in Britain. That is, voters consistently voted for the party with which they identified, or to which they felt loyal. Kavanagh (1985a: 106) observes that "The strong party identifiers, compared with other identifiers, are more likely to agree with their parties' policies, vote, participate in politics, and believe in the usefulness of the electoral process. They are . . . likely to remain loyal, however unpopular the party is." Class was thought to be the medium which bonded the voter both to association with the party and its program, and to the act of voting for the party.[2] Party identity was thought to be established, not through the perceived confluence of party programs and individual voter self-interest, but through early socialization experiences. Parents' class and party identification were believed to be the major determinant of their childrens' later identification and voting behavior. Party identification may be further shaped by the socializing experiences of young adulthood—e.g. the Labour converts of the 1930s and 1940s. Once established, party identification tends to exert an increasingly powerful influence on the voter as he or she ages (Dalton 1988: 182).

Strong party identification—"my party right or wrong"—is a bit like strong patriotism—"my country right or wrong." Even in recent years, amidst talk of decline of support for party, both the Labour and Conservative parties have benefited from votes cast by supporters who disagree with key elements of their programs. Stability, or inertia, is the rule, as "most voters are unwilling to abandon their preferred party in response to short term changes in the economy" (Whiteley 1986: 58). And even when they do, there is a "homing tendency" that brings them back to the fold (Harrop 1988: 36).

Over the past generation, views of voting in Britain have changed in a way that challenges both the class and party identification models. There is widespread agreement that (1) the Labour-Conservative duopoly has eroded and that the old two-class, two-party model no longer fits reality, (2) conventional notions of class have lost much of their predictive value for voting behavior, and (3) the national electorate is no longer territorially homogeneous (Scarbrough 1987: 219–20). In the 1987 parliamentary elections, notes Rose (1989: 167), "less than half the electorate voted as would be predicted by their class." Class size and composition have changed along with the rise of public sector employment, the decline in size of the old industrial proletariat, and changing proportions among the traditional occupational grades. Budge and McKay (1988: 79) note a "significant decline . . . in manual workers' willingness to identify with the working

Table 6.2

Between and Within Class Divisions of the Vote, 1987

	Percent of Electorate	Con	Labour	Alliance
Middle Class	39	52	20	26
Solid Middle	16	56	17	26
Lower Middle	23	50	23	26
Working Class	61	37	39	21
Skilled	30	44	33	21
Semiskilled; unskilled	31	31	45	21

Source: R. Rose, 1989. *Politics in England*, 5th ed: Table V1.4, p. 167. Glenview, IL: Harper Collins. Reprinted with permission of Harper Collins Publishers.

class, which has declined from 46 per cent in the 1960s to 39 per cent today. Non-manual workers are more inclined than previously to identify with the middle class."

Furthermore, despite Britain's relatively poor economic performance, affluence has spread in patterns that cut across old class divisions. It remains true that the greater the number of class characteristics a voter possesses, the more likely he or she is to vote for the appropriate "class party." A small minority of the British conform to any ideal set of class characteristics (Rose 1986c: 174). These factors are eroding old notions of class, and with them, the old class-party nexus. The consequence is that the Labour and Conservative parties are less able to win votes based on traditional class voting patterns. Sarlvik and Crewe (1983) observe that "The boundaries of the traditional social bases of the two major parties are being blurred and, as they have come to be seen as less significant, they have become easier to transgress" (cited in Scarbrough 1987: 221). Other parties, such as the Liberal Democrats, are the beneficiaries.

The fortunes of British parties are seen to parallel, if not to depend on, the above changes in class composition and loyalty (Scarbrough 1987: 221). The diminution of voter identification with both Labour and Conservatives is known as partisan dealignment. Denver finds that a modest decline, from 81 percent to 70 percent, occurred in the proportion identifying with either the Labour or Conservative parties between 1964 and 1983. Others have cited a more significant decline (Norton 1984: 90). But the drop has been steepest among strong identifiers—from 40 percent to 23 percent—over the same period (Denver 1987c: 239). Alt (1984: 300) calls the decline of strong identifiers "precipitous." Heath and Topf (1987: 51) tend to stress the emergence of greater volatility, as "support for the political parties seems to fluctuate widely from month to month, and even week to week."

The net result of class and party dealignment is that the old social cleavages model no longer appears as compelling as it once did (Denver 1987c: 239;

Scarbrough 1987: 220). As "the stabilizing factors" of class and party have weakened, voting behavior has become more volatile (Kavanagh 1985a: 109). The exception to the pattern seems to be among nonwhite voters, who still exhibit strong party (Labour) loyalty, with 81 percent indicating that they always vote for the same party (Charlot 1985: 149). Party dealignment is seen to have seriously eroded the partisan basis for voting choice over the past thirty years. Dealignment seems to affect voters regardless of age (Clarke and Stewart 1984: 695).

Recent elections suggest the extent of change within the traditional class bases of the Conservative and Labour parties. Some "new" members of the middle class—public sector, white-collar trade unionists have been defecting from the Conservatives, while more affluent, home-owning manual workers have been defecting from Labour. Conservatives have been losing votes among the British intelligentsia and public-sector employees, who in the 1980s defected to the Social Democrats and Liberals. Middle-class government workers can no longer be relied upon to vote Conservative (Alt 1984: 305). The decline of traditional working-class deference, and the loss of the traditional advantage among women voters, further contribute to a softening of the Conservative base. These losses have more than been compensated for, however, by Conservative gains among skilled workers and working-class homeowners. The "new working class" of private-sector laborers who own their own homes, cars, and telephones are more likely to vote Conservative than those who lack these characteristics (Kavanagh 1985a:112). How permanent these "cross-class" loyalties will prove, however, still remains to be seen, even after more than 13 years of Conservative government.

Evidence from recent elections supports the view that the class composition of support for the two main parliamentary parties has indeed changed. In 1987, the 36 percent Tory share of the manual workers' vote "was the largest for any postwar election" (Crewe 1987: 53). The much smaller middle class sharply divided its 1987 vote, with nearly two-thirds of those in the private sector voting Conservative, but only 44 percent of those in the public sector (Crewe 1987: 53). On balance, the 1987 election results suggest that the Conservatives still narrowly qualify as a "class" party, especially among the upper strata of the middle class (see Table 6.2).

Not even this cautious a claim can be made for Labour. If one accepts the traditional measures of working class, it is hard not to conclude that the Labour Party's class base has seriously eroded, rendering it no longer the party of choice for a majority of working-class Britons. Not only has the working-class Tory vote reached record levels, but, more significantly, the Labour Party no longer can count on a majority of working-class votes (see Table 6.2). Labour's vote was still largely working class, "but the working class was no longer largely Labour" (Crewe 1987: 54). If the Conservatives are marginally a "class" party, it would seem that Labour has virtually ceased to be a class party, even among what some call its "core identifiers."[3] It cannot help that, shifts in allegiance aside, the traditional working class is an ever-shrinking proportion of the British population (Table 6.1). Even if the "homing tendency" noted by Harrop should materialize, Labour will need new recruits from outside its traditional class territory if it is to rebound electorally. Ironically, while recruits to the middle-class, white-collar unions of government workers are increasingly likely to vote Labour, working-class defectors from the old manual trade unions are more likely to vote Tory. As Table 6.2 shows, the Conservatives were the party of choice for skilled manual workers in 1987. McAllister and Rose (1984: 7) have even concluded that "The 1983 election broke the mould by denying Labour's claim as the opposition party" based on the greater proportion of second place constituency finishes by Alliance candidates. As Table 6.2 clearly demonstrates, the Alliance parties are not class parties, but rather draw their strength in relatively equal proportions from all occupational classes.

Whiteley (1986) believes, based on the class decomposition and dealignment noted above, that "the sociological account of electoral behaviour is clearly obsolescent if the aim is to explain and predict electoral outcomes" (cited in McAllister and Mughan 1987: 48). Changes throughout society—contraction of the traditional working class, reconstitution of social classes, failed performance by both parties, increased affluence and changing consumption patterns, increased home ownership, more widespread education, media coverage, and resurgent nationalism have been cited among other factors to account for the erosion of traditional expressive voting behaviors. According to Franklin (1985: 125), "support for class based voting is very fragile."

But others have argued, to the contrary, that while the precise nature of the social cleavages has altered, expressive factors, including class, still prevail. The British still perceive themselves as members of traditional classes, and perceive the nation as divided by class. By many accounts, class continues to account for voting behavior more than any other single factor. Crewe (1987: 53) finds that "class, rather than age or sex, remains the primary shaper of the vote," if on a reduced scale. In fact, he sees "a sharpening of class polarization." Robertson (1984), Kelley et al. (1985), and McAllister and Mughan (1985) "find the continued importance of class albeit weakened over time" (Wellhofer 1986: 371). Scarbrough (1987: 220) believes that "much has changed but little is different—questions of class are still at the heart of the debate about British electoral politics." Citing the facts that "relative class inequalities remain broadly unchanged," and that the Conservatives have "all but torn up" the postwar social agreements that ensured full employment and economic security, she suggests "developments since the later 1970s would lead us to expect a revival of the class cleavage" (Scarbrough 1987: 221). In their controversial voting study of the 1983 election, Heath et al. (1985: 37) argue that relative class voting is still the rule, even though the size and composition of classes may be in flux or, in the case of the manual working class, decline. They assert that "our main argument ... is that the class basis of politics, if not the strongest it has ever been, nonetheless shows no good evidence of secular decline," and they reject the theory of "dealignment" in favor of fluctuations in party support based on political influences.[4] If they are right, Labour's electoral fortunes are not beyond redemption, nor are the Liberal Democrats' gains firmly enough rooted to qualify as yet as a voter realignment. The revival of the Labour Party and the rapid fade of the "third force" at the end of the decade reminds us to hold in abeyance any final conclusions about the demise of class voting. Particularly in contrast to Japan, we can say that voting in Britain still has a class base. However, in light of changes in the shape of class composition, this base has become somewhat more complex, if it has not eroded.

By the same token, it is important to keep in mind that even if partisan identification and loyalties are weakening, the electoral choice of voters is still structured by parties. Party names appear on the ballot, parties nominate the candidates, determine (in the case of Labour) the election manifesto, and pay for and run the campaigns. Party labels still exert a pull on voters that can overcome personality and issue preferences (Crewe 1985b: 175), even if they are not "the primary and almost exclusive influence" (Norton 1984: 82). Both the Conservatives and Labour continue to gain a percentage of the vote that is significantly higher than the percentage of people agreeing with many of their major policy positions. Even amidst obituaries for strong class identity, Crewe (1985b: 175) could find that in the 1983 election "deep-seated Labour loyalties" induced many to cast "a vote of the heart rather than the mind."

Socioeconomic class and class cleavages are not only less important in Japan as independent variables affecting voting behavior, their effect is almost universally considered to be negligible (Richardson and Flanagan 1984: 246; White 1982: 225; Watanuki 1980: 24). Japan prides itself on being an egalitarian society and, as has been noted in previous chapters, roughly 90 percent of Japanese survey respondents identify themselves as being members of the middle class. Not only is there a lack of class consciousness in Japan, but the homogeneity of Japanese society precludes the social group cleavages, such as race, ethnicity, nationality, language, and religion, often found in Western countries. Richardson and Flanagan (1984: 246) find that while social cleavage models are popular in Western Europe, they are "ill suited to the Japanese context." Murakami (1982: 42,45) goes so far as to argue that in Japan the economic classes are being melded by mass consumption, mass media, and mass education, and the postindustrialization of the economy into one giant "new middle mass" that will be completely nonideological and interest-oriented in its politics.

Even given problems of comparability of the data, a comparison of the split in Japanese party support in Table 6.3 with the British two-party split (Conservative-Labour) in Table 6.4 suggests the differences in occupational class voting in Japan and Britain. In Japan, the LDP garners a majority support among all but industrial workers, but even in this one case, the LDP has twice the support of

Table 6.3

Party Support in Japan, 1986 (in percent)

	LDP	JSP
Office workers	53	20
Managers	68	8
Industrial workers	46	23
Service workers	58	13
Merchants and business owners	72	5
Self-employed	71	13
Farmers	74	9
Other	55	15

Source: Asahi Shimbun poll, as reported in Gerald L. Curtis, 1988. *The Japanese Way of Politics*: Table 6.3, pp. 204–5. New York: Columbia University Press. Used with permission.

Table 6.4

Vote by Social Class, Britain 1983

	Conservative	Labour	SDP/ Liberal
Professional, managerial (AB)	62	12	27
Office and clerical (C1)	55	21	24
Skilled manual (C2)	39	35	27
Semiskilled, unskilled manual (D)	29	44	28
Trade unionists	32	39	28
Unemployed	30	45	26

Source: I. Crewe, 1985. "How to Win a Landslide Without Really Trying: Why the Conservatives Won in 1983." In *Britain at the Polls, 1983*, ed. Austin Rainey: Table 7.6, pp. 170–71. Washington, D.C.: American Enterprise Institute. Reprinted with permission of the American Enterprise Institute for Public Policy Research, Washington, D.C.

the JSP, its main rival. In the case of Britain, on the other hand, something of a class vote was preserved in the cases of semi-skilled and unskilled manual workers and labor-union members, who gave a plurality of their vote to the "natural" party of the working class.

The contrast between the class-party connection in Britain and that in Japan is well illustrated by the dilemma of the JSP. According to Hrebenar (1986: 12), "One of the severe problems for the JSP is that this party of the working class is poorly supported by that class. Only 28 percent of the labor union members in the Kansai area supported the JSP, according to a 1977 poll by the Labor Research Institute. Even if we examine just the party support of the members of Sohyo (the labor confederation supporter of the JSP), we find that only 44 percent were willing to identify themselves as JSP supporters." Because of the relative unimportance of manual and nonmanual class identities in Japan, and the

Table 6.5

Emphasis on Candidate or Party in Voting Choices in Japanese General Elections (in percent)

	Candidate	Party	DK
1958	45	32	23
1960	43	33	24
1963	51	31	18
1967	47	37	16
1969	33	49	18
1972	38	48	14
1976	40	46	14
1979	46	41	13
1980	38	49	13
1983	42	47	11
1986	39	49	12

Source: Bradley M. Richardson 1988. "Constituency Candidates versus Parties in Japanese Voting Behavior." *American Political Science Review* 82: Table 1, p. 698. Used with permission.

weakness of occupational class-party links, we would not expect such social changes as are occurring throughout the industrial democracies to have the same impact in Japan as in Britain.

In the past, party identification was not generally perceived to be of great importance to voting behavior in Japan (Hrebenar 1986: 20). Partisanship in Japanese voting behavior has always been relegated to secondary importance because Japanese society and its electoral system are so supportive of constituency and candidate relationships. Murakami believes that the nonpartisanship of Japanese politics will increase as nonideological interest groups become the center of focus for Japanese politics (Murakami 1982: 46).

There is reason to believe, however, that party identification is becoming a much more important factor, if not the primary factor, in Japanese voting behavior. In Japan, as in Britain, party identification is strongly correlated with the vote, with 70 percent of partisans in Japan voting for the party with which they identified in the 1983 election (Miyake 1986a: 43). Bradley M. Richardson (1988: 695), previously one of the main proponents of the importance of candidate and constituency variables, wrote in a 1988 article in the *American Political Science Review*, "[L]ocal candidate imagery, exposure to constituency campaigns, and the effects of vote solicitation within local social networks have a significant impact on the decisions of many Japanese voters. However, my findings show conclusively that party identification, party images, and party-focused habitual voting are the main determinants of the vote." Table 6.5 demonstrates how the effect of voters' perceptions of the importance of candidate and party has changed since the 1950s. Thus it would appear that Japan presents a contrast to Britain, where the movement is away from strong party identification and partisan mobilization.

Richardson (1988: 698–701) attributes the increasing importance of partisanship in voting to a number of factors: (1) the continuity and longevity of the LDP and its main opposition party, the JSP; (2) the increased visibility of parties, as opposed to candidates, in the mass media; (3) the diffusion of the mass media, especially television, throughout Japan; (4) the increasing urbanization of Japan; (5) the industrialization of the countryside; and (6) the increased level of educational attainment for most Japanese. The potential increase in partisan identification is made more important by the fact that in both Japan and Britain, it is quite strongly related to vote. In Japan, 70 percent of self-identified partisans voted for their party in the 1983 elections (Miyake 1986a: 43). Furthermore, stability in party identification is positively related to stability in voting behavior (Miyake 1986b: 52).

Richardson and Flanagan (1984: 173) see a trend toward an increased impact of party identification that is especially noticeable among voters for the major opposition parties—Komeito, Japan Communist Party, and Japan Socialist Party—and among young, highly educated, urbanized, male salarymen. Gerald Curtis (1988: 201), on the other hand, argues that the "new independents" who are dropping party identification are drawn from exactly the same pool—young male and female salarymen who are highly educated and urban. Although the picture is obviously muddled, what does seem to stand out clearly is that the JSP has suffered a loss of hard core supporters since the 1960s. In 1969 the JSP received 21.4 percent of the popular vote and that has decreased incrementally in every election since (with the exception of the 1972 election in which there was a 0.5 percent increase) until the JSP reached its postreunification (1955) nadir of 17.3 percent in 1986. This trend was finally reversed in the 1990 lower-house election, when the popular vote for the JSP rose to 24.4 percent (equivalent to the levels of the late 1960s), but the results of that election were an anomaly. After heavy losses in local elections in the spring of 1991 an Asahi Shimbun poll (June 12, 1991:1) had support for the Socialist Party back down to its lowest level, 17 percent. Generally the JSP gets few votes from outside the strong identifiers, but many voted for the JSP in the 1990 lower-house election because they wanted to send a message that they were finally fed up with the scandals and arrogance of the LDP. The LDP, for its part, has been increasing its level of party identification (Curtis 1988: 204–5), but it is much less strong than is party identification for the JSP and other opposition parties.

Traditionally low levels of party identification and instability of party identification have, for Richardson, tended to mask the importance, and independence, of two significant factors often linked to party identification—party images and consistent voting habits. He finds that a significant percentage (13 percent) of the voting public are not firm identifiers, but do hold positive images of parties and that about 20 percent of the voters vote habitually for the same party (Richardson 1988: 698, 713). White (1982: 221–22) also found in his study of Tokyo citizens that the party model of voting behavior seemed best suited to his data, and that voters emphasized party over candidate when asked their reason for selecting a particular candidate.

Although the rise of party voting in Japan brings it more in line with Britain, there are important differences in the specific operation of party identification on individual voting behavior. White (1982: 222), for example, believes that when discussing party or candidate identification in Japan it may be more reasonable to speak of the party acting as a "focusing device which directs voter attention" to a group of specific candidates; the "voter then chooses from among this group on non-party grounds." Watanuki (1986: 21) also found that party identification was a stronger factor than *koenkai* identification and also stresses the importance of party identification as an initial eliminator in Japan's multimember district system. Indeed Japan's single nontransferable vote system would facilitate such a scenario. "It seems that in the U.S. [or British] single-member constituency system, many voters can do a paired comparison of two competing candidates and U.S. candidates conduct their campaigns in such a way as to make themselves highly visible. Whereas in the Japanese multimember constituency system, comparison of all the candidates is impossible for most voters" (Watanuki et al. 1986: 23). Party identification is very important when selecting out those for whom you do not want to vote, but when it comes to the final choice, especially if it happens to be between two candidates from the same party, there are other factors that come into play.

Despite what appears to be evidence of increased partisan identification, the fortunes of the LDP and the JSP in particular do exhibit some tendencies toward dealignment. In 1955 when the parties of the right coalesced into the Liberal Democratic Party and the right and left wings of the Socialist Party reunified to form the Japan Socialist Party, it appeared to many students of Japanese politics that the time of the two-party system had arrived. This was a reasonable assumption given the strength of these two parties in the elections of 1958 relative to the only other viable party, the Japan Communist Party. The two-party system in Japan, however, was not destined to last very long as the left began to split—beginning with the formation of a moderate left party, the Democratic Socialist Party (DSP) in the election of 1960. The DSP was formed from a right-wing faction of the JSP, never truly comfortable with the alliance formed in 1955. The final split with the main body of the party followed a policy dispute over the revision of the Security Treaty, although "differences between the two wings went well beyond this one issue" (Hrebenar 1986: 182). The formation of the DSP began to chip away at the JSP in the election of 1960, and the process was continued with the formation of the Komeito (Clean Government Party) (KMT) in 1964. While this party is an anomaly in Japanese party politics in that it is the offspring of a Buddhist sect, Soka Gakkai, its supporters tend to be female, young, lower middle-class, manual workers who are less educated (Hrebenar 1986: 152)—i.e., people who had previously tended to support the JSP. By the election of December 1969, the fourth election for the DSP and the second for the KMT, the JSP's popular vote had been cut from its high of 33 percent in 1958 to 21.4 percent. As was stated before, the JSP has continued gradually to lose support, as evidenced through the popular vote in House of Representatives elections, but this seems a result of the decline in the number of those socialist and other unions who have always formed the core supporters of the party, as a result of the postindustrialization of the Japanese economy. Of course, the coalition of socialists in postwar Japan bore little resemblance to the older and more successful Labour Party in Britain, and its breakup in the 1960s cannot be said to have represented a disjunction in the pattern of political competition to the extent the breakup of Labour in Britain did in the early 1980s.

The LDP, for its part, has suffered a loss in popular votes since 1958, but it has not lost ground to the JSP. The gap between LDP and JSP popular support in 1958 was 24.9 percentage points, in 1983 it was 26.3 percentage points and in 1986 it was 32.2 percentage points (Curtis 1988: 200), although it decreased to 22 percentage points in the 1990 election. The LDP's loss in popular votes was similar in percentage points to that of the JSP (10–13 percent), but, not only did it have a larger base at the beginning of the slide, it has also lost votes for different reasons. Richardson and Flanagan (1984: 245–55) reflect the belief of many scholars (Hrebenar, White, Ward, Curtis, Reischauer) that the decline of the LDP is due to three important changes which occurred in Japan—decline of employment in the primary industries and increased employment in secondary and tertiary industries, migration from rural to urban and suburban locations, and the modernization of Japanese values. The LDP is the party of traditional values, and has long enjoyed strong support from the agricultural and rural sectors of the population. As values change and the number of people in rural areas and in the primary industries decline, so does the support for the LDP.

White outlines the distribution of Japanese votes in three somewhat different ways—temporal, spatial, and systemic—although the conclusions he draws are similar. Temporal distribution is described as the decline of LDP votes over the 1950s and 1960s, stagnation of the JSP at around 20 percent of the popular vote, and the growth of third-party votes and the fragmentation of third parties (White 1982: 220–21). Spatial distribution is described in two ways: (1) the rural-strong–urban-weak dichotomy of the LDP; the even distribution of votes for the JSP throughout the country; and the overwhelmingly urban support for third parties. In addition, (2) he describes an interesting pattern of LDP strength in the inner city changing to opposition support as one approaches the suburbs, until LDP support increases once again as one approaches the countryside (White 1982: 220–21). The systemic distribution he describes is the tendency for the Japanese to vote for the LDP in national elections and for the opposition parties in local elections (White 1982: 221).

A question which most certainly has to be answered is why support for the LDP seems to have reached a precipitous decline by 1972, taking one deep dip following the Lockheed scandal, coming back to the previous plateau, then skyrocketing again in the 1986 election. And even though twenty-three seats were lost in the 1990 election, that result was still much stronger than expected given the problems facing the LDP in that election. As we will see below, it may be possible that elements of electoral politics that have traditionally been classified as rural, such as *koenkai*, have been transferred to cities with urban migration, and that the LDP can now be legitimately classified as an urban party (Hrebenar 1986: 23). It also appears that some of the loss of support for the LDP comes from an increase in nonvoters and inconsistent voters, most of whom are ex-LDP voters (White 1982: 229).

In the past, voters with no party affiliation tended to be rural, poorly educated and not very interested in politics. They also tended to support the LDP when they did vote. Newer independents tend to be younger, educated salary workers who have made a conscious decision to be independent, and who have left the JSP and progressive side of the spectrum and come to support the LDP to a greater extent (Curtis 1988: 201–2). Indeed, one might say that there is no swing vote in Japan as, "[m]ost independents who do not vote for the LDP do not vote" (Curtis 1988: 202). This also means that LDP performance is directly related to voting rates. This is indicated by the LDP's showing in double elections (simultaneous elections for the upper and lower houses) and their effect is to raise the voting rate. In the only two double elections ever held, 1980 and 1986, the LDP has done much better than in other recent elections. When the voting rate decreased, as in 1979 and 1983, so has the LDP's share of the vote decreased. Gerald Curtis (1988: 195) estimates that for every three people who cast ballots in 1980 but stayed home in 1983, two had cast ballots for the LDP.

Murakami (1982: 59–60), like Curtis, also explains the resurgence of the LDP in the 1980s as a turning toward the LDP by "modern," nonpartisan independents. His "new middle mass" is seen as supporting the LDP because (1) crises of the 1970s reawakened their tradition-oriented conservatism, and (2) it broadened itself into a much more inclusive party in response to the increased interest orientation of the Japanese voter. This second factor is very much in accord with Kent Calder's theory of the LDP's broadening its "circle of compensation" which will be discussed in Chapter 7. Murakami (1982: 70) differs, however, with Curtis's belief that there is no swing vote in Japan in that he predicts that the future of Japanese party politics is headed toward "a competition between major interest-oriented catch-all parties . . . one conservative in origin and the other progressive in origin." It certainly appears as if the independent nonpartisan vote played an important role in the 1990 election, but this one election does not yet make a trend.

In any case, it would certainly appear that the demographic, occupational, and values changes that affected a reduction in voting for the LDP and an increase in nonvoting and more independent voting have stabilized and, given the results of elections in the 1980s, it appeared until the Recruit scandal as though the LDP was gaining strength with a new, but less stable, base of supporters. The JSP, on

Table 6.6

The Regional Vote in the 1987 Parliamentary Elections

	Percent of Vote				Percent Change since 1979			
	Con	Lab	All	Nat	Con	Lab	All	Nat
Scotland	24	42	19	14	−7	+8	+10	−3
North of England	37	42	21	—	−4	−3	+7	—
Wales	30	45	18	7	−3	−3	+7	−1
South and Midlands	51	24	25	—	—	−9	+10	—

Source: Adapted from *The Economist*, June 20–26, 1987:60. Used with permission.

the other hand, will continue to struggle in the long run unless it can become much more of an inclusive, catch-all party on the *Murakami model.*

Regionally Based Voting

Regional variations are an increasingly visible result of British electoral behavior today. "The national electorate," concludes Scarbrough (1987: 220), "is no longer the homogeneous body, responding to short-term forces in much the same way, that led Butler and Stokes to talk of a 'national uniform swing.' " A national pattern of the vote has been replaced to some extent by different territorial, and even constituency-wide patterns of electoral competition (McAllister and Rose 1984: 27). The most significant of these is referred to as the "North/South" cleavage that is regarded as having created "two political nations" (Scarbrough 1987: 220), corresponding to the "variation in the post-war distribution of economic well-being in Britain" (Curtice and Steed 1982: 264). The pattern of territorial voting, while fairly recent, is indeed so entrenched that it has forced the two traditional parties into largely regional molds, as is demonstrated by Table 6.6.

Neither the Labour Party nor the Conservative Party is a geographically "national" party. In 1983, Labour held a 2:1 advantage in seats in Scotland, Wales, and the north, while the advantage was 4:1 in favor of the Conservatives in the south (Kavanagh 1985a: 99). Only the Alliance in the 1983 election appeared to have relatively homogeneous support by region. The Conservatives have become the party of the suburban and rural south of England, while Labour has become the party of the cities and the periphery of Britain in the north and west. The north/south dimension can be seen as reinforcing class-based models—since the north, Labour's stronghold, has become increasingly working class (Curtice and Steed 1982: 261). Budge and McKay (1988: 81) find that where "society and economy have continued on traditional lines . . . class consciousness is higher: in Glasgow over three-quarters of electors spontaneously identify with a class compared to slightly over half in London. Here again we find regional and class differences entwined." But Hechter (1975) has argued instead that "reactive ethnic cleavages," between the "Celtic fringe" and the "Anglo-Saxon center," have combined with class "to undergird counter-center politics" (cited in Wellhofer 1986: 370). Thus "pre-industrial, non-class structuring of mass politics" was never fully displaced by industrial class politics (Wellhofer 1986: 373). It would appear in any case that region is not an independent variable, reflecting instead other factors such as class, social milieu, nationality, and unemployment (Harrop 1988: 58). But the fact remains that, electorally at least, Britain has become "two nations." It is precisely Labour's strong, if limited, territorial base that spared that party a catastrophic drop in parliamentary representation during the 1980s. The fact that the Liberal Democrats lack such a base accounts in part for their frustratingly low parliamentary representation.

Internal migrations have had little impact on these territorially based cleavages. Britain remains a relatively immobile society, geographically, so that population movements have not been politically significant in recent decades. Such population movements that have been significant, such as continued immigration of New Commonwealth citizens, have tended to reinforce existing territorial party preferences.

As was noted in Chapter 2, there are few regional and national differences in Japan that would lead to territorial differences in voting. Nationwide increases in affluence, as a result of continuing economic growth, further would seem to preclude the development of cleavages like those in Britain. However, the drastic demographic changes that occurred in Japan from the mid-1950s to the mid-1970s have had a far greater effect on voting than is the case in Britain. The migration of the Japanese population from rural villages to urban areas and a simultaneous suburbanization of the Kanto and Kansi areas significantly reduced the vote for the LDP. The effects of this seem to have ended by the mid-1970s, however, and support for the LDP has since been gradually growing. This is perhaps due in part to a transference of LDP loyalties and campaign mechanisms from rural areas to urban which took place during the migration. The different territorial dimensions of the vote, in combination with differences in apportioning parliamentary representatives among constituencies, remains one of the most significant contrasts between British and Japanese election systems.

Social Milieu and Group Process

In the case of Britain, a number of social-psychological explanations have challenged the individual class characteristics (sociological) model. In these models, "group membership alone is insufficient to explain voting patterns ... psychological factors, linked to group membership, play a major part" (Heath et al.

1985: 8). In these "environmental," "social milieu," "contagion," "neighbour-hood," and "consensual" models, face-to-face contacts influence many voters to copy the attitudes of the majority of the people with whom they live and work (Franklin 1985b: 50). The desire for conformity is therefore a powerful shaper of the vote, as it is of other social behaviors. According to Curtice and Steed (1982, cited in Kavanagh 1985a: 99), these environmental effects "dispose voters, re-gardless of their class, to support the dominant local party." Occupational or class majorities at the constituency level somehow convert an important segment of the local minority to their views. The result is a homogenization of the vote at the constituency level. For example, middle-class residents in largely working-class constituencies would be more likely to vote Labour than members of the same class in a middle-class constituency. By the same token, working-class residents in largely middle-class constituencies would be more likely to vote Tory. According to Miller (1978: 265), "People with similar characteristics and interests are more likely to come into contact with one another and these con-tacts, if not all contacts, are likely to produce discussions leading to consensual tendencies in political attitudes and partisanship." The operative mechanism for this process is the proportion of the "core class" of employers and managers in the constituency, rather than the proportion of middle and working classes as traditionally defined. This would suggest that "social processes" are more im-portant to partisan choice than individual membership in social groups, such as class (Miller 1978: 279, 284). Franklin (1985b: 126) concludes that "group pro-cesses of opinion formation and dissemination are the props which sustain what is left of the British class vote." These processes are generally described at the constituency level, where the tendency for one-party dominance seems greatest. But these local processes have cumulative regionwide and national repercussions and may help explain the emergence of "two Britains" in electoral politics. For example, among skilled workers, Labour had a 32 percent lead over the Conser-vatives in the north, but only a 6 percent lead in the south in the 1983 election (Norton 1984: 93). The Conservatives in 1983 picked up support only on their own "turf," and Labour, despite its national drubbing, witnessed some increases in support in large urban areas, predominantly in the north. Such an effect seems likely to accelerate the territorial polarization of the vote in Britain. Politics, concludes Miller (1978: 283), "has become more and more about 'people around here'."

At least for the time being, there is little available evidence of precisely how "contagion" or "neighbourhood" effects operate to enforce conformity. Until there is better evidence, we should be cautious about accepting such effects as an important factor in British voting behavior. Further, we need to know why a social mechanism that might seem more appropriate in traditional, closed rural communities can survive in an environment of weakening class ties, mobility, erosion of neighborhoods and traditional families, the homogenizing effects of the national media, and the disruptive effects of Boundary Commission decisions on communities over the years (see Dunleavy and Husbands 1985: 208; Scarbrough 1987: 240; Kavanagh 1985a: 100). It may be that we can find support for these theories in the successful transplant within Japan of the traditionally rural *koenkai* into modern, urban settings.

Even with the above caveats, British group-process models suggest that British and Japanese voting behavior may have more in common than has traditionally been assumed. In the case of Japan, group processes have long been accorded a leading role in determining voting behavior. Indeed, the Japanese emphasis on consensus, conformity, and harmony is clearly manifested in voting behavior. While little has appeared in the political science literature about the underlying mechanisms that produce voting conformity in Britain, in Japan they are at the center of much of the voting literature. When the operation of group process on voting in Britain is discussed, it is still often in the context of occupational class, and the interaction of class and social milieu. In Japan, class is a minor part of both social group identities and social-psychological processes. Furthermore, a comparison between the relevant groups in the two countries suggests a contrast between the nebulous British "class" and "neighborhood," and the more clearly defined Japanese associational groups such as workplace, and *koenkai* that shape the vote.

"[F]or many Japanese, voting is not so much a political activity as it is a part of general social behavior" (Kuroda cited in Hrebenar 1986: 15). What Richardson and Flanagan (1984: 247) call the "social network" model "stresses the role of both formal organization and informal small-group networks in shaping individual voting preferences." The social network is so important because Japan is a personalistic society. There are very "extensive and complex hierarchical and lateral communication networks that broaden the reach of interpersonal messages in Japan," a great deal of group conformity, and "well-developed, institutionalized procedures for transmitting partisan communications" (Richardson and Flanagan 1984: 247). Though these factors operate in both the countryside and in cities, and affect voting for all parties, social networks and the *koenkai* have been especially important in rural support for the LDP.

The importance of personalism in voting behavior is that "voting is likely to be based more on the individual's relationship to the candidates or his assessment of the candidates' personalities and attributes than on party labels, issues or ideologies" (Richardson and Flanagan 1984: 171). Although it was noted in the section on party identification and partisanship that this is changing, personalism is still the dominant influence for the old, those who live in rural areas, those with low education, farmers, and women (Richardson and Flanagan 1984: 173).

White (1982: 221) speaks of personal appeal and describes it more in charismatic terms. However, he also stresses the importance of personal ties in socially cohesive urban neighborhoods. "JCP and CGP backers in particular lamented the manipulation of personal obligations and human emotions by conservative politicians who contributed food and sake to *chokai* (neighborhood association) functions and played upon long-standing, personal relationships to elicit votes, never attempting to raise issues" (White 1982: 225).

When a Japanese voter is confronted with the choice of voting for a candidate or a party, the social environment, traditional practices, and the structure of the Japanese electoral system all tend to emphasize the former. Candidates of the same party may run against each other in a multiple member district. Therefore, the party does not want to take sides in running campaigns against fellow members, and so most aspects of the campaigns are left to the candidates and their factions. The initiative for the campaign comes from the candidate. In addition, Japan has traditionally had small, relatively isolated communities, with dense populations controlled by a hierarchical elite and populated by a conforming mass. Within these communities, personal obligation, loyalty, and social relations have been far more important than the abstract ideals, or even specific issue-oriented policies, of political parties (Richardson 1988: 697). Finally, because each ballot must be filled out by hand, it sometimes seems as if the individual candidate's sole concern is to ensure name recognition and proper spelling of his or her name. Given these conditions, it is not surprising, even with the inroads made by political parties, that a third of Japanese voters still contend that the individual candidate is more important in determining their vote than the political party (see Table 6.5).

One of the most important factors in the social network model is the candidate's personal support group, or *koenkai*. To use Watanuki's (1980: 31) definition, the *koenkai* is a "personal sponsoring association of a particular candidate, which is based on a network of various kinds of social ties and through which a variety of benefits are distributed to its members—both tangible and intangible, material and spiritual—in exchange for support for the candidate at election time." The *koenkai* complements other "social networks based on community kinship, occupational, school and other ties" (Watanuki 1980: 31). As we saw in Chapter 5, membership in *koenkai* is a significant form of political participation in Japan.

Watanuki et al. (1986: 6) reveal some interesting findings from the 1983 JES survey data as a result of extensive analysis of the role of *koenkai*. Nearly 30 percent of the respondents were affiliated with *koenkai*, and that translates into about 24 million Japanese. Joining, however, is often perfunctory and is undertaken at the request of friends, relatives, neighbors, company, or union. Thus, membership does not automatically mean a vote for the candidate, as only one out of every three *koenkai* members actually voted for the candidate supported by the group (Watanuki et al. 1986: 7). Even at that, it is the third highest factor in his ranking of campaign-related variables (Watanuki et al. 1986: 16).

Koenkai affiliation is highest in average population concentration districts, (small- to medium-sized cities), as has tended to be the case in the past. In addition, there is little difference in the percentage of members who actually voted for their *koenkai* candidate between the various types of electoral districts

(Watanuki et al. 1986: 8). Although, as we would expect, the occupation group with the largest proportion of affiliation to *koenkai* are farmers, other occupation groups, especially those that are considered urban occupations, have higher than expected percentages of *koenkai* affiliation. The percentages of those who voted for their *koenkai*'s candidate varied little across occupation (Watanuki et al. 1986: 8).

"Successful candidates are those who cannot only rely on the votes of their *koenkai* members at the polls but who utilize the group as a campaign organization to obtain votes from the electorate at large (Watanuki et al. 1986: 7–9). When determining the effect of *koenkai* on electoral behavior, their power beyond social pressure on the membership must be considered. *Koenkai* members use their individual persuasion skills and bonds of obligation and loyalty to sway their friends, relatives, co-workers, and neighbors, as well as acting as staff in mailing out postcards. Both these activities are very important, as 55 percent of the electorate is contacted by friends, etc., soliciting votes for their *koenkai* candidate, and 23 percent of those contacted responded as requested. The receipt of campaign postcards was second only to that of personal contact as a campaign-related variable (Watanuki et al. 1986: 11). Door-to-door canvassing is illegal in Japan and so *koenkai* members must draw a fine line between politicking and "just chatting" about politics.

Koenkai have continued to grow over the sixteen years of information gathering by the Japan Election Survey and their mobilization of support for their candidates has been "an essential factor for success in elections" (Watanuki et al. 1986: 13). This is another interesting indication that important segments of the Japanese political system may not be "modernizing" in a Western sense, in that political development as defined by Almond and Verba indicates that institutional and association influences take precedence over interpersonal and community pressures as a political system matures (the same potential contradiction is presented by British "neighbourhood" voting theories).

Our discussion of the role of group process and social behavior in Japanese voting behavior brings us back to a topic discussed at length in earlier chapters, namely, the spectator nature of Japanese political culture. The social nature of voting behavior, in combination with distrust of politicians, cynicism, and removal from the political system discussed above is at the heart of the passive spectator culture. According to Shupe (1979: 244–46),

> It seems likely that . . . this electoral climate [a climate of *jiban* and *koenkai* forces exerting personal and parochial pressures directing the vote] . . . gave many individuals less than complete opportunities to make the vote an act of 'their own,' i.e., one in which they invested their personal decision efforts and more of their political selves. The structure of the voting act itself, rigidly prescribed and confined to infrequent occasions, makes such a 'depersonalized' form of participation possible. There is reason, therefore, tentatively to regard Voting as a measure of behavior that required relatively

less personal initiative and personality involvement than the other measures of Political Participation; hence *passive* [author's italics] . . . Voting as an act reflects on the 'face' of the community. . . . Communities that cannot turn out high voting rates lose prestige or 'face' in the sense that their 'deficiencies' in solidarity are exposed. Voting, in this sense, is more a measure of community integration than of Political Participation. . . . Finally there remains the apparent inconsistency of the significant associations of Voting with Political Cynicism and Political Distrust. . . . Negative orientations can be interpreted as results of the dissonance between ideal and actual factors determining voting choice. [And here follows an excellent description of spectator political culture in operation.] This interpretation of dissonance regards the cynical, distrustful evaluations of government and politicians as the consequence of voting within a context having two competing culturally distinct sets of expectations: one emphasizing formal norms, definitions, and patterns of overt behavior transplanted from a Western cultural tradition; the other with its own operating ground rules, understandings, and forms of organization that often contradict the overt behavior.

Other Expressive Variables

Education

Education affects the vote in Britain in two ways. First, it weakens partisanship. As we saw earlier, "cognitive mobilization" increasingly replaces "partisan mobilization." According to Shively's (1979) model, less educated voters use parties as "an information-economizing device," while the spread of education means a smaller proportion of the electorate needs the shortcut of party identification (Alt 1984: 303). But Alt believes that, with the relatively small proportion of the British pursuing further education, this effect is not likely to explain very much of the dealignment that has occurred (1984: 304). Second, education might influence the choice of party. It is sometimes claimed that those with more years of schooling above the minimum are somewhat more likely to vote Conservative (Norton 1984: 95). But some evidence contradicts this view. For example, in 1987, the Alliance parties secured a larger proportion of the vote among university graduates than the Conservatives (Rose 1989: 164). Another way in which education might affect voting in the future is through its association with the development of new, nonclass values, such as postmaterialism, that we examined in Chapter 1. At the moment, however, the association of education with such values is not matched by the association between education and vote since political debate in Britain is still largely defined in terms of class (Heath et al. 1985: 67).

Watanuki (1980: 24), in keeping with his value cleavage theory of "cultural politics," believes that increased education in postwar Japan has led to greater holding of modern values, which leads to increased leftist voting. Although this relationship still holds true for those in the 35–49 age bracket, it appears as though education as an explanatory variable is losing its relevance in urban Japan.

Trade Union Membership

In light of the class theories of politics applied to Britain, one would expect trade union membership to be highly correlated with Labour support. Indeed, union members are still somewhat more likely, according to Table 6.4, to vote Labour (39 percent), than Tory (32 percent), or Alliance (28 percent), but it is difficult to escape the fact that 60 percent of union members did not vote Labour in 1983. As Franklin and Page (1984: 534) point out, trade union membership might be expected to reinforce class attitudes and voting inclinations "by bringing together persons with similar class characteristics in an additional group context." But, if such a reinforcing mechanism were at work, members of largely middle-class, white collar unions should be more likely to vote Tory than non-union. This is not, however, the case, with "white collar union members . . . more likely to vote Labour than white collar non-union members, just as do their blue collar counterparts" (Franklin and Page 1984: 534). For at least the past twenty-five years, "public sector radicalism" has been in evidence. It is the relative increase in public service employees relative to private sector employees that gives this factor increased electoral weight (Harrop 1988: 43). In other words, there is evidence that union membership itself, rather than the class characteristics of the specific unions, influence voting. Unfortunately for Labour (see Table 6.1 above), trade union membership as a percentage of the workforce continues to be in decline overall, as increases in white collar union membership are more than compensated for by declines in working class union membership.

In Japan, blurred class distinctions carry over into the identity of industrial unions. White and blue collar employees of the same company usually belong to the same union, and even distinctions between employers and employees are far less salient than in Britain: "about 16 percent of the members of boards of directors in large companies are former trade union leaders" (Maruo 1986: 67). Union membership and occupation used to be a relatively stable measure of party support, but that too is changing. The JSP claimed the support of more that 50 percent of blue collar workers in the early 1960s, but now claims only about 20 percent, while the percentage of blue collar LDP voters has risen from 20 percent in the early 1960s to 46 percent today (Curtis 1988: 210–11). The only occupational group in a 1978 poll conducted in Tokyo that gave greater support to the JSP than the LDP was transportation and communication workers, occupations with (at that time) nationalized industries and with strong unions (Hayashi as reported in Curtis 1988: 211). Former progressives are becoming nonvoters, and independents, but an even greater problem for the left is the weakening of the unions. Union membership is on the decline: privatization in the communication and transportation sectors dealt a blow to the heart of unionism in Japan, and union leadership has been less than successful in dealing with its problems (Curtis 1988: 210–21).

Home Ownership

Home ownership has joined class, parents' party affiliation, and union membership as a significant independent predictor of the British vote, although its increased prominence may be relative, as the other variables decrease in importance, rather than absolute (Franklin 1985b: 68). In the past, home ownership was closely linked to class. Hence home ownership was correlated with Conservative voting; council tenancy with Labour voting. But with the help of the Conservative government's policy of offering council flats for sale, the class pattern of home ownership has changed. The proportion of council tenants has fallen, while owner-occupiers increased by 1986 to account for 63 percent of households (*Social Trends* 18 1988: 132). In the 1987 election, among working-class homeowners, Conservatives led Labour 44 percent to 32 percent; among those who had bought their council houses, by 42 to 31 percent (Crewe 1987: 53). Thus home ownership among a portion of the working class is clearly one factor working against traditional working-class identification with Labour. It is this "new working class" that is growing, posing a specific threat to the future Labour vote. In the view of Franklin, "secondary or supportive variables (particularly housing and union membership) carried forward the appearance of class voting" (Scarbrough 1987: 222). No similar effect of home ownership has been noted in Japanese voting literature.

Age

Age is of relatively little importance in British voting patterns today. Butler and Stokes (1969) placed a great deal of emphasis on differences in voting behavior among generational cohorts. As each generation was shaped by different formative experiences, its views and party allegiances were expected to differ. Thus the generation socialized during the period of Labour dominance after World War II sustained its early Labour loyalties into the years of Labour government in the 1960s (Franklin 1985b: 70). In a similar vein, older voters socialized in the pre-Labour era continued to lean to the Conservatives (Kavanagh 1985a: 107), and more recently the large pro-Conservative swing among new voters in 1983 also suggests that the Conservative electoral surge in the early 1980s may itself have constituted a similar formative experience. Considering the age effects on partisan dealignment, Crewe et al. (1977, cited in Clarke and Stewart 1984: 694) conclude that "the picture that emerges clearly is one of uniform partisan decline across the entire electorate." Rose finds "age-related differences are matters of degree, not kind, and are often small" (Rose 1989: 159; and see Norton 1984: 91).

In Japan, it would also appear that the "life cycle theory" of voting behavior—that people tend to vote for parties of the left when young and become increasingly supportive of conservative parties when they grow older—no longer has much validity (Curtis 1988: 203). In the 1960s, the young gave most of their support to the parties of the left, but since the 1970s they have either opted for nonpartisanship or have become more supportive of the LDP. The belief that Japan's youth is becoming increasingly conservative, a belief well covered in the mass media, was reinforced by two surveys of incoming freshmen to the University of Tokyo, the hotbed of student radicalism in the late 1960s. A 1978 survey done by the college student newspaper found that of those who supported a political party (37.1 percent), 45.2 percent supported the LDP (Curtis 1988: 205). In 1983, Inoguchi Takashi and Kabashima Ikuo surveyed the same sample and found that, of those who preferred a political party, 28.5 percent preferred the LDP and 10.5 percent preferred the JSP, while 35.4 percent expressed no preference (Inoguchi and Kabashima 1986: 106). By all measures, it certainly appears as though Japanese youth are becoming more conservative, and that is a trend which may continue the above-mentioned disparity between the LDP and the JSP.

Gender, Race, and Religion

Once women voted slightly more Conservative than men, but since 1979 this effect "has now ceased to be a tradition" (Crewe 1987: 52). On the other hand, Rasmussen (1987: 112, 118) identifies a possible "sex penalty," albeit a limited one, for female candidates. But the causes of this penalty appear to be complex, and the differences small when other variables are taken into account. On balance, he concludes, "the electorate seemed unconcerned with a candidate's gender and went about voting in its usual way unaffected by this factor." Because of lower registration rates among New Commonwealth citizens, the impact of the racial vote is not significant outside a small number of constituencies. However, despite some discrepancies in the figures, it does appear that both Asian and Afro-Caribbean voters are staunchly in the Labour camp. According to a 1987 BBC/Gallup election study, 64 percent of black voters voted for Labour candidates (Husbands 1988: 301). Religion has long since disappeared as a serious factor, though nonmembership in the Church of England appears to reduce support for the Conservatives to a degree. Concentrations of Irish and Polish immigrants in certain regions in the north of England may also have an impact on the local vote.

Japanese women are becoming slightly more conservative in that they are increasing their support for the LDP and decreasing their support for the JSP. According to polls run by the *Asahi Shimbun* (Curtis 1988: 204–5), women in the mid-1960s supported the LDP over the JSP by a moderate margin, 42 percent to 35 percent, but by 1986 support for the LDP had grown to 56 percent while JSP support had dropped to only 15 percent. In the case of women, it appears that the LDP was a direct beneficiary of decreased support for the JSP, as women increased their support for other opposition parties by only 8 percent, and nonpartisanship decreased by 2 percent. This finding is especially interesting in light of the increased power of the women's movement worldwide during the 1970s and 1980s. One would expect that the two parties that are perceived as being ahead on women's issues, the JCP and the JSP, would have gained the most from increased consciousness concerning those issues. However, one can think of a number of mitigating factors for the female Japanese population. Japanese women have traditionally controlled the household finances and tend to be fiscally conservative. This, in turn, would give them a tendency to vote according to their pocketbooks and the past economic performance of the government. Secondly, radical feminism has never had much of an impact in Japan.

The effect of religion on voting in Japan is minimal. Those Japanese who believe in any religion make up only about 25 percent of the population and all Japanese, believers or nonbelievers, have a very high tolerance for those of any religion. The religious cleavages that tore the West apart as it emerged from the feudal period, and which, to some extent, remain today have not played an important role in Japanese history. Exceptions to the nonrole of religion in contemporary Japanese politics include the conservatives' attempts to reinsert Shinto into the political system, some Buddhist sects' support for the LDP, and the support that the Komeito receives from its parent, the Soka Gakkai (Watanuki 1980: 37–38). About half of all Komeito votes come from Soka Gakkai members, but beyond voting, Soka Gakkai members are also instrumental in fund raising, campaigning, and proselytizing for the party.

Consumption Cleavages

The "consumption cleavage" theory has been offered by Dunleavy and Husbands (Dunleavy and Husbands 1985) to explain contemporary voting from a nontraditional perspective. As Franklin and Page (1984: 523) describe the theory in a British context, "the key distinction within any particular consumption process is whether one is dependent upon the state for the provision of this good or service through public housing, education, transport, or the National Health Service, or whether one makes provision for consumption within the private sector through owning a house and car, or by paying for a private health insurance scheme or for private education." "Real political interests," rather than socialization or group pressures, shape the vote (Harrop 1988: 41). And these interests are viewed as linked to the growth of the state and related cleavages between public and private sectors, dependency on and independence from public services and the state (Harrop 1988: 42). Private-sector consumption patterns are said to be associated with Conservative voting, while public-sector patterns are said to be associated with Labour, Liberal, and Social Democratic voting. If these relationships are valid, then the increase in state intervention after World War II, and the

Table 6.7

Percentage Distribution to Households of State Welfare Benefits in Britain, 1984

Benefit description	Receive	Do not receive
Dependent on public transport	38	62
Pension	36	64
Regular treatment, doctor	35	65
Education	34	66
Housing	30	70
Hospital care in past year	29	71
Unemployment benefits	23	77
Personal social services	5	95

Source: R. Rose and R. Shiratori, eds., 1986. *The Welfare State in East and West:* Table 4.10, p. 101. 1986. Oxford: Oxford University Press.

rising importance of the state as a provider of personal income, should have worked against the Conservatives, and the curtailment of the welfare state under Thatcher should in time work in their favor.

In Britain today, the state supplies a plurality of income through direct public employment and through transfer payments. This share rose from 25 percent in 1951 to 38.5 percent in 1981 (Rose 1986b: 83). Even under Thatcher, the state also provided major social services to an overwhelming 89 percent of all British families. In 1985, the average household benefit was £1460 (U.S. $2044 at an exchange rate of $1.40) for education, National Health Service benefits, travel and housing subsidies, and welfare foods (*Social Trends* 18 1988: Table 5.15, 93). Table 6.7 illustrates the distribution of a variety of welfare services in Britain.

On the other hand, public employment as a percentage of the total has grown only slowly, from 26.6 percent in 1951 to 28.2 percent in 1985 (Rose 1989: 308). And while Britain spends 23.7 percent of its GDP on social expenditures, this places it well behind Sweden, France, Italy, and West Germany, and not far ahead of Japan (Rose and Shiratori 1986: Appendix Table D, 209). Despite its "welfare state" image, Britain, like Japan, places a "distinctive emphasis" on the family "as a source of social services" (Rose 1986a: 26). It is important to keep in mind, too, that in the future, Britain's relatively slow growth rates are likely to curtail increases in both state and private-sector–provided welfare (Rose 1986b: 100). Given the above, the operation of "consumption cleavages" faces a number of limiting factors for the foreseeable future. And, as we saw above, while government unions have indeed proved, like their working class counterparts, to vote Labour, increasing membership in government unions has been offset by decreasing membership in the traditional working-class unions. Budge and

McKay (1988: 79) conclude that there is no evidence in the last two elections to support "the possibility of a new political-economic cleavage between those workers supported by public taxes and those who gain no direct benefit from them." Franklin (1985b: 53) is more categorical when he finds that "consumption cleavage theory does not explain anything that cannot be explained with existing theoretical constructs."

If the electoral impact of state employment and state dependency is to be limited anywhere in the OECD, it is in Japan. As Maruo (1986: 68) notes, "the provision of welfare in modern Japanese society, drawing upon non-state as well as state resources, remains distinctive by comparison with European countries in such fields as family care, education, and labor-management relations." Though the share of welfare expenditures as a percent of GDP has grown very rapidly in recent years, it is still the lowest in the OECD—17.5 percent (Rose 1986a: 26). A greater proportion of social services is provided by the private sector or by families than in Britain, even though the role of the private sector is greater in Britain than in many other European countries. "[T]he market continues to play a major role as a producer of welfare, funding pensions and retirement benefits through corporate employers, health care through partial payment by patients, and education through a large private university system and schools providing additional tuition for younger pupils" (Maruo: 1986: 76). In addition, the structure of the national pension and health insurance schemes in Japan are such that benefits are widely distributed across the population. The continued relatively small share of the state as bursar and social service agency suggests why the "consumption cleavages" model has attracted little attention in Japanese voting studies. Murakami's "new middle mass" theory, however, does somewhat parallel the concept of consumption cleavages. "[T]he NMM is a quasi-propertied class because social security, preferential policies, and so on have given the people guaranteed income streams over their life time, something that could have been provided only to the relatively rich before the war. However, unlike private-property rights, these entitlements are not free from the effects of major changes in the political scene" (Murakami 1982: 45). Therefore, the new middle mass is forced to participate in the political system, through voting and joining interest groups, to protect its stake in the "guaranteed income stream."

Although Murakami believes that the need to maintain a continued flow of state benefits will directly influence the voting behavior of many Japanese in the future, there is as yet no direct evidence to support that contention.

To summarize the comparative aspects of the effects of social and demographic variables on voting in Japan and Britain, age, education, home ownership, occupation, and trade union membership have never been as important in Japan as in the Western countries. Partisan differentiation by socioeconomic status as found in the United States (Auh 1978) and the class-based voting of Britain have never had as much impact on voting in Japan (Watanuki 1980: 24). And today, as a result of dealignment and the reorientation of the independent swing voter toward the LDP, the importance of age, education, occupation, and population density on voting behavior has been reduced even further (Curtis 1988: 203). In neither Britain nor Japan is there sufficient evidence that consumption cleavages have a significant impact on voting behavior.

A final note on the impact of the electoral system itself is in order. Certain aspects of the structure of Japanese electoral procedures are substantially different from those in Britain and most other Western electoral systems. These differences affect voting strategies and behavior. In Britain, the single-member constituency, first-past-the-post system structures voting choice in important ways. Most important, the system is held to have been a crucial prop of the two-party system. Votes for third party candidates may lead to representation in Parliament, provided votes are concentrated, but they are most unlikely to lead to the election of a majority. This suggests that votes for such parties are not intended to elect a government, but have other objectives, such as protest or election of regional blocs of MPs. A second effect is that because electors choose only their own MP and not the national political leaders, the question of leadership personalities does not enter into voting to anything like the extent in presidential systems such as the United States.

Hans Baerwald (1986: 88) has concluded in his analysis of voting behavior in Japan that "it is the multi-member district systems (in both houses) which provide a more persuasive explanation of electoral outcomes than, for example, analyses of slowly changing attitudes and policy preferences among Japanese voters." Watanuki also points to the influences on voting of the structure and conditions of the Japanese single nontransferable vote electoral system, especially the single-ballot multimember constituency, and the need for all ballots to be handwritten. As was mentioned above, the single-vote, multiple member constituency has an effect on both party identification and the persistence of personalism. These structural factors also reinforce voters' greater concern with individual candidates than political parties (Watanuki et al. 1986: 1). Even though a voter may identify with the LDP, once in the voting booth, the voter gets but one vote. Since the LDP may run two or three candidates from that constituency, party preference only narrows the range of candidates. The voter will then have to apply other criteria in making his or her choice. In addition, candidates competing against other candidates from the same party in their constituency are more likely to run their campaigns with minimal help from the party. Other parties may also run more than one candidate per constituency, but it is most often done by the LDP. Indeed, the party's decision concerning how many candidates to run is itself of great importance. One possible explanation for the poor LDP showing in the 1983 election was over-optimism in running too many candidates. The party ran 339 candidates in the 1983 election, more than they had run in any election since 1967. However, the voting rate dropped, so there were not enough LDP voters to support that large a number of candidates (Curtis 1988: 196). Conversely, there is no doubt that the JSP underestimated its support in the 1990 lower-house election and wasted votes by not running enough candidates.

The fact that all ballots are handwritten is also important when it comes to voter choice and the effect of campaigning on electoral behavior. During a campaign many candidates will concentrate on name recognition almost above all else in order to ensure that voters can write his or her name properly. The most prominent feature in campaign posters, literature, and sound-truck speeches is the candidate's name. Another way in which the electoral system may affect voter choice is that the national constituencies for some of the seats in the House of Councillors permit the functional mobilization of votes by large interest groups. Effective groups can succeed in having their own candidates elected to these seats (Richardson and Flanagan 1984: 306).

Instrumental Factors

As the explanatory power of expressive theories has appeared to decline, a number of observers have concluded that short-term, rational factors are of increasing importance to British voters. McAllister and Mughan suggest that by 1983, "the role of political attitudes was greater . . . and the role of socio-economic status less than in 1966." "[A]ttitudes," they say, "were a substantially more powerful electoral force in 1983 than were the class variables, even taking account of the tendency for individuals' class characteristics to shape certain of their attitudes (McAllister 1987: 62, 65). Franklin (1985: 150–52) believes that "the decline of class voting in Britain has permitted a more or less equivalent rise in issue-based voting choice. . . . No longer constrained to the same extent by characteristics largely established during childhood, British voters are now more open to rational argument than they were in the past" (see also Kavanagh 1987: 109; Scarbrough 1987: 222). At least this may be so of voters outside the remaining committed core of party supporters.

One of the clearest arguments for the rise of issue voting in Britain was not merely the dealignment affecting Labour and the Conservatives, but the rise of the Social Democrats after 1981. Their appeal was widespread, neither class nor regionally based (see above, Tables 6.2. 6.4, and 6.7). And as they were a relatively new party, it is difficult to attribute their vote to early socialization into class or party, though socialization may obviously still play a role in the learning of values to which the new party appeals. Figures suggest that voters who objected to the movement of Labour and the Conservatives away from the political center were the most likely to defect to the Social Democrats, even though a great many former Labour and Conservative supporters defected despite a perception that their party had not shifted to the right or left (Heath et al. 1985: 149–50).[5] On the other hand, it now seems clear that many voters who agreed with Alliance positions nevertheless failed to cast a vote for Alliance candidates—though this fact alone does not rule out "rational" motives for this failure.

By 1990, splits in the Social Democratic movement and a dramatic decline in the popularity of the Conservative government cast strong doubt on the future of the "third force," and by the same token, on its explanatory value for voting change.

While many believe rationality plays an ever-larger role in British voting decisions, at least among a substantial segment of the voting public, there is no agreement on the decision rules that guide voting choice (Scarbrough 1987: 231). Retrospective judgments, "investment" and "consumer" decisions, "overall ideological stance," and "issue voting," among others, have all been suggested. To the extent that British voting motives are instrumental, we may not be able to do better than Crewe's observation that "what moves voters is a diffuse impression of each party's track record, policy package, and leader all rolled into one—in a word, its overall 'image' " (Crewe 1985b: 183; and see Heath et al. 1985: 172; Norton 1984: 95). Whatever the underlying mechanism of choice may be, Heath et al. (1985: 99) are rightly skeptical when they point out that efforts to elicit these rules from voters are plagued by the tendency of survey respondents to provide answers "that have little or no relevance to their behavior simply in order to be cooperative." Voter confusion, feelings of lack of issue saliency, and sheer ignorance complicate any effort to penetrate the mysteries of voting behavior. Kavanagh (1985a: 113) uses as an example a 1963–1964 survey of a panel of voters that revealed "only 39 percent gave similar responses in successive interviews" on a major policy question. And, we might add, voters may wish to avoid confessing decision rules that reveal ignorance or venality or, more likely, they may be unaware of why they made a particular choice. There is little convincing evidence that many voters, however well informed, make elaborate cost/benefit calculations. Rather, their choices are likely to follow relatively "rudimentary decision rules" such as "simple retrospective judgments" (Hibbing 1987: 26–27). It is not even clear that voters vote on the basis of the issues they say are most important. Heath et al. found that in 1983 "had people voted according to the detailed stances of each party on the most important issues of the day, Labour would not in fact have gone down to defeat at all" (Heath et al. 1985: 89).

If we cannot be certain of the prevalence of instrumental voting, or generalize about the precise mechanism for rational choice among British and Japanese voters, we can at least suggest what sorts of issues and positions are generally believed to be of importance from election to election.

The Economy

Economic issues play a role in British voting, though a review of the evidence is not conclusive about their importance or the mechanism by which their influence is exercised at the ballot box. In one important respect, the milieu in which economic issues play themselves out has been very different in Britain and Japan. In Japan, most elections in the past thirty years have been held amidst relatively steady economic expansion and emergence of Japan as an economic leader of the industrial world. In Britain, the trend has been the other way: slow and intermittent growth, and steady decline in relative economic position.

One view of the role of economic issues is that voters respond to aggregate national economic statistics—growth, unemployment, inflation (Harrop 1988: 54)—rewarding the incumbent party that establishes a good record in these areas, and punishing the party that fails to meet expectations. The attraction of aggregate economic models, writes Scarbrough (1987: 232), "is their parsimony; if the popularity of governments is a function of the macroeconomy, many of the more tortuous questions about voting would be resolved almost at a stroke." Frey and Schneider found "highly significant relationships between inflation, unemployment and the governing party lead in the polls" (cited in Whiteley 1986: 45). Goodhart and Bhansali even worked out a formula for predicting the vote based on government performance in employment and price inflation (cited in Heath et al. 1985: 161). Alt (1984: 299) believes that party dealignment has been the result of "the failure of both parties to produce the economic growth they promised since at least 1959." Others have found that the relationship depends on the specific economic indicator. For example, Hibbing (1987: 27) states that "the more real per capita income is increasing, the worse the 'in-party' fares in elections," while "unemployment and inflation . . . are related in the predicted direction to the electoral performance of the party in power." Budge and McKay (1988: 88) also suggest a more variegated voter response to economic performance, in which "electors punish governments for economic downturns," but do not necessarily reward them for good performance. The continued relative decline of the British economy that continued at least through the first Thatcher term should, it would seem, have worked equally against both incumbent Labour and Conservative administrations. Precisely because neither party had a very good track record in economic performance through the 1960s and 1970s, retrospective comparisons could offer little voting direction as long as the two-party mold held, and should, logically at least, have led to aimless alternations in power between one failed set of policies and another (very similar one).

The fact that the Gallup polls found 80 percent of the electorate believed unemployment the "most urgent problem" while the Conservatives were winning their 1983 landslide certainly suggests limits to the impact of specific macroeconomic issues on voting (Scarbrough 1987: 233). Voters may even reward what is by many measures a poor economic performance. Although the "misery index" (inflation plus unemployment) rose in the first Thatcher government, "the 1983 election not only rewarded the Conservatives with a second term, but added the bonus of a massively increased majority in Parliament" (Crewe 1985b: 155). In addition to factors of party loyalty that we identified above, perhaps the explanation for the ability of either Labour or the Conservatives to win a national election lies in the fact that, as Alt (1980) has shown, voters seem to have adjusted to the anemic state of the economy by lowering their expectations. As a result, economic voting has yet to nudge Britain out of the two-party parliamentary model.

Many feel that perceptions of individual well-being are a better predictor of voting behavior in Britain than aggregate economic performance (Hibbing 1987: 28–29). "[I]ndividual-level economic voting seems to be slightly more common in the United Kingdom than in the United States" (Hibbing 1987: 27). As we saw in chapter 5, the electorate is overwhelmingly concerned with its own personal standing. "Electors' private preferences," say Budge and McKay (1988: 89), "relate primarily to the stability and well-being of the family and of its relatives and friends." Crewe puts it this way, "when answering survey questions on the important issues, respondents think of public problems; when entering the polling booth they think of family fortunes" (Crewe 1987: 55; and see Kavanagh 1985a: 106,108; Hibbing 1987: 27).[6]

It is this self-interested voting behavior that is said to lead to the observed electoral business cycles, punctuated by government-engineered rising standards of living during election years. "Most recent general elections have been held in years which saw living standards rise faster than in non-election years" (Kavanagh 1985a: 108: and see E. Tufte 1978). Governments should take note, however, of Budge and McKay's (1988: 88) point, made above, that voters do not necessarily reward governments "for giving the population more." It is unclear, however, how such cycles affected the vote during times of secular decline. "If voters were deciding on the basis of their achieved economic benefits under Labour and Conservative governments," writes Kavanagh, "then both parties would have suffered even more drastic falls in support (Kavanagh 1985a: 108). It is something of a truism that the Conservatives are the party of the rich and Labour the party of the poor. Such a belief is "deeply rooted in the popular consciousness." At least in recent years, Conservatives have favored "a free-enterprise economy tailored to the more prosperous regions, whereas Labour endorse subsidies and protection from foreign competition in order to reduce unemployment in the peripheries"(Budge and McKay 1988: 74). But while there is some truth to this image, standard of living was not sufficient to " 'deliver' either the Conservative or Labour vote" (Sarlvik and Crewe 1983: 99). The struggling emergence of a "third force" in party competition during the 1980s made generalizations about the link between standard of living and vote even more difficult to determine.

One of the most consistently important election issues in Japan since 1963 has been the economy, at both the macro- and micro-levels. The most visible evidence of LDP success has been economic performance, for which the LDP is given much credit. Not only do short-term improvements in the Japanese economy bring about greater support for the LDP (Miyake 1986b: 62), but the conservatism of the Japanese also makes them reluctant to tinker with the long-term economic well-being they have enjoyed under the LDP (Hrebenar 1986: 22). Japanese voters would seem to be firm believers in the old axiom, "If it ain't broke, don't fix it." The effect of short-term and microeconomic policies on specific elections is important, and that effect is not always beneficial to the

Table 6.8

Recognition and Vote for Candidates Distributing Local Benefits in Japan
(in percent)

	Recognized	Voted
Highly concentrated electoral district	10.7	3.9
Lowly concentrated electoral district	26.2	13.9
Farmer	27.7	17.4
White-collar worker	12.3	5.0
Voted LDP	24.9	15.4
Voted JSP	10.9	2.5

Source: Joji Watanuki et al., 1986. *Electoral Behavior in the 1983 Japanese Elections*, p. 4.
Tokyo: Institute for International Relations, Sophia University.

LDP. Decreasing support for the LDP in 1988 and 1989 can be attributed in part
to economic factors (as well as to the series of scandals that has beset the LDP),
for example, anger on the farm toward the LDP policy of relaxing some agricultural import restriction under pressure from the United States, and to nationwide
anger at the tax reform package passed in early 1989 and the nonconsensual
manner in which the tax reform package was passed.

Inoguchi Takashi is one of Japan's leading experts on the relationship between economic conditions and voting behavior and he has found:

> 1) that macro-economic variables do matter in altering political support
> patterns despite all cultural and other differences from other OECD countries,
> but not as strongly as some other studies have shown for their countries,
> including the United States;
>
> 2) Japanese micro-economic management reveals more market-conforming
> features than market-driving features, which are stressed in studies on political
> business cycles;
>
> 3) Government support tends to be affected more by the consumer price
> index than by all other major macro-economic indicators;
>
> 4) Conservative resurgence since the late 1970s seems to be based on the
> narrowing gap between economic aspiration and performance when the eco-
> nomic growth rate have [*sic*] gone down drastically, encouraging economic
> conservatism and then political conservatism toward protecting the status quo
> (Inoguchi 1986: 87).

Inoguchi's analysis suggests that in Japan, as in Britain, individual-level economic voting is present. Japan, too, has its "misery index," even though voters
are concerned almost exclusively, as Watanuki found, with its inflation dimension. In addition, there is a specific "instrumental" dimension of social voting
(see above). Benefits may be bestowed either by the candidate or by local leaders

who campaigned for the candidate (Richardson and Flanagan 1984: 255–56). If not "economic" voting in the usual sense, this behavior certainly reflects the instrumental concern for material well-being normally associated with it. A different view is offered by Watanuki, who states that, on the whole, Japanese voters do not vote for candidates who "come through" for them in terms of bringing local benefits. As can be seen by Table 6.8, only 16.6 percent of the total electorate recognize that candidates have the ability to distribute local benefits and of those who do realize it, only half actually vote for that candidate.

Gerald Curtis (1988: 222) adds further support to the argument by stating that *koenkai* and other individual-based organizations do not constitute patron-client relationships. Japanese politicians are not powerful leaders demanding compliance, they are supplicants promising to deliver what is needed, and/or reminding the voter of family, obligation, or other social ties that bind them. The patron-client relationship still does exist in specific cases, such as the continued support for ex-Prime Minister Tanaka in Niigata even after his conviction on bribery charges and the local support for politicians implicated in the Recruit scandal.

Ideology and Principles

While stands on specific election issues may determine voting behavior, some feel that general principles, ideological stance, or overall "image" is more likely to be decisive. Rose and McAllister indicated that this was the case in the 1983 election, in which economic self-interest was less important than political principles and party performances (Scarbrough 1987: 235). A number of analysts have suggested that voting choice is centered on a dichotomous choice between two broad families of issues. Such issues might be grouped according to support for government intervention, or socialism, or, especially in recent years, its polar "free enterprise" alternative (Heath et al. 1985: 111). The cognitive model also identifies two issue groupings, one based on "familiar political and economic issues, the other on questions of law and order, immigration and social liberalism" (Himmelweit et al. 1981: 141). Others have made a distinction between "moral traditionalism" and "economic egalitarianism" (Topf 1989: 69). The latter would seem to favor Labour, the former the Conservatives.[7] On both issues, voters are suspicious of change "except where it is immediately beneficial" (Budge and McKay 1988: 86). Table 6.9 provides greater detail about these issues.

The actual outcome of a specific election will depend on the balance between those two broad families of concerns at the time for a plurality of voters. When class and party loyalties are strong, the scope for individual movement between these two sets of issues from election to election is small, since "personal and social circumstances render one policy area of paramount and enduring importance" to most voters (Budge and McKay 1988: 99). The effect of dealignment, on the other hand, has been to increase volatility to the point where not only are voters more likely to switch their emphases on the major issues, but they may

Table 6.9

Areas into Which Electors Classify Issues (Britain)

Broad Policy Area	Specific Issues Corresponding to Each Area	Party Favored
Civil Order	Law and order; measures against crime; death penalty; rioting; strikes and demonstrations; anti-system parties and problems caused by their strength	Conservative
Traditional	Support of traditional/Christian morals and Church; abortion and birth control; temperance; religious schools and education	Conservative
Ethnic	Immigration and foreign workers; attitudes to minority groups and their advancement; discrimination; school and housing integration; language questions	Conservative
Regional	National unity; devolution and regional autonomy; regional equalization of resources	Conservative
Socioeconomic Redistribution	Social service spending; importance of social welfare; housing as a problem; housing subsidies; rent control; health and medical services; social reform; pensions; aid to other services such as education; action in regard to unemployment; employment guarantee	Labour

Source: Ian Budge and David McKay, 1988. *The Changing British Political System: Into the 1990s,* Table 4.3, pp. 92–93. London: Longman. Used with permission.

break out of the two-party model altogether (Budge and McKay 1988: 99–100).

The ideological attitudes of the British voter tend, as we have seen, more to the center and right than elsewhere in Europe. Rose (1989: 267) goes so far as to say that "The Conservatives won the last [1987] election because twice as many voters see themselves on the right as on the left." Yet this fact alone does not explain Conservative party strength, especially in the Thatcher years. Under Conservative governments since 1979, the electorate has consistently endorsed views on specific policy questions like education, the health service, and others that are to the left of the Conservative position. While this fact may suggest, as noted above, that party loyalties tend to override specific issues, another explanation is that on those issues which voters believe most salient in a particular election, the Conservatives have been more in tune with national opinion than the opposition. Hence, while McAllister and Mugharn (1987: 60, 63) found relatively little deterioration in support for the Labour Party's traditional socialist principles in 1983 when compared to 1974 and 1979, it was the nuclear disarmament issue, not these principles, that crossed "the threshold of electoral salience."

The percentage of Japanese voters who can identify their own ideology (85 percent) and that of the parties (70 percent) is high, and the distribution of the ideologies of Japanese voters is normal, 37.7 percent responding as moderate liberals and 46.4 percent as moderate conservatives (Kabashima 1986: 64, 68). This does lead to a relationship of ideological identification with party voting, but it is stronger for the LDP than the parties of the left. Whereas 25 percent of those who classified themselves as liberal in the 1983 House of Representatives election voted for the LDP (as compared to 70 percent for the JSP and 31 percent for the JCP), only 10 percent of conservatives voted for the JSP and 2 percent voted for the JCP (Kabashima 1986: 84). There is an interesting parallel here between Japan and Britain, in that the ideological center in Japan is also middle-right and that, as noted above, one of the major problems the JSP has in getting votes is that their policies are out of the mainstream generally, but especially as they apply to defense and U.S.-Japan alliance policy. No ideologically based "issue clusters" similar to those Budge and McKay identify for Britain have been identified for Japan. However, Watanuki (1980: 15) suggests an analogous influence. He argues that the central cleavage in Japanese politics is not class, but a values cleavage between conservatives, who support "traditional and prewar values of Emperor worship, emphasis on hierarchy and harmony in the belief in a strong armed nation" and those on the left, who support "modern, postwar values of individualism, equality and fear of military build up and war." Not everyone agrees with Watanuki that there is even a values cleavage in Japan, as there is a remarkable similarity in value orientation between supporters of all political parties, including the JCP (Curtis 1988: 227).

Consensus

Though consensus is rarely identified as an election concern in Britain, the persistence of ideological moderation and collectivist traditions do explain public dislike of the fractious and polarizing behavior of Labour and the Conservatives. Rose (1986c: 294) believes that popular dissatisfaction with "confrontation politics" is at least partly responsible for dealignment of support for the Conservatives and Labour. And it is possible that the Liberals and Social Democrats have benefited to some extent from public protest against the polarizing trend of the 1970s. Heath et al. (1985: 165) suggest that "one of the positive attractions of the Alliance may be its reputation for concern with all groups in society rather than a narrow sectarian concern for the interests of its supporters alone." The British voter still seems to value consensus more than politicians of either of the two traditional parties, and while this fact may not explain party choice (e.g. this or that party is less divisive than the others), it may partly explain the phenomenon of dealignment, or abandonment of former identification with either Conservatives or Labour and the growth in support for the Alliance parties (Heath et al. 1985: 166).

Consensus in Japan is not just another value of the system, but is, as discussed in previous chapters, a dominant feature of social and political culture. In voting behavior there seems to be a perceived need on the part of a large number of voters for nationwide consensus on leadership, as well as a belief that consensus should guide government policy making. Together, these factors have contributed to the electoral dominance of the LDP. While the role of consensus in policy making will be discussed at length in Chapter 7, the extent to which the LDP works to build a consensus in policy making may be one factor that determines whether some members of the electorate vote for or against the LDP. Japanese voters love to hate a strong LDP, and are reluctant to love a weak LDP. They are wary of the former and uncomfortable with the latter. Sixty-five percent of respondents to an *Asahi Shimbun* poll said they thought the LDP had won too many seats in the 1986 election (302 of 512 seats), including 53 percent of those who had voted for LDP candidates. Forty-five percent of respondents to a 1984 NHK poll said that they want a narrow LDP majority, and 35 percent responded that they want a stable majority (reported in Curtis 1988: 197). These findings are replicated in a poll taken by the *Yomiuri Shimbun* following the July 1989 upper-house election (Sept. 16, 1989: 12). This supports the contention that there are many voters who want to keep the LDP balanced on the edge: enough members of the Diet to continue to control the government, but not enough to be able to act without consensus. Thus, when the LDP has a strong majority these voters are worried about its having too much power (e.g., after the 1980 election), and so they remove their support in the next (1983) election. When the LDP rule seems precarious (e.g., after the 1983 election) they are worried about an opposition role in government and so vote for the LDP in the next (1986) election (Curtis 1988: 197). When voters make a choice based on the belief that their party or candidate will maintain a consensual style of government, then they are acting instrumentally. When the consensual values of society operate on them to influence a choice, they are acting expressively.

Public Morality

Corruption plays a very small and intermittent role in British national elections. As we have seen, since the late nineteenth century, electoral corruption has virtually ceased to be a concern. And while the British are no less prone to human failings than others when it comes to politics, those scandals that do arise there more regularly involve sex and spy scandals than financial malfeasance. It has been the former, like the Profumo affair, rather than the latter, that has on occasion caused electoral problems for British governments. In the mid-1980s a major scandal developed over a decision about the fate of the Westland Company, which focused on questions of government defense contracting, but the issue was tinged with British nationalism and cabinet rivalries. Ultimately, the scandal was over whether the prime minister had been involved in a cover-up. There have been classic money and influence scandals, like the Poulson affair in the early 1970s, and one can only speculate how often the convention of secrecy has concealed or mitigated scandals in government that, in a country with a less effective regime of confidentiality, might have been campaign issues.

On the contrary, aside from the economy, the most consistently important issue facing the Japanese voter has been corruption (Hrebenar 1986: 237). The two issues may act in voters' minds as counterweights on a balance used to calculate their support for the LDP. The LDP may well be one of the most scandal-ridden parties in the developed world, but, in contrast to Britain, where the scandals tend to be about sex, the scandals in Japan have tended to be about money. Stringent campaign financing laws and the lack of mass media advertising notwithstanding, it is very expensive to be involved in Japanese politics. Campaigns cost in the hundreds of millions of yen and between campaigns one has to keep up a veritable flood of gifts to the wakes and marriages of constituents, donors, supporters and their families. The JSP has unions to support its members and the JCP has its very popular and profitable publication, *Akahata* (Red Flag), whereas LDP politicians rely upon donations from businesses. The LDP politician relies upon his faction to do most of the money raising, and the factions are always thinking of new ways to sidestep the letter and intent of the campaign financing laws in order to support their members. While the LDP factions are always looking for new ways to receive money, Japanese commercial interests are always looking for a way to give it to them. This combination has ensured a continuing saga of "dirty money" political scandals—the Lockheed scandal and the Recruit scandal having been only the two most publicized. Thus, while other factors were at work, one has to say that the reaction to the Lockheed scandal caused the popular vote for the LDP in the 1976 election to drop to its lowest level in the party's history. It also seems certain that the LDP suffered another precipitous drop in votes in 1983 because the election followed Tanaka's conviction for bribery and the party's reluctance to remove his influence from the party, by only two months. The Recruit scandal has had an obvious and direct impact on voting behavior in the 1989 upper-house election and the 1990 lower-house election. Although there were many factors involved, there seems little doubt that the Recruit scandal was a major factor in the LDP's loss of its majority in the upper house and its loss of twenty-three seats in the lower house. The importance of the scandal in the eyes of the voters is demonstrated by the fact that the LDP chose a relative outsider, but a squeaky clean outsider, Kaifu Toshiki, to lead the party and the nation. Even when he removed many of the largest factions' most powerful members in the cabinet due to their involvement in the scandal, those factions were not able to remove him for fear of reidentifying the party with the scandal.

Parochialism

It has long been axiomatic that British voters gave little attention to local issues. Voters, as we have seen, choose parties, not candidates, and residency in a constituency has not even been a requirement. Still, nearly half the respondents in one survey thought it important for their MP to have been brought up in his or her constituency (Young 1984: 20). Furthermore, there is some evidence of change in the importance of the personal vote (Cain et al. 1984: 304–10). As a result of the rising demand for constituency services that we noted in Chapter 5, the constituency parties now encourage MPs to take more interest in local affairs, and even to live in the constituency (J. Marsh 1985: 79). Marsh (1985: 70) asserts that incumbents command a small personal vote, based on the accumulated credit of their constituent service, but one which nevertheless could be decisive in a closely contested election. Others perceive a trend toward an increased personal vote (Cain et al. 1984: 308). Notwithstanding this view, there is still no clear evidence that local issues are important to a great majority of voters' decisions.

Parochialism has far greater significance in Japanese voting behavior than in the case of Britain. As we have seen, local factors may be of growing significance, especially in marginal seats, but they are still small relative to issues such as partisan identification and class. "[A] local rather than a national political consciousness, an emphasis on special benefits for one's local area (*jimoto rieki*), and an inattention to the language and issues of debate over which national politics are being fought" (Richardson and Flanagan 1984: 175–76). This model, one that has been posited by many other scholars of Japanese politics (e.g., Hrebenar 1986: 19), holds that the Japanese are much more interested in local politics than in national politics for those reasons we have labeled the national political culture a spectator culture. The authors believe, however, that this factor is changing. In the 1976 JABISS data, 45 percent of respondents were more interested in local politics than any other level, and voters also tended to be concerned with the candidates' stands on local issues (Richardson and Flanagan 1984: 173–75). Our own 1987 survey, however, found a much higher percentage of the respondents interested in international issues (86 percent), because national and international issues were seen as impinging on local issues (Stronach 1988: 7). More Japanese generally now see the international prestige of Japan as an issue that has a direct impact on them individually, and rural farmers, those most likely to be parochial, have a greater understanding of the importance of international policies (e.g., the trade policy with the United States) on their livelihoods.

Postmaterialism and Value Change

As we have seen, a much-debated topic over the past ten years has been the extent to which "post materialist values" (Inglehart 1977)—such as greater polit-

Table 6.10

What Do British Constituents Expect Their MPs to Do?

Role	Percent of Respondents
Ombudsman	19
Protecting constituency	26
Oversight	5
Information	24
Lawmaking (debating and voting)	11
All equal	10

Source: James Marsh, 1985. "Representational Changes: The Constituency MP." In *Parliament in the 1980s,* ed. Phillip Norton: Table 4.1, p. 77. Oxford: Basil Blackwell. Used with permission of Basil Blackwell.

ical openness, freedom of speech, and environmental protection—have been replacing "materialist" concerns, such as prices and physical security, and what effect these attitudinal changes have on behavior. This debate has been carried on both with respect to the Western democracies and to Japan, though each has its own distinctive variants. One area of political life that stands to be most affected by the new values is electoral politics and voting behavior.

We saw that postmaterialism among the British had been found to lag behind many other European states, but that by the late 1980s it was about average for the European Community and had grown over the past twenty years. Franklin and Inglehart found in a study in the early 1970s that in Britain the emergence of a group supporting these values "had remarkably little impact upon the balance of party support" (Franklin 1985b: 164). In a 1984 *Eurobarometer* survey, the British were substantially less likely than average to support an "ecologist" party—whose potential electorate is "likely to be post-materialist" (Inglehart and Rabier 1986: Table 1, 466; 476). Not surprisingly, critics who largely reject the Inglehart analysis do not find "postmaterialism" to have been a factor in British elections (Heath et al. 1985: 66). Election results from both British and European elections seem largely to have borne out this conclusion. It is certainly less likely in Britain than in Japan, and other states with variants of proportional voting, that these new attitudes, however they are classified and whatever the root causes of their appearance, could manifest themselves in more than limited electoral success for a Green Party.

Notwithstanding the claim of relatively weak postmaterialism among the British, the "new politics" that postmaterialism represents—based on issues such as environment, women's rights, disarmament, and increased participation—does appear to have made an impact in Britain. Even if postmaterialism is still not very widespread, postmaterialists bring a new set of attitudes toward participation and voting. "A consistent pattern of political alliance is apparently developing between postmaterialists and Leftist parties," including Labour (Dalton 1988:

170–71). Values change can be seen as one of the causes of disenchantment with the party programs of the major parties, and new politics issues have been found to be a strong influence among younger British voters (Dalton 1988: 172). The strength of the environmental movement is itself evidence of the impact of the new issues. While Britain's own Green Party languished for the first fifteen years of its existence, it experienced a dramatic increase in votes in the 1989 European parliamentary elections, capturing 15 percent of the British vote (but no seats), a figure higher than in any other European Community member (*The Economist* June 24, 1989).Whatever their electoral prospects, some of the issues the Greens champion have already had an effect on the political debate, for example, Mrs. Thatcher's announced conversion in 1988 to the cause of environmentalism.

In Chapter 1, we found that Japan, like other industrial states, is undergoing values change, though the emphasis is somewhat different in Japan from elsewhere. There, the cluster of postmaterialist (or postindustrial in Japan) values includes a shift to libertarian, cosmopolitan, and universalistic values. As we have seen, the importance of social networks as a motivation for voting in Japan has in the past tended to diminish the role of issue voting. But as Richardson and Flanagan (1984: 255) point out, the growth of libertarian values in Japan has contributed to changing voting behavior for many Japanese. The new voters are not so likely to be moved by the traditional style of campaigning, based on the expectation of personal benefit, but are concerned instead about the range of postindustrial objectives. A wide discrepancy in LDP support appears between traditionally oriented voters and postindustrially oriented voters, and in contrast to Britain, new, small parties have arisen reflecting the new value orientation (Richardson and Flanagan 1984: 256, 257).

Competence

While many specific policy issues may dominate elections—unemployment, inflation, law and order—another general instrumental criterion is perceived competence (Harrop 1988: 52). The voter is not just interested in the party stand on the issue, but how well the party can govern. The distinction between the issue position and perceived competence is yet another factor that helps explain why, for example, many people could vote for the Conservatives in recent elections, though they disagreed with many of their policies. The Conservatives, like their Japanese counterparts the LDP, have assiduously cultivated their image as the competent party, the natural party of government. This image is incorporated into their electoral strategy. That it has met with some success can be seen from opinion surveys and voting results. In Britain, Kavanagh (1985a: 113) found that on those issues for which the public perceived a "competency" differential between Labour and the Conservatives—law and order and taxation—the Conservatives gained in 1983 at the expense of Labour.

One complication in the competence hypothesis is that, as we saw in the

Table 6.11

Japanese Opinions of Best Party (in percent)

	LDP	JSP
Best candidates	39	10
Best leaders	38	8
Best policies	37	9
Best represents people in your occupation	32	15
Best understands people and problems in your district	38	6
Best able to eliminate political corruption	15	10
Best able to stabilize economy	29	11
Best in handling international diplomacy	51	3
Most capable of governing	54	6

Source: Joji Watanuki, 1986. *Electoral Behavior in the 1983 Japanese Elections*, pp. 203–5. Tokyo: Institute for International Relations, Sophia University.

One complication in the competence hypothesis is that, as we saw in the section on economic voting, by some very important economic measures the Conservatives in Britain did not perform consistently well, certainly not between 1979 and 1983. Here we must begin with the recognition that "why the Conservatives won" involved many factors, not the least of which was the split between Labour and the new Social Democrats. It is worth positing the distinction between competence as defined by some threshold of achievement (4 percent unemployment, or a cut in unemployment of 2 percent, for example), and perceived competence, defined either as an act of faith in future managerial success, or perhaps more important, as a comparative judgment about the future. Labour, it might be said, was felt by some significant number of voters to be potentially more incompetent than the Conservatives.

Competence is a central factor in explaining why the LDP remains in power year after year in Japan, even though it is often beset with financial scandals, problems in the U.S.-Japan relationship and unpopular microlevel economic policies. The belief held by many Japanese that the LDP is the only party able to govern and the inability of any of the Japanese opposition parties, especially the "major" opposition party, the JSP, to present themselves credibly as a viable government party is one of the major factors that distinguishes the British two-party system from the Japanese system of having one predominating party in a multiparty system. Table 6.11 clearly shows the disparity in perception of competency between the LDP and the JSP by a very wide margin, even on the question of eliminating corruption.

Although the Conservatives have been in power for more than a decade under Margaret Thatcher and John Major, frequent transfers of power between the Conservatives and Labour have occurred in the postwar period, and it would be a brave soul who would bet that another Labour government will not be formed sooner or later. By the 1990s, Labour's prospects already looked better than they had since the 1970s, although they were unable to cash in on their seeming advantage in the 1992 general election. There has been no ruling party in Japan other than the LDP since its formation in 1955 (all previous postwar governments but one were formed by the conservative parties that eventually melded into the LDP), and few people believe that the JSP will ever be able to form its own government in the future. Although the possibility of coalition government among the opposition parties was much discussed in the Japanese press from the mid-1970s to the mid-1980s, even that possibility seems to be very faint, and not even the Recruit scandal has changed the attitude of the Japanese electorate. Come what may, the Japanese have perceived the LDP as dependable and safe in the past (Hrebenar 1986: 22), and will probably continue to do so in the future.

There are many reasons that explain the perception of LDP competence: the success of the LDP's economic policies, the pragmatism of the LDP, the range of issue orientation within the factional system of the LDP, the conservative nature of the Japanese people, and the close ties between the LDP, the bureaucracy, and Japan's commercial interests. But perhaps the most important element in the perception is simple longevity. No other party has ruled in thirty-nine years. The perception of incompetence in the opposition parties is the mirror image of the perception of LDP competence. The JSP, Komeito, and JCP have never ruled and so are perceived as being unable to do so. They have been removed from real power for so long, and they have so few contacts in the bureaucratic and commercial halls of power, that there is a fear that the nation would collapse if they were ever brought to power (Hrebenar 1986: 10–13). On the other hand, the JSP and JCP have done nothing to help their own cause. Their policies have been out of the mainstream and have been essentially reactive to LDP initiatives, and one senses that there is not a great deal of optimism in their own ranks concerning a future JSP-led government.

The Campaign and the Media

In the past, neither the election campaigns themselves, nor the personalities of leaders were seen to be of particularly great importance in influencing the vote in Britain. But that view has been revised of late. Kavanagh (1985a: 111) claims that "the election campaigns, even if not decisive—except where the parties are evenly matched—are more important than were allowed for in the 1950s and 1960s." To underscore the point he notes that, "Enoch Powell's speeches against new-Commonwealth immigration and the release of the poor balance of trade figures in 1970, the miners' strike in January 1974, the industrial disputes and disruption in the winter of 1979, and the recapture of the Falklands in 1982 were all given massive coverage by the mass media and influenced some voters" (Kavanagh 1985a: 108). And while Crewe (1987: 55) finds that "leaders made little difference" to party vote in the 1987 election, Clarke and Stewart (1984: 701) conclude that "reactions to party leaders may have been of some importance in the late 1970s." While there is some evidence that the personalities of party leaders and the campaign strategies of the respective parties have increased impact on voting decisions in Britain, these factors are still felt to be overwhelmed by class and by concern for policies (Crewe 1985b: 175).

In traditional voting models the media were believed to accomplish little more than to reinforce existing predispositions. This view was especially plausible in the years prior to 1964, when the BBC was prohibited from airing election coverage during the campaign. However, Crewe (1985b: 163) found the impact of television in the 1983 election to be considerable, and preelection broadcasts were cited by more people (20 percent) than any other factor in the campaign in influencing how they "finally decided to vote." While such subjective evaluations of voting motives must be viewed with the same caution as any self-reported survey results, they are nevertheless an indication of how people perceive the importance of television in politics. News broadcasts themselves have also taken on some importance in framing the election. Harrop (1988: 45) goes so far as to say that "television no longer covers an election; television is the election," and that the weakening of party loyalties, the rise of new issues, and the credibility of the media have combined to make the media "full members of the family of influences on voting behaviour." It is not "how television 'frames' the news" that matters, but its powerful ability to "project" a story or a party's problems "into voters' living rooms with a directness which no other medium could match" (Harrop 1988: 46). From the political left, the media appeared to play a key role in maintaining the dominant values of the polity (Dunleavy and Husbands 1985). Still, the fact that party identification still carries more weight than the telegenic personality tends to limit television's role more than in the United States. It would seem that in its effects it is neither neutral nor determining, but the media's, especially television's, "visibility" in the election process suggests an important role.

In Japan, there has not been much to cover concerning the personality and leadership style of party leaders. Japan's political leaders have always emphasized their group identity, and the privacy of one's personal life has always been highly valued by all Japanese. The only political leader who broke this mold was Nakasone. He was a very outgoing and aggressive prime minister, who did not fear breaking party traditions and bucking the consensus of the party and public opinion. Although his personal life was never a matter of public attention, he did create an individual leadership style beyond the traditional "team player." It is arguable that the Japanese people saw in Nakasone a leadership style more in keeping with their place at the top of the international hierarchy—a leader who could hold his own, charismatically and intellectually, with the political leaders of the West. His policies and his actions during the Recruit scandal eventually brought him into disrepute, but for a time he did receive the highest level of popularity recorded in postwar polls. Post-Nakasone prime ministers seem, however, to have reverted to more traditional styles of leadership.

It is fair to say that the electronic news media have had less effect on campaigns and voting behavior in Japan than in any other developed nation (Curtis 1988: 169). Individual candidates are forbidden to buy ads in any mass medium and television news reporting tends to be very evenhanded in balancing the presentation of LDP and opposition views. Politicians are often on television talk shows, but the show's host is always a moderator and never a commentator. The print media have more of an impact in creating public opinion through analysis and opinion articles in both the national newspapers and the influential news weeklies, but even here it is rare for an individual politician and his or her campaign to be the subject of print-media reporting. Indeed, newspaper reporters in Japan have the image of being a part of the inside elite and not given to ruffling the feathers of politicians who allow them their insider status (Baerwald 1986: 121). The Japan Election Survey of the 1983 general election found that newspaper reporting was not significantly related to voters' candidate recognition or evaluation (Watanuki et al. 1986: 16). This is not to say that individual campaigns never receive intensive coverage by the news media, for example the 1990 lower-house election campaign of Hamada Makiko received a tremendous amount of coverage, but such examples are the exception to the rule.

Summary and Conclusions

What makes the British-Japanese comparison so interesting is that it demonstrates on the one hand how varied voting behavior can be in two parliamentary systems with relatively similar political institutions, and on the other how alike modern polities, even from vastly different historical backgrounds, have become. In both the British and Japanese cases, it is clear that considerable debate still characterizes our understanding of individual voting behavior, and that no single model of voting behavior can give full understanding to that process within any one political culture, let alone across cultures.

In both political cultures it appears that "expressive" factors such as class attributes, territorial parochialism, group socialization, party identification, and even the structure of the electoral system itself form a framework of initial motives to vote for one candidate or another, within which behavior is either reinforced or redirected by more immediate, conscious and "rational" considerations such as reward, past performance, future competency, and economic well-being. While the interplay between rational and expressive factors seems to be generally similar in both cases, the differences between Japan and Britain are in which factors, both general and specific, have the greatest impact in each country.

Table 6.12 summarizes and compares what we have found to be the most important factors influencing voting behavior in Japan and Britain.

There are significant differences in the relative importance of specific expressive factors in each country. In Britain, class cleavages have been considered the

Table 6.12

Voting Behavior Matrix for Britain and Japan

	Expressive	Instrumental
More influential in Britain	Class cleavages Territorial-based voting Housing tenure Ethnicity	Ideology and issue clusters Relative economic decline
Affect both	Party identification Electoral structure Occupational change	Individual-level economic performance Macroeconomic performance Competency Mass media
More influential in Japan	Group process Personalism Increased education Urbanization	Corruption Parochialism Consensus Global status; economic success

most important factor, and while class dealignment, the rise of the "working" middle class, and the decline of the trade unions has somewhat lessened its impact, it is still the central point of focus. Voting in Japan, however, has never been much affected by class cleavages, and remains innocent of their effect today. On the other hand, there the most important expressive factor is the group process—the pressure of the group on the individual to conform to the consensus, the essentially social and passive nature of voting participation in Japan, and the influence of the obligation/loyalty interpersonal nexus. We have argued that the group process is more important in Britain than may have been assumed in the past, but it is still relatively less important than in Japan where the mechanisms of group dominance are more central to the culture, and in particular, to the political culture.

In both Japan and Britain, party identification is a very good indicator of voting behavior, and according to one major figure in the field, Bradley Richardson, "partisan attitudes are the dominant force in Japanese parliamentary voting" (Richardson 1988: 695). The prevailing view is still, however, that, while party identification is becoming increasingly stable in Japan, it is less so, and there are more nonidentifiers than in Britain. An interesting contrast is that while strong partisan identification is associated in Britain with traditional attitudes, and contrasted to "cognitive mobilization," in Japan increased partisan identification actually seems to be related to modernization and increased levels of cognitive mobilization.

The major differences in the role of party identification in Japan and Britain stem in part from structural differences in the electoral system and historical differences. In Britain, the single-member constituency, first-past-the-post system, tends to emphasize the role of parties. In Japan's SNTV, multiple-member constituency system, party identification tends more to be only an initial selector for the voter. In addition, the relatively long histories of the two major parties in Britain, each identified with the most important classes in a class-based society, give stability to voter identification in a number of ways, as for example through the socialization process. In Japan, however, political parties and party government as a concept have a very short history (only about 100 years), prewar parties were perceived as corrupt, incompetent, and overly partisan, and the parties that exist today have only been around for a few decades and have not yet shaken the mistrust of the past. Under these conditions, one can hardly expect the Japanese to form strong identifications with their parties as the British do.

Another expressive factor affecting voting behavior in Japan but not Britain is the drastic demographic changes that occurred in Japan from the mid-1950s to the mid-1970s. The migration of the Japanese population from rural villages to urban areas and a simultaneous suburbanization of the Kanto and Kansi areas has significantly reduced the vote for the LDP. The effects of this seem to have ended by the mid-1970s, however, and support for the LDP has been since gradually growing. This is perhaps due in part to a transference of LDP loyalties and campaign mechanisms from rural areas to urban areas, which took place during the migration. Britain remains a relatively immobile society, geographically, so that population movements have not had a comparable electoral effect. Such population movements that have been significant, such as continued immigration of nonwhites, have tended to reinforce existing territorial party preferences. On the other hand, the impact of class and occupational shifts has been at the heart of the debate on voting behavior. While the greatest shifts in voting preference have occurred within the working class, so that recent votes have been relatively evenly divided among the Conservatives, Labour, and the Alliance parties, that class is itself diminishing in size. The future battleground of politics would appear to be the increasing middle class, or classes, with their large component of public employees and professionals. Like Britain, Japan has experienced significant change in the composition of the workforce, with important political implications. A reduction of the workforce in primary industries from one-third of the working population to one-tenth of the working population has combined with the demographic factors cited above to weaken LDP support.

Neither consumption cleavages nor territorially based voting have an impact on voting behavior in Japan. As we saw, the constituency of state-dependent voters is probably the smallest in the OECD, and the structures of the national pension and health insurance schemes in Japan are such that benefits are widely distributed across the population. As was noted in Chapter 2, there are few regional and national differences in Japan that would lead to territorial differences in voting. This, in combination with nationwide increases in affluence as a result of continuing economic growth, precludes the development of Scottish-English or Yorkshire-Kent cleavages that occur in Britain. Although Murakami believes that the need to maintain a continued flow of state benefits will directly influence the voting behavior of many Japanese in the future, there is as yet no direct evidence to support that contention. While consumption cleavages show no signs at present of emerging as an important election factor, regional cleavages certainly have, as Britain has become, electorally speaking, "two Britains."

Before turning to the differences and similarities in the roles that rational factors play in these two political systems, let us restate that there is not much evidence to show that British and Japanese voters make elaborate cost/benefit calculations as they enter the voting booth, and it is not even clear that voters vote on the basis of the issues they think are most important. There is a traditional variant on the cost/benefit analysis which has had importance in past Japanese voting behavior, the patron-client relationship. The patron-client relationship is commonly found in hierarchical societies with strong loyalty/obligation interpersonal bonds, but it is one aspect of Japanese society that does seem to have changed with the above-mentioned demographic and occupational sector changes.

The rational factors of which we have been speaking are, in actuality, categories of issues which tend to have more importance than other categories of issues. Ideology and principle seem to play a much larger role in British than Japanese voting, again a factor that one would expect when comparing a class-based to an egalitarian society. Many of the political issues of the past thirteen years have polarized around socialism and free market economics. Government policies, especially those policies intended to excise the remnants of socialism, have certainly heightened the sensitivity of many British voters to this polarization. It is interesting to note that while the policies of ex-Prime Minister Nakasone's government in the mid-1980s also featured the privatization of national industries, they have not created as intense a national debate as was the case in Britain, nor did they tend to kindle greater ideological orientations. Those on the left who were already ideologically oriented were enraged, but, in general, the nature of the policy issues facing the public did not increase the impact of ideology on voting.

Consensus, like group process, is not uniquely Japanese, but it has a much greater effect on voting in Japan because it is so much more deeply ingrained as a social and political value. Consensus as a value is actually an expressive factor of voting behavior. It is expressive when one believes that the ruling party should act according to the national consensus (something which is much more reasonable to conjecture in Japan than in Western societies), and that the ruling party should bring together other political parties and institutions into the decision-making process. It is rational when the voter casts a ballot for or against a particular candidate or party because they have taken a particular action to support or disregard the consensus.

Parochialism is still a factor in Japanese voting behavior, but it may be that this is changing as, again, rural to urban migration takes effect, and as the issues that have a direct impact on all Japanese, rural and urban, farmer and salaryman, become more national and international. Thus, while the authors have included parochialism in the matrix of important factors that influence Japanese voting, they also believe its importance to be waning. In contrast, parochialism has had a limited role in Britain, although there is some evidence of an increase in its importance, particularly in marginal constituencies, that may reflect the overall changes in British political behavior we examined in Chapter 5.

Those rational factors which have an important impact in both Japan and Britain are economic issues and competence, but again there are differences. In Japan, the trend of LDP domination has been sustained over decades and many factors work for the continuation of that trend. There is little doubt that the voters will not trust the JSP with a government, will not trust a coalition of the opposition with a government, and, although they may intensely dislike the LDP, its attitudes, and its behavior, it will continue to maintain itself in power because of its aura of competence. Part of that aura of competence derives from the success of its economic policies in the past, and its ability to work with both private enterprise and the bureaucracy to ensure continued economic success in the future. The accumulated goodwill derived from this success, the general feeling of well-being among most Japanese, and the Japanese aversion to change that which is not perceived to need changing, weighs heavily on the Japanese voter who is not absolutely committed to one of the opposition parties. While this is the most important element of the economic factor in voting behavior in Japan, the fact that specific economic issues do affect voting behavior is best proved by the exceptions to the rule. When the LDP supports an unpopular economic policy, like the tax reforms discussed in Chapter 7, there will likely be a decrease in support for the LDP. The biggest threat to the LDP as regards economic issues, however, is the law of rising expectations. Many Japanese believe that their personal affluence and the quality of their lifestyle is not commensurate with the amount of money that has entered the Japanese economic system.

The situation in Japan is in many ways quite different from the falling expectations of economic performance identified in British election literature. Voters had concluded that neither Labour nor the Conservatives offered a particularly credible prospect of reversing Britain's fortunes. Reduced voter expectations may have had the effect of making economic issues less salient to electoral choice, thereby shielding the two traditional parties from even further loss of support. But it seems reasonable to suggest that these changed voter attitudes benefited the party in power when they became manifest, that is, the Conservatives. Even improved aggregate economic performance for a time under the Thatcher governments, including a drastic reduction of inflation, did not disguise the fact that Britain's unemployment remained at among the highest rates in Europe. The full employment consensus of the postwar period had been rendered a dead letter, without serious cost to the Conservative party's fortunes. In 1992, the Tories even managed to retain their majority despite what many believed to be the worst recession since the 1930s. Among other things it might appear for now, especially after the 1992 election, that the British voter defines competence to embrace more than successful economic policies. The Conservatives' tax reduction policies, including reduction of top rates and abolition of local rates in favor of the "poll tax," would seem designed to strengthen the Tories' existing core constituency, rather than to expand support within the lower income brackets. As such, they reflect the view that individual-level economic voting in Britain is more important than macro-performance.

Notes

1. Another synthetic model is offered by Heath, Jowell, and Curtice (1985: 10), who describe an "interactionist" interpretation. "Any act of voting must involve both expressive and instrumental elements, and we very much doubt whether the balance between these two elements has changed much in the course of this century . . . It is the interaction between the social and the political that determines how people vote."

2. Heath et al. (1985: 112) remark that the shaping of values is a two-way process, and that "the parties help to shape class values" as well.

3. Heath et al. (1985: 29) dissent from the prevailing view that Labour is no longer a party of the working class. In their view of the 1983 election, "Labour remained a class party . . . it was simply a less successful class party than before."

4. "The absolute level of class voting," they conclude, "has declined as Labour has become less successful, but the relative level of class voting shows few signs of secular decline. Class has by no means withered away. Nevertheless the class structure has changed in several respects. The working class has contracted, reducing Labour's electoral base. The salariat has expanded, in particular its liberal wing of educated, public sector professionals who are out of tune both with the free enterprise ideology of the entrepreneur and with the interventionist ideology of the working class. This group provides fertile soil for the Alliance . . ." (Heath et al. 1985: 87).

5. Heath et al. (1985: 150) are quick to point out that it is impossible to infer from the data that the reason for an individual's switch in voting preference was the perceived ideological movement of their former party.

6. Others reject the role of economic self-interest in British voting. Scarbrough (1987: 235) concludes that the evidence "does not point to the priority of economic self-interest in the concerns of the electorate, despite the persistent erosion of traditional party ties." From a different perspective, Heath et al. (1985: 166) challenge the self-interest theory by concluding that "a government's record is evaluated as much in terms of its fairness and social justice as in terms of its contribution to the individual voter's personal well-being."

7. "Overall, a large-impact issue such as civil order, or welfare and redistribution, when it emerges in an election, produces a net change of about 2.7 per cent in favor of the party to which it 'belongs.'. . . In 1987, for example, the Conservatives gained 4.5 per cent of their vote of 42.2 per cent from the issue prominent in the campaign" (Budge and McKay 1988: 99).

Part III

Policy Making

In Parts I and II we were concerned with the mass political cultures of Japan and Britain—the political values, attitudes, and behaviors prevalent in each.

In Part III we turn to the question of policy making—the process by which the needs, desires, and demands of the public are combined, weighed, and reconciled, and the process by which elites finally choose some policies, and favor some interests, over others. This is not to imply that government only reacts to demands from below. Government elites have their own agendas, and retain considerable initiative in goal setting, rule making, and allocation of resources. Policy making requires a system of institutions and processes that ensure (1) identification of salient interests and problems, (2) development of feasible policies to deal with the problems identified, (3) the ability to resolve conflict, and (4) successful implementation and legitimacy.

The central question is how the elites who occupy official positions in national government make the choices that shape public policy—that determine "who gets what" in the political system. In light of the political culture approach of the present study, we will focus on the network of *relationships* (including authority relations), *patterns of interaction*, and *rules* that shape the policy process and ultimately determine outcomes (getting on the agenda, processing the agenda, deciding among options, implementation). This network includes relations among elites in core institutions like the cabinet, between officeholders and officials of their party organizations, between elected politicians and bureaucrats, between cabinet and parliament, between party and government leaders and factions, between the government majority and its opposition, between government and interest groups, between government and electors, and finally, between government and international and regional bodies.

Discussion of institutional structure and powers will be incorporated into discussion of these relationships and the norms that govern them. Organizational charts and lists of formal powers may misrepresent or obscure underlying processes. In Japan, the distinction between formal, public politics and informal, behind-the-scenes politics is embodied specifically in the concepts of *omote* and *ura*, but it is a distinction that, in one form or another, may be observed elsewhere. What is different is the prominence attached to the *omote-ura* dimension in Japan (Ishida 1984). Still, there are aspects of British politics that also reflect, in a broader sense, the contrast between appearance and reality, formality and informality, that is captured by these concepts. Examples are provided in the contrast between Walter Bagehot's "dignified" and "efficient" parts of the constitution—that which appears to exercise power and that which really exercises power (Bagehot 1966: 64–65). These are visible not only in the contrast between the "theatrical" elements of the royal family and the efficient work of the cabinet that Bagehot had in mind, but in the contrast between the publicly assumed constitutional conventions of parliamentary sovereignty and the realities of delegated legislation and group power, or between public disagreement and private accord as well. As Richard Rose (1979: 142) has emphasized, the adversarial politics often stressed in the media, and enshrined in one of many "models" of British politics, obscures a policy process that at the elite level is still remarkably consensual.

By focusing on norms and process we hope better to relate elite behavior to the mass norms and behaviors that we have examined up to now. Certainly elites are the purveyors of the many of the political values and attitudes of society at large. And elites tend to shape the language of political debate. Despite the advantages possessed by the elites in shaping political culture, influence operates in two directions. Mass values and attitudes cannot help but affect how elites behave and the range of choices that is likely to be perceived, considered, and presented. The process of government is shaped by the extent of nationalism, trust and respect for authority, political participation, and voting behavior, even if, as we admit, causality remains exceedingly difficult to establish. At best, we can attempt to place the decision process, as it is described in the existing literature, within the larger cultural context that we have presented in the first six chapters. Chapter 6 already established a link between mass political culture and decision making, in that electoral behavior is both input into specific public policy decisions (expression of public wishes) and a decision output (a referendum on who rules). A governmental decision is merely a different type of decision, made by a different set of actors. Just as electoral behavior must reflect to a degree the national historical experience, values, and attitudes, so elite decisions cannot escape the same influence. Of course, elite values and attitudes are bound to differ in some respects from mass values and attitudes. Not only are social backgrounds of elites different from the national norm, but their work surroundings and associations generate norms of their own—for example, the "village" culture some writers identify in Britain's national bureaucracy.

From this political culture perspective, how does the process of reaching authoritative decisions flow from the mass polities that we have described in chapters 1–6? What is the machinery for resolving conflict and building support in countries where the parliamentary majority is usually guaranteed? How is government made strong enough to govern, but rendered democratically accountable? How hierarchical is the decision process, and how open? What is the balance in the system between government and interests, between government and parliament, between government and party? How do political values, such as collectivism and consensus, shape public choice? What effect do levels of compliant/subject support, and the levels and types of participant/citizen support have on the expectations and decision-making practices of elites?

In no country is there one decision-making process. The pathway of decision, the relevant circle of actors, and even the norms will vary from one set of issues to another, from one administration to another, and from one time to another, and will depend on the complexity of the issue at hand. These differences need not be perceived as reflecting strongly held and competing philosophies of policy making, though they may. How an issue is resolved can be affected by numerous accidental environmental factors: a coming election, a scandal, a policy crisis.

In choosing to focus on the aspects of policy process we have described we invariably neglect other important aspects of decision making, such as organizational structures, patterns and norms of local decision making, implementation strategies, and policy outcomes themselves. The choice is deliberate and reflects our interest throughout the present study in the attitudes and behavior of political actors in national politics.

A final word is necessary. The task of comparison, as always, is a difficult one, but in the case of policy making norms and practices, there are even fewer quantitative guideposts that can be relied on for comparison than we found in the case of mass attitudes and electoral behavior. A great deal of judgment must be exercised in making comparisons concerning the degree of conflict and consensus in decision making, the role of interest groups, the power of the central elites, and numerous other characteristics of the decision-making process.

7

Policy Making in Britain and Japan

This chapter compares the most salient features of the policy-making process in Britain and Japan through the analysis of five clusters of institutional relationships: relations among the central executive elite of cabinet, ministers, and (in Japan's case) party officials, followed by executive elite/bureaucracy relations, executive elite/legislative relations, executive elite/interest group relations, and executive elite/local government relations.

Both Britain and Japan are constitutional democracies, in which elected governments are responsible for making and administering national public policy, organized political parties offer policy programs and contest elections, and basic civil liberties are recognized and protected by a combination of constitutional and cultural sanctions. With respect to how basic democratic institutions function, Japan and Britain enjoy more similarities than differences. A core of elected politicians works closely with the bureaucrats of the civil service to formulate national policy. In both, career civil services play an important and respected role in government. Core executive institutions, reinforced by collectivist traditions, are responsive to the pressures generated by organized interests, but retain great discretion in determining which interests become participants. While government/interest relations have pluralistic aspects, they also exhibit characteristics of corporatism. In both, the central elites concentrate policy-making power, while granting considerable discretion to public and private institutions in implementation. Values of consensus and harmony influence policy-making practice in both polities, and government/opposition agreement prevails a surprising amount of the time on the *ura* level. Yet neither is immune from often intense political conflict, and legislative debate displays an adversarial style of party politics. Despite differences that can be attributed to the contrast between the

Liberal Democratic Party's electoral dominance in Japan and alternating party government in Britain, the two countries have developed norms and practices whereby the opposition's views are taken into account. However, these consultative practices embrace both elements of *tatemae* and elements of *honne*.

Important contrasts may be found as well. Broadly speaking, the British postwar consensus was centered around the welfare state, while the Japanese consensus was centered around economic growth and the "developmental state." In Britain, neither a tradition of government planning nor a common societal goal of "nation building" has been present behind the scenes to lend authority to government dirigism. Nor has Britain given to government the same regulatory powers as Japan's government commands. Industrial self-regulation remains the rule. The respective roles of the civil service are quite different, with the Japanese bureaucracy playing a significant (though perhaps declining) role in the formulation of major policies, and the British bureaucracy eschewing a policy-initiating role in favor of a policy-screening and drafting role. Reflecting this difference, British ministers may exert more control over policy formulation than their Japanese counterparts. There is generally less circulation of elites in Britain than in Japan, where a larger proportion of former civil servants enter the Diet or industry. The roles of the major political party organizations in policy formulation are quite different. After thirty years of governing Japan, the LDP has developed influential policy-making machinery, exemplified by the Policy Affairs Research Council (PARC or *Seimu Chosakai*), which is closely tied to the government bureaucracy and the Diet. In Britain, by contrast, party control over policy formulation tends to wane, with the assumption of the responsibility of governing. Finally, some comparisons are difficult and ambiguous. For example, while consultation is central to the political process in both Britain and Japan, Japanese methods for creating consensus, such as *nemawashi*, or rootbinding, are different both in origin and in practice from British "consultation."

Characteristics of British Policy Making

Britain has no codified constitution that neatly outlines the powers of governmental institutions, spells out the rules of the political game, and guides institutions in their relations to one another and to the people. Britain's constitution is a collection of statutes, legal precedents, conventions, treaties, and edicts, often extending back hundreds of years, that govern the rules of the game and the nature of political institutions. As a result, Searing (1982: 241) observes, "British constitutional norms cover much more ground than do the constitutions of other nations." New legislation must always be scrutinized in light of old (Rose 1989: 299). At the heart of the constitutional order is the doctrine of parliamentary supremacy, by which Parliament can make or unmake any law it wishes. This power is conferred by law. But conventions, rather than laws and statutes, govern many of the networks, relationships, and processes of government with which we are concerned. Norton (1984: 63) defines conventions as "rules that are considered binding by and upon those who are responsible for making the Constitution work, but rules that are not enforced by the courts or by the presiding officers in either house of Parliament." These conventions include royal assent to legislation, selection of the cabinet members from Parliament, collective and individual ministerial responsibility to Parliament, and resignation of governments that lose parliamentary support. In general, conventions have tended to reinforce "strong government" rooted in the legally sanctioned "absolute" powers granted Parliament in the Bill of Rights and the Act of Succession. Modern conventions of party government have greatly enhanced the power of cabinet and prime minister at the expense of Parliament. It is they who exercise the vast legal powers of the Parliament itself. In its deep historical roots, labyrinthine complexity, and evolutionary character, the British constitution stands in marked contrast to the modern, Americanized constitution of Japan.

To a greater extent than in the United States or Japan, the constitution *is* practice. What politicians do, how they behave, is not dependent on constitutional exegesis. Practice may deviate from conventions, or even replace them with new conventions, in that change is a basic characteristic of Britain's organic constitution. A new reality, and constitution, replaces the old, without "amending" the higher law, as is necessary in Japan or the United States. Many once-powerful conventions have eroded or lapsed over the past two decades. To the Japanese, for whom constitutional prescriptions retain a large measure of *tatemae*, such a casual erosion of basic constitutional norms would not be terribly surprising, while to Americans it would be nearly unthinkable.

As a consequence of the constitutional tradition discussed above, both institutions and policy-making procedures have tended to be jury-rigged, and to leave much to the discretion of the decision maker or makers. Admirers find in this system a rugged, stable, and flexible means of adapting to a changing world. Some critics find in it a hopelessly antiquated and conservative Rube Goldberg contraption, a prisoner of administrative "satisficing" (Simon 1976) that is neither effective nor democratic. They find its conventions increasingly undermined, its processes increasingly fragmented and divorced from accountability, and its outputs confused or inadequate. Still other critics see the system as an instrument of class hegemony.

British policy making reflects the values and attitudes of the political culture, particularly acquiescence and strong government. But just as Britain's mass political culture is characterized by a mix of established and often opposed traditions—defiance of authority and deference, "self-help" and paternalism, individualism and collectivism—it is not surprising that the institutions and processes of government reflect a similar mix. In commentary on government, one is as likely to find words like "conflict," "strife," "battle," and "sabotage," as one is to find terms like "risk-aversion," "consultation," and "compromise." There is disagreement over the basis and importance of the constitution, the relative importance of institutions of policy-making and policy-influencing bodies, the means and effectiveness of group influence, and the extent to which British politics is "adversarial" or "consensual," "pluralistic" or "neo-corporatist," to name a few (Dunleavy 1988).

Recognizing that British policy making is characterized by complexities and contradictions, we propose nevertheless that the following traits are diagnostic: (1) strong government, reinforced by secrecy, on the one hand, and (2) limited government, encouraged by the pressure of "ongoing realities" and fragmentation of authority, and exercised through self-restraint and norms of consultation with interest groups, on the other, and (3) the primacy of politics over law in the resolution of conflict. The result is a polity that vests considerable power and discretion in the leaders of the day, but which tends, even under a relatively dynamic leadership, to incrementalist policies rooted in what Putnam (1973: 150–51) has called a "problem-solving" approach.

Strong Government

Strong government is intrinsic to the concept of parliamentary sovereignty. To control Parliament is to command a tremendous arsenal of constitutional powers. The traditional "strong government" model of British policy making entails a competitive two-party system in which elections confer a popular mandate on one of the parties, and a dependable majority in Parliament, with which to enact its election manifestos. Policy decisions are made by leaders of the party that won the last election (though less so in the case of Labour), and implemented by a loyal and competent civil service. As a result, there is expected to be a clear line of accountability between government action and the electorate. The government sets the direction, while other actors are limited to effecting shifts, delays and halts, not initiating or giving direction. The strength of central elite institutions is upheld by the ability of government to maintain a large degree of exclusivity in its policy-making networks. Compared to most democratic political systems, says Ashford (1980: 61),

> one cannot help being impressed with the ease with which leaders can exclude other political actors and political forces from policymaking. Party manifestos are written by the labor [sic] leader and, in turn, used selectively at his discretion; MPs labor in committees whose work is seldom debated and whose advice is easily ignored; once constituency associations have chosen a candidate, they are for the most part quiet spectators of the policy process; local politicians are swamped with tasks imposed by national government, and are either unable or unwilling to use their collective force to influence national policies. Cabinet and ministerial powers are exercised behind a cloak of confidentiality, which, of course, they may lift with impunity, but others may not draw aside. In addition, they have at their disposal an array of patronage, honors and favors that, if less costly than patronage in the United States and France, are no less well orchestrated to tap the political values and motives that prevail in British society and politics.

Strong government is exercised by an "oligopoly" of bureaucrats, politicians, and organized interests, who maintain their control through exclusivity of membership, internal consensus and trust, and manipulation of information made available to the rest of society (Goodin cited in Grant and Nath 1984: 33). Even after years of alarm over "pluralistic stagnation," examples of strong government are not difficult to find. The Thatcher government's enactment of union reforms, reductions of powers of local authorities, and suspensions of civil liberties in cases of political violence in Northern Ireland are examples of strong government at work. It is even possible to view the frequent "U-turns" by governments in the 1960s and 1970s—during the height of immobilism—as representative of the power of central government authorities to make major decisions, including mistaken ones, without serious challenge from Parliament.

A major pillar of strong government has been secrecy, or confidentiality. In comparison with the relatively leak-prone American executive, the inner workings of the British executive, both at the cabinet and the bureaucratic level, are shrouded from public, and often parliamentary, scrutiny. At the heart of the secrecy is Section 2 of the 1911 Official Secrets Act, which prohibits unauthorized disclosure of official information. Budge and McKay (1988: 41) have observed that "the British government is one of the most secretive in the world." As of 1982, there were eighty-nine laws on the books making unauthorized disclosure of various sorts an offense (Michael 1982: 18). Secrecy is supported by a host of forces beyond the statutes themselves, including the unwritten nature of the constitution, court decisions, parliamentary and bureaucratic practice, media acquiescence, and the acquiescent tendencies of the wider political culture (Gray 1987: 25–27). The result has been to insulate the central policy-making organs against most outside pressures (Ashford 1980: 7).

Although one might be tempted to equate strong government traditions in Britain with the authoritarian traditions of prewar Japan, to do so would be incorrect. Strong government reflects a democratic development over three centuries, in which accountability to the electorate, as opposed to institutional or legal constraints, comprises the principal check on governmental power. While the government of Japan has considerable constitutional powers, and while it can occasionally take strong, centralized action, its exercise of power does not stem from factors analogous to those at work in Britain, except perhaps to the extent that acquiescent attitudes and behavior give government in both countries wide latitude to act without close popular scrutiny.

Limited Government

Critics of Britain's strong government tradition claim that the system creates "an elected dictatorship," and one that in recent years has not even had the support of a majority of the electorate, that it encourages wild policy swings with alternations of party control, and that it even permits policy "U-turns" within the life of a Parliament (Budge and McKay 1988: 25; McAuslan and McEldowney 1986: 509). Despite all the evidence of the prevalence of strong government, however, a number of constitutional conventions, cultural norms, and environmental realities conspire to restrain the government in Britain. As Vogel (1986: 287) puts it, "Legally, the British government—that is the Crown acting through Parliament—is more powerful than that of any other democracy. In reality, the relative power of the British state vis-à-vis British society is sharply limited." Limits are imposed by the need for governments to submit regularly to the judgment of the electorate, by strong elite norms of "auto-limitation," by a risk-averse civil service, by entrenched inhibitions against "dirigist" practices, and by a tradition of delegated administration. Further, the consensual values of the culture exert no small pull, and the government's reservoir of powers must be exercised without disturbing the still-pervasive "societal consensus" that supports the political system (Ashford 1980: 267). The dramatic rise of the welfare state and the extension of government responsibilities after World War II strengthened government as a whole, as throughout most of the industrial democracies. But the multiplication of responsibilities was on such a scale that prime ministers were compelled to yield substantial discretion to ministers, ministers to civil servants, and civil servants to proliferating quasi-governmental bodies and organized interests. This spillover of authority is one of the centrifugal forces serving to limit British government. Like strong government, limited government has no direct Japanese equivalent. In contrast to Britain, civil liberties in Japan are protected by a bill of rights, but as in Britain, the protection of liberties tends not to be played out in the courts. As in Britain, restraints are observed often as the result of cultural norms. In Chapter 5 we saw that in both Britain and Japan, there is evidence of reduced acceptance of authority and increased citizen activism. Yet at the elite level, government still largely reflects the older deferential norms, and restraints remain a matter of culture rather than law.

Consultation with affected interests is another characteristic of British government practice that upholds limited government. Consultation proceeds both among affected individuals and departments within government, and between departments and affected private interests. Some consider government consultation with organized groups central to the British system, and indeed Prime Minister Wilson referred to it as a duty. For a time, some observers saw the practice evolving into a formal "corporatist" system of consultation among government and major industrial and labor organizations. The obligation to consult has roots in politics, law, and culture, and it is a pervasive and resilient norm. The courts, while generally reluctant to intervene, have tended to uphold the practice of consultation. Extensive consultation, and the resulting constraint on government, helps maintain the balance between the need for central authority and the need for openness. While intragroup norms are highly significant for the practice of government in Japan, and while major interest groups play an important role, the norms of government-group consultation are quite different. There is no corresponding expectation, let alone "right," to be consulted on the part of affected interests. The boundaries between insider and outsider groups are variable and fluid in Japan, while they tend to be relatively more fixed in Britain.

Even with regard to the practice of secrecy, some of the above restraints play a role. Government is expected to be accountable, and a degree of openness is provided through extensive publication of data on public affairs, and by the inclusion of interests in the decision process. The weakening of the two-party system in Parliament during the 1980s, wider access to and less anonymity in the civil service, and the advent of the select committee system also have tended to work toward somewhat greater openness, as have, in a few cases, statutory constraints such as the Public Records Act (Gray 1987: 27–29). The media, too, have played a part by pursuing investigatory pieces more than in the past. In keeping with the rise of direct democracy, a Campaign for Freedom of Information was founded in 1984 to seek repeal of Section 2 of the Official Secrets Act.

Primacy of Politics

"Political rather than judicial control is a central feature of Britain's unwritten constitution" (Ridley 1984: 3). This is true both in the sense that Britain has no overarching constitution granting powers to and imposing limits on government, and in the sense that political, rather than judicial or administrative resolution of disputes, is the norm.[1] In Britain, "the rule of law" does not reflect a narrow legalism, but rather an extension of politics through "fair administrative practices; recognition of the rights of political opposition and dissent; complying with constitutional conventions; adequate means of individual redress of grievances about government action" (McAuslan and McEldowney 1986: 500). Official discretion is a basic modus operandi of British policy making. Officials do not expect to follow prescribed procedures for making decisions. In his discussion of environmental politics, Vogel (1986: 24, 29) identifies a British regulatory style less grounded in fixed rules and standards, like the Japanese or American, and more in self-regulation, informality, and ultimately, a cooperative relationship between regulator and regulated. Still, the "political" settlement of disputes employed by the British bears some resemblance to the "personalism" and "administrative guidance" that are central to the Japanese approach.

Decision-making norms, processes, and styles are likely to vary with the issues, institutions, and personalities involved. This fact applies especially to the degree of openness in the process. As Hogwood (1987: 47–50) points out, policy may be imposed by the central elite, generated through an internalized process of debate, determined through consultation with outside interests, derived from below as a result of experience "in the field," or developed through public debate. But even accepting this variability, the elite norms of decision making characteristically have tended toward the more consensual side, if it is also understood that by custom the circle of consensus is relatively exclusive. Still, few policies will be made by cabinet or prime ministerial preemption. And, as elsewhere in the industrial democracies, the more important the issue is to significant nongovernmental interests, the wider the circle of decision participants. British politics is a mixed decision-making regime when it comes to the poles of openness and unity of decision, but, with its powerful norms of secrecy, it is in many ways less open than the other industrial democracies.

Characteristics of Japanese Policy Making

While the concepts of "strong government," "limited government," "consultation," and "supremacy of politics over law" have some relevance to Japan, they are not the terms in which Japanese government is discussed. Where they do apply, the Japanese context and meaning require careful explanation. Modern Japanese government is certainly strong government, in the sense that central elites operate with considerable authority and discretion, and notions of direct democracy are, as in Britain, feebly developed. Britain's obsession with group consultation has its analogy in Japanese consensus building, but the meaning and operation of consensual norms is quite distinctive in Japan.

The central premise of this book, that culture is a major influence on politics, is especially evident with respect to policy making in Japan. Although Japan may not be unique in either its institutions or the fact of cultural influences on those institutions, there are both absolute differences and differences of degree between Britain and Japan. Specifically, Japanese patterns of behavior in group formation and decision making, including the need for consensus, bottom-up (*ringi*) decision making, and the tendency toward factionalism in Japanese organizations separate it from many Western models. That is not to say that similar phenomena do not exist in Britain and the West. To quote Chalmers Johnson (1978: 11),

> It is true that the Japanese cultural and historical experience is unique, and it colors modern Japanese political and economic life. But to elevate this heritage into an intellectual construct called 'national character' and to use it to explain virtually all differences between Japan and other open, advanced industrial societies is both tautological—since no one knows precisely what national character is—and unprofitable, since it precludes making the kinds of serious comparisons that will reveal the genuine strengths and weaknesses of Japanese institutions. Conversely, to deny that there is much difference between Japan and, say, the political economy of the United States is simply uninformed, given the cultural and historical differences between the two countries.

In the area of Japanese policy making, as in every area of contemporary Japanese studies, scholars have had to reexamine accepted theories in the light of changes in the polity over the past ten to fifteen years. Where an elite consensus once reigned, scholars now see a growing pluralism. The bureaucratic dominance over policy making which began in the Meiji era is now challenged by the LDP and interest groups, and as the number of groups participating in the process increases, so does factionalism. However, regardless of the changes that are occurring, consensus, bureaucratic dominance, and pluralism still remain the foci of the Japanese policy-making process.

There are some important contrasts between Britain and Japan in the roles of major political institutions and the postwar contexts in which they evolved. While the political institutions of Britain and the United States remained essentially intact after the war, those in Japan were radically altered in two ways. First, the relationship between the political institutions (party, government, and Diet) and the civil administrative service developed in an economic environment dominated by rapid, over-heated, economic growth, and a belief that national economic policy making was the prerogative of the bureaucracy. As a result, even in postwar Japan, the bureaucracy retained a dominance largely absent in Britain, even with the onset of the welfare state. Second, the growth of democratic institutions and relationships was accomplished in a far more compressed time span in Japan than in Britain, and required sudden and dramatic shifts of power within the system. The bureaucracy, nurtured by the old authoritarian political system and still dominant in the first postwar years, now had to adapt itself to life amongst democratic institutions. The democratic institutions, in turn, were shaped by a dominant and authoritatively structured bureaucracy.

Characteristic of the development of Japanese democracy has been the inclusion of a larger number of inputs into the policy-making process as democratic political institutions in the country matured and the norms of participation developed. This progression from fewer to more participants is captured in what Kosai Yutaka has described as the models of "the one, the three and the many." "The sequence of these models reflects the changes in the structure of policy formation in Japan. The first, the bureaucracy-led model, captures the essential characteristics of the polity of the prewar period and of the years immediately following World War II. The second, the ruling-triad model [consisting of bureaucracy-LDP-commercial interests] describes the policy making of the 1950s. The last, patterned pluralism, is useful and effective for examining the latest stage of the Japanese political economy, which began around 1960" (Kosai 1987: 557). There has been an analogous, but considerably more muted, trend in Britain with the rise of pluralism and direct democracy in the 1970s. But it must be remembered that Britain began the postwar period with a far more advanced pluralism than what existed in Japan.

Another major distinction between postwar political institutions in Britain and Japan is the imposition of the constitution by the Americans during the occupation. We have addressed ourselves previously to the role of the constitution in Japanese politics, but a few major points will bear repeating in the context of policy making. Japan's constitution occupies the middle ground between Britain's "constitution of practice" and the American *rechtstaat*. While the allocation of policy-making power under the constitution is quite clear, practice does not always follow form. The Japanese constitution, as a written document, is precise in the formal allocation of policy-making power to dignified institutions, and can only be changed by amendment—an event which has yet to occur. In this there is less flexibility than in Britain. However, there is even greater flexibility in the ability of those institutions to contravene the spirit, and even the letter, of the law, or to use authority not found in statutory or constitutional law. The clearest example of this is administrative guidance, as will be discussed later in the chapter.

Of all the Japanese cultural influences upon the policy-making process, perhaps the most commonly emphasized is the need for consensus. Intense pressures on the individual to conform to the group are transferred from individual norms of behavior to institutional norms of behavior. Japanese decision making is justifiably noted for its reliance on behavior that will bring about a unanimous, consensual decision. Contentious subjects that can create conflict are usually avoided in the formal decision-making setting. Instead, opinions are usually expressed in more informal settings, most commonly over an after-hours drink with co-workers, so that those who express the opinions do not have to be held to them. At the same time, the participants can get an understanding of who supports which position and line up behind a forming majority. It is also outside the formal decision-making environment that superiors understand the need to go along with decisions agreed upon by subordinates and subordinates understand the need to conform to the rules of seniority. Proposals are widely distributed both horizontally and vertically so that everyone feels included in the process. By the time a formal meeting is held, the decision is often a foregone conclusion, and yet the consensus is reinforced one more time by having everyone in the group, down to the most junior member, included in the process by allowing them to state their positions. While the British cabinet system also mandates consensus as an output, cabinet-level deliberation is, by all accounts, far more contentious. In fact, often the most nettlesome problems, deadlocked at lower levels, find their way onto the cabinet agenda.

While most Japanese learn both the need to conform and the means of creating a consensus within their groups, the same consensus-building behavior is often attributed to interactions between groups as well. Consensus as the dominant theme in Japanese group relations is the foundation for the "ruling triad" or "Japan, Inc." models of Japanese policy making. However, at this level of policy making there cannot exist the unanimity that exists within the small group. For example, in the above models, public opinion, consumer groups, and any group outside the government that is not a "prime contractor" (to use Johnson's terms) is going to have very little influence on policy (Johnson 1986: 51). But, given the pervasiveness of consensus in Japan, and the expectation of the citizenry that their leaders should rule with consensus, it still plays an important role in policy making at the institutional level.

The broadest and most general models of consensus formation in Japanese policy making are those with the least validity. It is easy to conjure up a picture of an overlapping elite from the political parties, the bureaucracy and private enterprises meeting in geisha houses and other informal settings to reach a consensus on national policy. Certainly there are close ties among the members of these three elites, but there is no special cohesiveness in their social backgrounds, and the role of private enterprise may be rather limited (Muramatsu and Krauss 1984: 144; Johnson 1986: 52). There are many conflicts between the LDP and the bureaucracy, between the LDP and private enterprise, between private enterprise and the bureaucracy and among factions within all three of these broader institutions (Muramatsu and Krauss 1984: 144; Pempel 1982: 26).

The ideal of Japanese consensus has its greatest validity when applied on a more limited basis. When the LDP is attempting to pass legislation it will call on the opposition parties to join them in a unified coalition as means of expressing to the Japanese public that they are attempting to create a consensus. On the other hand, the Japan Socialist Party and other opposition parties will boycott Diet committee meetings as a signal to the public that a consensus does not exist, thereby placing the onus of not having formed a consensus on the LDP—if they do pass legislation regardless of opposition concerns (Richardson and Flanagan 1984: 334). As we will see later in the chapter, while this battle over policy and the claim to true consensual behavior is being fought in public, a very different relationship between the members of the LDP and opposition parliamentary parties is often carried out behind the scenes. *Shingikai*, as we will also see later in the chapter, are another important example of institutional consensus building in that they are used by the ruling party and the bureaucracy as a means of bringing all relevant elements of the Japanese polity into the policy-making process.

If consensus is a relationship among the members of a group, then factions are the ideal representation of the Japanese group. Factions, or *habatsu*, are formed by people who have common associations, e.g., university ties, regional ties, ideological ties, and who have common needs. Japanese factions are hierarchical and are generally formed around strong individual leaders, such as leading politicians in the LDP and those in the upper levels of the civil administration. Within the faction, strong group solidarity and consensus is supported by a patron-client relationship between the leaders and subordinates and the loyalty associated with the common attribute that the membership may have in common. Backbenchers in the LDP may be attracted to a particular faction for ideological reasons, or because the leader comes from the same prefecture, but it is most likely that the benefits of prestige, help with campaign funds, and a leg up on important party positions serve as the most significant inducements. Similarly, a new member of the civil administration will likely join a faction based upon university affiliation, but once in the faction will expect his seniors to help him along up the ladder of promotion and into his fields of interest. In return, the junior members of the faction follow the leadership in supporting policy, voting on bills in the Diet, supporting their leader for higher office, and in helping to raise funds for the party faction.

Factions illustrate well the importance of the level of consensus. While there is consensus within the faction, the factions themselves can be forces for fragmentation as well as consensus. When a policy is being considered, there must be coordination between the party and the civil administration. Within the civil adminstration there must be coordination between ministries and bureaus and among the factions within them. There must be coordination in the party between the various policy-making committees, such as PARC's Deliberation Commission, PARC itself, and the Executive Council, which, in turn, depends upon coordination among the factions. The faction system can be beneficial in that coordination and agreement among relatively few people, the leaders of the factions, is all that is necessary. Once the faction leaders are in agreement, everyone gets their shoulder behind the wheel. But, it must be remembered, factions are by their very nature fragments of an institution, and if the leadership cannot come to agreement, then serious ramifications will ensue. For example, the LDP failed to get a majority of seats in the House of Representatives in the 1979 election and had to turn to independents to fill out their majority. In this atmosphere, the party split between two factions, one led by Ohira Masayoshi and one led by Fukuda Takeo, both of whom ran for prime minister before the Diet. Ohira was finally elected on a run-off ballot, but his government fell in the spring of 1980 when members of the Fukuda faction abstained from voting during a Socialist-sponsored vote of no-confidence—the only successful vote of no-confidence in the LDP era.

Policy Actors: Relationships and Process

The Central Executive Elite

One of the institutional clusters we have chosen to compare is the central elite: prime minister, cabinet, and ministers (and in the case of Japan, the Liberal Democratic Party). In both countries, the power of the executive is considerable, but relationships and powers within the executive reveal differences. In British political science literature, debate often concerns the relative powers of the prime minister, cabinet, ministers, and civil service. Parties have their role in the making of policy, but it is not a central role. In Japan, by contrast, the power of the central governmental elite is rivaled by that of LDP extraparliamentary organizations. Another significant difference is the much greater policy-initiating role of the Japanese government bureaucracy. It is much harder in the Japanese case, in fact, to distinguish the traditional executive elites of the cabinet and ministries from the influential government and party bureaucracies.

Prime Minister

At the apex of the British political system are the institutions of the prime minister (PM) and cabinet. Both institutions have considerably greater importance in Britain than Japan. In Britain, the hierarchy of decision-making power follows rather closely the formal hierarchy of governmental institutions: prime minister, cabinet, ministries, and bureaucracy. In Japan, this is far less the case, as the powers of formal power holders are challenged by both the party organization of the ruling LDP and by the traditionally more influential bureaucracy.

The basic roles of the British and Japanese prime ministers are quite similar. The British PM is chief decision maker and diplomat, government manager, party leader, and broker. As head of government, it is his or her job "to choose the people who make most of the day-to-day decisions of government, to orchestrate the overall pattern of government," to impose "an overall sense of direction and purpose" (Rose 1989: 74–75). At the same time, in making appointments, attending to factional disputes, consulting with MPs and secretaries, defending the government in "question hour," issuing public statements, and making media appearances, the PM is exercising the party leadership role—in effect preparing to contest the next election. Consideration of the merits of policy must be reconciled with the other tasks of governing: staying in power, maintaining government unity and loyalty, and holding up the morale and commitment of the faithful.

These roles have long made the PM primus inter pares, but there is a difference of opinion between "the presidential school" and "the chairmanship school" over how "primus" the PM really is (Barber 1984: 73). In the former view, he or she may be far more powerful, far more independent, indeed in a quasi-presidential position (Grant and Nath 1984: 31; Wolf-Phillips 1984 : 400). R.H.S. Crossman observes not only that the postwar epoch witnessed "the final transformation of Cabinet Government into Prime Ministerial Government," but that the cabinet, "joins the other dignified elements in the Constitution" (Crossman in Bagehot 1966: 51, 54). This power could be attributed to the increased size and scope of government, which, in the view of Crossman, redounded to the benefit of the official at the center, the prime minister (Barber 1984: 75). The PM may pick and choose his or her closest colleagues, within, and even outside of, the cabinet, and may on occasion even fail to inform the full cabinet of decisions (Kavanagh 1987: 13). Ministers are too dependent upon prime ministerial support to offer a real challenge. Mrs. Thatcher, in particular, was frequently criticized for riding roughshod over her cabinet colleagues in pursuit of her objectives. The chairmanship school, by contrast, takes altogether a different view, in which the prime minister operates in a very constrained environment, beset by opponents and rivals, and in which he or she is dependent on the support of others to be effective (Barber 1984: 76). The massive extent of government, which the presidentialists see as a source of power, the chairmanship school sees as a drag on the prime minister, while the great powers of patronage must be used "to satisfy the ambitions of other party interests rather than those of the Prime Minister" (Barber 1984: 77).

It does not appear at the present time, however, that the power of the PM has undergone a permanent transformation. Most important, Mrs. Thatcher did little to enhance the institutional powers and resources of her office (Budge and McKay 1988: 30–31). And, to some extent, the apparent increase of prime ministerial power reflects differences of style, for example between what Kavanagh calls "mobilizers" and "reconcilers" (Kavanagh 1985a: 61). Attlee and Wilson were examples of the latter in their approach to the Labour movement. The more unconventional "mobilizer" style of Mrs. Thatcher in many ways illustrates what is not, by tradition, political leadership in Britain. That style, by which the prime minister foregoes collective support of the cabinet, can carry significant political costs in the event of a crisis. In the Westland affair, Mrs. Thatcher found herself with no one else to share the blame (Burch 1987: 34–35). Mrs. Thatcher's successor, John Major, showed signs of a return to a more conciliatory style of leadership. Yet even under Thatcher herself collective decision making was not "totally pushed aside" (Riddell 1989: 102).

Japan has barely had a prime ministerial government, let alone a "quasi-presidential" prime ministership. Although there have occasionally been active, high-profile prime ministers, like Yoshida Shigeru in the immediate postwar years, or Nakasone Yasuhiro, who led the government from 1982 to 1987, prime ministers in the consensual style of Britain's Attlee are more the norm. The Japanese PM has extensive formal powers of appointment and decision, but is hemmed in by many of the same constraints as in Britain, and by some peculiar to Japan. To a far greater extent than in Britain, the PM is vulnerable to factional politics. His continuation as PM and president of the LDP depends directly upon politics. The PM holds office only by the sufferance of an intraparty coalition, and organized policy groups within the party may further restrain the prime minister's "freedom of choice in policy matters" (Richardson and Flanagan 1984: 337). Rotation in office is considerably more frequent than in Britain. In Britain since 1945 there have been ten prime ministers, in Japan eighteen, and if the two longest serving prime ministers, Sato and Thatcher, are excluded, the average prime ministerial term in Britain has been forty-four months as opposed to twenty-seven months for Japanese PMs. As has been noted in previous chapters, there was an expectation that Nakasone's reign would open the way for stronger prime ministerial leadership, not only in terms of policy making, but also vis-à-vis the party factions and their leadership. That expectation has vanished, however, as a reinvigoration of the factions during the tenure of Nakasone's successor, Takeshita, and several scandals led to a total of three PMs serving in 1989 alone.

For those Japanese PMs who are willing to break the traditional social and political bonds that restrain their behavior, there are, on paper and in traditional practice, many powers available to them. He (the male pronoun is used as there has never been a female PM) is the elected head of his political party, he appoints the other members of the cabinet, he is the leader and initiator in domestic and foreign policy making, and is the arbitrator in policy disputes between the government and the bureaucracy, and within the party factions. However, those PMs who have demonstrated a willingness to combine and use these powers, such as Yoshida, Kishi, Tanaka, and Nakasone, tend to leave office under a cloud and to be succeeded by group-oriented "team players."

Cabinet and Ministers

Often policy making is discussed in terms of the interplay of bureaucrats and politicians—the elected officials of Parliament and government. Aberbach et al. (1981: 110–11) describe the perspective of the politician in Western democracies this way: "The politician is informed by a broad gauged view of society, inclined to see conflict and group differences, and prone to formulate policy that distinguishes between groups in society. . . . In sum, the key policy question that politicians are likely to ask is 'What ends will be served and whose interests will be satisfied?' Politicians are generalists motivated by political ideals and broad interests, and the world view of the generalists is usually keyed to simple explanations." This description could aptly be applied to Japanese politicians as well.

The most important policy bodies through which politicians in Britain operate are the cabinet and the various ministries of government.

The cabinet retains great formal importance in Britain. It can still prevail on occasion over the will of the prime minister, and it provides a "centripetal coordinating force to the bureaucracy" (Aberbach et al. 1981: 229). As Rose (1989: 97) indicates, "Endorsement by the Cabinet is the strongest sanction that a policy can have." This reflects what is undoubtedly the most important constitutional convention underlying cabinet government—"collective responsibility." The unity, and thus the authority, of government decisions is to be ensured by the practice of ministers to grant unanimous support for, and to assume responsibility (to Parliament) for, decisions taken in cabinet. But cabinets are no longer likely to resign unless faced with loss of a vote of confidence, and open disagreement within cabinets has increased in frequency (Kavanagh 1977: 14). More important, the cabinet faces significant limitations. Its authority is greatest on a rather small number and narrow range of issues, and both ministers and the prime minister may have their reasons for not bringing an issue to the full cabinet. The cabinet or its subcommittees may deal perfunctorily with decisions already "made" at the ministerial level, and the cabinet's main remaining function is to "broker" issues not resolved at a lower level. According to Richard Crossman, the cabinet "becomes the place where busy executives seek formal sanction for their actions from colleagues usually too busy—even if they do disagree—to do more than protest" (Barber 1984: 74). Because a problem is often politicized when it comes to the cabinet, it is not necessarily the objective importance of an issue that decides, but its political importance and the degree of intraparty controversy that it generates (Hogwood 1987: 98–99). The vast majority of "cabinet" decisions are in fact taken by cabinet committees, specialized subcabinet bodies composed of ministers whom the prime minister wishes to appoint. The decisions made by these committees, even where the full cabinet may not be informed of them, carry the same weight as decisions of the full cabinet (Norton 1984: 178). Ministers rarely interfere in agreements forged in cabinet committees or bilaterally between departments, in the expectation the courtesy will be extended to them in turn. As a result, the cabinet's role may be said to be reduced to "legitimating and endorsing" policies made elsewhere (Burch 1987: 25).

Prime ministers and cabinets can take extraordinary measures under the aegis of strong government. It has followed that limited government in Britain is to a large extent "auto-limitation." Government is expected to exercise self-restraint because that is the norm, and because no government would risk, by authoritarian excesses, its chances in the next election. Despite the rise of reform movements like Charter 88, which has called for a written bill of rights, the evidence we have reviewed to this point suggests that the public still appears prepared, by and large, to defer to the judgment of government.

Restraint is not just a consequence of the good intentions of the governors. We have already noted that prime ministers face limits on their power. British government is limited both by conventions of behavior and by the realities of the policy environment. Many factors internal to government exert a restraining influence: a workload that exceeds the capacity of core institutions, fragmentation of authority, competing institutional interests, prior commitments, limited resources, the climate of opinion in the legislature, bureaucratic conservatism, and a "hands-off" tradition in public administration. Limits are also imposed by the fact that governments rarely have the opportunity to make "new" or "discreet" decisions. Mrs. Thatcher was relatively successful in implementing a new set of policies. But an overwhelming number of decisions in all governments involve perpetuating or modifying past decisions on which there is widespread agreement. Outside government, pressures from interest groups, the electorate, media, economic conditions, and foreign events exert considerable restraining influence. Even the principle of parliamentary supremacy itself, which undergirds so much of the tradition of strong government in Britain, has been challenged, internally by trade union and local government defiance and calls for constitutional reform, and externally by the powers of the European Community and international monetary institutions.

In a highly centralized state with a skilled and loyal civil service, one would expect fragmentation to be a minor problem. But even within the central core of institutions, fragmentation exists. It is, says Rose, more the network of institutional relations than the preferences of one institution that determine policy. As he frames the process (Rose 1989: 105), "Few policies of major importance can be formulated or carried out by a single ministry, let alone a single minister. Information and opinions must be exchanged within this network in order to create a policy that takes into account financial and administrative problems, difficulties within the governing party in Parliament and often difficulties abroad. Discussion is also helpful in mobilizing the political resources to overcome difficulties."

Like other industrialized countries, Britain experienced a tremendous growth in the public sector after World War II. And yet the British did not to the same extent adopt the planning, directing, and coordinating roles that emerged elsewhere, including Japan. Government proliferated, but it did not fundamentally reorient itself to the "guiding" role that was to be so important to Japan. Britain remained, more than elsewhere, subject to centrifugal forces (Budge and McKay 1988: 21–23). For example, one way Britain responded to the increasing demands of the welfare society was to create a network of quasi-nongovernmental organizations (quangos), not under the direct control of ministers or Parliament, to administer a great variety of government services and programs. This act of delegation has given these bodies considerable decision-making power.

From the foregoing discussion, it seems that for most issues, most of the time, Britain does not have government by collective cabinet. "Indeed," says Norton (1984: 183), "there is a case for arguing that, far from having prime ministerial or cabinet government in Britain, one has a form of ministerial government." In Britain, the minister may entertain fairly high expectations of his or her powers in the department. Within the confines of the party program, ministers may initiate policies as well as decide them, though this may vary with the differing styles of ministers and the responsibilities of the department. The doctrine of ministerial responsibility—whereby individual ministers take responsibility before Parliament for all the successes and failures of their departments—creates a mutually beneficial dependency between minister and civil servant which neither side is anxious to disrupt. Ministers alone have the power to announce decisions and speak publicly for the department (Rose 1989: 84). Furthermore, the secrecy sanctioned by ministerial responsibility, though often breached today, is an important weapon in the arsenal of the minister. A minister who knows what he or she wants, has sufficient confidence and time, is willing to be concerned with administrative matters, and has the political skill to pilot proposals through the political "shoals" can make policy (Christoph 1975: 40, 44; Rose 1989: 82). Such paragons are not the norm, however.

Like the prime minister, ministers face their own constraints. Ministers have a great deal of latitude in matters that do not impinge too closely on their colleagues' bailiwicks, but, on major policies, ministers are constrained by collective responsibility to pursue the policies of the government and by the need to consult affected departments and interests. Just as the prime minister is dependent upon his or her ministers, ministers are dependent on their departments for advice, support, and implementation. The minister's "single most continuous source, and the one he tends to rely upon for factual information and estimates of feasibilty, is his departmental machine," and there is some risk of becoming prisoners of the "departmental view," or even the view of the senior civil servants (Christoph 1975: 42, 43, 46). As a result of the erosion of ministerial control over senior civil servants, Crossman goes so far as to assert that "the minister must normally be content with the role of public relations officer to his department, unless the Premier has appointed him with the express purpose of carrying out reforms" (Crossman in Bagehot 1966: 51). Also like the prime minister, ministers will find the pressures of time and multiple responsibilities constrain their ability to take the lead on policy. Furthermore, the prominence of consensual values in the political process, the need to bring together competing interests and demands in the search for consensus, tend, as in Japan, to require a long gestation period for policies. Given an average two-year stint on the job, ministers inevitably run afoul of the fact that it takes three years to see a new policy implemented (Rose, cited in Christoph 1975: 38). Loyalty to the PM, who appointed the minister in the first place, is another factor tending to limit the independence of ministers (Crossman in Bagehot 1966: 52). Despite the limits, opportunities for ministerial leadership are greater than in Japan, where ministers do not expect to, and do not, lead their departments.

In Japan, a ministerial appointment is more honorary and reflects the need for factional balance even more than in Britain. Ministerial tenure is even briefer than in Britain—on average less than the two years typically enjoyed by a British minister. Ministers are "enormously dependent on the bureaucracy for information, advice, and cooperation in handling the myriad of details involved in policy making and implementation. . . . Other groups, including powerful interest groups and the opposition parties, also exercise important checks on the policy-making initiative of the Japanese central executive elite. . . . These restraints on executive power common to all pluralistic democracies have been enhanced in some periods by the Japanese cultural norm that leadership should not be too autocratic in style. This norm appeared to be at work in the favorable press reception of Prime Minister Ikeda's 'low posture' in comparison with the frequent condemnation of the less conciliatory political style of his predecessor" (Richardson and Flanagan 1984: 339). Emphasis on conformity necessitated by the Japanese faction system also reduces the probability of strong individual leadership. The result is that ministers are little more than conduits for proposals generated by their departments. In the words of Robert Ward (1978: 138), "Cabinet ministers are in no position to exercise effective or continuing control over national policies."

Despite restraints, the central elite plays the important role of broker in resolving the proposals advanced by groups, ministries, Diet groups, the LDP and even, on occasion, the opposition. Where differences are significant, they must be settled by negotiation, often involving the PM. In this process, solutions are arrived at by informal, behind-the-scenes discussions between at least some of the various parties involved. The role of the executive elite as a policy broker is a subtle and complex one, which involves the exercise of great manipulative skill and extremely delicate use of the prime minister's influence, with the result that his leadership is not open and explicit even though his authority may be considerable in such situations. "A second role of the executive elite in Japan involves ratification of decisions made elsewhere, typically within the bureaucratic ministries" (Richardson and Flanagan 1984: 341). This is done when decisions are relatively minor and fall within one ministry's jurisdiction. The PM or relevant cabinet member will be consulted, often pro forma, but sometimes to be sure the policy conforms to overall policy orientations. Or it is done when a powerful ministry, such as finance or MITI, undertakes a major initiative (Richardson and Flanagan 1984: 342). There are some situations where the central elite is not passive. Prime ministers usually have at least one important policy initiative with which they are identified, or have had sufficient interest in economic policy, or have intervened in budget decisions (Richardson and Flanagan 1984: 342).

Political Parties

In Britain, the central political role assumed by cabinet and ministers (who happen to be members of the parliamentary majority party), contrasts with "the comparatively low capacity of parties to formulate and influence policy" (Ashford 1980: 54). In Japan, the Liberal Democratic Party (which is the governing party) is more likely to assume this role. The party/government connection is far more important in making policy in Japan. It is extensive, and is manifested in greater circulation of elites, formal bureaucratic and executive-level consultation and joint policy making, as well as innumerable informal social contacts and *giri* networks. Indeed, party and government are nearly inseparable from an institutional point of view.

In both the British Labour and Conservative parties particularly, the parliamentary party has enjoyed considerably more autonomy from the party conference or its executive organs than has been the case in Japan. There is, unlike Japan, no formal machinery for processing legislative proposals for the government within the parties, and no formal consultation procedures among government, MPs, and party in the generation of legislation. In his study, *Do Parties Make a Difference?*, Rose (1979: 148) emphasizes that, in the end, "how limited is the part that party politics plays in the political system of Britain." This is particularly true in the making of policy, in the sense that central party organs play a far more modest policy-making role than in Japan. The policy function of the central organs of the extraparliamentary party is to draft, or participate in drafting, the election manifesto. In a political system in which a party may be called upon to form a government on short notice, it would seem quite important to have devised policies for the event, and yet the two governing parties have performed unevenly in this regard. At times, this role may assume some significance, as in the case of policy innovation in the new Labour government in 1945 or the Conservative government in 1970 (Brown and Steel 1979: 205; Ashford 1980: 54). But this role better qualifies as "preprocessing" or agenda setting rather than policy making (Hogwood 1987: 77). Without access to the civil service, the opposition has inadequate information or staff resources to engage in drafting legislation for the time when it will govern. The party bureaucracy thus ceases to play a significant role once its party's leaders become the government. For the party in power, the traditional preeminence of the parliamentary party, and the limits that secrecy puts on the information available, tend to limit the role of the national party organization. As a result, the party organization's input is carried out through placement of its members in government, rather than through formal bureaucratic linkages between party and civil service. Britain's MPs have traditionally had far greater independence from either national or constituency organizations, though this has been less true of Labour, where the delegate view of representation is more likely to prevail.

In Japan, the party/bureaucracy relationship parallels the minister/bureaucracy relationship in Britain. In comparing the policy-making powers of the LDP versus the bureaucracy, we will assume for the time being, that there is a zero-sum game of power sharing between these two institutions. Later in the chapter, the number of players in the game will be expanded. Because of its long tenure, the LDP's party bureaucracy established a far more formal place in the policy process, and a more significant one, than the Diet. Although earlier models of Japanese policy making have usually stressed the importance of the bureaucracy as the dominant institution, the LDP's input has been steadily increasing. Muramatsu and Krauss (1984:142) conclude that "[P]oliticians, parties and the Diet are perceived by the elites themselves to play a much greater role in policy making than most models of Japanese politics have described. . . . [A] model of shared and equal influence between bureaucrats and politicians or even of party superiority is more appropriate." The arguments they put forward to support their conclusion are fundamental to the "revisionist" contention of the increased, perhaps even superior, policy-making power of the LDP. They are as follows: (1) Although the bureaucracy came through the occupation relatively unscathed, the prime ministership and the Diet emerged from the occupation with extremely strengthened and expanded powers, powers with the potential to rival those of the bureaucracy. (2) The unification of the LDP vastly strengthened LDP politicians by centralizing the government in the hands of one party. That party then created an "extensive and powerful apparatus comprised of Diet members within the party structure (especially the Policy Affairs Research Council) which debates and ultimately shapes legislation and legislative priorities" (Muramatsu and Krauss 1984: 143). (3) Top party leaders have a great deal of leverage over the bureaucracy to ensure that their ideas prevail. Bureaucrats who want to be elevated to the highest levels of the civil service, who want to "descend from heaven" into the LDP or even into private corporations, are often vetted by the party leadership. (4) The very longevity of the party's rule has ensured that the bureaucracy is going to be sensitive to the party's needs. The close working relationship between LDP politicians and bureaucrats is a two-way street which facilitates the ability of LDP members to win over their bureaucratic counterparts. In addition, the long, and often absolute, control over the Diet by the LDP gives it the final authority to implement or reject the policy goals of the bureaucracy. (5) Because the LDP had a much greater need to compromise with the opposition at those times in the late 1970s and early 1980s when the LDP's majorities were slim, the deliberative process of the Diet became much more important in policy making. The specter of a Socialist-led coalition government added spur to the bureaucracy's support for the LDP. (6) Finally, the bureaucracy's control over information and expertise is now being challenged by the LDP's leadership. In the early post-occupation years the bureaucracy did have a monopoly on the technical and administrative expertise needed for efficient and effective policy formulation, but more than thirty years of LDP rule in the cabinet and in Diet committees, in addition to the participation of party members in the policy study groups that have arisen within the party, have given party members a much greater expertise (Muramatsu and Krauss 1984:142–43).

Those "revisionists" who stress the increased role of the LDP in policy making have chosen various dates to mark its beginning, but the most common, and most important, seems to be the oil shock of 1973 and its attendant economic slump. In post-oil slump Japan, government income dropped and debt increased. This left the government in a position such that it was unable to consistently maintain funding for pre–oil slump programs and tough political choices had to be made. As Hrebenar (1986: 274) puts it,

> As long as fair shares kept coming to the constituencies and clientele groups, the conservatives seemed to be content with the fact that bureaucrats made the allocative decisions. However, when the economy slowed down, the political bargaining process changed, because the 'pie' is smaller and the crucial decisions are not allocational, but the protection of existing subsidies and grants against cuts concerns politicians and bureaucrats alike. Under these new rules, the bureaucrats are not well equipped to deal with the situation. In the politics of 'who loses what,' any decisions made by the bureaucrats will easily become politicized and expose them to the danger of losing the respect and credibility they had gained over the years. In this new environment, the bureaucracies tend to follow a cautious path by avoiding controversial political decisions. They also appear to feel that it is the responsibility of the LDP to resolve these various tough questions, and thus the weight of policymaking has shifted from the bureaucrats to the LDP.

These arguments dovetail nicely with Kent Calder's theory of "crisis and compensation." In his book of the same name, Calder argues that previous theories of policy making in Japan, especially those based upon rational planning led by a technocratic bureaucracy, cannot explain why there have been so many innovations in policy and so many abrupt changes in the distribution of budget allocations in those policy areas outside economic policy and foreign policy. Within the latter, policy formulation has tended to conform to the Johnsonian developmental state with its technocratic, state/adminstrative bureaucracy-guided model. But outside these two policy areas, both innovation and compensation have been higher where there have been "patterns in the domestic sectors where the bureaucracy . . . was forced to accommodate the political world, thus intensifying the importance of distributive politics and political-party intervention in these sectors" (Calder 1988: 23).

"Japanese politics . . . operates largely in terms of institutionalized networks of players engaged in special reciprocal relationships of obligation and reward with public authority. Expectations on both sides are relatively pragmatic and accommodating, analogous to what Tilley calls the 'politics of the polity member.' Government provides benefits to private sector participants, in return for their consistent political support" (Calder 1988: 23). Outside these circles, the obligation/reward paradigm doesn't work, decisions tend to be ad hoc, there is much conflict, and uncertainty prevails. The crisis and compensation model is "the complex process of accommodation between government and its opponents—both intraparty and interparty opponents. That accommodation occurs at crucial junctures, when either the continuance of a given adminstration's tenure in office is perceived to be severely threatened, or internal political unrest seriously impairs its international credibility" (Calder 1988: 23).

LDP policies have been creative (i.e., they have compensated various sectors of the polity with traditionally nonconservative policies, like the social welfare state) because conservative politicians are insecure and are preoccupied with stabilizing their own positions. Thus they have reacted to threatening crises by extending the circles of compensation, shifting resources, sometimes radically, when necessary (Calder 1988: 20–21, 26). Both big business and the bureaucracy have acquiesced to the (for them) economically irrational policies of compensation to unions, agriculture, and small business when the LDP has pressured them to do so. The image presented by Calder is one of the LDP following the lead of the bureaucracy until there is a crisis which threatens its rule, at which time it takes over the reins and adopts a policy that will compensate the aggrieved sector of the public (whether or not the bureaucracy agrees with the policy). That policy then gets locked into place until it is supplanted by the need to compensate some other group which is creating a crisis (Calder 1988: 27).

In Britain, where no party has been able to establish quite such a lengthy hegemony, the mechanism of "circles of compensation" does not operate in precisely the same way. But in the normal process of electoral bidding, governments exchange benefits and insider status for consent and electoral support. In Britain, where electoral competition puts more overt pressure on the parties to seek votes, such politically motivated policies—an obvious example being the Conservative embrace of the welfare state—would not seem exceptional.

The increased power of the LDP in policy making would not be possible if the members of the party, leadership, and backbenchers had not been able to develop their own abilities and expertise in policy formulation. Gerald Curtis (1988: 112) believes that there is a new "political leadership culture" in Japan. Younger members of the party are much more inclined to get involved in the policy-making process beyond the traditional pork barrel, constituency-reward level. In the past, one of the major intraparty divisions within the LDP has been between those members who were ex-bureaucrats and those who were politicians who came up from the ranks. The contrast to Britain, where the division between a civil service and political career remains virtually complete, is obvious. The policy-making duties within the party were controlled by those who were ex-bureaucrats. Today, however, the distinction has less meaning for younger members of the party. They believe to a greater extent that the duty of the LDP is to take the lead on policy, and they have a higher level of educational attainment than their *sempai* (especially among those who work their way up from the ranks) that allows them a greater technical understanding of the issues involved, without spending years of training in Diet or party committee work. Indeed, while most theories of the increased power of the LDP in policy making stress the importance of time as a factor in the increased policy expertise of LDP members, Curtis believes that it is not time that is important—it is the new desire for policy involvement among younger members and their belief in the LDP's preeminence in policy making (Curtis 1988: 112). In Britain, where the role of Parliament has declined, and the party offers no analogous channel for policy activism, we noted the tendency of MPs to become increasingly inclined to seek their rewards in constituency service rather than policy making.

The desire of the new leadership to exert its, and the party's, authority over policy making is manifested through a reinvigoration of existing policy-making institutions within the party. The most important of these institutions is the Policy Affairs Research Council. PARC is a complex organization for policy study, research, formulation, and planning. There are seventeen divisions within the PARC, one for every ministry and, similarly, for every standing committee in the Diet. These divisions and their subcommittees bear the brunt of investigating, researching, and formulating policy that may become a cabinet bill. In addition to the divisions and their subcommittees there are many (thirty-two in 1987, according to Curtis) commissions dealing with broader policy questions (Curtis 1988: 112–13; Thayer 1973: 207–36). It can be argued that an LDP Diet member's greatest impact on government policy formulation comes not through his or her activities in the Diet, but through his or her participation in the PARC. In the words of John Stern, an American lobbyist in Japan, "The fact is, before bureaucrats get anything done, they make sure they run the proposal past the policy bureau of that LDP that's in charge of the issue" (*Japan Times*, January 10, 1991: 12).

Another important, but completely informal, organization that has helped increase the LDP Diet members' policy-making power is the *zoku*, or policy tribe. This was the sobriquet given in the 1970s to those Diet members who had served in the leadership of enough party and Diet policy-making institutions in one issue area to enable them to rival their bureaucratic counterparts in expertise. The *zoku* today refer to very loose policy factions with almost no definable structure, comprised of Diet members—both the types of leaders described above and interested/expert backbenchers—who use their commitment and expertise in a particular issue area to work with the bureaucracy and interest groups to realize a particular policy (Curtis 1988: 114–16).

Bureaucrats and Politicians

Just as power spills over from prime minister and cabinet to ministers, power spills over from ministers to civil servants, and beyond them to innumerable quangos. "The relationship between ministers and civil servants is one of the most crucial aspects of British government. On that relationship depends the ability of voters through their elected government to influence public policy" (Budge and McKay 1988: 35). The argument is frequently made, in fact, that the top civil servants, or "mandarins," really run Britain, and it is certainly true that they "wield enormous influence" (Ashford 1980: 38). In fact, Ian Gilmour once estimated that "only about one Minister in three runs his Department" (cited in Norton 1984: 193). It could be argued further, then, that Britain has bureaucratic, rather than ministerial, government, and that it is "the large agglomeration of complex bureaucracies that in practice carry out the work done in the name of Cabinet ministers" (Rose 1979: 141). The bureaucracy remains, in Bagehot's terms, one of Britain's "efficient secrets" (Greenaway 1987: 38). In fact, by convention the minister takes responsibility for all sorts of decisions of which he or she may know nothing, made by countless middle and lower-level civil servants.

The legendary reputation of the British civil service has been secured essentially through its practice of entry by competitive examination (also true in Japan) and by the tradition of nonpartisanship, or neutrality (a concept largely irrelevant to LDP-dominated Japan).[2] In fact, it is this neutrality that justifies politicians' heavy reliance on the civil service mandarins (Ashford 1980: 38). In spite of attempts over the years to encourage greater specialization and technical expertise at this level, "British civil servants continue in the main to conceive of themselves as general administrators rather than specialists, to promote circulation between departments and ministries rather than dedication to a particular specialty" (Budge and McKay 1988: 32). Brown and Steel (1979: 187) attribute the practice to the desirability of cultivating the "organizational wisdom" necessary to solve problems "too complex for the individual specialist to grasp." As a result of the generalist tradition in the civil service and Parliament, and the predominance of a parliamentary career path to cabinet positions, Britain has lacked, by and large, a technically trained core elite. This is one of the reasons, as we shall see, that government has come to rely so heavily on consultation with organized interests and outside advisers. The Thatcher government established civil service reform as one of its priorities, and it made a sustained and partially successful effort to change the "culture of the Civil Service," by encouraging greater specialization, commitment and managerial efficiency (Greenaway 1987: 53).

The central policy role of the top civil service is not to initiate policy, but rather to "respond to ministerial initiatives sympathetically but not uncritically" (Rose 1989: 88). It is to provide ministers with advice and options, to build a policy consensus, to defend the department, to "influence discreetly the climate of opinion about the department" in interdepartmental committees and other forums, and to make decisions that are in accord with the minister's overall objectives (Rose 1989: 89). The norms of the civil service are an excellent showcase for consensualism and incrementalism in British politics.[4]

Vital to an appreciation of power sharing between bureaucrats and politicians is their perception of the political system and their role in it. Do bureaucrats favor the rational world of the bureaucracy or do they favor the pluralism of politics? Aberbach et al. (1981: 110) have found in their study of Western democracies that just as cabinet and other ministers reflect the "broad gauged," "visionary" world view of the politician, the civil servant will reflect a more narrowly focused and conservative bureaucratic view. As the minister asks "What ends will be served and whose interests will be satisfied?," the bureaucrat asks "Is it do-able?" (Aberbach et al. 1981: 111). Often, their role is to point out to the minister the impracticality of what he or she is considering, to find "one more snag than anyone else has found in a proposal for change" (Rose 1989: 90). The result of this bifurcation (in actuality a matter of degree) of attitudes has tended to be something of a "division of labor" in which each provides a per-spective lacked by the other (Aberbach et al. 1981: 93).

In the eyes of the classical bureaucrat, "a perfect world would be a world without politics" (Putnam 1975: 103). While such bureaucrats exist in Britain, however, many top civil servants exhibit a somewhat more positive attitude concerning politics than many of their European peers. In one cross-national study (Putnam 1975: 99), British civil servants were substantially more likely than their Italian or West German counterparts to rate political factors more important than technical factors. This emphasis is confirmed in Table 7.2, below, which finds top British civil servants far more likely than their Japanese counter-parts to adopt a positive view of politics. Despite the "neutrality" of the civil service, political advice is as important as a technical assessment of a measure's feasibility, and the civil service is not averse to giving it (Michael 1982: 75).

Despite the "Yes Minister" portrayal of the conservative and conniving civil servant, the British civil service is a less powerful player than the Japanese, at least in policy initiation. Britain has no strong "bottom-up" tradition comparable to Japan. "Civil servants in Britain are trained, to a greater extent than their counterparts in many other democracies, to obey political masters. The British civil servant has neither the French and Japanese bureaucrat's confidence in the superiority of his judgment to the politician's nor the American civil servant's belief in the legitimacy of using the legislature (Congress) against the political leadership of the department" (Budge and McKay 1988: 34). The civil servant does not expect to dominate (see Table 7.2). Despite its generally reactive role, the bureaucracy certainly has its policy-making functions, and civil servants "are not mere instruments of a political will" (Brown and Steel 1979: 201). Given the logic of ever-increased pressures on prime ministers and ministers, it is inevitable that the civil service be called upon more and more to fill in policy-making functions. This may be seen clearly in the widespread and increasing use of "delegated legislation," by which civil servants wind up drafting the details of policies that Parliament has delegated to ministers (Christoph 1975: 29). But in the end, the policy views of civil servants "complement, rather than compete with, those of politicians" (Brown and Steel 1979: 201).

To recap what has already been written about the historical roots of contemporary bureaucratic power in Japan, the bureaucracy retained a great deal of power after the occupation because of what might be termed "system hangover." The dominant authority of the bureaucracy in policy formulation and the prestige accruing to the emperor's servants remained intact, while the occupation forces were not successful in carrying out major reforms of the civil adminstrative bureaucracy. On the contrary, the occupation forces tended to rely upon the bureaucracy to carry out the governing of Japan, and through a top-down, centralized, and authoritative adminstration further demonstrated to the Japanese the universality and effectiveness of this type of bureaucratic rule. When the LDP was formed and began its long rule, the bureaucracy was able to dominate the party because many political leaders were so inexperienced that they needed the guidance and expertise of technocrats, and because many other new members of the party were ex-bureaucrats who believed that the party was *sempai* (senior) to the *kohai* (junior) bureaucracy, and should thus follow its lead. It must be remembered, however, that within the confines of a new democratic system, the bureaucracy needed the LDP to carry its policies through the legislature and to mediate disputes within the bureaucracy (Misawa 1973: 20).

Another factor that played a role in the continued dominance of the bureaucracy in the postoccupation period, and which also distinguishes the Japanese case from contemporary policy making in Britain and the United States, was the drive for economic development. This concept is best explained by Chalmers Johnson's exposition of the "developmental state" in his classic book, *MITI and the Japanese Miracle*. In that book, Johnson presents an analysis of the "miracle" of postwar Japanese economic development based upon the role of the developmental state. Postoccupation Japan found itself in the position of a late-developing nation with a weak economy plugged securely into an international trading system, dominated by a fully developed and economically powerful

United States. Given its economic situation and past political history, the road to rapid economic development and more equitable competition lay in a state-dominated, plan rational political economy. In the Japanese developmental state the bureaucracy set "substantive social and economic goals" (Johnson 1986: 19), within the context of a capitalist economy, and then guided the nation toward the achievement of those goals. Thus, the economic "miracle" was the result of the Japanese bureaucracy setting specific, rational (as opposed to political) goals and implementing plans for the attainment of those goals for the ultimate benefit of the public—economic development. The role of the LDP in the process has been to legitimize the policies created by the bureaucracy by passing them into law through the only law-making institution in the political system—the Diet. The LDP has also been helpful in fending off interest groups and constituent appeals that were viewed as being particularistic and therefore antinational policy (Johnson 1986: 49).

Finally, leaving aside the expansion of military bureaucracies necessitated by the Cold War, a factor in the United States and Britain but not Japan, all three countries, and many others, have been forced to expand their bureaucracies to cope with increasingly complex social and economic problems and the need for the central government to become more directly involved in their solution. While there has been no benchmark event in Japan similar to the expansion of the British bureaucracy following postwar socialization, there has been a similar expectation in Japan that it is the duty of the central bureaucracy to become directly involved in the solution of problems that had previously not existed, e.g., the regulation of new technologies, or had been handled on a more primary level, e.g., aging.

It was argued above that in Japan the LDP assumed a much larger role relative to the formal institutions of cabinet and the prime minister than is the case in Britain. However, the power of the party needs to be understood in relation to the power of the government bureaucracy. Whatever the role of political institutions in the early postoccupation years, there were few who doubted that the bureaucracy was acting as both policy maker and administrative organ. But there are many who continue to believe that the bureaucracy still takes the lead in initiating policy, in researching policy, and in debating policy. What is it that enables the bureaucracy to maintain such power over political institutions in the policy-making process?

Unlike the case in Britain, where cabinet officials and ministers themselves have considerable policy-initiating powers, in Japan, the initiatives of the ministries originate with the bureaucracy, in "bottom-up" fashion. Thus, to assert cabinet ascendency over the Diet is really to assert bureaucratic ascendency over the Diet. "Cabinet bills originate and are drafted exclusively within the ministries. They are then passed on to the LDP for its approval and introduction into the Diet. As a matter of routine, ministerial officials are also present in the Diet to explain their legislation and answer questions" (Johnson 1986: 47). Johnson

Table 7.1

Proportion of Cabinet Bills to Member Bills in Japan, 1946–1979

	Cabinet	Bills	Member Bills
1946–55	2.204	835	72.5
1956–69	2,574	1,218	67.9
1970–74	624	315	64.0
1975–79	437	329	57.0

Source: Bradley Richardson and Scott C. Flanagan 1984. *Politics in Japan:* Table 9.2, p. 347. Boston: Little, Brown. © Bradley Richardson and Scott C. Flannagan. Used with permission of Harper Collins.

believes that the trend has been toward greater approval of cabinet bills as opposed to private member bills (1986: 47). To take a relatively recent example, in the thirty-sixth session of the Diet (July 1980–November 1983), 269 bills were presented by the cabinet and 89 percent of them passed, but of the 177 bills sponsored by private members, only 27 percent passed (Hrebenar 1986: 272). While this is not out of line with Richardson and Flanagan's assertion that the ratio of cabinet bills to private member bills introduced into the Diet is decreasing (see Table 7.1), cabinet bills still account for somewhere between 60 and 75 percent of all legislation passed in the postwar period (Flanagan and Richardson 1984: 347).

Thus, while the domination of government bills in the British Parliament is used to underscore the subservience of Parliament to cabinet, in Japan the same relationship may be used as well to underscore the subservience of the LDP to the government bureaucracy. In essence, the bureaucracy uses the LDP to legitimize its policies through what has been called the "puppet Diet" (Wildes quoted in Johnson 1986: 50). "The fact is that the party's election platforms as well as its overall policies usually are a mere rearrangement of a list of policy proposals submitted by the ministries, thus revealing the total dependency of the party on the organized bureaucracy" (Misawa 1973: 20).

Bureaucratic power also emanates from powers delegated by the Diet to the cabinet and the ministries by way of the power to issue ordinances. While ministerial and cabinet ordinances are not uncommon in any state, in Japan their number, and their importance to the Japanese policy-making process, is substantial. The ratio of laws passed by the Diet to ordinances issued by the ministries has increased from 1.5 ordinances for every law in the early postoccupation years to 4.2 ordinances for every law by the mid-1970s (Richardson and Flanagan 1984: 349). The rules of the policy-making game, as well as the policies that are finally translated into action, are more often than not, even if filtered through the cabinet, a product of the civil administrative bureaucracy.

Muramatsu Michio and Ellis Krauss's study of the relations between Japanese bureaucrats and politicians in policy making found that Japanese bureaucrats and politicians resemble Western European bureaucrats and politicians in their social backgrounds and also in that the roles of the two are converging. Japanese bureaucrats make a larger contribution to the policy-making process than do their British counterparts, but, looking at the problem from a different perspective, Japanese politicians have less influence over policy making than the prevailing models of a "bureaucracy dominant" or "ruling triad" would allow (Muramatsu and Krauss 1984: 131). Muramatsu and Krauss (1984: 142) also argue that the increasing role of the bureaucracy in developed nations is universal, but in a system like Japan where the bureaucracy has always been a dominant sector, the policy-making power of politicians and the bureaucracy are converging as politicans increase their power to equal that of the bureaucrats, thus making the policy-making process, and the political system as a whole, more pluralistic.

Table 7.2 confirms what we noted above about British top civil servants: more so than the norm among European bureaucrats, they favor political over technical approaches to problems. It also confirms that Japanese bureaucrats' preference for technical considerations conforms rather closely to the Aberbach scheme, noted above, for European civil servants as a whole. The table clearly demonstrates that Japanese bureaucrats are much more antipluralist than their British counterparts. This data provide a very clear insight into the oft-cited theory that bureaucrats perceive their role, and the role of their ministries, as a stabilizing factor in the political system. Political parties are seen as serving the needs of only a segment of the nation, while the bureaucracy represents and serves the needs of the entire nation. This idea obviously still remains strongly implanted in the minds of contemporary bureaucrats. The perceived superiority of Japanese bureaucrats over politicians is also reinforced by their respective socioeconomic backgrounds. As Table 7.3 illustrates, Japanese politicians are more likely to come from working-class backgrounds, are more likely to come from families with lower levels of educational attainment, and are more likely themselves to have a lower level of educational attainment. The fact that a similar dichotomy separates British politicians and civil servants, without leading to a visibly superior attitude on the part of the latter, suggests the importance of context in interpreting the impact of social background. In Britain, the tradition of subordination of bureaucratic authority to political authority is well established. Although Japanese bureaucrats seem to be opposed to pluralism in a general sense, there is not much difference between their perceptions and politicans' perceptions of the role of the bureaucracy. Forty-four percent of higher bureaucrats, 34 percent of middle bureaucrats and 44 percent of LDP politicians believe the role of the bureaucracy is to "lay the groundwork for political decisions" and 27 percent of higher bureaucrats, 40 percent of middle bureaucrats, and 24 percent of LDP politicians believe that the role of the bureaucracy is to "coordinate competing interests and views." However, only 9 percent of higher bureaucrats, 10 percent of middle bureaucrats, and 16 percent of LDP politicians believe that the role of the bureaucracy is to "implement Diet and party policy" (Muramatsu and Krauss 1984: 134). Although a greater per-

Table 7.2

Japanese and British Bureaucrats' Attitudes toward Pluralism
(percent agreeing)

	Japan	Britain
Interest groups' conflict endangers country's welfare	69	18
Political parties exacerbate conflict	96	54
Civil service guarantees reasonable public policy	80	21
Technical considerations should outweigh political	49	21

Source: Michio Muramatsu and Ellis Krauss, 1984. "Bureaucrats and Politicians in Policymaking: The Case of Japan." *American Political Science Review* 78: 132. Used with permission.

Table 7.3

Comparison of Social Backgrounds of Politicans and Bureaucracts in Britain and Japan (in percent)

	Bureaucrats		Politicians	
	Britain	Japan	Britain	Japan
Father's occupation				
Managerial or professional	68	64	64	59
Other nonmanual	21	21	12	11
Manual	13	7	25	27
Father's education				
None or primary	29	21	—	48
Intermediate	43	30	—	14
University	27	45	—	31
Education				
University	83	98	71	67
Less than university (includes two-year junior colleges and technical schools)	16	2	29	27

Source: Michio Muramatsu and Ellis Krauss, 1984. "Bureaucrats and Politicians in Policymaking: The Case of Japan." *American Political Science Review* 78: 132. Used with permission

centage of LDP politicans perceive the role of the bureaucracy to be implementing policy for the Diet and the party, a majority of them also believe that they are more influential in policy making than bureaucrats, whereas bureaucrats see it as being about equal. Neither gives any other group much credit for influence.

One of the most important means of bureaucratic control in the policy-making process is "administrative guidance" (*gyosei shido*). Administrative guidance is a term which covers a wide variety of bureaucratic behaviors, but, in essence, it is what an American would call "jaw-boning," backed by all the strength of the ministries stretched to, and sometimes over, the limits of their legal authority. The intent of administrative guidance is to align the behavior and/or policies of local governments, interest groups, companies, individuals, or any one else in disagreement or conflict with the ministry's policy goals. Administrative guidance has been used to regulate building codes and broadcasting hours, to control and allocate the production of companies when competition is overheating the economy or when conflict results from the competition of new and old industries, or to promote the ministry's policies.

The location of administrative guidance at the very core of the bureaucracy's policy-making power is demonstrated by a MITI memorandum (administrative guidance has been most often linked to MITI, although it is not by any measure the only ministry to use it), "The Concept of Administrative Guidance," reproduced here in translation from Hiroshi Shiono's chapter in Kiyoyaki Tsuji, ed., *Public Administration in Japan* (1984: 212).

> From the standpoint of the national economy, it is important to implement the following measures in a proper manner:
>
> Request voluntary controls on the prices of goods related to life despite hikes in oil prices.
>
> Request voluntary control on exportation in order to avoid trade frictions.
>
> Recommend production increases in case of tight supply-demand conditions.
>
> So far the Ministry has managed to carry out the aims of industrial policies and tide over the difficulties. The aim of administrative guidance is to implement an effective measure in a flexible manner on the basis of agreement and cooperation with other parties, without excessive interference. Therefore, administrative guidance has played an important role in the development of the Japanese economy and will continue to be effective in the future. The Ministry of International Trade and Industry intends to implement administrative guidance if necessary. It is natural that the implementation of administrative guidance should not lead to joint action in any industry which is deemed to be contrary to the provisions of the Antimonopoly Law.

Although administrative guidance deals with policy making based upon bureaucratic interpretation at the highest levels of the state and private enterprise, similar practices exist at all levels of administration. For example, under Japanese law in the early 1980s, anyone riding a motorcycle with an engine displacement larger than 50 cc was required to wear a helmet, but motorcycles with an engine displacement of 50 cc or less could be ridden without a helmet. Nevertheless, policemen at traffic checkpoints often stopped those riding 50 cc motorcycles without helmets to issue a warning that such a practice was dangerous, if not illegal. This case illustrates that guidance from civil administrators which is not based on statutory law can, and does, take place at all levels of the administrative hierarchy. The relationship between statutory law and administrative guidance has been frequently examined by both the courts and scholars, and while scholars have questioned its legality, the courts have frequently supported it to the extent of specifying "that local governments can and should promote administrative guidance even when they are not vested with statutory authority" (Shiono 1984: 209). Indeed, administrative guidance is an excellent example of the primacy of effective and/or traditional practice in the Japanese political system over statutory and constitutional law. Although the British observe an analogous "administrative discretion," central authorities are normally reluctant to press their clients as hard as "administrative guidance" implies. The "hands-off" and "self-regulation" approaches to administration suggest more limited regulatory power than is the case in Japan.

Personnel practices also enable the bureaucracy to maintain a strong influence on policy making. There are many bureaucrats who leave their positions to become LDP members of the Diet and, eventually, cabinet ministers. This arrangement is suitable to the party as it maintains open channels of communication with the bureaucracy, but it also ensures a strong faction within the party leadership that supports the bureaucracy's preeminence in policy making. Since the 1960s, the percentage of LDP ex-bureaucrat members of the Diet has been about 25 percent in the House of Representatives and 35 percent in the House of Councillors (Curtis 1988: 91–92).

Looking at the other side of the coin, the party has little influence over the administrative civil service. Ministers are the only political appointments to the bureaucracy and so the PM can only make approximately twenty appointments, all at the ministerial level. Neither are they really his to make as they must be allocated according to faction and by the number of elections the individual has won (Johnson 1986: 52; Curtis 1988: 93). After their appointment, ministers are often at the mercy of the civil servants around them, as in Britain, because of the minister's short tenure and lack of knowledge in the ministry's area. They also face, unlike Britain, the pressure of policy initiatives rising from below and an ingrained respect for the primacy of the bureaucracy (especially in the case of ex-bureaucrat ministers). "Were a minister to veto a draft proposal approved by his subordinates who have many years of technical and administrative experience, not only would his entire bureaucratic force distrust him, but they might drive him out of office. Hence, he is bound to rubber-stamp a draft proposal. Conversely, the system of *pro forma* approval of draft proposals enables incompetent ministers to remain in office" (Misawa 1973: 31).

Government and Legislature

The Powers of the Legislature

One could almost say that the British Parliament is a sovereign body whose sovereign power resides elsewhere. In the late nineteenth century, the age of the "independent" MP, Parliament was at the peak of its legislative power. Yet, today, Parliament lacks the responsibility either for originating government legislation, or for exercising policy choices. "The function of the legislature has been to sustain and examine the executive," observes Riddell (1989: 110), "rather than to replace it." In this respect, it is much closer to the Japanese Diet than to the American Congress. Furthermore, party loyalty, ministerial responsibility, civil service anonymity, and minimal career overlap between Parliament and civil service translate into relatively little parliamentary contact with or leverage over the bureaucracy (Aberbach et al. 1981: 98, 229–33). Even the influence Parliament retains is circumscribed. Except in the limited case of "private members' bills" on which the majority leadership takes no position, MPs no longer have responsibility to draft legislation. As in Japan, a large percentage of government bills is passed—between 80 and 100 percent. And while a larger number of private members' bills is introduced, these normally deal with less weighty matters, and less than 10 percent are likely to pass (Punnett 1988: 261). Even when Parliament expresses a distinct position, government may ignore it, as the government did in the case of the House of Commons' vote in 1985 against placing the third London airport at Stansted. What policy-initiating and policy-debating roles Parliament has have been undermined by government consultation with organized interests, governmental secrecy, and even, in the 1970s, resort to public referenda. Perhaps the remaining policy-making role of Parliament is best described by the function of the House of Commons as "an acute barometer of the mood both of MPs and of the nation generally" (Riddell 1989: 112). Brown and Steel (1979: 226) suggest that MPs themselves may sometimes fail to exploit even those opportunities for influence that do come along. Perhaps the fact that Parliament does not assert itself more, given the blank check of parliamentary supremacy, is, according to Ashford (1980: 50), the "most compelling evidence of the durability and depth of political consensus within Westminster." The growing importance and authority of the European Community, striking as it does at the heart of parliamentary supremacy, should further accelerate the trend toward a declining policy role for the British Parliament.

If Parliament does not make policy, it gives its assent to, or legitimizes legislation that originates elsewhere. This is true both in the sense of formal assent by division, or vote, and in the sense of "latent legitimization" that arises from the cabinet being "elected through" the House of Commons. Parliament also legitimizes through "tension release," provided by the airing of different views, and through "support mobilization" or the mobilization of public support for government-sponsored measures (Norton 1985b: 5). Even the legitimizing and assent roles are exercised relatively late in the game, often coming after government consultation with interests. And these roles, too, are threatened by the legitimizing and consent functions of organized groups, by the willingness of a few groups to disobey parliamentary laws, and by questions about the legitimacy of the electoral system and the House of Lords.

Parliament is more likely to have its impact on policy through its ex-post facto exercise of scrutiny of existing policy. Traditionally, this function has been carried out through question time, and other formal opportunities for debate which serve to underline "the role of ministers as the link between government and parliament" (Ridley 1984: 8). In the face of government secrecy, even the principle of accountability through parliamentary questioning of ministers is difficult to realize. Certain topics are taboo. If a minister will not answer on a subject for two successive parliaments, "it goes on a more or less permanent list of taboo subjects on which the Table Office will not accept questions" (Michael 1982: 62). The growing complexity and amount of legislation has strained Parliament's ability to deal with the broad scrutiny function. MPs too busy to intervene on all but a fraction of issues may seek at best "to keep the possibility of review constantly in the minds of administrators and departmental Ministers" (Brown and Steel 1979: 223). Nongovernmental corporations and bodies, not in the administrative chain, are largely beyond the control of Parliament. The use of "delegated legislation" or "outline legislation" that confer "broad powers while leaving the details and safeguards to regulations" are yet another way in which both parliamentary input and scrutiny have been by-passed (McAuslan and McEldowney 1986: 506). As a result of these limitations, Parliament has been at best a policy-influencing, not policy-making body. Parliament has become only "one of several specialized channels through which ideas, information, and pressures are legitimately applied to the development of public policy," and one that on specific issues may be overshadowed by other policy inputs (Brown and Steel: 1979: 203). Though Parliament's impact on Britain's public policy is not great, some writers have proposed a "transformative model," which claims a modest revival of parliamentary influence. The assertiveness of backbenchers in the 1970s and 1980s, and the reforms that created new "select committees" with the power to call government officials to testify and to present policy recommendations, led Beer (1982a: 180) to refer to the "rise of Parliament" and Norton (1985b: 2, 41) to assert that Parliament had become "a relatively more significant policy-influencing body."

In the difference between its constitutional powers and its practical impact on policy making, the Japanese Diet is very similar to the British Parliament. According to the Japanese constitution, the Diet is the only law-making organ of the state, and, according to law, it establishes all administrative organs from ministries down to the regional level, it determines the scope and authority of those organs, and it regulates the number of personnel in the civil administrative bureaucracy. The above notwithstanding, it has long been assumed that the Diet is the poor stepsister of the bureaucracy and the LDP. Previous figures given in Table 7.1 that demonstrated the preponderance of cabinet bills over private member bills, and the overwhelming success of government legislation indicate that no matter who formulates policy—the LDP, the bureaucracy, or both—the Diet's role in formulating policy is reactive. The Diet does not initiate policy, it reacts to initiatives from the governing party and the bureaucracy. The strength of its input into the policy-making process depends upon the ability of the opposition parties to alter or kill legislation.

Policy making that does take place in the Diet takes place in its committees. There are sixteen standing committees which parallel the ministries and the PARC divisions. The committees debate legislation, propose alternative legislation, and make amendments to legislation. While on the surface the committee system in Japan was crafted through the American-written constitution to resemble that of the United States, in actuality it more resembles the British committee system in which the governing party controls the leadership of the committees and the debate within the committees through its majority in the Diet. Thus, as most legislation is drafted either by LDP policy-making institutions like the PARC or by the government bureaucracy before it reaches the committees, the input into policy formulation by the committees is limited. Richardson and Flanagan (1984: 355) argue that it is a fallacy to assume that the Diet is merely a rubber stamp of the LDP, by pointing to the fact that only 56 percent of all cabinet bills submitted between 1960 and 1980 were passed without being postponed, amended, or shelved. John Stern's statement, "Bureaucrats may run Japan, but the Diet runs the bureaucrats" (*Japan Times*, January 10, 1991: 12) may be a bit of hyperbole, but it does remind us that the control of legislation, and of the bureaucracy, is ultimately in the hands of the Diet.

Dissent and Opposition in Parliament

At one time, "All accepted that the majority party in the House of Commons had the right to govern and the minority party the right to oppose" (Denver 1987b: 78). The role accorded the official legislative opposition—Her Majesty's Loyal Opposition—has long been one of the most widely recognized features of the British system. Since two-party alternation in government has been the rule for most of the last 150 years, it is not surprising that many of the norms of parliamentary conflict resolution and decision making start from that premise. The majority of the day has had to govern in the recognition that the opposition might win the next election, and the opposition has had to behave in the knowledge that it might soon be called upon to govern. However, the opposition has no significant role in the making of specific policies.

In general, the constitutional role of the opposition is a political one, rather than a legislative one, centering on holding the government of the day accountable, as well as demonstrating its readiness to assume the reins of government. The system guarantees that government and opposition are electoral foes, and the desire to win elections and the constitutional need for government accountability requires that the opposition take its role seriously. The bi-weekly question hour, the debate on the Queen's speech, frequent "supply days," and the second reading debates give the opposition ample opportunities to air their views. However,

Table 7.4

Support for Selected Constitutional Attitudes (in percent), British MPs

	Support for Attitudes and Items	
	Conservative	Labour
1. Vigorous and Critical Opposition	64	97
Opposition criticism a duty	78	93
Give opposition better resources	75	99
2. Favor individual ministerial responsibility	38	80
Greater opportunity to question ministers	54	87
Ministers reveal all information	36	67
Too much concentration of power in PM	31	66
3. Parliamentarism	82	53
Support policy by MP deliberation	72	54
Disagree with referendum	90	73

Source: Adapted from D. Searing, 1982. "Rules of the Game in Britain: Can the Politicians Be Trusted?" *American Political Science Review* 76: Table 5, p. 253. Used with permission.

the opposition's lack of sufficient information consistently and effectively to challenge government ministers reinforces this political role. As Table 7.4 shows, both Conservative and Labour MPs strongly support the concept of vigorous and critical opposition. Vigorous opposition is desirable "because it punctures complacency and guards against Bonapartism in relationships between Government and citizen" (Searing 1982: 242). Enshrined as it is in the legitimate constitutional order, adversarial politics, far from suggesting an exception to consensual politics, "is heavily geared toward generating and maintaining support for the system" (Ashford 1980: 264).

In contrast to the claims that adversarial politics best characterizes British elite behavior, however, Rose has argued that "Consensus best describes the legislative process. To see government in Adversary terms is to mistake for the whole a relatively small part of its action leading to occasional divisions in Parliament" (Rose 1979: 89). The fact is that parliamentary politics in Britain has tended to moderation. This moderation exists both in the general comity of relations among MPs (Putnam 1973), and in the continuities of policy rooted in "ongoing reality." As Searing (1982: 242) notes, despite the greater prominence of the adversarial values of opposition, "political compromise and trust . . . are nevertheless, important rules of the game, for without willingness to work with the other side and give it its due, parliamentary government would grind to a halt." Only rarely will opposition MPs vote with the government. But on most bills, the opposition's decision not to call for a division tends to create a "tacit consensus" (Rose 1979: 79, 86). Even "On social affairs, an area of major potential difference between the parties, the proportion of consensual bills was virtually average, 77 percent. . . . Even in the contentious field of the economy, there were no divisions on two-thirds of all government bills" (Rose 1979: 81). Finally, when the opposition does obtain power, it repeals only a small proportion of the legislation of the previous government. Government is not indifferent to the opposition, and "The division record of the House of Commons shows that both Conservative and Labour governments have usually put forward bills that will be acceptable to all sides of the House of Commons" (Rose 1989: 285).

As we have noted in previous chapters, the perennial control of the Japanese Diet by the LDP has created an opposition unable effectively to oppose government policy and with little hope of attaining control of the government. On the public level, the opposition parties, and especially the JSP and the JCP, tend to work against any LDP legislation, to the extent that it sometimes appears as if their opposition is to the LDP, rather than the policy embodied in the legislation. They enjoy the similar privileges and forms of opposition to the British in the reading of bills and question periods. However, that opposition is only effective when the LDP's majority is slight. When the LDP has a stable majority, opposition to its legislation can be blithely overridden, but it must be courted when their majority is thin. Given the mood of the Japanese public in 1990, it would appear that the latter will be the case for some time to come.

The Japanese people expect a high degree of consensus in the formulation of policy, especially as it finds its way through the Diet in the form of legislation. This expectation has given greater impetus to the LDP to reach accommodation with the opposition parties and it has given the opposition parties a weapon with which they can threaten the LDP. The LDP understands that the legitimacy of their policies depends upon the public's perception of the consensus involved in their formulation and passage by the Diet. When, for example, the government submitted a bill designed to allow SDF participation in United Nations Peacekeeping Forces following the invasion of Kuwait, it was forced to back down after withering questioning and debate from the opposition in both plenary sessions and committee sessions. Although a clear lack of public support for the bill and political maneuvering within the LDP also aided its downfall, the government has stated that the next such bill will emerge only after consultations with the opposition parties. The need for consensus allows the opposition parties to "play to the gallery" when opposing legislation in the Diet. Obstructing the passage of legislation by boycotting committee meetings and plenary sessions, calling for votes of no confidence, and deliberately slowing the voting process in the Diet are all means by which the opposition attempts to communicate to the Japanese people their lack of support and consensus for any particular piece of legislation. Up until the late 1960s there were even attempts physically to intimidate the LDP on the floor of the Diet and in the halls outside, but that tactic has not been used frequently of late. At any rate, it tends to negate the effect of painting the LDP as the bullies of the political system.

For all of the *tatemae* appearances of conflict in the Diet between the LDP and the opposition parties, there has actually been much real cooperation *honne*. While this battle over policy and the claim to true consensual behavior is being fought in public, a very different relationship between the members of the LDP and opposition parliamentary parties is often carried out behind the scenes. While some have criticized Japan of wearing a "mask of consensus," in this case we can accuse the political parties of wearing a "mask of contention." The LDP and the opposition parties maintain their "face" by continuing a public conflict over policy, but behind the scenes, in informal settings, they are working together closely to set the terms and the limits of the debate—creating consensus (Thayer 1973 : 289–90; Kishima 1987: 103–10). In this contrast between public contention and private agreement, we see a significant parallel to the British elite political behavior described by Rose. Kishima found, in her in-depth study of Watanuki's Finance Committee, that "government-proposed bills that are finally enacted more often than not represent a merger of views and interests of the Opposition and the LDP government. Moreover, since resolutions attached to bills have political [*sic*] binding power to direct the future course of the administration, the Opposition's views and principles actually constitute a part of the basis of the government policy making well before concrete bills are drafted" (Kishima 1987: 109). The declining majorities of the LDP since the 1970s have given more power to the opposition parties in Diet committees. As the opposition parties take more seats and chairmanships of the committees, the LDP is forced to accept concessions in order to get their legislation passed. Bills passed by LDP support alone has declined to about 5 percent in the 1977–1980 period and increased JSP and Komeito support for successful legislation to 80 percent and JCP support for successful legislation to about 70 percent (Curtis: 1988: 39). Before the public is presented with the ritual legislative drama of obstructive tactics by the opposition, followed by the railroading of the bill through the legislature by the LDP, the content and timing of the conflict may be planned by the LDP and the opposition parties in informal gatherings and off-the-record meetings (Curtis 1988: 37–38). Thus the LDP gets de facto support for the policy and the opposition parties, while acting constructively in the passage of legislation, get needed concessions and maintain their image of David fighting Goliath.

Intraparty Dissent

Party dissidents can cause more of a problem for a government than the official opposition, although the promise of patronage is a valuable weapon against rebellion (Barber 1984: 75). In Britain, "Only in the 1951–55 Parliament, when the Labour opposition was unusually divided by the Bevanite controversy, did opposition MPs dissent more than government MPs" (Rose 1979: 83). The ability of the government to count on majority support for its programs is the key link that is thought to provide effective and accountable government. In a parliamentary vote, a significant number of party votes are not cast by the officeholders on the "front benches" of Parliament, but by members who do not hold office—the backbenchers. Not holding positions of power themselves, backbenchers are in a sense "outsiders" to government who must, like an interest group, make their views known to the leadership. Backbenchers have their own organizations, such as the Conservatives' 1922 Committee. Despite their power to do so, MPs of the majority rarely will vote to bring down their own government.

Though the norm is still party discipline, MPs are more critical of government than in the past, and this is one of the factors explaining what some see as the rise of Parliament. Between 1970 and 1984 the government suffered over 500 defeats—some on important issues—in both houses (Norton 1985b: 13). That level of dissent is without precedent in the twentieth century. Because of the weakening of party loyalty, the Labour governments of the 1970s decided not to treat their regular defeats as a loss of parliamentary confidence, and did not resign. Drucker and Gamble (1988: 67) suggest that "The significance of MPs' change in attitude is felt not so much in lost government bills, but in governments' increased need to consult with and seriously consider the attitudes of their backbenchers." Despite her reputation for combativeness in cabinet, Mrs. Thatcher attempted to work closely with the executive of the backbenchers' 1922 Committee (Burch 1983: 409). Still, concessions to the back benches have, by and large, been "at the margin" (Riddell 1989: 111).

Dissent and opposition within the Japanese Diet differ from that in Parliament primarily due to the effects of one-party domination and factionalism within the LDP. At first glance it appears as if most dissent in the Diet does come from the opposition parties, but there is intraparty opposition as well. Intraparty opposition to government legislation in the Japanese Diet comes not from a leadership-backbencher dichotomy, but from the division of the party into factions. Party discipline is a misnomer in the case of the LDP. It is actually factional discipline that is important. Party harmony and discipline within the Diet is maintained through consensus by the factional elite. Factions within the LDP are divided into mainstream and anti-mainstream factions. Mainstream factions are the largest factions and represent the majority of LDP members. They also tend to be the most conservative. Antimainstream factions represent the minority and serve as the opposition to the mainstream factions. Although the process of consensus building and group decision making within the party usually does an adequate job of bringing conciliation on points of difference, and of spreading party and government positions equitably, there are also many examples of intraparty opposition that have had dire consequences for the LDP. To name but two of the most important examples, in the early 1970s a young LDP politician whose father had been an LDP leader, Kono Yohei, led a drive among younger party members to reform corruption within the party. The futility of his efforts and the Lockheed scandals led him to split from the LDP and create a new party, the New Liberal Club (NLC). The other came with the previously mentioned 1980 vote of no-confidence against the Ohira government, in which two anti-mainstream factions long in contention with Ohira over both party leadership and policy abstained from voting, allowing the no-confidence motion to pass.

Center-Local Relations

Britain and Japan are both unitary governments, but local authorities retain a considerable amount of responsibility for government. For example, in Britain, local government accounts for a quarter of public expenditure and over a third of public employees (Punnett 1988: 411). There are many different local authorities, but most important are the county, district, and borough councils. As in Japan, Parliament has the power to constitute all subordinate political institutions and endow them with their powers. Central government controls local government through statutory instruments, administrative methods, budgetary control, and the court system. Whatever powers local government has are statutory, and they include both prescriptive and permissive policy powers. These responsibilities include housing, education, fire, police, transport, and social services. Nonetheless, many consider local government to be "vital to diffusion of power and limitation on central government" in Britain (McAuslan and McEldowney 1986: 502). Local government can deliver some kinds of services more effectively than central authorities, and, by the same token, can relieve some of the burden on the center. Devolution of control over education saved government the expense and difficulty of running schools directly but, at least until the Thatcher government, limited the degree to which the secretary of state for education "could make real decisions about what happens in schools" (Budge and McKay 1988: 40). Local government also serves as an important means of bringing citizen and government into closer contact, and as a means of political recruitment for Parliament (Punnett 1988: 408–9). Finally, the delegation of certain powers to the local authorities and an independent, at least until the 1990 reforms, tax base through local rates (property taxes) allowed localities a certain autonomy from the center.

As in the case of government-group relations, government-local relations have traditionally been characterized by a consultative relationship. "[C]entral governments generally accepted that they should act in 'partnership' with local authorities, drafting legislation in ways which at least took account of majority local government opinion" (Dunleavy and Rhodes 1988: 118). "Because previous post-war governments depended upon councils for increased public housing or large school building programmes, they trod carefully around 'local autonomy' issues, and relied more on 'partnership' relations with councils than on the full exercise of Whitehall's control powers" (Dunleavy and Rhodes 1988: 126).

While it is possible to describe center-periphery relations in terms of partnership, it is also possible to describe the traditional attitude of the center as one of "detachment." According to Dunleavy and Rhodes (1988: 112), "Britain is characterised by 'hands off' control systems which lay down general rules for

Table 7.5

Proportion of Taxes Collected at the National and Local Levels, 1986
(in percent)

	Japan	Britain
National	66	89
Local	34	11

Source: Calculated from OECD *National Accounts, 1974–1986*, vol. 2. Paris: OECD, 1988: pp. 67, 68, 504, 505.

Table 7.6

Sources of Local Revenue, 1986 (in percent)

	Japan	Britain
Direct taxes	25	—
Indirect taxes	33	35
Transfers	40	54

Source: Calculated from OECD *National Accounts, 1974–1986*, vol. 2. Paris: OECD, 1988: pp. 68, 505.

dealing with whole classes of sub-central agencies in the same way. . . . This system means that the gulf between central ministries and municipal government in terms of lack of personal contacts or administrative involvements is far wider in Britain than in countries which have supposedly been more centralist, such as France. Whitehall's relations with local councils have consistently been characterised by a concern to stay out of those aspects of policy questions which are not salient for national political elites." The Thatcher government demonstrated the scope of central control, and a disregard for the traditional local-central relationship, in cutting grants, abolishing the Labour-controlled Greater London Council and seeking to discipline other councils that were seen to be uncooperative, and implementing educational reforms that include a national curriculum and the ability of local comprehensive schools to "opt out" and become self-supporting, and in implementing reform of the local tax rate system. The Rates Act of 1984 was perceived as undermining local tax authority, and interfering with the elective principle by requiring councils to consult with business before fixing rates. Some have even seen the Conservatives' policies on local government as seriously undermining the Constitution (Bogdanor 1989: 137–38).

As has been the case with other aspects of central control over policy making, it would appear that in Japan the occupation reforms decreased the strength of the center and vastly increased the strength of local institutions (prefectural, county, and municipal). The American occupiers came from a culture steeped in local autonomy and they were inclined to pass that tradition on to the Japanese. Decentralization of the police and the education system were important elements of the democratization program, but both were soon recentralized after Japan regained sovereignty. Chapter VIII of the constitution deals specifically with local self-government. It forbids the Diet from passing special laws pertaining to one public entity without the consent of that entity, guarantees elections for all local executive and legislative offices, and lends general support to the principle of local autonomy.

For the most part, however, local autonomy and local input in the national policy-making process have been lacking. Japan has a unitary administrative system in which power is concentrated in the organs of the central government. Local governments cannot pass ordinances that contravene national laws. By tradition, central organs forward "recommendations" for action to the local level, and in some cases local officials become agents for the national government. There is little precedent for decentralized power in modern Japanese history, and the fact that 70 percent of local government financing comes from Tokyo does little to encourage local autonomy (Richardson and Flanagan 1984: 56–57).

Richard Samuels identifies two aspects of centralization, first, a "lack of autonomy, inability of localities to pursue independent policy initiatives," and second, the "idea of vertical administration" (Samuels 1983: 245). As an example, he cites the Japanese policy of regionalism. While a form of regional organization would seem designed to give greater power to subnational governments, regionalism has actually increased the power of the center. It has done so by concentrating on bringing various communities together for the joint implementation of policies directed by the national bureaucracy—always a high priority for Japan. Thus regional administration is a means of control, not a means of decentralization. The horizontal interdependence among communities is a result of vertical tutelage from the center (Samuels 1983: 243–44). Centralization and local autonomy may not be mutually exclusive in the case of Japan, however. The above translocal contacts, although sponsored by the national bureaucracy, also bring about a sharing of policy-relevant information, which is important both for the carrying out of administration, and for the formulation of some policies at the regional level (Samuels 1983: 244). In addition, "bureaucratic politics at the center and horizontal interdependence at the periphery may vitiate the most onerous of the direct controls of the central state" (Samuels 1983: 246). Conflict over local policy at the center can produce different plans, each supported by its sponsoring ministry, which then gives the local administration the opportunity either to choose between them, or to play them off against each other. The ministries are susceptible to this because local allegiance to their scheme gives it weight in its contest with other ministries' schemes (Samuels 1983: 247).

As "creatures of the state and under the influence of extralocal interests" localities act like interest groups in a corporate context, but "in sponsoring elections and pursuing interests at the national level with shifting pragmatic alliances" they appear to be interest groups in a pluralist context (Samuels 1983: 242). As we have seen in other contexts, there is a tendency to move away from the almost absolute control of the earlier postoccupation Japanese politics to a situation in which local governments have found a stronger voice in articulating their needs and demands to the central authorities.

A case involving a host community for American military installations provides a good example of center-periphery relations. The city of Atsugi is home to one of the largest U.S. naval air bases in Japan. Night air traffic and night touch-and-go (take-off and landing) training exercises were creating a number of problems for residents who live near the base. After years of petitioning the national government to get the Americans to change their training schedule or move it elsewhere, including a civil suit to ban night flights by Japanese and American military aircraft over Atsugi, the government responded. It has attempted to maintain the policy, but moved the exercises to the more remote islands of Miyake and Iwojima. Although a district court has upheld the Atsugi plaintiff's suit against the government, the Tokyo High Court rejected it saying that administrative policy cannot be changed through a civil suit (*The Japan Times* April 4, 1989).

The above case demonstrates that when the central government is in conflict with local governments, it is willing to compromise but not capitulate, bend but not break. From the local perspective, it is obvious that citizens were not hesitant to let their local governments know of their opposition to the actions of those governments.

The Mechanisms of Group Participation, Consultation, and Mobilization

In virtually all modern polities, the role of nongovernmental organizations that articulate and aggregate interests is a significant component of the policy process. This role has been magnified in the industrial states, where the increased intervention of government has been accompanied by a correspondingly greater dependency upon groups for information, for implementation, and for consent. Which groups have influence, and how is it exercised? We shall find that the British and Japanese approaches to interest group roles have significant points in common with most other industrial democracies. Both accord a significant role to interests in the formulation of policy, yet both restrict access to the "inner circle" to what amounts to "approved" groups. Both have witnessed the evolution (if not the entrenchment) of forms of corporate representation, in which organizations representing major functional interests engage in bargaining with the state. Representative of a very different trend, both have witnessed a proliferation of "cause" groups, a fragmentation of group interests that suggest a more open and pluralistic approach to government than has traditionally been the case. In both Britain and Japan, the collective expression of demands is more firmly established than in the United States. And it is considered normal for organized interests to have an institutionalized relationship with government. Numerous advisory councils regularly put interest representatives in touch with government officials. In both, the limited roles of the legislature in the policy-making process tend to focus group pressure on other institutions such as the bureaucracy and (in the case of Japan) the party.

There are important differences between the two countries as well. Because of the greater prominence of the party organization in Japanese policy making, both interest group–party links, and group ties to the legislature are generally more important in Japan than Britain. In Japan, interest group membership in the Japanese inner circle is more likely to vary with political necessities than is the case in Britain. The greater importance of personalism in political relationships, and the relatively lax campaign regulations, combine to give Japanese groups a potentially larger arsenal of persuasions upon which to rely. The flow of cash and gratuities from groups to politicians have played a significantly greater role in Japan than in Britain. On the other hand, the obligation of government to respond to legitimate group pressures is much stronger in Britain than Japan. Group/bureaucratic agreement is on occasion a sufficient condition for policy to be approved in Britain.

Hogwood (1987: 57) says it is "virtually part" of the British constitution "that groups affected by government proposals should be asked for their opinion on them and that the government should consider altering proposals in the light of representations made by the groups." Even if not everyone agrees that consultation has constitutional status, it is certainly true that the norm of consultation has a pervasive influence on British government. And while formal institutions of cabinet and departments are major and, on occasion, decisive role players, it is more commonly specialized policy communities or "subgovernments" of government and group actors that, according to Ripley and Franklin, "effectively make most of the routine decisions in a given substantive area of policy" (cited in Jordan and Richardson 1987: 92). These policy communities are composed of civil servants, ministers, local authorities, and representatives of approved interest groups (Hogwood 1987: 18).

What Groups?

Although a number of distinctions can be made among types of groups, the difference between sectional and promotional groups is particularly salient in the case of Britain. Sectional groups represent an identifiable economic or professional interest, or function, such as trade unions, business and financial institutions, physicians, barristers and solicitors. Promotional groups advocate particular causes and are open to anyone in agreement with their orientation.

Examples of the latter would be the Royal Society for the Prevention of Cruelty to Animals (RSPCA), the Campaign for Nuclear Disarmament (CND), and various environmental groups such as Greenpeace. There are thousands of both types of groups in Britain today. Needless to say, the two types of groups may overlap. Many sectional groups promote specific causes. The tendency until quite recently, in class-based English politics, was for the most important sectional interests to be aggregated through political parties and large "peak" organizations such as the Trades Union Congress (TUC) and the Confederation of British Industries (CBI). The TUC (founded in 1868) represents over 100 affiliated unions and 95 percent of all trade unionists (Norton 1984: 154). The former retains close organizational links with the Labour Party, while the CBI has never developed such close links with the Conservatives. Although these organizations suggest the potential for a high degree of integration, they are really quite ineffective as coordinating and directing bodies. Many large British companies, what Grant and Nath (1984: 61) call "capitalist aggressive" firms, deal directly with government, rather than through the CBI.

As we saw in Chapter 5, there has been both a proliferation of organized interest groups, and an increased concern by citizens for protecting their own individual interests, not necessarily as part of a collective. Public corporations, though reduced in number, exert their influence, as do the "quangos" or "fringe organizations"—bodies that are not "line" organizations headed by elected officials, but which are public-financed (Rose 1989: 329). They may have responsibility for delivering a government service, such as the BBC, the Manpower Commission, or the Commission for Racial Equality, or they may be merely advisory, like the Scottish Food Hygiene Council. The government itself has created many "countervailing pressure organizations," such as the Health Education Council, and Action on Smoking and Health that have become part of the group politics scene (Hogwood 1987: 63).

Consultation in Britain is pervasive but far from universal. There are both "insider" groups to whom government regularly turns for consultation, and "outsider" groups, to whom it does not (Grant 1984: 132–34). In the matter of determining which groups are "insiders," observes Hogwood (1987: 57), "Government, however, is not just another actor but can in part write the rules of the game, determine who can play, and even (in the case of both local authorities and 'campaign' groups or research bodies) create or abolish the people with whom it is 'playing.' " By limiting which groups are admitted into policy making, government has yet another means to reduce the visibility, and hence the potential contentiousness, of policy making. As Vogel (1986: 25) notes of industrial regulation, "by controlling nonindustrial access to the regulatory process and insulating many of its regulatory bodies from public scrutiny, Britain has attempted—with a fair degree of success—to defuse much of the political conflict associated with government regulation in the United States. Only the "inside" or "legitimate" groups are allowed to become official players, to get on the departmental "lists" referred to above. The power of government to determine who is consulted and who is not suggests that consultation is a privilege, rather than a right, and that the older deferential and paternalistic norms of British culture are still quite influential at the elite level.

A number of considerations determine whether a group will be recognized as legitimate, and thus consulted. Government is more likely to confer with sectional, rather than promotional, interests (especially those campaigning for change rather than the status quo). Lacking the assets of "monopoly of information and expertise," promotional groups "are without the attributes enjoyed by the sectional interest groups in achieving leverage in their relationship with government" (Norton 1984: 161). Groups should also be seen to be representative of their constituency. Discretion and "responsible behavior," as in all British politics, is a requirement of insider status—a fact that greatly complicates the acquisition of information about group politics (Kavanagh 1985a: 155). Groups who do not adhere to the "unwritten code of conduct," who leak confidential information, or are too strident may be punished by expulsion from the inner circle (Grant 1984: 129). In some cases, even groups with a prior reputation for stridency and confrontation have been given consultative status, though this may be accomplished more at the periphery rather than at the center of government (Lowe and Goyder 1983: 177, 180). But gaining admission to the club is likely to take time, and meanwhile, groups will be more likely to resort to "outsider" strategies such as publicity and protest. In some instances, as when the RSPCA refused in 1979 to participate in the new Farm Animal Welfare Council (FAWC), groups may actually elect not to be insiders.

The size of the policy community consulted may vary greatly, although "there seems to be a low threshold of accessibility" (Jordan and Richardson 1987: 131). In cases of "open" consultation, government may consult a wide spectrum of groups and even invite public comment, as it did in 1985, with respect to its social security proposals (Hogwood 1987: 55). Some consultations will involve many hundreds of organizations, as in the case of VAT legislation, but others will be more intimate, involving only a small number of specialized interests (Hogwood 1987: 59).

Not only are some groups consulted and some not, but group influence may vary from issue to issue, and on any given issue, groups will not all be accorded equal influence. As Jordan and Richardson (1987: 131) point out, *"access is different from influence"* (their italics). In some cases, groups enjoy a virtual veto. For example, CBI members on the Health and Safety Commission "were given a veto over new regulations" (Jordan and Richardson 1987: 189). While some groups are regularly invited to submit their views, others "are at best tolerated to the extent that they are allowed to send occasional deputations to the relevant department" (Grant 1984: 133). Yet even among the more influential sectional interests, governmental discretion as well as the differing levels of resources controlled by groups will lead to variable influence. Groups that have a monopoly of information, and groups, like the British Medical Association, that have a high density membership (comprising a high percentage of individuals from the potential group), will tend to have easier access and greater influence (Kavanagh 1985a: 155). Influence will also depend on the issue concerned. On questions of partisan importance, consultation may take place, but be "cynical and merely cosmetic" in nature (Jordan and Richardson 1987: 141). However, other issues may allow significant group input. This is most likely where the government has no strong views of its own and is inclined to act as "referee" among interested parties (Hogwood 1987: 50–51). On issues like foreign affairs and defense, outside groups may have little influence. In the end, government discretion is decisive. After decades of close tripartite consultations among labor, business, and government, the Thatcher government's policy was to deal at arms length with both labor and business.

The distinction between sectional and promotional groups made in the British case also applies to Japan. Unlike Britain, Japanese labor and industry have not been represented by single peak organizations like the CBI or the TUC. Industry is represented to some extent by traditional umbrella organizations such as the Federation of Economic Organizations (Keidanren), the Federation of Employers' Organizations (Nikkeiren), the Japan Chamber of Commerce and Industry, and the Keizai Doyukai. Industrial labor has traditionally been represented by the General Council of Trade Unions (Sohyo) and the Japanese Federation of Trade Unions (Domei), however, a new peak organization, Shin Rengo (the Japanese Trade Union Federation), has recently been formed. Shin Rengo incorporates both the old Domei and Sohyo and includes 8 million of the 12 million union workers in Japan. It also promises to move labor a little to the right, increasing labor's power in both the government and opposition camps as it does so. However, labor in Japan is still far from unified as the left wing of Sohyo has refused to join Shin Rengo and Communist Party affiliated unions have created their own new Federation of National Labor Unions (Zenroren) to stand as an alternative.

Agricultural interests are represented in the Central Association of the Federation of Agricultural Cooperatives and the National Land Improvement Association. As in Britain, physicians and other professionals have their organizations, too.[5] Although it is difficult to estimate their membership, many grass-roots, anomic, nonassociational interest groups representing consumers, minority groups, peace activists, environmental concerns, women, and others outside the traditional elite exist in Japan. "There are hundreds if not thousands of important organized interest groups which regularly petition national government for consideration of their needs" (Richardson and Flanagan 1984: 293). National organizations, such as women's groups, have been active and successful. However, those promotional groups which tend to be organized horizontally—such as consumer groups—have been at a relative disadvantage to those in Britain because of the greater prevalence of vertically organized groups—businesses, communities, etc.—that has tended to inhibit growth of nationwide consumer organizations. Often, then, it is local organizations that will fight pollution or unpopular land use. Such was the case in protests against routing of the *shinkansen* and the appropriation of land for Narita International Airport. Generally, the influence of these promotional groups on the political system and the number of members, while difficult to estimate, seems to be minimal. That will remain the case until they can demonstrate their impact on the political system in such a way as to make the LDP realize the necessity of incorporating them into, in Calder's words, their circle of compensation. An example of this process is provided by the impact of women on the July 1989 House of Councillor's election. Prior to that election, the LDP demonstrated little interest in women's issues and took relatively little action in mediating women's interests with the bureaucracy or representing their interests through legislation. Their one major piece of legislation, the equal opportunity law, finally passed in a very watered-down version and did little to affect the role of Japanese women in the workplace. However, the role of women's groups in making the relationship between then Prime Minister Uno and his mistress into a national scandal and a women's rights issue in the 1989 upper-house and 1990 lower-house campaigns, in addition to the drastically increased number of women who ran successfully in that election on those issues, seems to have made the LDP realize that it now must be more responsive to women's groups, their constituents, and the issues they represent, if they want to survive as the ruling party. The first Kaifu government to be formed following the 1989 election loss included two female cabinet ministers.

As in Britain, the government has a great deal of influence over which groups are admitted into the inner circle of policy making and what influence they have. In the view of the Japanese government that stresses a corporate structure, government is believed to have established a mutual dependency with the major business and agricultural interests, while others, especially labor, are excluded. In Pempel's view of the "conservative coalition," consensus in Japanese politics is to be found in the close relationship between the LDP, the peak organizations of big business, and organized agriculture. "This consensus is, of course, a limited one. The cohesiveness between the conservative coalition and the strong state makes for ease of adjustment particularly because the major challengers of that cohesiveness [e.g., labor] can be systematically excluded from policy making roles" (Pempel 1982: 41).

In the "circles of compensation" view of Calder, the LDP retains control over admission to insider status, but who is in and who is out depends on the current circumstances, especially the perceived electoral needs of the LDP. In this view, the circles of compensation contract and expand according to political need, and the changing ability of groups to benefit the party. In Britain, the inner circle may expand to accept new members as new groups prove their "reliability," but its composition does not fluctuate. In Japan, membership in the inner circle does fluctuate much more widely in an effort to shore up the LDP's electoral fortunes.

Only interests that can get the attention and backing of the bureaucracy and ruling party are likely to be compensated (Calder 1988: 25). Though political considerations no doubt affect the recruitment of new "insider" groups in Britain, there is no analogous "circles of compensation" theory to suggest that the granting of insider status is as overtly partisan as in Japan, or as closely tuned to the electoral cycle.

Motives for Consultation

There are a number of explanations for the pervasive consultative behavior in British policy making—including constitutional norms, statutory requirements, legal decisions, pragmatic considerations, and consensual aspects of the political culture. As noted above, some observers assign consultation the status of constitutional convention, and in a relatively small number of cases, consultation is mandated by law (Jordan and Richardson 1987: 94, 134). In order to comply with such legal requirements, departments keep lists of approved organizations. The courts, while not playing a very aggressive role in shaping interest group–government relations, have defended consultation on occasion, even establishing "the obligation to consult" (Hogwood 1987: 57). In the case of the government's ban on unionization of workers at the Cheltenham communications headquarters, the court found in 1984 that only grounds of national security excused the government from its obligation to consult beforehand with the unions, and again in 1985, the court criticized the Department of Health and Social Services for inadquate consultation (Jordan and Richardson 1987: 137).

The impulse to consult is also a result of the perceived benefits of group consent. Prior consultation and consent certainly facilitate compliance, and groups are often key agents of implementation whose cooperation is essential. In the 1930s, E. P. Herring observed that "The greater the degree of detailed and technical control the government seeks to exert over industrial and commercial interest, the greater must be their degree of consent and active participation in the very process of regulation, if regulation is to be effective or successful" (Beer 1974: 181). The aggregative capacity of groups allows government to use them "to communicate government policy . . . and secure their adherence" (Grant 1984: 126). In Britain, a great deal of implementation is left to interest groups rather than government. For example, detailed implementation of health and safety policy is controlled by a commission dominated by the Confederation of British Industry, and the Trades Union Congress (Budge and McKay 1988: 36). There may even be cases where "subcontracting" tasks to pressure groups may be most cost-effective (Grant 1984: 126). Furthermore, given the on-going character of consultation, both government and interest groups recognize that "disputes could jeopardize their relationship as well as pass the problem on for others to resolve" (Norton 1984: 160). Groups often provide the expertise that is, in the tradition of the British generalist, inconspicuous at the top of the civil service, and are often a source of information that is necessary to allow the government to determine its own agenda. The lack of technical training and expertise within the civil service tends to increase administrative reliance on groups (Ashford 1980: 58). Consultation may also be facilitated by the fact that, increasingly, former top civil servants enter second careers in industrial management or as directors of pressure groups (Grant 1984: 126), though this appears to be a considerably more pervasive factor in Japanese consultations. In short, the government-group relationship is one of mutual dependency, as well as habit.

But neither statutes, nor court enforcement, nor pragmatism account for the pervasiveness of consultation. Also important are the influences of the political culture. Aspects of British political culture, as we have seen, emphasize political resolution of disputes, and encourage consultation and consensus. Goodin writes that "consultation and cooperation are decisively preferred over compulsion; advice and accommodation are decisively preferred over adversarial relations" (cited in Jordan and Richardson 1987: 287). Though such a view has to be qualified by the example of British industrial relations and the "impulse to defy" (Dore 1985: 204), characterizations of the British preference for accommodation strongly resemble similar characterizations of the Japanese. Even if we conclude, as we must, that consensual and consultative norms are even stronger in Japan than in Britain, both display the consensual norms we identified in Chapter 1.

It is important to understand, then, that group consultation is widely perceived as an obligation. Even beyond the sense of moral or legal obligation, however, policy makers perceive very pragmatic motives to pay attention to organized interests. Some groups have proven their capacity to "veto" government decisions more effectively than the parliamentary opposition, as did the unions in their campaign of noncompliance with the Industrial Relations Act under the Heath government (Rose 1979: 91). Even if they cannot directly "veto" government action, they have "a potential for noise and nuisance" (Jordan and Richardson 1987: 93), and if the government can secure the agreement of the relevant interest groups, it significantly reduces the chances of a damaging dispute over its policy (Budge and McKay 1988: 36).

A major difference between British and Japanese motives for consultation is the absence in Japan of legal obligations to consult affected interests. On the other hand, as in Britain, consultation reflects pragmatic considerations, especially the mutual dependence of interests and government. Of major importance is the impetus for cooperation created by the modern interventionist state. Specifically, the pursuit of state-led development stimulates government-interest collaboration. And while groups seek benefits for their members from government, "permanently organized interest groups provide many cues to government officials and play a large role in the interest articulation stream. Politicians normally pay special attention to these groups and cultivate their representatives in their efforts to gather information about their own political environments" (Richardson and Flanagan 1984: 294). Japanese interest groups are also brought into the policy-making process by the bureaucracy itself in order to gain help in policy implementations, as a means of providing information and advice, and to provide, at a minimal level, the appearance of consensus (George 1988: 122–23).

A further similarity, reflecting the importance of consensual norms in both Britain and Japan, is that consultation in Japan is seen as a means of reinforcing social consensus and harmony. However, in Japan, the appearance of consultation may have relatively greater importance than in Britain. As in the case of LDP/opposition "consultation," consultation with interests reflects the fact that it is important to be seen as having listened to different views, even if the policy outcome does not reflect group inputs.

Personal ties also play a major role in reinforcing group/government interaction. Business may exert influence because of the values, personal ties, and even overlapping personnel that it frequently shares with the LDP. The practice of *amakudari* (retiring from the bureaucracy to take up lucrative positions in private enterprise) and other forms of personnel sharing tend to reinforce group/bureaucracy contacts. It is not surprising that group and interest representatives frequently share a common conservative ideological orientation. They are simultaneously bound to the LDP through the same ties, with the addition of financial and organizational support for the LDP qua political party. "The most senior *amakudari* positions—for example, the postretirement landing spots of MITI's vice ministers—are bases from which to coordinate the strategic sectors. At this point, the Western distinction between public and private loses its meaning. . . . At the level of the supreme leadership of the business community, the primary concern is that the relationship between government be managed effectively for the good of all. *Amakudari* is significant here only in that it contributes to a common orientation—as does education at Todai, golf club memberships, and the common experience of the war and its aftermath" (Johnson 1986: 71). *Amakudari* also helps to form an interpersonal network between the LDP and the bureaucracy. As noted earlier, ex-bureaucrats have always played an important role in the LDP, they comprise a significant percentage of the total LDP Diet membership, and are brought into the cabinet earlier in their careers than members without experience in the bureaucracy (Curtis 1988: 93).

When and How Do Groups Interact with Government?

Interaction between British civil servants and representatives of major interest groups may be almost daily, long term, and continuous (Hogwood 1987: 60). Consultation is likely throughout the policy process, from initiation to promulgation (Jordan and Richardson 1987: 127). In some cases, government may solicit group opinion early in the policy process, as a "trial balloon," even before drafting has begun. In others, government may seek group views in order to find out, absent an established position of its own, what policy it should pursue. Government may have a position, and meet with groups in order to "sell" its policies or to negotiate an acceptable joint position. Finally, consultation may take place after policy is decided, whether or not there was prior discussion. If there was, this follow-up consultation may concern the implementation of the policy. If there was no prior consultation, it may represent a government effort to explain and gain legitimacy for a decision taken on its own.

Consultation takes place most often between groups and ministries, but groups may use Parliament, the parties, or the public as channels of communication. A 1980 report listed over 1500 advisory bodies and sixty-seven "tribunal systems" in Britain, many of which "allow and encourage group participation" (Jordan and Richardson 1987: 182). The number of these bodies increased dramatically in the 1960s and 1970s, and even after the Thatcher government set out to abolish many of them, the numbers remain substantial and include such high-profile entities as the National Economic Development Council and Royal Commission (Jordan and Richardson 1987: 187–88). Despite the myriad of formal consultation mechanisms, most consultation is informal, and undertaken on an ad hoc basis. The existence of the consultative committees noted above "should be regarded as complementary to more informal consultation" (Hogwood 1987: 59). Indeed, the British prefer informal to formal, mandatory consultation. Government-group contact, observes Norton (1984: 161), "is less systematic, less professional, and less obvious than in the United States. It takes place on a smaller scale, and the use of professional lobbyists is virtually unknown."

Most policy in Britain, as we noted above, is made at departmental and subdepartmental level, and most group negotiations take place at the ministry level or in the consultative committees created by the ministries. Where consensus is not reached at the lower levels, group influence will still make itself felt indirectly at the level of debate on Cabinet committees, with groups finding a voice through "their" ministry. As Budge and McKay (1988: 27) put it, "Many of the major departments have links with approved interest groups, and the clashes between departments in Cabinet committees constitute one of the most important ways in which outside demands are voiced and combined into an overall policy. Government action usually follows group consent." "The right time for a government to act on a particular problem or issue is often when the appropriate advisory committee has come to a collective agreement that there is a problem to be solved, and to a broad consensus on what should be done" (Jordan and Richardson 1987: 185).

How government sees its role in consultation varies greatly. Government may treat consultation as a cosmetic means of compliance with statutory requirements for consultation (Hogwood 1987: 53), and both government and interest may treat a particular consultation in a ritualistic fashion (Grant 1984: 139). Government may act as referee, where it has no clear goal or stake (as when auto registration dates were changed). It may act as negotiator (but greater than an equal partner) when it has a view of what it wants, "but is prepared to bargain about the policy to secure the agreement of groups or at least to minimize their opposition" (Hogwood 1987: 52). Where consultation grants interests real power, they do not just "air their views, they then go away, and the government makes up its mind. Rather, it would be better in some cases to regard the process as one of negotiating or bargaining in which compromise is sought on both sides" (Hogwood 1987: 61). Finally, government may act as partner in corporatist arrangements, of which we shall say more below, in which groups and government jointly and co-equally make policy, and in which the consulted groups are then entrusted with a major role in policy implementation.

Whether bilaterally or through consultative committees, groups exert pressure more generally through the ministries rather than through Parliament or the party organizations. The relationship between parties and interest groups in Britain presents a mixed picture. The relatively strong party system in Britain, and the resulting curtailment of the legislative influence of MPs serves to devalue group contacts with Parliament. However, as Jordan and Richardson (1987: 238) point out, "Particular groups do use parties as a means of access and as a means of getting issues on to the political agenda. And in one particular case—the trade unions—party links may be said to be of central importance." But aside from the Labour–TUC relationship, enshrined in the party conference and electoral college, groups exert little influence on election manifestos themselves (Kavanagh 1985a: 153), though they may attempt to do so. However, electoral volatility (which seemed more characteristic of the 1970s) has increased the risk factors of groups becoming too closely associated with one party (Jordan and Richardson 1987: 236). In addition, Moran suggests that another reason for the decline of parties vis-à-vis groups is that "Rich and sophisticated groups are perfectly capable ... of organising representation independently of parties ... with the result that groups now seriously rival parties in the system of representation" (cited in Jordan and Richardson 1987: 238).

While the legislature is far less likely a target of interests than in Japan or the United States, occasionally groups will include parliamentary lobbying in their strategy. The Police Federation's campaign for extension of the widow's pension is a case in point (Brown and Steel 1979: 218–21). Some writers even suggest increased interest group attention to Parliament in the recent past (Grant 1984: 140). However, the relatively strict party discipline in Parliament limits the possibilities for groups to affect individual MPs' votes. Unlike the United States or Japan, groups lack the leverage on individual MPs provided by campaign donations, which are channeled to parties rather than to candidates (Norton 1984: 163). It remains true that the Labour and Conservative parties remain largely dependent upon unions and corporations, respectively, for much of their funding, though the impact of this relationship on policy remains problematical (Jordan and Richardson 1987: 243). However, asserts Rose (1989: 227), "[M]oney does not buy favors from public officials or parties." Though MPs do receive considerable outside income from consultancies, the opportunities for reciprocal favors that are so integral to Japanese politics are far less frequent. And while circulation of elites appears to be less than in other countries, MPs do have to keep an eye on prospects for employment after they leave Parliament (Punnett 1988: 171).

As we have seen, all kinds of groups are likely to rely on public strategies to a greater or lesser extent. Groups may hope to shape public opinion on an issue, and through it Parliament or even the government. More likely, they will attempt to use the media to influence specialized publics (Grant 1984: 141). However, because of the great importance of working within the system in Britain, such public strategies are usually not the preferred method, and are most likely to complement, rather than replace, more traditional forms of consultation, as in the case of radio and television interests campaigns for commercial broadcasting (Punnett 1988: 160,163). Mobilization of public opinion, coupled with inside group pressure, was essential in the effort to abolish the death penalty. Groups do attempt to get the public on their side, but the effect of public opinion is so nebulous that often the best result groups can hope for is to create a favorable public climate of opinion which can then be used as leverage with politicians. Public demonstrations on the part of specific groups have on occasion been cited as actually costing a group support in government (Grant 1984: 134).

Group consultation in Japan takes place with a wider spectrum of governmental actors than in Britain. This is so because of the relatively greater policy role of the governing party, and because of the continued inclusion of the Diet in the scope of interest group pressures. "Mass groups have approached the political parties in the Diet, whose rank-and-file members then became carriers of interest demands to the parties' decision-making bodies; in addition, such groups have approached party or bureaucratic elites directly to request resolution of their problems. Meanwhile, business groups have regularly submitted lists of policy recommendations to party and government organs, while corporation presidents have mentioned their needs to governmental colleagues in informal 'discussion group' meetings in Tokyo's prestigious hotels and restaurants. Other interest group representatives have presented claims directly in Diet committees or in government advisory councils" (Richardson and Flanagan 1984: 321). According to data on Diet membership for 1980–1983 reported by Aurelia George, "there were 144 politicians in the lower house ... who either held or were holding official leadership positions in interest groups. In the upper house there were 102 interest group officials . . ." (1988: 108). The *zoku* also act as effective contact points for interest groups desirous of influencing the legislative process.

As in Britain, many groups and companies are represented on advisory councils (*shingikai*). Japan had 162 such councils in the early 1980s. Within the ministries, the *shingikai* play an important role in the policy-making process as a channel for public opinion and as a means of creating consensus. They also provide an insight into how pluralist elements can be incorporated into what is still essentially an elitist policy-making process. Every ministry has a standing deliberation council, in addition to many temporary advisory councils called to discuss policy on relevant topics and then disbanded when recommendations are made. The total number of *shingikai* at any given point in time is well over one hundred. The membership in *shingikai* is distributed among many different groups, depending upon the policy discussed, but generally includes members of the business community, academics, government officials, and specialists in the area under discussion. Interest groups and public interests are well represented, but there are questions as to what effect participation on these advisory commissions has on the policy-making process. Although *shingikai* do seem to have an important input into that process, many people argue that they are often controlled by their members who represent business and government interests, while others argue that they are just a *tatemae* institution used to present a picture of public opinion gathering and consensus formation to the general public while business as usual continues within the ministries (Johnson 1986: 48).

In Japan as well, what groups communicate in private is more important than what they communicate in public. Despite the predominance of private consultations, however, groups in Japan frequently make use of public channels. In fact, group demonstrations are considerably more important in Japan than in Britain, where we saw that in general public expression of demands varied more or less inversely with private access. In Japan this is not the case, as "public demonstrations appear to be as much a legitimate mode of interest articulation in Japan as they are a last resort of frustrated radical groups and movements on the left or right" (Richardson and Flanagan 1984: 320). As we saw in Chapter 5, protest demonstrations in Japan have become ritualized to a large extent. In addition to rallies, "Most large interest groups express their demands in statements in the media, in annual policy papers and resolutions, and in organizational publications, in addition to submitting vollies of petitions to government officials and parliamentarians" (Richardson and Flanagan 1984: 319–20).

A greater variety of Japanese groups have successfully used the electoral process as a means of acquiring influence than is the case in Britain, even allowing for the fact that the Labour Party was founded as a working-class party and is still sponsored by working-class unions. The direct representation of interests by forming specific, issue-oriented political parties takes place primarily in the context of elections for the House of Councillors. Only parties, not individual candidates, can run in national constituency elections for the House of Councillors. It has been accepted as normal procedure that obscure and narrow parties such as the "Green and Life Network" (Midori to Inochi no Network), the "Tax Affairs Party" (Zeikinto), and the "People Who Don't Need Nuclear Power Party" (Genpatsu Iranai Hitobito) will be formed in every run-up to upper-house elections. Some of the parties, for example, the Zeikinto (four members in the upper house) and Rengo (12 members in the upper house), can build a constituency that keeps them in power from election to election. Although Diet membership gives groups a direct legislative role, the minuscule size of the parties almost guarantees an insignificant (if any) role in policy making. Exceptions to this rule would occur if the group is large enough, and carries enough political weight, to make its entrée into the policy-making process meaningful. Large groups, such as Rengo, often succeed in electing their own officials to the Diet, and there is a real fear in the socialist camp that the increasing strength of Rengo will be yet another significant drain on the JSP's support.

Interest group money is far more important to government-group relations than it is in Britain. This is especially true in the case of the LDP. In 1984 72.4 percent of its revenues came from corporate contributions with more than thirty-five of the largest corporations in Japan contributing well over ¥2 billion (Hrebenar 1986: 58, 61). The LDP claims that only about 20 percent of their campaign contributions come from big business. However, the LDP and the Keidanren jointly own a subsidiary organization, the National Political Association, which raises about U.S. $100 million per year for the LDP. As Masaya Miyoshi, director general of Keidanren, was quoted in *The New York Times*, "When the Liberal Democratic Party needs money, we are ready to listen" (January 29, 1990).

The flow of funds is not simply part of electoral politics. Money and favors remain fundamental to the group-politician relationship after elections are over. One of the remarkable things about the Recruit Company scandal in the late 1980s is that it reflected politics as usual. Industry associations or individual corporations, rather than the peak business organizations themselves, fund the Liberal Democratic Party and, occasionally, other parties. Some research has suggested a declining role for personalism, and a more complex relationship in government-business relations. What remains without doubt is that business, as in Britain, is the principal financial backer of the conservative party, while other interests are political contributors to the opposition. Sohyo is the main contributor to the JSP, Domei is the main contributor to the DSP, and the JCP relies on the sales of its newspaper, *Akahata*.

While in Japan, as in Britain, groups are considered a more important articulator of interests than the public at large, there are many organizations within the Japanese bureaucracy, such as the Public Opinion Research Bureau of the Prime Minister's Office, whose job it is to keep up with public opinion, and there is a great concern within the government in general about opinion polls and public hearings, but that does not ensure that public opinion is translated directly into policy. Policy making still tends to be a "downward conversion" in that satisfying vested interests and increasing the regulatory powers of the bureaucracy itself seems to be more important than adjusting policy in accordance with public demands (Misawa 1973: 28). The LDP and the bureaucracy have long "heard" public opinion through polls, surveys, and contacts with the mass media, but those opinions that are not in agreement with the values of the LDP or the programs of the bureaucracy are likely to be ignored until they demonstrate the strength necessary to force the LDP to listen.

The Corporatist/Pluralist Debate

We have put forth a number of policy-making models for both Japan and Britain, but a final question remains: To what extent are Britain and Japan pluralist or corporatist? Both terms have been subjected to lengthy debate and diverse interpretation. In pluralist systems, atomistic groups outside government compete on an equal footing for influence on government policy. Legitimacy is achieved through the inclusiveness of the system. In corporatism, the principal sectional groups, labor and capital, are highly organized and integrated into the governmental structure, where decisions of high policy emerge as the product of bargaining. Since groups are assumed to speak for, and to be able to ensure the cooperation of, their membership, the system could be assumed simultaneously to achieve popular consent and cooperation in policy implementation. Depending on one's point of view, corporatist arrangements are a tool of government co-optation and control, or a source of group power over government. From the former perspective, "In exchange for monopoly the groups discipline and control members, enforce policy, and make a more manageable environment for the government" (Jordan and Richardson 1987: 96). Keehn argues, less optimistically, that "Corporate forces, which have accrued their own power capability, can render government by consent impotent by disagreement. The power of elites and collectivities is therefore determined by the extent to which they can modify the government's commitment, bridle its action, and alter its goals" (Keehn 1978: 541–42).

Speaking of Britain in the 1970s, Keehn (1978: 543) declared, "It is accepted that corporatist groups have a right to be consulted and to exercise veto power over decisions detrimental to their interests." Within this structure, the government is variously described as partner, broker, or in the more negative interpretations, either prisoner or "co-opter" of interests. In the 1960s and 1970s the British government often discussed economic policy with representatives of peak organizations (especially the unions). Wages and prices policies were negotiated, and new tripartite bodies were created. Particularly since 1979, it has become much more difficult to argue the case for corporatism, as quasi-corporatist arrangements like Labour's "social contract" unravelled, as government has eschewed comprehensive, high-level negotiations over macro-economic policy with both labor and business, and as the collective membership and power of unions appeared in decline. Unions haven't had the resources to take advantage of the consultative structures that do exist (Budge and McKay 1988: 38). While consultation may still take place, there was virtually no evidence of an institutionalized tripartism under the Thatcher government. "Insofar as it exists at all," concludes Grant (1984: 131), "corporatism in Britain seems to have been not so much an immutable feature of the operations of the state as a style of government, reflecting choices by politicians in power."

It may be said that even if corporatism as a system does not exist in Britain, some specific consultative values and relations embody an element of corporatism. Vogel (1986: 273) argues that British corporatisim involves "granting of semiofficial status to specific interest groups," but not the "centralized bargaining among interest groups" that is often associated with formal corporatist arrangements. It is a corporatist conception of society, rather than a formal, institutionalized corporatism that, if anything, is relevant to the British experience, for corporatism is "a conception of society as consisting primarily not of individuals, but of sub-societies, groups having traditions, occupational and other characteristics in common" (Eckstein cited in Vogel 1986: 273). Jordan and Richardson (1987: 189) argue that the potentially conflicting groups that make up policy communities may even develop their own sense of corporate identity. To illustrate the point, they cite the willingness of the TUC to grant employer representatives on the Health Services Commission a veto over safety regulations, despite the obvious importance of safety issues to the unions. This interpretation of "corporatist" is certainly consistent with the collectivist traditions of the British political culture that we have identified in earlier chapters.

Pluralists, like corporatists, accept that modern interventionist government makes close government-group cooperation essential. But, unlike corporatists, they "emphasize the extent and range of groups, their access to government, and the competition between them" (Norton 1984: 164). In this decentralized system of "balance among groups," government plays the role of arbiter of interests, with the result that public policy tends to change incrementally (Norton 1984: 164). This model contradicts not only the more traditional strong government model, but also corporatist and neocorporatist models, and radical models of class hegemony. But among pluralists, there is disagreement over whether the system of fragmented interests is a positive contributor to democratic policy making or whether it has contributed to a policy stalemate and obstruction of needed reforms.

The authors believe that the corporatist-pluralist debate in Britain matters less than the fact that groups retain considerable influence, bolstered by strong consultative norms. There seems little doubt that policy by consultation and consensus has often left government the follower, rather than the leader. All recent governments have occasionally abandoned or compromised policies rather than antagonize some interest. While pluralism has much to recommend it, Kavanagh (1985a: 320) is correct to conclude that the need to take the group and other actors into account "limits the Government's area of manoeuvre and produces what often appears to be an immobilism in policy." Despite evidence that government had become the hostage of interest groups, however, Britain's central government elites have considerable autonomy if they choose to exercise it, or as Norton argues, in British political culture "the orientation to cooperation" provides "a breathing space" for governments willing to search for solutions to Britain's economic woes (Norton 1984: 363). The Thatcher government more than many in recent times ignored or overrode strongly held group preferences, in no case more dramatically than in the 1984 miners' strike. But a "conviction" government also points up the costs of straying from the consultative norm. When things go badly, fewer people will be around to share responsibility, and resentment of what is perceived as policy by fiat may boil over, as it did in the antitax riots of 1990.

Corporatism has been one of many models applied to British policy making, but it has been a dominant model of Japanese policy making. A major trend in the study of Japanese policy making has been to isolate the influence of the interest groups representing big business. What some have labeled the "ruling triad" model presents a picture of Japanese policy making in which major corporate interest groups, such as the Keidanren and the Nikkeiren, also have a major impact on the formulation of policy. These organizations can use their influence over their member individuals and corporations to pressure both the bureaucracy and the LDP by withholding support for their policies. While there is no doubt that organizations like Keidanren wield power in the policy-making process, there is significant doubt as to the extent of that power, the level of consensus between the bureaucracy, the LDP, and the corporate interest groups, and the primacy of their influence in comparison with other interest groups representing labor, agricultural, consumer, and environmental interests.

Perhaps a more realistic approach to the role of interest groups in policy making can be found in Muramatsu and Krauss's "patterned pluralism," or Richardson and Flanagan's "structured corporatism." Both of these approaches reject the simple corporatist model of the ruling triad as described above, arguing instead that a variety of interest groups have gained power and influence in the Japanese policy-making process since the late 1960s. As Muramatsu and Krauss put it (1987: 537–38),

> Patterned pluralism is pluralistic in fundamental ways: influence is widely distributed, not concentrated; interest groups have many points of access to the policy-making process; and although interest groups are definitely tied to the government, there are elements of autonomy and conflict in the relationship. We are not dealing here with classic pluralism in which policy was merely the outcome of open-ended, competitive lobbying by pressure groups on a relatively weak government. . . . Rather we have in mind a new type of pluralism, as follows:
> 1. The government and its bureaucracy are strong, but the boundaries between state and society are blurred by the integration of social interest groups with the government and by the intermediation of political parties between social interest groups and the government. The government is not weak, but it is *penetrated* by interest groups and political parties.
> 2. One of the reasons for this integration between state and society is that one party is perpetually or nearly perpetually in power. This is a pragmatic, catchall party at least partially responsive to a wide variety of sometimes competing social interests.
> 3. There is an ideological cleavage in the system with the dominant party and its social allies in a more or less antagonistic relationship with the

opposition parties and their interest group allies over important value issues. Unlike the situation under classic pluralism, ideology plays a somewhat greater role, and, consequently, party-interest group alliances are more fixed. However, the opposition has some influence on policy, even if it is through indirect means.

Patterned pluralism in Japan manifests itself through the relationship between the LDP, the bureaucracy, older, more entrenched interest groups and new interest groups. Recently the LDP has become the mediator between the bureaucracy and interest groups that have either sprung up around new social, economic, and environmental issues, or have formerly been associated with the opposition parties. This, in combination with the recently increased power of the LDP in the policy-making process, means that a greater variety of interest groups are having a greater impact on that process (Muramatsu and Krauss 1987: 539–40). The pluralist model is supported by Calder's theory, noted above, of broadening circles of compensation, and by Richardson and Flanagan's model of "structured corporatism" (Richardson and Flanagan 1984: 327).

Most contemporary scholars would argue that while the influence of interest groups on the political system in the past has been essentially corporatist, pluralism in Japan seems to be on the increase. And yet, as all of the above authors point out, one should be very careful when applying the concept of pluralism to the Japanese policy-making process. Aurelia George's research "supports the pluralist contention that the Japanese political system is an open one," but her "analysis does not endorse the notion implicit in the pluralist thesis that because there are various institutional channels of access to policy makers which a range of interest groups utilise in observable ways, then all groups enjoy equal access" (1988: 132).

The increased pluralism in Japan stems from a number of factors. (1) The larger, traditional, umbrella-interest groups representing business, labor, and agricultural interests are being fragmented by more specific interest factions from within. (2) As LDP members become more technically proficient, better educated, and better administrators, they are also splitting the party into policy factions (*zoku*). (3) A number of new concerns—rural-urban, consumer, environmental—are not easily articulated through the old corporatist interest group-government relationship. However, it does not appear that the increase is as much a push from the bottom up for more representation in the policy-making process as it is a fragmentation of elite groups already plugged into the system. The debate over the merit of interest group politics, while present in Japan, is more a feature of British politics, where the poor economic performance has encouraged a search for villains, including groups.

Summary and Conclusions

A major factor in any comparisons of decision-making machinery is the contrasting historical origins of the two political systems. Japan's political institutions were radically altered after the war by the American occupation and the MacArthur constitution. Given the nonorganic nature of the constitution, its powers were less important in many instances than traditional practices and, as the need for economic development began to drive policy, than practical result. British institutions of government and the conventions by which they exert their power are more closely entwined in the cultural heritage and traditions of the nation and are, therefore, less likely to be in conflict with them than in Japan. This is not to say that changing culture and constitutional practice do not conflict or grow out of balance. The contemporary importance of issues of nationalism, race, and a bill of rights testify to that. But in Britain, resistant as the elite culture and the governmental institutions may be to the pressures of cultural and social change, the "unwritten" character of the constitution has in the past permitted significant constitutional change. In Japan, contradictions between the formal constitution and the policy-making reality cannot so readily be translated into constitutional change. They are often accommodated instead through the recognition of *tatemae* and *honne*. While there is a great deal of informality in the policy-making processes of both countries, in Britain it is manifested through the flexibility of the constitution and its conventions to allow interinstitutional relationships to change without the necessity of formal amendment of procedures. In Japan, however, the informality is manifested in the primacy of human relationships, the communication network that exists behind the facade of constitutional institutions.

In neither Britain nor Japan does the institution in which formal responsibility for policy making resides—the legislature—exercise significant power in that process. In Britain, this reflects a secular decline in parliamentary power, but in Japan, it reflects the historical norm. But, if power does not lie with the legislature in either Britain or Japan, it does not follow that the true seat of power in the two countries is ultimately the same. On the contrary, in Britain the most important policy-making institutions are still the prime minister and cabinet, at the formal center of gravity of the constitutional order. Policy making in Japan, by contrast, is to a great extent controlled by two institutions toward the periphery of the constitutional structure—the bureaucracy and the Liberal Democratic Party. In Britain, the pecking-order follows, if somewhat loosely, the formal hierarchy of executive institutions: prime minister, cabinet, ministers, bureaucracy. In Japan, the prime minister and the cabinet are challenged by both the party organization of the ruling LDP and by the bureaucracy. The higher turnover rate of Japanese prime ministers is evidence of the fact that they are more beholden to their factions and are somewhat more likely to be expected to subordinate themselves to the group—to be "team players"—than is the case in Britain. While prime ministers in both systems act as a policy broker and a ratifier, British prime ministers are much more likely to be policy initiators. They have had greater freedom than Japanese prime ministers to choose between "mobilizer" and "reconciler" styles. The same basic statements can be made about ministerial influence as well. Japanese ministerial appointments are more honorary and reflect even more than in Britain the need for factional balance. Ministerial tenure is short in both countries, but even briefer in Japan than in Britain. Japanese ministers are little more than conduits for proposals generated by their bureaucracies, while in Britain, ministers can exercise initiative and can count on a tradition of bureaucratic deference to political institutions.

In Japan the party/government nexus is far more important in making policy than in Britain. The links are extensive, and manifest in greater circulation of elites, formal bureaucratic and executive-level consultation, and joint policy making, as well as innumerable informal social contacts and *giri* networks. Indeed, party and government are nearly inseparable from an institutional point of view. In Japan, the party/bureaucracy relationship parallels the minister/bureaucracy relationship in Britain, and the policy-making power of the LDP vis-à-vis the bureaucracy continues to grow with party institutions, such as the Policy Affairs Research Council and the policy *zoku* having become significant forces in policy making. Britain, unlike Japan, has no formal machinery for processing current legislative proposals within the parties, and no formal consultation procedures among the government, MPs, and party in the generation of legislation.

Prewar bureaucratic authoritarianism and the lack of expertise in early postwar Japanese elected officials has given way to a greater inclusion of the ruling party and, through the LDP, interest groups, in the policy-making process. These developments may be seen as proof of the successful cultivation of democratic norms and an increasingly pluralistic polity. They may in this sense also suggest that the political culture is catching up to the formal constitutional order. British government practice, which had long since established its modern democratic norms and institutions before World War II came along, certainly changed less in the postwar years than Japan. However, the size, scope, and complexity of government grew, as we have seen, after 1945, as state-run enterprises and new intermediary governing institutions, such as quangos, took their place alongside the civil service. But this more extensive government had a mixed impact on the relative roles and powers of central institutions in Britain. The resulting fragmentation of responsibility clearly weakened the traditional civil service. At the same time, as government became increasingly concerned with technical questions, the civil service came under attack for the inadequacy of its generalist traditions. So, there is some evidence for bureaucratic "decline" in both Britain and Japan. However, British central executive elites may not have gained significantly at the expense of the bureaucracy, as in Japan. As we have seen, the same forces that have weakened the civil service also have worked to siphon off some of the former power of the prime minister and cabinet.

The different relative strengths of the Japanese and British bureaucracies in policy making represent more than different postwar trends. They also reflect different traditions and outlooks within the administrative civil services. The British civil service has no strong "bottom-up" tradition comparable to Japan. Although the popular image of British civil servants is as tenured manipulators of a transient interloper (the minister), in fact they are trained to help their minister get policy through the bureaucratic maze. Their concern is more to stop "bad" policy than to originate "good" policy. The Japanese bureaucrat has traditionally believed, and still does today, that superior training and expertise enables him or her not just to facilitate policy, but to initiate as well (see Table 7.2).

In both Britain and Japan, consultation between central and local government exhibits two facets. While there are norms of consultation, central government may exhibit an aloofness from, or even an indifference to, local feeling. In Japan, the central bureaucracy does work to build consensus among local governments on national policy, but if local entities are not willing to go along, then protracted conflict, such as that over Narita Airport, are likely to occur. In Britain, government may consult extensively with local interests, as in the case of the third London airport, but then decide not to consult over the channel tunnel.

The British and Japanese approaches to interest group roles have significant points in common with most other industrial democracies. Both are a mixture of corporatist and pluralist elements that accord a significant role to interests in the formulation of policy, yet both restrict access to the "inner circle" of policy making to what amounts to "approved" groups. In both, the center tightly controls who can play. Both have witnessed the appearance of some form of corporatism, in which organizations representing major functional interests engage in bargaining with the state, though such arrangements never became as well established in Britain as they have in Japan. In both Britain and Japan, the collective expression of demands is more firmly established than in the United States. And it is considered normal for organized interests to have an institutionalized relationship with government. Numerous advisory councils regularly put interest representatives in touch with government officials. In both systems, the limited roles of the legislature in the policy-making process tend to focus group pressure on other institutions such as the bureaucracy and (in the case of Japan) the party, though in the case of Japan the legislature continues, more than in Britain, to be included within the scope of interest group pressures. Representative of a very different trend, both have witnessed a proliferation of "cause" groups, a fragmentation of group interests that suggest a more open and pluralistic approach to government than has traditionally been the case.

There are differences, however, in the two countries' approaches to consultation. Consultation in Britain is an attempt to include those governmental institutions and private groups which policy is likely to affect and which will have significant responsibility for implementation. Japanese consultation is actually less inclusive of institutions and groups directly affected by proposed government policy. For example, even though both Japan and Britain have a highly centralized unitary administrative system, the British policy-making process includes a greater breadth of groups and the values they represent. Japan's historically strong central bureaucracy and the one-party predominance of the LDP have tended to inhibit government responsiveness to consultations. Group consultation in Japan is wider than in Britain in some respects. Both governments have resorted to "cosmetic" consultations. But the practice seems more prevalent in Japan than in Britain. And yet, the reality of Japanese consultation is still more a consensus-building process among elites than a process of consultation among institutions and groups. As in the case of LDP/opposition "consultation," consultation with interests reflects the fact that it is important to be seen as having listened to different views, even if the policy outcome does not reflect it. There are both similarities and differences in the motives for consultation. Constitutional norms, statutory requirements, legal decisions, consensual aspects of the political culture, and pragmatic considerations all contribute to the pervasiveness of consultation in Britain. Group consultation is widely perceived as an *obligation*. Even beyond the sense of moral or legal obligation, however, policy makers perceive very pragmatic motives to pay attention to organized interests. While social norms play a significant part in both countries in encouraging consultation and consensus, in Japan they play a relatively larger role. Although consensual norms are of great importance in both Britain and Japan, consensus building in Japan includes the additional dimension of reinforcing social consensus and harmony. In Japan, there are even fewer, if any, legal obligations enforcing consultation than there are in Britain. As in Britain, consultation partly represents pragmatic considerations, especially the mutual dependence of interests and government. Of major importance is the impetus for cooperation created by the modern interventionist state. The need for constant collaboration in the carrying out of state-led development is a major stimulus to interest group consultation in Japan. This particular stimulus has been largely absent in Britain. On the other hand, the drive for consultation occasioned by the building of the welfare state after 1945 in Britain was much less prominent in Japan. In any case, in Japan there is not as much concern about a lack of serious consultation limiting the ability of the government to maintain the legitimacy and support for policies. Again, the one-party predominant system and traditionally strong bureaucracy decrease the need for true consultation.

Both the Japanese and British systems have responded to the rise of postindustrial values and the call for participation, but both the rise of postindustrial values themselves, and the opening up of government to wider participation have proceeded slowly. One conclusion of this study is that the cases of Japan and Britain bear out the assumption of political culture as a conservative force. Mass values, attitudes, and behavior are changing slowly, and the political rules of the game are resistant to change. A complementary conclusion is that government institutions and processes lag behind values change at the mass level. A major finding of recent research on Britain's political culture has been the decline of deference, yet the core institutions of government still operate on the assumption of mass deference to core decision makers. What we have seen is that popular acquiescence is still sufficient, even lacking true deference, to sustain a polity that in most aspects is bent on avoiding erosion of the basic consensus on elite policy making (Ashford 1980: 8–9).

Finally, the increasingly transnational character of the world economy cannot help but affect policy making. Britain and Japan are no exceptions. But while internationalist, and even integrative, pressures operate increasingly in the world economy, Britain's membership in the European Community exerts influence on policy institutions and processes for which there is no Japanese counterpart. While the direction of change within the European Community is even less predictable in the 1990s than it was at the end of the 1980s, the British have already become less sovereign than in the recent past, as the result of the rise of European institutions and efforts at harmonization of policies. The closed loop of government and insider interests has been forced open by economic reality and by treaty obligations under the Treaty of Rome and the Single Act of 1985.

To sum it all up, both Japanese and British decision making rest on the foundations of strong elite consensus and control, buttressed by tenacious, though different, collectivist norms and traditions, and by an acquiescent citizeny. In both, policy is often about maintaining consensus. Both central elites, in somewhat different ways, regulate access to and/or knowledge about the inner circle. What the Japanese do mostly through social conventions, the British are more inclined to do through political conventions.

Notes

1. Ashford (1980: 15) links the absense of either a written constitution or a body of administrative law to the desire of Parliament over the centuries to avoid putting "the slow accumulation of parliamentary power in jeopardy."

2. Despite their purported neutrality, it is clear that top civil servants do give political advice, and that this is an important part of their duties (Michael 1982: 75). The neutrality of the civil service was placed under additional strain both from the efforts of Mrs. Thatcher to promote greater programmatic loyalty and from within, where there is some evidence of a stronger political self-concept among younger civil servants (Putnam 1975: 117).

3. While Mrs. Thatcher engaged in open warfare on the "consensus mongering" in the civil service, she was not always impervious to the bureaucratic realities. After the 1983 elections, she cancelled plans to introduce certain education reforms because "the administrative consequences would be colossal." In this case, the establishment prevailed over the government's ideological preferences, but only because it had broad support from the Local Educational Authorities and could show that vouchers would damage "other central Conservative objectives" (Ambler 1987: 97–98).

4. One of the reforms that has made possible this small increase in parliamentary influence has been the advent of the select committee system. Since 1979, fourteen select committees, one for each major ministry, have exercised considerably more independence than the existing standing committees. They can call ministers and civil servants to testify, and can issue reports, occasionally critical of government policy. The new system is still restricted by party discipline, but it "does draw information out of government" and occasionally leads to a policy change, as in the case of the Education Committee in the 1979–1980 Parliament (Drucker and Gamble 1988: 69). The influence of the select committees, as befits a government still grounded in auto-limitation, "relies not upon sanctions

or threats but normally upon the expertise and cogency of their investigations and reporting, and upon how far government is prepared to accede to 'mere' recommendations" (Downs 1985: 50). Giddings (1985 cited in Hogwood 1987: 80) concludes cautiously, that "the effect of these committees on minister[i]al and department policy making has been indirect and marginal, contextual rather than substantive."

5. Government officials themselves constitute interests, as in Britain, and bureaucrats may organize to defend their interests within government (Richardson and Flanagan 1984: 293).

References

Aberbach, Joel D., Robert D. Putnam, and Bert A. Rockman. 1981. *Bureaucrats and Politicians in Western Democracies*. Cambridge: Harvard University Press.

Abrams, M., D. Gerard, and N. Timms, eds. 1985. *Values and Social Change in Britain*. London: Macmillan.

Abramson, Paul R. 1983. *Political Attitudes in America: Formation and Change*. San Francisco: W. H. Freeman.

Airey, Colin. 1984. "Social and Oral Values." In *British Social Attitudes: the 1984 Report*, ed. Roger Jowell and Colin Airey: 121–56. Aldershot: Gower.

Alderson, John. 1987. "Police and Public Order." In *British politics: A Reader*, ed. Martin Burch and Michael Moran: 314–25. Manchester: University of Manchester Press.

Almond, Gabriel. 1980. "The Intellectual History of the Civic Culture Concept." In *The Civic Culture Revisited*, ed. Gabriel Almond and Sidney Verba, 1–36. Boston: Little Brown.

Almond, Gabriel, and G. Bingham Powell, Jr. 1978. *Comparative Politics: System, Process and Policy*. Boston: Little Brown.

Almond, Gabriel, and Sidney Verba. 1963. *The Civic Culture: Political Attitudes and Democracy in Five Nations*. Princeton: Princeton University Press.

———, eds. 1980. *The Civic Culture Revisited*. Boston: Little Brown.

Alt, James E. 1979. *The Politics of Economic Decline: Economic Management and Political Behaviour in Britain since 1964*. Cambridge: Cambridge University Press.

———. 1984. "Dealignment and the Dynamics of Partisanship in Britain." In *Electoral Change in Advanced Industrial Countries*, ed. Russell Dalton et al.: 298–329. Princeton: Princeton University Press.

Alt, James, and B. Sarlvik. 1974. "Partisanship and Policy Choice: Issue Preferences in the British Electorate." *British Journal of Political Science* 6: 273–90.

Ambler, John S. 1987. "Constraints on Policy Innovation in Education." *Comparative Politics* 20: 85–106.

Amery, L. S. 1949. *Thoughts on the Constitution*, 3d ed. New York: Oxford University Press.

Anchordoguy, Marie. 1988–89. "The Public Corporation: A Potent Japanese Policy Weapon. *Political Science Quarterly* 103: 707–25.

Approaches and Interpretations in the Study of British Politics [review]. 1984. *Parliamentary Affairs* 37: 109–13.

Asch, Solomon E. 1952. *Social pyschology*. New York: Prentice-Hall.

Ashford, Douglas E. 1980. *Policy and Politics in Britain: The Limits of Consensus*. Oxford: Basil Blackwell.

Auh, Soo Young. 1978. "Japanese Political Participation in Comparative Perspective." Ph.D. dissertation. University of Michigan.

Austin, Lewis. 1975. *Saints and Samurai*. New Haven: Yale University Press.

Austin, Rodney. 1985. "Freedom of Information: The Constitutional Impact." In *The Changing Constitution*. Oxford: Oxford University Press.

Baerwald, Hans H. 1986. *Party Politics in Japan*. Boston: Allen & Unwin.

Bagehot, Walter. 1966. *The English Constitution: With an Introduction by R. H. S. Crossman*. Ithaca: Cornell University Press.

Banks, Arthur S., ed. 1989. *Political Handbook of the World: 1989*. Binghamton: SUNY Press.

Barber, James. 1984. "The Power of the Prime Minister." In *British Politics in Perspective*, ed. R. L. Borthwick and J. E. Spence: 73–101. New York: St. Martin's Press.

Barnes, Samuel H., Max Kaase, et al., eds. 1979. *Political Action: Mass Participation in Five Western Democracies*. Beverly Hills: Sage.

Beasley, W. G. 1984. "The Edo Experience and Japanese Nationalism." *Modern Asian Studies* 18: 555–66.

Beer, Samuel H. 1974. *The British Political System*, 1st paper ed. New York: Random House.

———. 1982a. *Britain against Itself: The Political Contradictions of Collectivism*. New York: W. W. Norton.

———. 1982b. *Modern British Politics: Parties and Pressure Groups in the Collectivist Age*, 1982 ed. New York: W. W. Norton.

Beer, Samuel, and Adam Ulam, eds. 1973. *Patterns of Government: The Major Political Systems of Europe*, 3d ed. New York: Rodman.

Birch, Anthony H. 1980. *British Government and Politics*, 4th ed. Boston: Allen & Unwin.

———. 1984. "Overload, Ungovernability and Delegitimization: The Theories and the British Case." *British Journal of Political Science* 14: 135–60.

Blaker, Michael K., ed. 1976. *Japan at the Polls: The House of Councillors Election of 1974*. Washington D.C.: American Enterprise Institute for Public Policy Research.

Bodman, A. R. 1984. "The Neighbourhood Effect: A Test of the Butler-Stokes Model." *British Journal of Political Science* 13: 243–49.

Bogdanor, Vernon. 1989. "The Constitution." In *The Thatcher Effect* eds. Dennis Kavanagh and Anthony Seldon: 133–43. New York: Oxford University Press.

Bogdanor, Vernon, and David Butler, eds. 1983. *Democracy and Elections: Electoral Systems and Their Political Consequences*. Cambridge: Cambridge University Press.

Borthwick, R. L., and J. E. Spence, eds. 1984. *British Politics in Perspective*. Leiscester: Leiscester University Press.

Bozeman, Ada. 1984. "The International Order in a Multi-cultural World." In *Expansion of International Society*, ed. Hedley Bull and Adam Watson. Oxford: Clarendon.

Brittan, Samuel. 1975. "The Economic Contradictions of Democracy." *British Journal of Political Science* 5: 129–59.

Broadbent, Jeffery. 1988. "State as Process: The Effect of Party and Class on Citizen Participation in Japanese Local Government." *Social Problems* 35: 131–44.

Brown, R. G. S., and D. R. Steel. 1979. *The Administrative Process in Britain*. London: Methuen & Co. Ltd.

Budge, Ian, and Dennis J. Farlie. 1983. *Explaining and Predicting Elections: Issue Effects and Party Strategies in Twenty-three Democracies*. London: George Allen & Unwin.

Budge, Ian, and David McKay. 1988. *The Changing British Political System: Into the 1990s*, 2d ed. London: Longman.

Bulpitt, Jim. 1986. "The Discipline of the New Democracy: Mrs Thatcher's Domestic Statecraft." *Political Studies* 34: 19–39.

Bull, Hedley. 1972. "International Relations Theory, 1919–1969." In *The Aberystwyth Papers: International Politics 1919–1969*, ed. B. Porter. London: Oxford University Press.

Bull, Hedley, and Adam Watson. 1984. *Expansion of International Society*. Oxford: Clarendon.

Burch, Martin. 1983. "Mrs. Thatcher's Approach to Leadership in Government." *Parliamentary Affairs* 36: 399–416.

———. 1987. "The Demise of Cabinet Government." In *Political Institutions in Britain: Development and Change*, ed. Lynton Robins: 19–37. New York: Longman.

Burch, Martin, and M. Moran. 1985. "The Changing British Elite, 1945-1983: MPs and Cabinet Ministers." *Parliamentary Affairs* 38: 1–15.

Butler, David, and Gareth Butler. 1986. *British Political Facts, 1900–1985*. New York: St. Martin's Press.

Butler, David, and Paul Jowett. 1985. *Party Strategies in Britain: A Study of the 1984 European Elections*. New York: St. Martin's Press.

Butler, David, Howard R. Penniman, and Austin Ranney, eds. 1981. *Democracy at the Polls: A Comparative Study of Competitive National Elections*. Washington, D.C.: American Enterprise Institute.

Butler, David, and Donald Stokes. 1969. *Political Change in Britain: Forces Shaping Electoral Choice*. New York: St. Martin's Press.

Cain, Bruce E., John A. Ferejohn, and Morris P. Fiorina. 1984. "The Constituency Service Basis of the Personal Vote for U.S. Representatives and British Members of Parliament." In *Controversies in Voting Behavior*, 2d. ed., ed. Richard G. Niemi and Herbert F. Weisberg: 292–313. Washington, D.C.: American Enterprise Institute.

Calder, Kent E. 1988. *Crisis and Compensation: Public Policy and Political Stability in Japan, 1949–1986*. Princeton: Princeton University Press.

———. 1989. "Japanese Agricultural Policy: The Wax and Wane of Rural Bias." Paper presented to the Association of Asian Studies, Washington, D.C., March 17–19.

Calesta, D. J. 1984. "Postmaterialism and Value Convergences: Value Priorities of Japanese Compared with Their Perceptions of American Values." *Comparative Political Studies* 16: 529–55.

Campbell, John C. 1977. *Contemporary Japanese Budget Politics*. Berkeley: University of California Press.

———. 1981. *Parties, Candidates and Voters in Japan: Six Quantitative Studies*. Ann Arbor: University of Michigan Press.

———. 1984. "Policy Conflict and Its Resolution within the Governmental System." In *Conflict in Japan*, ed. Ellis Krauss et al.: 294–334. Honolulu: University of Hawaii.

Charlot, Monica. 1985. "The Ethnic Minorities' Vote." In *Britain at the Polls, 1983*, ed. Howard Penniman and Austin Ranney: 139–54. Washington, D.C.: American Enterprise Institute.

Cheng, Peter. 1988. "Political Clientelism in Japan: The Case of 'S' " *Asian Survey* 28: 471–83.

Christoph, James B. 1975. "High Civil Servants and the Politics of Consensualism in Great Britain." In *The Mandarins of Western Europe: The Political Role of the Top Civil Servants*, ed. Mattei Dogan: 25–62. Beverly Hills: Sage.

Christopher, Robert C. 1983. *The Japanese Mind: The Goliath Explained*. New York: Linden/Simon Schuster.

Clarke, Harold D., and Marianne C. Stewart. 1984. "Dealignment of Degree: Partisan Change in Britain, 1974–83. *The Journal of Politics* 46: 689–718.

Clarke, Harold D., Marianne C. Stewart, and Gary Zuk. 1986. "Politics, Economics and Party Popularity in Britain, 1979–1983." *Electoral Studies* 5: 123–41.

Coles, R. E. 1985. "The Macropolitics of Organizational Change: A Comparative Analysis of the Spread of Small-group Activities." *American Journal of Sociology* 91: 593–615.

Conge, Patrick. 1988. "The Concept of Political Participation: Toward a Definition." *Comparative Politics* 20: 241–48.

Cotgrove, Stephen. 1982. *Catastrophe or Cornucopia: The Environment, Politics and the Future*. New York: John Wiley & Sons.

Cozens, Peter, and Kevin Swaddle. 1986. "Notes on Recent Elections: The British General Election of 1987." *Electoral Studies* 6: 263–88.

Crewe, Ivor. 1981. "Electoral Participation." In *Democracy at the Polls*, ed. David Butler, Howard R. Penniman, and Austin Ranney: 216–63. Washington, D.C.: American Enterprise Institute.

———. 1985a. *Electoral Change in Western Democracies: Patterns and Sources of Electoral Volatility*. Beckenham, Kent: Croom Helm.

———. 1985b. "How to Win a Landslide Without Really Trying: Why the Conservatives Won in 1983." In *Britain at the Polls, 1983*, ed. Howard Penniman and Austin Ranney: 155–96. Washington, D.C.: American Enterprise Institute.

———. 1986. "On the Death and Resurrection of Class Voting: Some Comments on How Britain Votes." *Political Studies* 34: 620–38.

———. 1987. "What's Left for Labour: An Analysis of Thatcher's Victory." *Public Opinion* July/August: 52–56.

———. 1989. "Values: The Crusade that Failed." In *The Thatcher Effect*, ed. Dennis Kavanagh and Anthony Seldon: 239–50. Oxford: Clarendon Press.

Crewe, Ivor, and David Denver, eds. 1985. *Electoral Change in Western Democracies*. London: Croom Helm.

Crossman, R. H. S. 1975. *Diaries of a Cabinet Minister*. London: Hamilton.

Crouch, Colin. 1983. "Pluralism and the New Corporatism: A Rejoinder." *Political Studies* 31: 452–60

Curtice, John. 1987. "Interim Report: Party Politics." In *British Social Attitudes: the 1987 Report*, ed. Roger Jowell, Sharon Witherspoon and Lindsay Brook: 171–86. Aldershot: Gower.

———. 1988. "One Nation?" In *British Social Attitudes: the 5th Report*, ed. Roger Jowell, Sharon Witherspoon and Lindsay Brook: 127–54. Aldershot: Gower.

Curtice, John, and Michael Steed. 1982. "Electoral Choice and the Production of the Government: The Changing Operation of the Electoral System in the United Kingdom since 1955." *British Journal of Political Science* 12: 249–98.

Curtis, Gerald L. 1988. *The Japanese Way of Politics*. New York: Columbia University Press.

Dahrendorf, Ralf. 1981. "The Politics of Economic Decline." *Political Studies* 29: 284–91.

Dalton, Russell J. 1984. "Cognitive Mobilization and Partisan Realignment in Advanced Industrial Democracies." *Journal of Politics* 46: 264–84.

———. 1985. "Political Parties and Political Representation: Party Supporters and Party Elites in Nine Nations." *Comparative Political Studies* 18: 267–99.

———. 1988. *Citizen Politics in Western Democracies: Public Opinion and Political Parties in the United States, Great Britain, West Germany, and France*. Chatham: Chatham House.

Dalton, Russell, Scott Flanagan, and Paul A. Beck, eds. 1984. *Electoral Change in Advanced Industrial Democracies: Realignment or Dealignment?*. Princeton: Princeton University Press.

Delafons, John. 1982. "Working in Whitehall: Changes in Public Administration 1952–1982." *Public Administration* 60: 253–72.

Dennis, Jack, Lem Lindberg, and Donald M. Crane. 1971. "Support for Nation among English Children." *British Journal of Political Science* 1: 25–48

Denver, David. 1987a. "The British General Election of 1987: Some Preliminary Reflections." *Parliamentary Affairs*: 449–57.

———. 1987b. "Great Britain: From 'Opposition with a Capital 'O' to Fragmented Opposition." In *Opposition in Western Europe*, ed. Eva Kolinsky: 78–115. New York: St. Martin's Press.

———. 1987c. "Predicting the Next British Election (or not, as the case may be). *Parliamentary Affairs* 40: 238–249.

Deutsch, Karl W. 1974. *Politics and Government: How People Decide their Fate*, 2d ed. Boston: Houghton Mifflin.

Dicey, A. V. 1959. *Introduction to the Study of the Law of the Constitution*. New York: St. Martin's Press.

Dogan, Mattei, ed. 1975. *The Mandarins of Western Europe: The Political Role of Top Civil Servants*. New York: John Wiley & Sons.

———, ed. 1988. *Comparing Pluralist Democracies: Strains on Legitimacy*. Boulder: Westview.

Doi, L. Takeo. 1986. "Amae: A Key Concept for Understanding Japanese Personality Structure." In *Japanese Culture and Personality*, ed. Takie S. Lebra and William P. Lebra: 121–29. Honolulu: University of Hawaii Press.

Doig, Alan. 1983. "Watergate, Poulson and the Reform of Standards of Conduct." *Parliamentary Affairs* 36: 316–33.

Dore, Ronald L. 1973. *British Factory, Japanese Factory: The Origins of National Diversity in Industrial Relations*. Berkeley: University of California Press.

———. 1985. "Authority and Benevolence: The Confucian Recipe for Industrial Success." *Government and Opposition* 20: 196–217.

———. 1987. *Taking Japan Seriously: A Confucian Perspective on Leading Economic Issues*. London: Althone.

Drucker, Henry, and Patrick Dunleavy. 1988. "The Party System." In *Developments in British Politics*, 3d. ed., ed.. Henry Drucker et al.: 60–87. New York: St. Martin's Press.

Drucker, Henry, Patrick Dunleavy, Andrew Gamble, and Gillian Peele, eds. 1988. *Developments in British Politics*. New York: St. Martin's Press.

Dunleavy, Patrick. 1988. "Topics in British Politics." In *Developments in British Politics*, 3d. ed., ed.. Henry Drucker et al.: 329–72. New York: St. Martin's Press.

Dunleavy, Patrick, and Christopher Husbands. 1985. *British Democracy at the Crossroads*. New York: Allen & Unwin.

Dunleavy, Patrick, and R. A. W. Rhodes. 1988. "Government Beyond Whitehall." In *Developments in British Politics*, 3d ed., ed. Henry Drucker et al.: 107–43. New York: St. Martin's Press.

Easton, David. 1965. *A Framework for Political Analysis*. Englewood Cliffs: Prentice-Hall.

Eckstein, Harry. 1960. *Pressure Group Politics*. Stanford: Stanford University Press.

———. 1988. "A Culturalist Theory of Political Change." *American Political Science Review* 82: 789–804.

The Economist. 1988. A Mandarin's Guide to Tokyo. January 9: 32.

The Economist, June 20, 1987.

The Economist, June 24, 1989.

Elkins, David J., and Richard E. B. Simeon, 1979. "A Cause in Search of its Effect, or What Does Political Culture Explain?" *Comparative Politics* 11: 129–45.

Eurobarometer, No. 24, 1985. Brussels: Commission of the European Communities.

Festinger, Leon. 1957. *A Theory of Cognitive Dissonance*. Stanford. Stanford University Press.

Finer, Sammy E. 1975. *Adversarial Politics and Electoral Reform*. London: Anthony Wigram.

———. 1980. *Changing British Party Systems, 1945–1979*. Washington, D.C.: American Enterprise Institute.

———. 1982. "Adversary Politics in the Eighties." *Electoral Studies* l: 221–30.

Flanagan, Scott C. 1978. "The Genesis of Variant Political Cultures: Contemporary Citizen Orientations in Japan, America, Britain and Italy." In *The Citizen and Politics*, ed. Sidney Verba and Lucian W. Pye: 129–63. Stamford, CT: Greylock.

———. 1979. "Value Change and Partisan Change in Japan." *Comparative Politics* 11: 253–78.

———. 1980. "Value Cleavages, Economic Cleavages and the Japanese Voter." *American Journal of Political Science* 24: 177–206.

———. 1982. "Changing Values in Advanced Industrial Societies: Inglehart's 'Silent Revolution' from the Perspective of Japanese Findings. *Comparative Political Studies* 14: 403–44.

———. 1984. "Electoral Change in Japan: A Study of Secular Realignment." In *Electoral Change in Advanced Industrial Countries*, ed. Russell Dalton, Scott Flanagan and Paul Beck: 159–204. Princeton: Princeton University Press.

Fogarty, Michael. 1985 "British Attitudes to Work." In *Values and Social Change in Britain*, ed. Mark Abrams et al.: 173–200. London: Macmillan.

Foreign Press Center. 1989. *Facts and Figures of Japan*. Tokyo: Japan Times.

Foucalt, Michel. 1981. *Power/Knowledge*. New York: Pantheon.

Franklin, Mark N. 1985a. "Assessing the Rise of Issue Voting in British General Elections since 1964." *Electoral Studies* 4: 37–56.

———. 1985b. *The Decline of Class Voting in Britain*. Oxford: Oxford University Press.

Franklin, Mark N., and A. Mughan. 1978. "The Decline of Class Voting in Britain: Problems of Analysis and Interpretation." *American Political Science Review* 72: 527–34.

Franklin, Mark N., and Edward C. Page. 1984. "A Critique of the Consumption Cleavage Approach in British Voting Studies. *Political Studies* 32: 521–36.

Frey, Frederick W. 1973. "Communication and Development." In *Handbook of Communication*, ed. Pool et al.: 337–461. Chicago: Rand McNally.

Friedman, David. 1988. *The Misunderstood Miracle: Industrial Development and Political Change in Japan*. Ithaca: Cornell University Press.

Frost, Ellen L. 1987. *For Richer, for Poorer: The New U.S.-Japan Relationship*. New York: Council on Foreign Relations.

Fry, Geoffrey K., 1984. "The Development of the Thatcher Government's 'Grand Strategy' for the Civil Service: A Public Policy Perspective." *Public Administration* 62: 322–35.

———. 1988. "Inside Whitehall." In *Developments in British Politics*, 3d. ed., ed. Henry Drucker et al.: 88–106. New York: St. Martin's Press.

Fukutake, Tadashi. 1982. *Japanese Society Today*, 2d ed. Tokyo: University of Tokyo Press.

Gamble, Andrew. 1982. *Britain in Decline*. New York: Macmillan.

Gamson, William A. 1968. *Power and Discontent*. Homewood, Il.: Dorsey Press.

George, Aurelia. 1988. "Japanese Interest Group Behavior: An Institutional Approach." In *Dynamic and Immobilist Policies in Japan*, ed. J. A. A. Stockwin et al.: 106–140. London: Macmillan.

Gerard, H. B. 1964. "Conformity and Commitment to the Group." *Journal of Abnormal and Social Psychology* 68: 209–11.

Gibbins, John R., ed. 1989. *Contemporary Political Culture: Politics in a Postmodern Age.* Newbury Park: Sage.

Girvin, Brian. 1987. "Conservatism and Political Change in Britain and the United States. *Parliamentary Affairs* 40: 154–71.

———. 1989. "Change and Continuity in Liberal Democratic Political Culture." In *Contemporary Political Culture: Politics in a Postmodern Age,* ed. John R. Gibbins: 31–51. Newbury Park: Sage.

Goldthorpe, J. H. 1980. *Social Mobility and Class Structure in Modern Britain.* Oxford: Clarendon.

Goodin, R. E. 1982. "Rational Politicians and Rational Bureaucrats in Washington and Whitehall." *Public Administration* 60: 23–41.

Grant, Wyn. 1984. "The Role and Power of Pressure Groups." In *British Politics in Perspective,* ed. R. L. Borthwick and J. E. Spence: 123–43. New York: St. Martin's Press.

Grant, Wyn, and Shiv Nath. 1984. *The Politics of Economic Policymaking.* New York: Basil Blackwell.

Gray, Andrew. 1987. "Secrecy and Openness in Government." In *Political Issues in Britain Today,* 2d ed., ed. Bill Jones: 20–31. Wolfeboro, N.H.: Manchester University Press.

Gray, Andrew, and William I. Jenkins. 1982. "Policy Analysis in British Central Government: The Experience of PAR." *Public Administration* 60: 429–50.

———. 1985. *Administrative Politics in British Government.* New York: St. Martin's Press.

Greenaway, John R. 1987. "The Higher Civil Service at the Crossroads: The Impact of the Thatcher Government." In *Political Institutions in Britain: Development and Change,* ed. Lynton Robins: 38–57. New York: Longman.

Greenleaf, W. H. 1983a. *The British Political Tradition: The Rise of Collectivism.* London: Methuen.

———. 1983b. *The British Political Tradition: The Ideological Heritage.* London: Methuen.

Greenwood, J. R., and D. J. Wilson. 1982. *Public Administration in Britain.* London: Allen & Unwin.

Gregory, Jeanne. 1987. *Sex, Race and the Law: Legislating for Equality.* Beverly Hills: Sage.

Grofman, Bernard, and Arend Lijphart, eds. 1986. *Electoral Laws and their Political Consequences.* New York: Agathon.

Gunter, Barrie, M. Svennevig, and M. Wober. 1984. "Viewers Experience of Television Coverage of the 1983 General Election." *Parliamentary Affairs* 37: 271–82.

Gwyn, William B., and Richard Rose. 1980. *Britain: Progress and Decline.* London: Macmillan.

Habermas, Jurgen. 1975. *Legitimation Crises.* Boston: Little Brown.

Halsey, A. H. 1985. "On Methods and Morals." In *Values and Social Change in Britain,* ed. Mark D. Abrams et al.: 1–20. London: Macmillan.

Halsey, A. H., ed. 1972. *Trends in British Society since 1900: A Guide to the Changing Social Structure of Britain.* London: Macmillan.

Harding, Stephen. 1985. "Values and the Nature of Psychological Well-being." In *Values and Social Change in Britain,* ed. Mark D. Abrams et al.: 227–52. London: Macmillan.

Harding, Stephen, and David Phillips. 1986. *Contrasting Values in Western Europe: Unity, Diversity and Change.* London: Macmillan.

Harrop, Martin. 1987. "The Changing Electorate." In *Political Institutions in Britain: Development and Change*, ed. Lynton Robins: 166–78. New York: Longman.

———. 1988. "Voting and the Electorate." In *Developments in British Politics*, 3d. ed., ed. Henry Drucker et al.: 34–59. New York: St. Martin's Press.

Hart, Vivien. 1978. *Distrust and Democracy: Political Dissent in Britain and America*. Cambridge: Cambridge University Press.

Hastings, Elizabeth Hann, and Philip K. Hastings, eds. 1983. *Index to International Public Opinion, 1981–1982*. Westport: Greenwood Press.

———, eds. 1984. *Index to International Public Opinion, 1982–1983*. Westport: Greenwood Press.

———, eds. 1985. *Index to International Public Opinion, 1983–1984*. Westport: Greenwood Press.

———, eds. 1986. *Index to International Public Opinion, 1984–1985*. Westport: Greenwood Press.

———, eds. 1987. *Index to International Public Opinion, 1985–1986*. Westport: Greenwood Press.

Hastings, Elizabeth Hann, and Philip K. Hastings, eds. 1988. *Index to International Public Opinion, 1986–1987*. Westport: Greenwood Press.

———, eds. 1989. *Index to International Public Opinion, 1987–1988*. Westport: Greenwood Press.

———, eds. 1990. *Index to International Public Opinion, 1988–1989*. Westport: Greenwood Press.

Heald, Gordon. 1982. *A Comparison between American, European and Japanese Values*. Paper presented at the Annual Meeting of the World Association for Public Opinion Research, May 21.

Hayachi, Chikio. 1988. "The National Character in Transition." *Japan Echo* 15 (Special Issue 1988): 7–11.

Heath, Anthony, and Geoff Evans. 1988 "Working-class Conservatives and Middle-class Socialists." In *British Social Attitudes: The 5th Report*, ed. Roger Jowell, Sharon Witherspoon and Lindsay Brook: 53–70. Aldershot: Gower.

Heath, Anthony, R. Jowell, and J. Curtice. 1985. *How Britain Votes*. New York: Pergamon Press.

Heath, Anthony, R. Jowell, and J. Curtice. 1987. "Trendless Fluctuations: A Reply to Crewe." *Political Studies* 35: 256–77.

Heath, Anthony, and Richard G. Topf. 1986. "Educational Expansion and Political Change in Britain: 1964–1983." *European Journal of Political Research* 14: 543–67.

———. 1987. "Political Culture." In *British Social Attitudes: the 1987 Report*, ed. Roger Jowell, Sharon Witherspoon and Lindsay Brook: 51–67. Aldershot: Gower.

Heidenheimer, Arnold J., Hugh Heclo, and Carolyn Teich Adams. 1990. *Comparative Public Policy: The Politics of Social Choice in America, Europe, and Japan*, 3d ed. New York: St. Martin's Press.

Held, David. 1987. "From Stability to Crisis in Post-war Britain." *Parliamentary Affairs* 40: 218–37.

Hibbing, John R. 1987. "On the Issues Surrounding Economic Voting: Looking to the British Case for Answers." *Comparative Political Studies* 20: 3–33.

Hibbs, Douglas A., Jr., and N. Vasilatos. 1982. "Economic Outcomes and Political Support for British Governments among Occupational Classes: A Dynamic Analysis." *The American Political Science Review* 76: 259–79.

Higgins, G. M., and J. J. Richardson. 1976. *Political Participation*. London: The Politics Association.

Himmelweit, Hilde, P. Humphreys, M. Jaegar, and M. Katz. 1981. *How Voters Decide.* Philadelphia: Open University Press.

Hogwood, Brian W. 1987. *From Crisis to Complacency? Shaping Public Policy in Britain.* Oxford: Oxford University Press.

Holmes, Martin. 1985. *The First Thatcher Government.* London: Wheatsheaf.

Hrebenar, Ronald J. 1986. *The Japanese Party System: From One Party Rule to Coalition Government.* Boulder: Westview.

Huntington, Samuel. 1968. *Political Order in Changing Societies.* New Haven: Yale University Press.

Husbands, Christopher T. 1988. "Race and Gender." In *Developments in British Politics,* 3d. ed., ed. Henry Drucker et al.: 295–312. New York: St. Martin's Press.

Ike, N. 1978. *A Theory of Japanese Democracy.* Boulder: Westview.

Impoco, Jim. 1988. "Who Runs Japan? Not its Politicians." *U.S. News and World Report* August 29/September 5: 78–79.

Inglehart, Ronald. 1977. *The Silent Revolution: Changing Values and Political Styles among Western Publics.* Princeton: Princeton University Press.

———. 1979. "Value Priorities and Socioeconomic Change." In *Political Action: Mass Participation in Five Western Democracies,* ed. Samuel Barnes, Max Kaase, et al.: 305–42. Beverly Hills: Sage.

———. 1982. "Changing Values in Japan and the West." *Comparative Political Studies* 14: 445.

———. 1984. "Post Materialism in an Environment of Insecurity." In *Controversies in Voting Behavior,* 2d ed., ed. Richard G. Niemi and H. F. Weisberg: 561–88. Washington, D.C.: Congressional Quarterly.

———. 1989. "Observations on Cultural Change and Postmodernism." In *Contemporary Political Culture: Politics in a Postmodern Age,* ed. John R. Gibbins: 251–56. Newbury Park: Sage.

———. 1990. *Culture Shift in Advanced Industrial Society.* Princeton: Princeton University Press.

Inglehart, Ronald, and Hans D. Klingemann. 1979. "Ideological Conceptualization and Value Priorities." In *Political Action: Mass Participation in Five Western Democracies,* ed. Samuel Barnes, Max Kaase, et al.: 203–14 Beverly Hills: Sage.

Inglehart, Ronald, and Jacques-Rene Rabier. 1986. "Political Realignment in Advanced Industrial Society: From Class-based Politics to Quality-of-life Politics." *Government and Opposition* 21: 456–79.

Inglehart, Ronald, and Scott Flanagan. 1987. "Values Changes in Industrial Societies." *American Political Science Review* 81: 1289–1319.

Inoguchi, Takashi. 1987. "The Japanese Double Election of 6 July 1986." *Electoral Studies* 6: 63–68.

Inoguchi, Takashi, and Ikuo Kabashima. 1986. "Status Quo Student Elite." In *Behavior in the 1983 Japanese Elections,* ed. Watanuki et al.: 103–117. Tokyo: Sophia University.

Ishida, Takeshi. 1984. "Conflict and Its Accommodation: *Omote-ura* and *Uchi-soto* Relations." In *Conflict in Japan,* ed. Ellis Krauss et al.: 16–38. Honolulu: University of Hawaii.

Ishida, Takeshi, and Ellis S. Krauss, eds. 1989. *Democracy in Japan.* Pittsburgh: University of Pittsburgh Press.

Itoh, Hiroshi, ed. 1973. *Japanese Politics: An Inside View.* Ithaca: Cornell University Press.

Janis, Irving. 1982. *Groupthink: Psychological Studies of Policy Decisions and Fiascoes,* 2d. ed. Boston: Houghton Mifflin.

Jansen, M. B. 1965. *Changing Japanese Attitudes toward Modernization*. Princeton: Princeton University Press.

Jenkins, Peter. 1988. *Mrs. Thatcher's Revolution: The Ending of the Socialist Era*. Cambridge: Harvard University Press.

Jervis, Robert. 1976. *Perception and Misperception in International Politics*. Princeton: Princeton University Press.

Jessop, Bob. 1971. "Civility and Traditionalism in English Political Culture." *British Journal of Political Science* 1: 1–24.

Johnson, Chalmers. 1978. *Japan's Public Policy Companies*. Washington, D.C.: American Enterprise Institute for Public Policy Research.

———. 1986. *MITI and the Japanese Miracle*. Stanford: Stanford University Press. Reprint. Tokyo: Tuttle Books.

Johnston, Michael, and Douglas Wood. 1985. "Right and Wrong in Public and Private Life." In *British Social Attitudes: The 1985 Report*, ed. Roger Jowell and Sharon Witherspoon: 121–48. Aldershot: Gower.

Johnston, Ronald J., and J. C. Doornkamp. 1982. *The Changing Geography of the United Kingdom*. New York: Methuen.

Johnston, R. J., and C. J. Pattie. 1991. "Tactical Voting in Great Britain in 1983 and 1987: An Alternative Approach." *British Journal of Political Science* 21: 95–128.

Jordan, A. G., and J. J. Richardson. 1987. *Government and Pressure Groups in Britain*. Oxford: Clarendon Press.

Jowell, Roger, and Colin Airey, eds. 1984. *British Social Attitudes: The 1984 Report*. Aldershot: Gower.

Jowell, Roger, and Richard Topf. 1988. "Trust in the Establishment." In *British Social Attitudes: The 5th Report*, ed. Roger Jowell, Sharon Witherspoon and Lindsay Brook: 109–126. Aldershot: Gower.

Jowell, Roger, Sharon Witherspoon, and Lindsay Brook, eds. 1985. *British Social Attitudes: The 1985 Report*. Aldershot: Gower.

Jowell, Roger, Sharon Witherspoon, and Lindsay Brook, eds. 1987. *British Social Attitudes: The 1987 Report*. Aldershot: Gower.

Jowell, Roger, Sharon Witherspoon, and Lindsay Brook, eds. 1988. *British Social Attitudes: The 5th Report*. Aldershot: Gower.

Kaase, Max. 1988. "Political Alienation and Protest." In *Comparing Pluralist Democracies: Strains on Legitimacy*, ed. Mattei Dogan: 114–42. Boulder: Westview.

Kaase, Max, and Alan Marsh. 1979a. "Political Action Repertory: Change over Time and a New Typology." In *Political Action: Mass Participation in Five Western Democracies*, ed. Samuel Barnes, Max Kaase et al.: 137–66. Beverly Hills: Sage.

———. 1979b. "Political Action: A Theoretical Perspective." In *Political Action: Mass Participation in Five Western Democracies*, ed. Samuel Barnes, Max Kaase, et al.: 27–56. Beverly Hills: Sage.

Kabashima, Ikuo. 1984. "Supportive Participation with Economic Growth: The Case of Japan." *World Politics* 36: 309–38.

———. 1986. "Ideological Identification and Belief Systems." In *Electoral Behavior and the 1983 Japanese Elections*, ed. Watanuki et al.: 63–86. Tokyo: Sophia University.

Kabashima, I., and Lynn T. White III. 1986. *Political System and Change*. Princeton: Princeton University Press.

Kavanagh, Dennis. 1971. "The Deferential English: A Comparative Critique." *Government and Opposition* 6: 333–60

———. 1977. "New Bottles for Old Wines: Changing Assumptions about British Politics." *Parliamentary Affairs* 30: 6–21.

———. 1980. "Political Culture in Great Britain: The Decline of the Civic Culture." In

The Civic Culture Revisited, eds. Gabriel A. Almond and Sidney Verba: 124–76. Boston: Little Brown.

———. 1985a. *British Politics: Continuities and Change*. New York: Oxford University Press.

———. 1985b. "Whatever Happened to Consensus Politics"? *Political Studies* 33: 529–546.

———. 1986. "How We Vote Now." *Electoral Studies* 5: 19–28.

———. 1987. "Margaret Thatcher: A Case of Prime Ministerial Power?" In *Political Institutions in Britain: Development and Change*, ed. Lynton Robins: 9–18. New York: Longman.

———. 1988. "Thatcher's Third Term." *Parliamentary Affairs* 41: 1–12.

Kavanagh, Dennis, and Anthony Seldon, Eds. 1989. *The Thatcher Effect*. Oxford: Clarendon Press.

Kawashima, Takegoshi. 1967. "The Status of the Individual in the Notion of Laws, Right, and Social Order in Japan." In *The Japanese Mind*, ed. Charles S. Moore: 262–87. Honolulu: East-West Center.

Keehn, Norman H. 1978. "Great Britain: The Illusion of Governmental Authority." *World Politics* 30: 538–62.

Kellas, James G. 1990. "The Constitutional Option for Scotland." *Parliamentary Affairs*, 43: 426–34.

Kervis, H. 1983. "Ethics and Elections." *Far Eastern Economic Review* 122: 28.

King, Anthony. 1975. "Overload: Problems of Governing in the 1970's." *Political Studies* 23: 284–96.

———, ed. 1977. *Why Is Britain Becoming Harder to Govern?* London: British Broadcasting Corporation.

Kishima, Takako. 1987. "Political Life Reconsidered: A Poststructuralist View of the World of Man in Japan." Ph.D. Dissertation. University of Wisconsin-Madison.

Klingemann, Hans D. 1979a. "The Background of Ideological Conceptualization." In *Political Action: Mass Participation in Five Western Democracies*, ed. Samuel Barnes, Max Kaase et al.: 255–78. Beverly Hills: Sage.

———. 1979b. "Measuring Ideological Conceptualization." In *Political Action: Mass Participation in Five Western Democracies*, ed. Samuel Barnes, Max Kaase et al.: 214–54. Beverly Hills: Sage.

Knutsen, Oddbjorn. 1988. "The Impact of Structural and Ideological Party Cleavages in West European Democracies: A Comparative Empirical Analysis." *British Journal of Political Science* 18: 323–52.

Kosai, Yutaka. 1987. "The Politics of Economic Management." In *The Political Economy of Japan: The Domestic Transformation*, ed. Kozo Yamamura and Yasukichi Yasuba: 555–92. Stanford: Stanford Unviersity Press.

Krauss, Ellis S., and James M. Fendrich. 1980. "Political Socialization of U.S. and Japanese Adults." *Comparative Political Studies* 13: 3–32.

Krauss, Ellis S., Thomas P. Rohlen, and Patricia G. Steinhoff, eds. 1984. *Conflict in Japan*. Honolulu: University of Hawaii Press.

———. 1984. "Conflict and Its Resolution in Postwar Japan." In *Conflict in Japan*, ed. Ellis Krauss et al.: 377–98. Honolulu: University of Hawaii Press.

Kyogoku, Junichi. 1987. *The Political Dynamics of Japan*. Tokyo: University of Tokyo Press.

Lebra, Takie Sugiyama. 1976. *Japanese Patterns of Behavior*. Honolulu: University of Hawaii Press.

Lebra, Takie Sugiyama, and William P. Lebra, eds. 1986. *Japanese Culture and Behavior*, 2d ed. Honolulu: University of Hawaii Press.

Lijphart, Arend. 1984. "Trying to Have the Best of Both Worlds: Semi-proportional and Mixed Systems." In *Choosing an Electoral System: Issues and Alternatives*, ed. Arend Lijphart and Bernard Grofman: 207–13. New York: Praeger.

Lijphart, Arend, and Bernard Grofman, eds. 1984. *Choosing an Electoral System: Issues and Alternatives*. New York: Praeger.

Lijphart, Arend, Rafael Lopez Pintor and Yasunori Sone. 1986. "The Limited Vote and the Single Nontransferable Vote: Lessons from the Japanese and Spanish Examples." In *Electoral Laws and their Political Consequences*, ed. Bernard Grofman and Arend Lijphart: 154–69. New York: Agathon.

Lowe, Philip, and Jane Goyder. 1983. *Environmental Groups in Politics*. London: Allen & Unwin.

McAllister, Ian., and Anthony A. Mughan. 1986. "Differential Turnout and Party Advantage in British General Elections, 1964–1983." *Electoral Studies* 5: 143–52.

———. 1987. Class, Attitudes, and Electoral Politics in Britain, 1974–1983. *Comparative Political Studies* 20: 47–71.

McAllister, Ian, and Richard Rose. 1984. *The Nationwide Competition for Votes: The 1983 British General Election*. London: Frances Pinter.

McAuslan, J. P. W. B., and J. F. McEldowney. 1986. "The Constitution under Crisis." *Parliamentary Affairs* 39: 496–516.

Marsh, Alan. 1975. "The 'Silent Revolution,' Value Priorities and the Quality of Life in Britain." *American Political Science Review* 69: 21–30.

———. 1977. *Protest and Political Consciousness*. Beverly Hills: Sage.

Marsh, Alan, and Wyn Grant. 1977. "Tripartism: Reality or Myth." *Government and Opposition* 12: 194–211.

Marsh, Alan, and Max Kaase. 1979a. "Background on Political Action." In *Political Action: Mass Participation in Five Western Democracies*, ed. Samuel Barnes, Max Kaase et al.: 97–137. Beverly Hills: Sage.

———. 1979b. "Measuring Political Action." In *Political Action: Mass Participation in Five Western Democracies*, ed. Samuel Barnes, Max Kaase, et al.: 57–96. Beverly Hills: Sage.

Marsh, James. 1985. "Representational Changes: The Constituency MP." In *Parliament in the 1980s*, ed. Philip Norton: 69–95. Oxford: Basil Blackwell.

Marshall, Gordon, David Rose, Carolyn Vogler and Howard Newby. 1985. "Class, Citizenship, and Distributional Conflict in Modern Britain." *British Journal of Sociology* 36: 259–84.

Maruo, Naomi. 1986. "The Development of the Welfare Mix in Japan." In *The Welfare State in East and West*, ed. Richard Rose and Rei Shiratori: 64–79. Oxford: Oxford University Press.

Matsushita, Keiichi. 1975. "Politics of Citizen Participation. *Japan Interpreter* 9: 451–65.

Mayer, Lawrence C. 1989. *Redefining Comparative Politics: Promise versus Performance*. Newbury Park: Sage.

Merkl, Peter H. 1988. "Comparing Legitimacy and Values among Advanced Democratic Countries." In *Comparing Pluralist Democracies: Strains on Legitimacy*, ed. Mattei Dogan: 19–57. Boulder: Westview.

Michael, James. 1982. *The Politics of Secrecy*. London: Pelican Books.

Middlemas, Keith. 1979. *Politics in Industrial Society: The Experience of the British System since 1911*. London: Deutsch.

Miliband, Ralph. 1982. *Capitalist Democracy in Britain*. London: Oxford University Press.

Miller, W. L. 1978. "Social Class and Party Change in England: A New Analysis." *British Journal of Political Science* 8: 257–84.

Masawa, Shigeo. 1973. "An Outline of the Policy-Making Process in Japan." In *Japanese Politics: An Insider View*, ed. Hiroshi Itoh: 12–48. Ithaca: Cornell University Press.

Miyake, Ischiro. 1986a. "Instability of Party Identification in Japan." In *Electoral Behavior in the 1983 Japanese Elections*, ed. Watanuki et al.: 26–49. Tokyo: Sophia University.

———. 1986b. "Partisan Instability and Correlative Factors." In *Electoral Behavior in the 1983 Japanese Elections*, ed. Watanuki et al.: 50–62. Tokyo: Sophia University.

Miyamoto, Shosun. 1967. "The Relation of Philosophical Theory to Practical Affairs in Japan." In *The Japanese Mind*, ed. Charles A. Moore: 4–23. Honolulu: University of Hawaii Press.

Moeran, B. 1984. "Individual, Group and Seishin: Japan's Internal Cultural Debate." *Man* 19: 252–66.

Moore, Charles A., ed. 1967. *The Japanese Mind*. Honolulu: University of Hawaii Press.

Moran, Michael. 1987. "The Changing World of British Pressure Groups." In *Political Institutions in Britain: Development and Change*, ed. Lynton Robins: 179–87. New York: Longman.

Moscovici, Serge, and E. Lage. 1976. "Studies in Social Influence III: Majority versus Minority Influence in a Group." *European Journal of Social Psychology* 6: 149–74.

Murakami, Yasusuke. 1982. "The Age of New Middle Mass Politics: The Case of Japan." *Journal of Japanese Studies* 8: 29–72.

Muramatsu, Michio, and Ellis Krauss. 1984. "Bureaucrats and Politicians in Policymaking: The Case of Japan." *American Political Science Review* 78: 126–46.

———. 1987. "The Conservative Policy Lines and the Development of Patterned Pluralism." In *The Political Economy of Japan: The Domestic Transformation*, ed. Kozo Yamamura and Yasukichi Yasuba: 516–54. Stanford: Stanford University Press.

Nakamura, Hajime. 1967a. "Basic Features of the Legal, Political, and Economic Thought of Japan." In *The Japanese Mind*, ed. Charles A. Moore: 143–63. Honolulu: University of Hawaii Press.

Nakamura, Hajime. 1967b. "Consciousness of the Individual and the Universal among the Japanese." In *The Japanese Mind*, ed. Charles A. Moore: 179–200. Honolulu: University of Hawaii Press.

Nakamura, Kikuo, ed. 1975. *Gendai nihon no seiji bunka* (Contemporary Japanese Political Culture). Kyoto: Minerva Shobo.

Nakane, Chic. 1986. "Criteria of Group Formation." In *Japanese Culture and Behavior*, ed. Takie S. Lebra and William P. Lebra: 171–87. Honolulu: University of Hawaii Press.

Neary, Ian. 1986. "Socialist and Communist Party Attitudes towards Discrimination against Japan's Burakamin." *Political Studies* 34 : 556–74.

Newton, Kenneth. 1988. "Mass Media." In *Developments in British Politics*, 3d. ed., ed.. Henry Drucker et al.: 313–25. New York: St. Martin's Press.

The New York Times, January 29, 1990.

Nie, Norman. 1974. "Mass Belief Systems Revisited: Political Change and Attitude Structure." *Journal of Politics* 36: 541–91.

Niemi, Richard G., and Herbert F. Weisberg, eds. 1984. *Controversies in Voting Behavior*, 2d ed. Washington, D.C.: Congressional Quarterly.

Nippon Hoso Kyokai Public Opinion Research Institute, 1982. *Nihonjin to Americajin* (Japanese and Americans). Tokyo: NHK Shuppankai.

Nordlinger, Eric. 1967. *The Working Class Tories*. London: McGibbon & Kee.

Norton, Philip. 1981. "The House of Commons and the Constitution: The Challenges of the 1970s." *Parliamentary Affairs* 34: 253–71.

———. 1984. *The British Polity*. White Plains: Longman.

————, ed. 1985. *Parliament in the 1980s*. Oxford: Basil Blackwell.

————. 1985a. "Behavioral Changes: Backbench and Independence in the 1980s." In *Parliament in the 1980s*, ed. Philip Norton: 22–47. Oxford: Basil Blackwell.

————. 1985b. "Introduction: Parliament in Perspective." In *Parliament in the 1980s*, ed. Philip Norton: 1–19. Oxford: Basil Blackwell.

————. 1987. "Independence, Scrutiny and Rationalization: A Decade of Changes in the House of Commons." In *Political Institutions in Britain: Development and Change*, ed. Lynton Robins: 58–86. New York: Longman.

Offe, Claus. 1985. *Disorganized Capitalism: Contemporary Transformations of Work and Politics*. Cambridge: MIT Press.

Organization for Economic Cooperation and Development. 1988. *National Accounts*, vol. 2. Paris: OECD.

Paicheler, Genevieve. 1988. *The Psychology of Social Influence*. New York: Cambridge University Press.

Parry, Gerraint. 1972. *Participation in Politics*. Manchester: University of Manchester Press.

Parry, Gerraint, and G. Moyser. 1984. "Political Participation in Britain." *Government and Opposition* 19: 68–92.

Patrick, Hugh, and Henry Rosovsky, eds. 1976. *Asia's New Giant: How the Japanese Economy Works*. Washington, D.C.: Brookings Institution.

Peel, Gillian. 1988. "The State and Civil Liberties." In *Developments in British Politics*, 3d. ed., ed.. Henry Drucker et al.: 144–75. New York: St. Martin's Press.

Pekonen, Kyosti. 1989. "Symbols and Politics as Culture in the Modern Situation: The Problems and Prospects of the New." In *Contemporary Political Culture*, ed. John Gibbins: 127–43. Newbury Park: Sage.

Pempel, T. J. 1982. *Policy and Politics in Japan*. Philadelphia: Temple University Press.

————, ed. 1977. *Policymaking in Contemporary Japan*. Ithaca: Cornell University Press.

Phillips, David. 1976. "Trust, Distrust and Consensus." *British Journal of Political Science* 6: 129–42.

————. 1985. "Participation and Political Values." In *Values and Social Change in Britain*, ed. Mark Abrams et al.: 146–72. London: Macmillan.

Pool, Ithiel de Sala et al. 1973. *Handbook of Communication*. Chicago. Rand McNally.

Porter, B., ed. 1972. *The Aberystwyth Papers: International Politics 1919–1969*. London: Oxford University Press.

Powell, G. Bingham. 1982. *Contemporary Democracies: Participation, Stability and Violence*. Cambridge: Harvard University Press.

————. 1984. "Voting Turnout in Thirty Democracies: Partisan, Legal, and Socio-Economic Influences." In *Controversies in Voting Behavior*, 2d ed., ed. Richard G. Niemi and H. F. Weisberg: 34–53. Washington D.C.: Congressional Quarterly.

Prime Minister's Office. 1986. *Public Opinion Survey on Society and State*. Tokyo: Foreign Press Center.

————. 1988. *Public Opinion Survey on the Self-Defense Force and Defense Problems*. Tokyo: Foreign Press Center.

————. 1989a. *Public Opinion Survey on Society and State*. Tokyo: Foreign Press Center.

————. 1989b. *Public Opinion Survey on the Life of the Nation*. Tokyo: Foreign Press Center.

————. 1990. *Public Opinion Survey on the Society and State*. Tokyo: Foreign Press Center.

Pulzer, Peter. 1967. *Political Representation and Elections in Britain*. London: Allen & Unwin.

Punnett, R. M. 1988. *British Government and Politics*, 5th ed. Chicago: Dorsey Press.

Putnam, Robert D. 1973. *The Beliefs of Politicians: Ideology, Conflict and Democracy in Britain and Italy*. New Haven: Yale University Press.

———. 1975. "The Political Attitudes of Senior Civil Servants in Britain, Germany and Italy." In *The Mandarins of Western Europe: The Political Role of Top Civil Servants*, ed. Mattei Dogan: 87–128. Beverly Hills: Sage.

Pye, Lucian W. 1972. "Culture and Political Science: Problems in the Evaluation of the Concept of Political Culture." *Social Science Quarterly* 53: 285–96.

Pye, Lucian W., and Sidney Verba, eds. 1965. *Political Culture and Political Development*. Princeton: Princeton University Press.

Ranney, Austin. 1981. "Candidate selection." In *Democracy at the Polls*, ed. David Butler et al.: 75–106. Washington D.C.: American Enterprise Institute.

———. 1985. *Britain at the Polls, 1983: A Study of the General Election*. Durham: Duke University Press.

Rassmussen, Jurgen. 1987. "Women in Politics." In *British Politics: A Reader*, ed. Martin Burch and Michael Moran: 109–26. Manchester: Manchester University Press.

Reed, Steven, and Gregory G. Bruchk. 1984. "A Test of Two Theories of Economically Motivated Voting: The Case of Japan." *Comparative Politics* 7: 55–66.

Reimer, Bo. 1989. "Postmodern Structures of Feeling: Values and Lifestyles in the Postmodern Age." In *Contemporary Political Culture: Politics in the Post Modern Age*, ed. John Gibbins: 110–126. Newbury Park: Sage.

Reischauer, Edwin O. 1978. *The Japanese*. Cambridge: Harvard University Press.

Rennger, N. J. 1989. "Incommensurability, International Theory and the Fragmentation of Western Political Culture." In *Contemporary Political Culture: Politics in the Post Modern Age*, ed. John Gibbins: 237–50. Newbury Park: Sage.

Rhodes, R. A. W. 1984. "Continuity and Change in British Central/Local Relations." *British Journal of Political Science* 14: 261–83.

———. 1987. "Mrs. Thatcher and Local Government: Intentions and Achievements." In *Political Institutions in Britain*, ed. Lynton Robins: 98–120. New York: Longman.

Richardson, Bradley, M. 1974. *Political Culture of Japan*. Berkeley: University of California Press.

———. 1988. "Constituency Candidates versus Parties in Japanese Voting Behavior. *American Political Science Review* 82: 695–718.

Richardson, Bradley, and Scott C. Flanagan. 1984. *Politics in Japan*. Boston: Little Brown.

Richardson, J. J., and A. G. Jordan. 1979. *Governing under Pressure: The Policy Process in a Post-Parliamentary Democracy*. Oxford: Martin Robertson.

Riddell, Peter. 1989. "Cabinet and Parliament." In *The Thatcher Effect*, ed. Dennis Kavanagh and Anthony Seldon. Oxford: Clarendon Press.

Ridley, F. F. 1980. "The British Civil Service and Politics Principles in Question and Traditions in Flux." *Parliamentary Affairs* 33: 400–21.

———. 1984. "The Citizen against Authority: British Approaches to the Redress of Grievances." *Parliamentary Affairs* 37: 1–32.

———. 1988. "There is No British Constitution: A Dangerous Case of the Emperor's Clothes." *Parliamentary Affairs* 41: 340–61.

Robertson, D. 1984. *Class and the British Electorate*. Oxford: Basil Blackwell.

Robins, Lynton., ed. 1987. *Political Institutions in Britain*. New York: Longman.

Robinton, Madeline. 1970. "The British Method of Dealing with Political Corruption." In *Political Corruption*, ed. Arnold J. Heidenheimer: 249–97. New York: Holt, Reinhart and Winston.

Robson, J. M., ed. 1977. *The Collected Works of John Stuart Mill*. Vol. 18. Toronto: University of Toronto Press.

Rose, Richard. 1964. *Politics in England: An Interpretation*. Boston: Little Brown.

———, ed. 1976. *Studies in British Politics: A Reader in Political Sociology*, 3d ed. New York: St. Martin's Press.

————. 1979. *Do Parties Make a Difference?* Chatham: Chatham House.

————. 1982. *Understanding the United Kingdom: The Territorial Dimension in Government*. London: Longman.

————. 1983. "Elections and Electoral Systems: Choices and Alternatives." In *Democracy and Elections*, ed. Vernon Bogdanor and David Butler: 20–45. Cambridge: Cambridge University Press.

————. 1984. "Proud to Be British." *New Society* : 379–82.

————. 1985. "National Pride in Cross-National Perspective." *International Social Science Journal* 36: 85–96.

————. 1986a. "Common Goals But Different Roles: The State's Contribution to the Welfare Mix." In *The Welfare State in East and West*, ed. Richard Rose and Rei Shiratori: 13–39. Oxford: Oxford University Press.

————. 1986b."The Dynamics of the Welfare Mix in Britain." In *The Welfare State in East and West*, ed. Richard Rose and Rei Shiratori: 80–106. Oxford: Oxford University Press.

————. 1986c. *Politics in England: Persistence and Change*, 4th ed. Boston: Little Brown.

————. 1989. *Politics in England: Persistence and Change*, 5th ed. Glenview, IL: Harper Collins.

Rose, Richard, and Ian McAllister. 1986. *Voters Begin to Choose*. London: Sage.

Rose, Richard, and Rei Shiratori, eds. 1986. *The Welfare State in East and West*. Oxford: Oxford University Press.

Royal Commision on the Constitution. 1973. *The Report of the Royal Commission on the Constitution,* Vol. 1, *Report*. London: HMSO.

Rustow, Dankwart A. 1970. "Transitions to Democracy: Toward a Dynamic Model." *Comparative Politics*. 2: 337–63.

Samuels, Richard J. 1983. *The Politics of Regional Policy in Japan: Localities Incorporated?* Princeton: Princeton University Press.

Sansom, George B. 1963. *A History of Japan*, 3 vols. Stanford: Stanford University Press.

————. 1965. *The Western World and Japan*. New York: Knopf.

Sarlvik, Bo., and Ivor Crewe. 1983. *Decade of Dealignment*. Cambridge: Cambridge University Press.

Savage, Stephen P. 1987. "Fighting the Enemy within: Law and Order under the Tories." In *Political Institutions in Britain: Development and Change*, ed. Lynton Robins: 230–44. New York: Longman.

Scarbrough, Elinor. 1984. *Political Ideology and Voting: An Exploratory Study*. Oxford: Clarendon Press.

————. 1987. "Review Article: The British Electorate Twenty Years on: Electoral Change and Election Surveys." *British Journal of Political Science* 17: 219–46.

Searing, Donald D. 1982. "Rules of the Game in Britain: Can the Politicians Be Trusted?" *American Political Science Review* 76: 239–58.

Shiono, Hiroshi. 1984. "Administrative Guidance." In *Public Administration in Japan*, ed. Kioyaki Tsuji: 203–16. Tokyo: University of Tokyo Press.

Shively, P. 1979. "The Development of Party Identification among Adults: Exploration of a Functional Model." *American Political Science Review* 73: 1039–1054.

Shupe, Anson, D. 1979. "Social Participation and Voting Turnout: The Case of Japan." *Comparative Political Studies* 12: 229–56.

Simon, Herbert A. 1976. *Administrative Behavior: A Study of the Decion-making Process in Administrative Organization*, 3d ed. New York: Free Press.

Smith, Anthony. 1981 "Mass Communications." In *Democracy at the Polls: A Comparative Study of Competitive National Elections*, ed. David Butler et al.: 173–95. Washington, D.C.: American Enterprise Institute.

Social Surveys, Ltd. 1986. *Gallup Political Index*. No. 306 (February). London.

———. 1986. *Gallup Political Index*. No. 307 (March). London.

———. 1986. *Gallup Political Index*. No. 308 (April). London.

———. 1986. *Gallup Political Index*. No. 316 (December). London.

———. 1987. *Gallup Political Index*. No. 320 (April). London.

———. 1987. *Gallup Political Index*. No. 323 (July). London.

———. 1987. *Gallup Political Index*. No. 326 (October). London.

———. 1987. *Gallup Political Index*. No. 327 (November). London.

———. 1988. *Gallup Political Index*. No. 329 (January). London.

———. 1988. *Gallup Political Index*. No. 330 (February). London.

———. 1988. *Gallup Political Index*. No. 331 (March). London.

———. 1988. *Gallup Political Index*. No. 333 (May). London.

Social trends 18:1988. London: HMSO.

Soma, Masao, ed. 1987. *Nihon no sosenkyo 1986-nen* (Japan's 1986 General Election). Kyushu: Kyushu University Press.

Steele, David. 1982. "Government and Industry in Britain." *British Journal of Political Science* 12: 449–504.

Steiner, Kurt. 1965. *Local Government in Japan*. Stanford: Stanford University Press.

Stockwin, J. A. A. 1983. "Japan." In *Democracy and Elections*, ed. Vernon Bogdanor and David Butler: 209–27. Cambridge: Cambridge University Press.

Stockwin, J. A. A. et al., eds. 1988. *Dynamic and Immobility Policies in Japan*. London: Macmillan.

Stoetzel, Jean. 1955. *Without the Chrysanthemum and the Sword*. New York: Columbia University Press.

Stronach, Bruce. 1980. "Achievement and Affiliation Motivation in Japanese College Women." Ph.D. dissertation. Fletcher School of Law and Diplomacy.

———. 1988. *Deference, Pride and Political Culture: The Social Context of Japanese Political Participation in Comparison with Great Britain*. Paper presented at the Annual Meeting of the Canadian Asian Studies Association, Windsor, Ontario, June.

Studlar, Donley T. 1976. "British Political Culture and Racial Policy." In *Studies in British Politics: A Reader in Political Sociology*, ed. Richard Rose: 105–14. New York: St. Martin's Press.

Studlar, Donley T., and Susan Welch. 1981. "Mass Attitudes on Policy Issues in Britain." *Comparative Political Studies* 14: 327–55.

Suzuki, Takao. 1984. *Words in Context: A Japanese Perspective on Language and Culture*, 2d ed. Tokyo: Kodansha.

Takabatake, Michitoshi. 1975. "Citizen Movements: Organizing the Spontaneous." *Japan Interpreter* 9: 315–23.

Thayer, Nathaniel B. 1973. *How the Conservatives Rule Japan*. Princeton: Princeton University Press.

Topf, Richard. 1989. "Political Change and Political Culture in Britain, 1959–1987." In *Contemporary Political Culture: Politics in a Postmodern Age*, ed. John R. Gibbins: 52–80. Newbury Park: Sage.

Tsuji, Kiyoaki, ed. 1984. *Public Adminstration in Japan*. Tokyo: University of Tokyo Press.

Tsunoda, Ryusaku, William Theodore de Bary, and Donald Keene, comps. 1958. *Sources of Japanese Tradition*. New York: Columbia University Press.

Tufte, E. 1978. *Political Control of the Economy*. Princeton: Princeton University Press.

Turner, Bryan. 1989. "From Post Industrial Society to Postmodern Politics: The Political Sociology of Daniel Bell." In *Contemporary Political Culture: Politics in the Post Modern Age*, ed. John Gibbins: 199–217. Newbury Park: Sage.

United Kingdom. Parliament. 1973. *Report of the Royal Commission on the Constitution, 1969–1973.* Vol. I. London: Her Majesty's Stationery Office.

Van Deth, J. W. 1983. "The Persistence of Materialist and Post-Materialist Value Orientations." *European Journal of Political Research* 9: 63–79.

van Wolferen, Karel. 1990. *The Enigma of Japanese Power.* New York: Knopf. Reprint. New York: Vintage Books.

Varley, Paul H. 1984. *Japanese Culture,* 3d ed. Honolulu: University of Hawaii Press.

Verba, Sidney. 1967. "Conclusion: Comparative Political Culture." In *Political Culture and Political Development,* ed. Lucian W. Pye and Sidney Verba: 512–60.

Verba, Sidney, and Norman H. Nie. 1972. *Participation in America: Political Democracy and Social Equality.* New York: Harper and Row.

Verba, Sidney, and Lucian W. Pye, eds. 1978. *The Citizen and Politics.* Stamford, CT: Greylock.

Verba, Sidney, Norman H. Nie, and Jae-on Kim, 1978. *Participation and Political Equality: A Seven-nation Comparison.* Cambridge: Cambridge University Press.

Vogel, David. 1986. *National Styles of Regulation: Environmental Policy in Great Britain and the United States.* Ithaca: Cornell University Press.

Wagatsuma, H. 1984. "Some Cultural Assumptions among the Japanese." *Japan Quarterly* 31: 371–79.

Wakiya, Michihiro. 1987. "Kokumin wa Genzai no Seito o Donoyoni Mite Iruka?" *Hoso Kenkyu to Chosa* (May 1987): 22–31.

Ward, Robert E. 1965. "Japan: The Continuity of Modernization." In *Political Culture and Political Development,* ed. Lucian Pye and Sidney Verba: 27–82. Princeton: Princeton University Press.

———. 1971. "Political Modernization and Political Culture in Japan." In *Political Modernization,* ed. Claude E. Welch, Jr.: 100–117. Belmont, California: Wadsworth.

———. 1978. *Japan's Political System,* 2d ed. New York: Prentice-Hall.

Watanuki, Joji. 1980. *Social Structure and Voting Behavior in Japan.* Tokyo: Institute for International Relations, Sophia University.

Watanuki, Joji. 1986. *Nihonjin no senkyo kodo* (Japanese voting behavior). Tokyo: University of Tokyo Press.

Watanuki, Joji, et al. 1986. *Electoral Behavior in the 1983 Japanese Elections.* Tokyo: Institute for International Relations, Sophia University.

Waterman, Harvey. 1988. "Sins of the Children: Social Change, Democratic Politics and the Successor Generation in Western Europe." *Comparative Politics* 20: 401–22.

Weisz, J. R. 1984. "Standing out and Standing in: The Psychology of Control in America and Japan. *American Psychology* 39: 955–969.

Welch, Claude E. Jr., ed. 1971. *Political Modernization.* Belmont, California: Wadsworth.

Welch, Susan, and Donley T. Studlar. 1983. "The Policy Opinions of British Political Activists." *Political Studies* 31: 604-19.

———. 1985. "The Impact of Race on Political Behavior in Britain." *British Journal of Political Science* 15: 528–39.

Wellhofer, E. Spencer. 1986. "Class, Territory and Party: Political Change in Britain, 1945–1974." *European Journal of Political Research* 14: 369–92.

White, James W. 1981. "Civic Attitudes, Political Participation and System Stability in Japan." *Comparative Political Studies* 14: 371–400.

———. 1982. *Migration in Metropolitan Japan.* Berkeley: Japan Research Monograph, Institute for East Asian Studies, University of California.

Whitely, Paul F. 1986. "Macroeconomic Performance and Government Popularity in Britain: The Short Run Dynamics." *European Journal of Political Research* 14: 45–61.

Widmaier, Ulrich. 1988. "Tendencies toward an Erosion of Legitimacy." In *Comparing Pluralist Democracies: Strains on Legitimacy*, ed. Mattei Dogan: 143–67. Boulder: Westview.

Wiener, Martin. 1981a. "Conservatism, Economic Growth and English Culture." *Parliamentary Affairs* 34: 409–21.

———. 1981b. *English Culture and the Decline of the Industrial Spirit*. Cambridge: Cambridge University Press.

Williams, David E. 1983. "Beyond Political Economy: A Critique of Issues Raised in Chalmers Johnson's *MITI and the Japanese Miracle*." Berlin: Occasional paper no. 35, East Asian Institute, Free University of Berlin.

Wolf, Sharon, and Bibb Latane. 1985. "Conformity, Innovation and the Psychosocial Law." In *Perspectives on Minority Influence*, ed. Serge Moscovici et al.: 201–15. New York: Cambridge University Press.

Wolf-Phillips, Leslie. 1984. "A Long Look at the British Constitution." *Parliamentary Affairs* 37: 385–402.

Worcester, Robert M. 1984. "The Polls: Britain at the Polls 1945–1983." *Public Opinion Quarterly* 48: 824–33.

World Opinion Update. 1989. Williamstown: Survey Research Consultants International.

Wright, Anthony. 1987. "British Decline: Political or Economic?" *Parliamentary Affairs* 40: 41–56.

Wright, Deil S., and Yasuyoshi Sakurai. 1987. "Administrative Reform in Japan: Politics, Policy, and Public Administration in a Deliberative Society." *Public Administration Review* 47: 121–33.

Wright, Maurice. 1977. "Ministers and Civil Servants: Relations and Responsibilities." *Parliamentary Affairs* 30: 293–313.

Yamamura, Kozo, and Yasukichi Yasuba, eds. 1987. *The Political Economy of Japan*. vol. 1, *The Domestic Transformation*. Stanford: Stanford University Press.

Young, Hugo, and Anne Sloman. 1982. *No Minister: An Inquiry into the Civil Service*. London: BBC Publications.

Young, Ken. 1984. "Political Affairs." In *British Social Attitudes: The 1984 Report*, ed. Roger Jowell and Colin Airey: 11–46. Aldershot: Gower.

———. 1985. "Shades of Opinion." In *British Social Attitudes: The 1984 Report*, ed. Roger Jowell and Colin Airey: 1–32. Aldershot: Gower.

Index

Curtis Martin is Professor of Comparative Politics and International Relations at Merrimack College, where he chairs the Political Science Department. Previously he was a research associate at the National Bureau of Economic Research. His research interests include comparative political culture and foreign policy decision making. He received his doctorate from the Fletcher School of Law and Diplomacy at Tufts University. He is co-author with Robert A. Leone of *Local Economic Development* (1977).

Bruce Stronach has recently joined the International University of Japan as an Associate Professor of Japanese Studies in the Graduate School of International Relations. Dr. Stronach was previously Assistant Professor of Political Science at Merrimack College and a visiting researcher and lecturer at Keio University. He received his doctorate from the Fletcher School of Law and Diplomacy at Tufts University. He has authored two books: *Changing America* (1986), and *Japan and America: Opposites That Attract* (1989). Dr. Stronach was also Associate Editor of *The Handbook of Japanese Popular Culture*.

For Product Safety Concerns and Information please contact our EU
representative GPSR@taylorandfrancis.com
Taylor & Francis Verlag GmbH, Kaufingerstraße 24, 80331 München, Germany

www.ingramcontent.com/pod-product-compliance
Lightning Source LLC
Chambersburg PA
CBHW071833270326
41929CB00013B/1980